Politics
and
Social Structure in
Latin America

Politics
and
Social Structure in
Latin America

by James Petras

New York and London

To the memory of my parents
Frank and Anthippy

Contents

Acknowledgments

I would like to acknowledge the generous financial support of the Louis M. Rabinowitz Foundation and the Ford Foundation which made possible the writing of many of these essays.

Innumerable discussions with students, workers, and peasants in Latin America helped me to understand the problems and issues considered in these essays. In seminars and meetings students and faculty members in the United States have, through discussion and criticism, helped to clarify many of my ideas. The growing awareness in the United States of the destructive consequences of U.S. expansion and penetration of Latin America is one of the most important developments in recent years. It is hoped that these essays can contribute to furthering the growth of this understanding.

I
Class
and
Politics

Class and Politics in Latin America

This essay will attempt to synthesize some of the relevant findings on class structure and politics and to speculate on the future prospects of some of the significant strata in Latin America. We will discuss primarily the political behavior of classes and segments within each class and the impact of inter- and intraclass relationships on political development.

Industrialization, Urbanization, and the Class Structure

Industrialization has not been a decisive factor in the development of the class structure of Latin America. Urbanization, bureaucratization, commercialization of agriculture, and the influence of external social, economic, and political forces have had a more significant effect on the emerging social structure. Industrialization has taken place largely in an environment established by other processes and forces.

The factory-employed working class emerged as a social force in most Latin American countries comparatively late in history.[1] Until World War I the urban industrial working class was almost exclusively composed of artisans in small workshops. Nuclei of workers employed in foreign-owned economic enclaves were found only in the larger countries, namely Argentina, Brazil, Mexico, and Chile. On the average, the artisan shops contained less than five workers. Few trade unions or working-class political organizations of any size existed except in the mining areas. Throughout Latin America radical organization and ideology were confined to a small number of workers in particular crafts, and had little or no impact on unskilled laborers or the rural labor force. Mass industrial unions and socialist parties hardly existed.

13

The industrial working class became more numerous with the advent of the Depression. Because of the Depression, which restricted their capacity to import key goods, most Latin American countries were forced to adopt measures to encourage and protect national industries. During the 1930's the state promoted the production of light consumer goods. These industries were largely labor-intensive and absorbed a substantial increment of the urban labor force. In the post-World War II period a few Latin American countries began producing heavy machinery and intermediate goods. However, while the use of modern technology and the growth of capital-intensive industries have resulted in an increase in per-capita output, they have provided comparatively few opportunities for new employment for the growing mass of rural migrants who are occupying the slum areas around the big cities.[2] Large-scale United States and European firms which locate in Latin America utilize the latest technology and hence provide opportunities for a small number of skilled employees but little or no employment for the vast number of disguised unemployed frequently found in the service sector.[3]

Beginning in the early part of the century and especially in recent decades there has been a growing exodus from the countryside to the cities. Those arriving most recently have been described as urban though many of them reside in areas outside of the city and continue to maintain a mixture of rural and urban values.[4] There is no clear spatial or psychological distinction between rural or urban styles of life. Urbanization has occurred for a variety of reasons, among which probably the most important are the lack of opportunities for the rural workers in the countryside, the presence of their relatives and friends in the city, and the hope of the previously rural people that they will secure employment. Urbanization has not resulted from the demands of industry for cheap labor.

Social tension and polarization in Latin America result in part from the fact that accelerated urbanization has coincided with a decline in the development of labor-intensive industry and an increase in the production of machinery through capital-intensive investments.[5] The relative decline in small artisan shops, which are unable to compete with the larger firms, is matched by the eclipse of labor-intensive industry by automatic machinery. In these circumstances, rural migration has resulted in the expansion of a large urban slum class which is employed neither by artisan shops nor by manufacturing firms. The nonindustrial urban proletariat is found in all Latin American countries, the more developed as well as the severely underdeveloped.

The nonindustrial slum proletariat has few political allies among the existing working-class organizations. Existing parties which claim to favor reforms have not been willing to undertake serious campaigns to alter the structurally induced socioeconomic condition of the slum proletariat.[6] One of the more striking features that emerges from an examination of Latin American politics is the lack of social solidarity in most countries among broad sectors of the urban working class. The causes of this social fragmentation are numerous and complex. One factor which may account for it is the economic inequalities existing within the urban working class; another is the numerical weakness of the factory proletariat.[7] An analysis of the socioeconomic divisions within the urban working class shows three distinct strata: white collar workers, both public and private employees; industrial workers; and nonindustrial workers who are usually classified in the service sector but who are largely semiemployed individuals active as penny vendors and personal servants.

Industrial Workers: Factory and Artisan Shop

The number of industrial factory workers employed by large firms is very small in proportion to the size of the economically active urban population, even if we consider firms employing as few as one hundred workers as large. Despite a rise in the number of factory workers employed by industry, almost half the industrial labor force is still composed of artisans (47.3 percent).[8] Artisans, or workers either self-employed or in shops employing less than five persons, still are more numerous than factory workers in most Latin American countries. The predominance of the artisan shop has not encouraged the development either of a class-conscious proletariat or of large-scale social movements. Paternalism and personal and family ties usually characterize the relationship between employer and employee in the artisan workplace. The dispersion of small numbers of workers among a large number of shops creates serious obstacles to the communication of ideas, experiences, or grievances which might create the bonds for social organization.[9] Workers in artisan shops may perceive themselves as transients who will become shop owners themselves and not infrequently may participate in commercial activities along with their manual work.

Factory workers are employed within a heterogeneous industrial environment. They are found in numerous inefficient and low-paying small firms and, in much smaller numbers, in large enterprises. Among the larger firms, workers are employed by the technologically backward and economically inefficient labor-intensive industries producing consumer goods as well as by much less numerous technologically modern capital-intensive industries producing capital goods. Unskilled workers outnumber the skilled. The wage differentials among workers employed in small factories, traditional, and modern industries are significant. In addition, the wage differences between skilled and unskilled labor are quite substantial.[10] The number of workers employed by large modern industries is less than 5 percent of the economically active population in Latin America, but the number of skilled workers is close to 1 percent.

The growth of large-scale industry in Europe and the United States, which concentrated large numbers of skilled and unskilled workers in factories, created the conditions for the emergence of massive working-class organizations.[11] These conditions are lacking throughout most of Latin America. A working-class culture based on the factory experience is lacking. The existence of small dispersed firms generates individual and personal approaches to problem-solving by segments of the urban working class because their political experience is confined to interaction with a small number of equally atomized workers.

Service Workers: White Collar and the Shirtless

Two related processes have also affected the relative political and social strength of the industrial working class: bureaucratization and urbanization. The growth of commercial capitalism and the central importance of the state in all aspects of economic and social life have generated a large white-collar group in Latin America.[12] In banking and trade (domestic and foreign), in private and public enterprises, in semiautonomous corporations and in government agencies (which proliferate after each change in regime), white-collar employees have multiplied despite the low industrial level of most countries in Latin America.[13] The service sector was not an outgrowth of an industrial technological revolution. The white-collar group expanded, especially earlier in the century, in order to service the growing commercial activities of the export sector of the economy, which was largely controlled by large landowners and foreign investors.[14] Following the Great Depression, increased government involvement in the economy and the rapid increase in the number of high school graduates substantially enlarged the number of white-collar employees in government offices. As a result, the number of white-collar workers has in some countries exceeded the number of industrial workers employed by large firms.

Lacking property, white-collar employees have frequently organized legal or quasi-legal trade unions or other similar types of organizations in order to advance their interests. In some countries, such as Uruguay and Chile, white-collar employees are among the best organized and most "militant" groups in the city.[15] Largely concentrated in the capital city, frequently in large offices, stung by inflation and austerity programs, they have shown considerable capacity to engage in social and political warfare. Through their organizations they have been able to achieve social welfare legislation and wage levels that set them distinctly apart from other segments of the urban wage-earning group.

In contrast to the factory and white-collar workers and at the bottom of the urban pyramid is the subproletariat—the largest single group in the city. Classified as part of the service sector, the subproletariat encompasses a large mass of semiemployed and irregularly employed individuals who scratch a living through a great variety of low-paying, unproductive activities: as penny vendors of a few cheap articles, personal servants, car watchers, shoeshiners, newspaper and lottery vendors, occasional day laborers, etc. The urban subproletariat is not directly related to industrial production, yet it numerically exceeds the number of all manufacturing workers, including artisans. Most of the low-paid service occupations are manned by rural migrants while most industrial workers are recruited from among already urbanized workers. Thus there are cultural as well as economic differences between the two groups which sometimes lead to political cleavages. The subproletariat has formed an increasing proportion of the economically active urban population, a trend which has become even more evident in recent years. Migration to the city, occurring as it does independently of the ability of industry to provide jobs, has created a class that would seem to be in an explosive social situation: a growing subproletariat with a very precarious existence, one in fact excluded from the benefits that may accrue to the nation through the expansion of modern technologically advanced industry. Yet the very socioeconomic position that the subproletariat occupies in society has been responsible for the largely nonrevolutionary role that it has played in Latin American political life.[16]

The relatively conservative political behavior of members of the subproletariat can be understood through an examination of their economic position and of the types of problems with which they have been concerned. A great many of the occupations in which they are engaged are "individual." The poverty-stricken penny capitalism of the street vendors encourages an identification with the commercial values of the petty bourgeoisie, not with the ideas of class solidarity found among industrial workers. Others are employed in personal service—hardly a member of the middle class lacks at least a washerwoman or a full-time maid—and are subject to the personal supervision and influence of the employer and his values. Payment is usually partially in kind as well as in money wages. The highly dispersed nature of these economic activities does not encourage a sharing of experience that might lead to collective action. In sum, the nature of the economic activity engaged in by the low-paid service workers generates personal dependence and paternalism, individualism and commercial values, in contrast to the class consciousness that is a more likely result of employment by large impersonal industrial firms, where the worker's link to the job is through wage payments exchanged for labor.

These urban masses differ from the industrial workers not only in terms of their economic position but also in terms of the immediate problems they confront and hence in their political and social orientation. In the first place, the industrial workers' immediate concern is with improvement: social insurance, wage increases, job security, promotion, etc. In contrast, the primary concern of the nonindustrial subproletariat is subsistence: finding a job in industry or any other type of institution that can provide secure employment; obtaining a site for building a shack and acquiring title to the land; securing some minimal sanitary services (potable water, electricity, etc.). The traditional factory-based organizations have not been particularly relevant to the urban nonindustrial slum dweller. It has been impossible to organize the subproletariat into trade unions, given the heterogeneous economic activity in which they are engaged. Secondly, to the extent that trade unions confine themselves to issues such as salary and working conditions within individual firms[17] they have little attraction for the subproletariat outside the factory. In the third place, legal and political restrictions inhibit broadly based socioeconomic organization and encourage social fragmentation. In addition, the labor policy of most Latin American governments fosters clientele relationships. As a result, labor organizations are encouraged to concern themselves with narrowly conceived issues for specific segments of the urban working class.

The major political appeals to the urban nonindustrial working class have been populist, corporatist, or a combination of both rather than class-oriented appeals.[18] The possibilities of creating class-oriented organizations among the migrants may be greater before they depart for the city rather than after they arrive in the slum. A relatively stable homogeneous labor force such as is found among rural laborers or in a mining community is susceptible to labor organization and to its ideology. On the other hand, the rural refugees who migrate to the city lose their social identity as part of a cohesive labor group. The amorphousness and transitoriness of labor and interpersonal relations in the new urban slum settlement make migrants susceptible to demagogic corporatist and populist movements.[19] The appeal of these movements lies in their ability to offer marginal services to individuals with desperate immediate needs. Peronism, Vargismo, the Alianza Popular Revolucionaria Americana (APRA) all appealed to the new urban slum dwellers, though of course not exclusively to them. The more rightist movements such as organized paternalistic dictatorships (those of Odría in Peru, Pinilla in Colombia, Jiménez in Venezuela, etc.) promoted large public works programs and supported legislation on welfare, job security, and price controls on basic food items such as flour.

The corporatist appeal is partially the result of traditional attitudes carried over from the countryside.[20] However, in some areas of Latin America leftism is growing stronger among the rural populace; this might have a radicalizing effect in the urban areas.[21] The corporatist appeal may also reflect the conservatism of individuals who experience upward mobility by moving from rural to urban areas. As a new generation of urban slum dwellers emerges, however, it is unlikely that their frame of reference for evaluating their social position will continue to be that of their parents. In any case, the type of upward mobility experienced is of a relative and subjective sort: in the city the nonindustrial subproletariat is at the bottom. The most plausible explanation of the corporatist appeal can be found in the dual position of the migrant slum dweller. Psychologically and physically he is part urban and part rural. He lives on the outskirts of the capital city and reflects the poverty of the countryside as well as the aspirations of the city. He experiences a loss of identity with the rural or mining community in which he originates and is not integrated into a trade union or an industrial setting. While urban paternalism in the form of the corporatist appeal provides a connection with his new social situation, liberal or leftist organizations offer little that is tangible. Corporatist and populistic movements rather than class-oriented Marxism have become the ideology of the Latin American masses because the traditional leftist groups have acted as defensive institutionalized organizations of particular segments of the industrial working class.[22] The traditional Left has not appealed to the nonindustrial workers and in most cases has hardly made an effort to articulate programs relevant to their needs.

Urban Working Class and Revolution

Thus far we have been examining the features of urban society which inhibit social solidarity and radical politics among the wage-earning and salaried classes. We have noted the absence of links among employees, industrial workers, and nonindustrial workers. We have also noted differences in organization, orientation, and behavior. Yet there are a number of important instances in which urban classes have joined together successfully in revolutionary activity, or at least in movements that have resulted in significant socioeconomic changes. These cases suggest that there are conditions under which the differences and obstacles outlined above have been overcome.

Industrial workers have played an important role in leading a social revolution (the tin miners in Bolivia, 1952), in providing support for a social revolution (the workers in Cuba's sugar *centrales*), and in backing a national-popular reform regime (the industrial proletariat in Argentina during the Peronist period).[23] In Cuba and especially in Bolivia the industrial workers, though a distinct minority of the economically active population, were concentrated in homogeneous occupational communities within which they were able to create a radical political culture. These workers were important agents for the diffusion of radical ideas. In Cuba, a political leadership that was able to combine revolutionary politics with a populist emphasis on living conditions, unemployment, powerlessness, etc., rather than on the job situation per se was able to mobilize masses and unite broad strata of the population, including industrial, nonindustrial, and white-collar workers. The target of the revolutionary populist movement was societal exploitation rather than capitalism. In the urban areas, conflicts were promoted largely though not exclusively at the point of habitation rather than at the point of production. The immediate consequence of this style of politics was to create in the street and in the outlying areas a sense of collective identity (the experience of sharing common problems and a common struggle) so clearly absent in migrant urban slums. The politics of class struggle were made relevant to the slum dwellers, who were exploited outside of modern industry, through revolutionary populist mobilization. In Argentina, the pattern of industrial development concentrated migrant and immigrant workers in a relatively small number of large firms in the province of Buenos Aires, which accounts for 66 percent of all Argentine industrial production.[24] Perón's ability to mobilize massive support behind his programs of income redistribution, social welfare, and industrial unionism was greatly enhanced by the concentrated nature of the industrial working class.

Throughout Latin America, wherever economic development has encouraged the concentration of workers it has usually generated social forces for mass radical political organization. In Chile the major base, past and present, for the Marxist Left has been the mining and industrial workers.[25] The miners, despite their limited numbers, have also been effective agents in politicizing other exploited strata, peasants as well as urban workers. This suggests that qualitative factors such as commitment and organizational skill as well as quantitative factors are important in determining the political role of industrial workers. Acción Democrática of Venezuela, during its early radical phase, drew considerable support from workers concentrated in the petroleum industry.[26] In Peru the agricultural workers on the largely foreign-owned sugar and cotton plantations provided the mass base for APRA during its early revolutionary struggles.[27]

The Dominican revolution of 1965 and the resistance to the United States military occupation are perhaps the best examples of interclass and intraclass solidarity: white-collar employees, industrial workers, the subproletariat, and the workers from the giant El Romano sugar mills were integrated into fighting brigades.[28] With the restoration of the old order, however, political fragmentation set in and social differences once again reasserted themselves.

The idea that labor in Latin America is not revolutionary is invalid if we consider the political experiences of a considerable number of countries.[29] What is obvious is that urban labor in Latin America is not a homogeneous entity ready to climb the barricades at any given moment in history. Segments of the labor movement, such as industrial workers, miners, or agricultural workers, have become the basis for larger revolutionary movements in situations where they were able to communicate with one another and to organize (in the absence of intense repression), where a sympathetic government sought to mobilize working-class support, and where revolutionary leadership emerged that recognized the specific character and needs of Latin America's urban labor force.

In some cases, such as in Peru with APRA, in Venezuela with Acción Democrática, and in Argentina with the Peronist trade unions, a dual process of deradicalization of the leadership groups and bureaucratization of the organization resulted in the shift of working-class demands away from structural changes to much more limited economic issues.[30] Despite the maintenance of revolutionary rhetoric these political groups have, through their policy of business unionism, widened the socioeconomic gap between industrial and nonindustrial workers, between organized and unorganized labor. Over time these differences have become accentuated. This has contributed to the indifference, on the part of some unionists, to the sea of social problems among their less fortunate countrymen.

If the urban working class has not always been the agency for structural change in Latin America, what has been and is today the role of the other urban classes? Are the urban elites better situated and are they oriented toward the promotion of dynamic social change and economic development?

The Urban Economic Elites: Industrialists and Businessmen

The shift from a rural to an urban society and from agricultural to commercial and industrial activity has also resulted in the increasing prominence of urban economic and administrative elites. Decisions affecting government policies regarding economic development and social change have been increasingly influenced by the behavior and attitudes of industrial elites.

The industrialists in Latin America are rarely self-made men who have risen from the bottom of society. The great majority are either drawn from the traditional ruling elites or else they are middle-class immigrants to Latin America. In his study of industrial managers of large industrial firms in Chile, Dale Johnson noted that ". . . this group of Chileans is largely composed of members of the nation's traditional elite families." [31] Studies of industrial elites in Peru, Brazil, Argentina, and Mexico contain similar findings.[32] Hardly marginal individuals, members of the urban industrial and commercial elites are an integral part of the social system. The entrepreneurs tend to be oriented toward conserving existing social relations and to seek the support of political and social groups which share their outlook. Most of Latin America's industrialists and businessmen were born in a relatively privileged setting, received an above-average education, and began their careers at a relatively high position. The entrepreneur by social origins and experience has little contact with the lower or popular classes and is not likely to develop any close identification with their problems and struggles. The social origins, educational training, and career patterns of the entrepreneurs expose them to the values of the traditional upper and middle classes and they largely identify with the goals of those groups with which they most closely associate. Through the bonds of kinship and friendship with members of the landowning elite the urban businessman is more likely to hold a conservative outlook than to want to modify the existing structure of society. Once established in the economy, the urban economic elites have become absorbed in protecting their newly established monopolies and oligopolies.[33] By the early 1960's few possibilities existed for new entrepreneurs to enter any established market.

Many of the practices and attitudes from the past continued alongside new modern industries: family-owned firms, paternalistic social relations between employers and employees, etc. Given their preponderant position in the new urban industrial complex, it is highly unlikely that the economic elites would seek to break down the barriers to economic development.

The new industrial elites are not autonomous but rather dependent in varying degrees on external economic forces.[34] The largest firms show the greatest attraction for foreign capital. Many of the goods produced are patented abroad and foreign investors hold substantial shares in many large enterprises. Latin America's industrial and commercial elites at most merely share control of their economies with U.S. corporations. This dependence on and linkage with foreign countries probably accounts in considerable measure for the lack of strong nationalist sentiment among the urban economic elites.

Heavy state intervention has greatly aided the large firms which have been the main beneficiaries of state financing and credit. The large established corporations receive preferential treatment in the purchase of profitable public enterprises sold to the private sector. Because of their connections with political institutions it is not likely that Latin American businessmen or industrialists will engage in innovative political activity which might upset established relationships with government agencies.

Managers of the larger firms usually hold directorships in several enterprises and banks; this leads to a high concentration of economic power.[35] The interlocking nature of the economic establishment limits the possible engagement of industrialists even in piecemeal social engineering.

One of the least analyzed areas in the development literature is the linkage between business and agriculture. The unstated assumption of most impressionistic accounts is that these two sectors are represented by distinct groups.[36] But data collected on Chile's largest businessmen indicate that almost one-half are either themselves landowners or are related through family to owners of large farms.[37] The extensive overlap between agricultural complexes and big business largely invalidates the notion that there are basic sectoral conflicts in Latin America between modern urban elites and traditional rural elites. One of the major political reasons why agriculture has not been reformed is that reform would require a frontal attack on politically influential urban big business. The absence of major conflicts between urban and rural elites at the advent of industrialization in the 1930's can be traced to this overlapping membership. The existence of kinship ties and property links between agriculture and business helps to explain the lack of support for agrarian reform among industrialists.

The conservatism of the urban industrial elites, however, is not confined to rural issues. One study of industrial entrepreneurs in Latin America indicated that their acceptance of trade unions was coupled with a demand for greater state control. The study observed that "a strong proportion of the entrepreneurs support the idea that the state must increase its control over the workers' organizations, above all in relation to the petitions for an increase in salaries and the right to strike." [38] A survey study of the Chilean entrepreneurial elite shows that over 82 percent are for maintaining the present system of fragmented unionism or of increasing state control in order to restrict further basic union activities.[39] Less than 15 percent favored more freedom for the trade unions. In present circumstances, what the entrepreneurs do accept is a weak, highly fragmented trade-union structure, in which, with a few exceptions, each factory has its own union and 85 percent of the labor force is not organized in truly independent trade unions.

Urban industrial elites maintain their position through a multiplicity of institutions and practices buttressed by state support. Essentially integrated into the economy, subsidized by the state, protected from outside competition, and controlling the internal market through monopolies and interlocking directorates, the entrepreneurs are basically a conservative force concerned with the stability of the social system. They generally have influence in most coalitions in political bargaining because they are represented by the political parties, and have direct access to state agencies. Embedded in the old coalitions, the entrepreneurs have come to identify their success with the maintenance of the traditional structure of power and authority.

Their association with the traditional elites puts the entrepreneurs in an unfavorable position when they must deal with the problems posed by economic stagnation and the exclusion of the rural populace from the polity. Their class rigidity circumscribes income, markets, opportunity, and mobility. The problems of economic development and social change are in large measure caused by the failure of the economy to provide greater opportunities for the mass of the lower class or to create new industries. The industrial progress achieved by the initial efforts of the industrialists, their successful manipulation of the state, their promotion of new enterprises have ended by creating new problems and barriers to further development. The problem is not the absence of industry but the difficulties generated by a complex of monopolies, oligopolies, and small inefficient firms.

These difficulties raise serious doubts about the ability of political movements which seek the support of the modern urban economic elite to reorient a group which is accustomed to limited changes and economic security into a dynamic force which would further basic social change, such as the integration of the peasantry into society, and economic development.

The Administrative Elite

It appears that the more modern the countries of Latin America have become the more difficult it is for middle-class parties to act as coherent political forces which could direct the economy toward a sustained and rapid growth of the society toward an expansion of social opportunities.[40] Increasing modernization has led to a greater fracturing of middle-class parties. Under conditions of growing social polarization the bureaucracy has become the major agency handling social problems and managing conflicts. While cabinets and coalitions change frequently and while parties experience abrupt shifts in strength, the continuity and stability of the political system are maintained by the bureaucracy.[41]

The major policy-making groups in the bureaucracy, the department and section chiefs and the professionals, closely resemble modern Western white-collar groups in their attitudes.[42] In terms of class identification they identify with the middle class. In a vague general way, they favor social change. In their life style, they are more consumption- than saving-oriented. Thus while the urban bureaucratic elites differ from the traditional Latin American middle class which identified with the old aristocracy, they show few similarities with the earlier Western bourgeoisie which was oriented toward savings and abstinence.

The specific kinds of innovations that the bureaucratic elites tend to favor, like their counterparts in other parts of the world, are incremental changes within the existing structure of society. They favor programs that call for the broadening of the educational base, economic stability, and full employment. Issues like agrarian reform, which would alter the structure of socioeconomic power, or massive low-cost housing programs, which would in effect redistribute income, are not given first priority by most bureaucrats, despite the obvious visibility of the basic problems. Development plans which attempt to go beyond the incremental approach and embrace structural changes will probably meet with resistance from the administrative elite. Thus while most top administrators frequently articulate a collectivist or statist ideology and express hostility to uninhibited free enterprise, in practice they follow policies acceptable to the dominant urban economic elites. The combination of radical rhetoric and commitment to short-range solutions found generally among liberal reformers characterizes the bureaucratic elite in Latin America.

The national industrialization effort necessary to overcome the chronic stagnation afflicting most of the Latin American economies is weakened by the conspicuous-consumer behavior of the administrative elites. The government exhortations to the workers and employees to work, sacrifice, and save go unheeded because these exhortations are contrasted with the life style of the top government officials. Actual behavior which stresses immediate satisfactions rather than abstinence surely will continue to influence the lower classes and serve as the model that guides their behavior. In this sense the values of the bureaucratic elite have a direct and indirect effect on the developmental process. There is little evidence that the administrative elite which largely serves the urban and rural economic elites is about to initiate any significant social or economic innovations.

Trends in Latin American Politics

Latin American politics are in continual flux. Periods of conformity (such as the past few years) in which military juntas or closely supervised civilian regimes are in ascendance, popular movements are dismantled, and labor and peasant organizations confine their activity to economic struggles have alternated with periods (the late 1950's and early 1960's) in which mass urban and rural mobilization and radical political changes seemed to be the order of the day. In recent years accounts which have attempted to define "the" political situation in Latin America or "the" role of labor, of the peasantry, or of the middle class usually have made generalizations on the basis of limited time periods and have been highly selective in the data presented.[43] As a result these accounts do not reflect the broader historical process. Repeatedly and erroneously, social scientists have generalized from particular attitudes and events without bothering to analyze the relationship between historical sequences and individual responses at a given moment of time. Social scientists have ignored the linkage between particular demands and the development of broad social and political movements. Strata of the urban working class have supported and in some countries continue to support radical and revolutionary political leaders, especially where they will not be shot or imprisoned for long periods of time for doing so. Peasants participate in reformist trade unions in attempts to achieve satisfaction of immediate needs, but continue to express support for programs which would basically restructure society.

Trade unions which have modeled themselves after United States business unions and which function merely to defend the standard of living of their members (and which are only slightly concerned with issues affecting the majority of poorly paid workers who are not members) are increasingly ineffective in achieving their limited goals. Economic stagnation and the increasing intransigence of business leaders who are backed by military regimes have in some cases forced even this labor elite to accept wage freezes and even cuts. The proportion of the economically active labor force represented by unions has declined. In the face of authoritarian regimes trade-union functionaries have shown little of the élan and combativeness necessary to mobilize labor to secure even the marginal gains that they had previously achieved. Bureaucratic, economically oriented labor organizations will have to face serious political problems which they appear singularly unequipped to deal with. The old-style bargaining at which labor bureaucrats were so adept has not worked with the conservative elites prominent today in several large Latin American states. The decomposition of the Peronist trade unions in Argentina, the collapse of the Labor Party in Brazil, the splits, defections, and expulsions from Acción Democrática and its associated trade unions in Venezuela, the disintegration of the National Revolutionary Movement and its unions in Bolivia, the emergence of radical urban and rural unions to rival the APRA-dominated unions in Peru are cases in point.[44] The demise of bargaining politics has been particularly visible in the more developed and industrialized Latin American countries which have more important and developed trade-union structures. Whatever the specific demands which Latin American workers may articulate, it is clear that in present political circumstances (in which over two-thirds of the Latin American population is ruled either by the military or by military-controlled civilian governments) the restrictions affecting organization and mobilization are decreasing the possibility of gradual incremental change. As a result, the moderate unions have been losing influence over their members, some of whom are becoming restive while others are turning cynical or apathetic.

The possibility of an interclass coalition, involving segments of the organized working class and the upper class, accomplishing changes in specific sectors of the economy such as agrarian reform or nationalization of foreign firms, is also less likely due to the interlocking of economic elites. Foreign investors, industrial and commercial entrepreneurs, and large landowners increasingly are found as directors and stockholders of the same enterprises.

There are indications, however, that new social forces are emerging which may energize reformist or radical political action. The growing number of white-collar workers in Latin America and their vulnerability to inflation, regressive taxation, and wage freezes have created a new social base for radical politics. In several of the more developed countries of Latin America, namely Uruguay and Chile, white-collar workers (bank employees, teachers, health workers, public employees of all sorts) have engaged in militant struggles and in some cases have resorted to general strikes. The majority of the active leadership of the white-collar union in each country is Marxist. The growth of a nonpropertied white-collar group, which is dependent on salary and affected by the same employer-employee relationships as are industrial workers in the more advanced countries of Latin America, has led to alliances between white- and blue-collar workers—an unusual phenomenon in the not too distant past. Rather than speak of the expansion of the middle class in Latin America it is more accurate to describe this process as the growing proletarization of the middle class. With the expansion of large-scale modern industry and the relative decline of the independent middle-class proprietor, organized white-collar employees have become increasingly important elements in national politics.

Another potentially dynamic political force is the second generation of urban slum dwellers: the children of the rural migrants now growing up in an urban environment. They have experienced neither the marginal gains nor the repression which inhibited their parents from participating in radical political movements. The unemployed slum youth played an extremely important role in the resistance to the occupation of the Dominican Republic by the United States.[45] However, although they are available for political mobilization on concrete issues, they continue to be difficult to organize on a continuous basis since most of them lack fixed places of employment. Further, with the recent wave of military takeovers, it is possible that conditions for mass political mobilization even on concrete issues will become difficult and that the trend away from clientele politics will be temporarily reversed —that paternalism and traditional personalistic relationships between subjects and rulers will reemerge, for a time, in urban settings.[46]

In the countryside, the push by United States policy-makers and Latin American elites is toward increased mechanization and rationalization of agricultural production.[47] In some countries, such as Chile and Peru, unsuccessful attempts have been made to create a class of small farmers as a counterweight to the increasingly militant landless peasants. In the rural areas the push toward modernization is undermining traditional loyalties and heightening social tension. While government repression has in recent years permitted a kind of modernization from above in the countryside, there is no certainty that insurgent rural groups can be contained for an indefinite period.[48] A new urban and rural insurgency involving white-collar, industrial, and rural workers could upset the delicate bargaining arrangements which have prevented some of the larger Latin American countries from experiencing thoroughgoing social and political change.

NOTES

1. The discussion in this section draws on data found in the following United Nations documents: Economic and Social Council, Economic Commission for Latin America, Symposium on Industrial Development, *The Process of Industrial Development in Latin America,* Vols. I–III (ST/ECLA Conf. 23/L.2, Santiago, Chile, December 1965); Economic Commission for Latin America, *Estudio económico de América Latina, 1963* (E/CN. 12/696/ Rev.1, New York, November 1964); *The Economic Development of Latin America in the Post-War Period* (E/CN. 12/659/ Rev. 1, New York, 1964).

2. For a general discussion of Latin American social development in the post-World War II period see United Nations, Economic and Social Council, *Social Development of Latin America in the Post-War Period* (E/CN. 12/660, Mar del Plata, Argentina, April 1964); and Andre Gunder Frank, "Urban Poverty in Latin America," *Studies in Comparative International Development,* II, No. 5 (1966–67), pp. 75–84.

3. For a detailed discussion of the impact of the new industrialization in Brazil see Glaucio Ary Dillon Soares, "The New Industrialization and the Brazilian Political System," in James Petras and Maurice Zeitlin, eds., *Latin America: Reform or Revolution?* (New York: Fawcett, 1968), pp. 186–201; and Anibal Quijano, "Dependencia, cambio social y urbanización en Latino-américa," *Cuadernos de Desarrollo Urbano Regional,* Marzo 1968, pp. 3–48.

4. DESAL, *América Latina y desarrollo social* (Santiago, Chile: DESAL, 1965), Vols. I and II; Armand Mattlelart and Manuel A. Garreton, *Integración nacional y marginalidad* (Santiago, Chile: Editorial del Pacífico, 1965). For a discussion of the urban-rural continuum and the new type of individual—the mixed Indian-Crede *cholos*—see Julio Cotler, "The Mechanics of Internal Domination and Social Change in Peru," *Studies in Comparative International Development,* III, No. 12 (1967–68), p. 240 *passim.*

5. John Friedmann, "A General Theory of Polarized Development,"

Ford Foundation—Urban and Regional Advisory Program in Chile, Santiago, Chile, December 1967 (mimeo).

6. Julio Cotler describes the split between strata as the "neutralization of the participants" and "segmentarian incorporation," *op. cit.*, pp. 240–241.

7. United Nations, Economic Commission on Latin America, *Estudios sobre la distribución del ingreso en América Latina* (E/CN. 12/770, March 1967), and *The Process of Industrial Development in Latin America*, pp. 124–136.

8. *Ibid.*, p. 125.

9. Frank Bonilla, "The Urban Worker," in John J. Johnson, ed., *Continuity and Change in Latin America* (Stanford, Calif.: Stanford University Press, 1964), p. 196.

10. The wage differential ratio varies from 1:2 in Brazil to 1:3 in Colombia. See *The Process of Industrial Development in Latin America*, pp. 131–133.

11. S. M. Lipset, *Political Man* (New York: Doubleday, 1963), Ch. 7.

12. Marcos Kaplan, "Estado, dependencia externo y desarrollo en América Latina," *Estudios Internacionales*, II, No. 2 (Julio–Septiembre 1968), pp. 179–213, and "Desarrollo socioeconómico y estructuras estatales en América Latina," *Cuadernos de Desarrollo Urbano Regional*, Diciembre 1967, pp. 1–27.

13. Eduardo Galeano, "Uruguay: Promise and Betrayal," in Petras and Zeitlin, *op. cit.*

14. Luis Ratinoff, "The New Urban Groups: The Middle Classes," in S. M. Lipset and Aldo Solari, eds., *Elites in Latin America* (New York: Oxford University Press, 1967), pp. 61–93.

15. On Uruguay see Roque Faraone, *El Uruguay en que vivimos* (Montevideo: Arca, 1965). Throughout 1968 weekly reports on strikes, general strikes, and conflict between public employees' unions and the government appeared in the Uruguayan weekly *Marcha*. On Chile see Jorge Barría Serón, *Trayectoria y estructura del movimiento sindical chileno 1946–1963* (Santiago, Chile: INSORA, 1963).

16. E. J. Hobsbawm, "Peasants and Rural Migrants in Politics," in Claudio Véliz, ed., *The Politics of Conformity in Latin America* (New York: Oxford University Press, 1967), pp. 43–65. Also see Helio Jaguaribe, "Brazilian Nationalism and the Dynamic of Its Political Development," *Studies in Comparative International Development*, III, No. 4 (1967–68), pp. 55–69; *Barriadas de*

Lima (Lima: Centro de Investigaciones Sociales, Ministro de Trabajo y Communidades, 1967).

17. For a discussion of the moderate "economist" side of Latin American trade-union activity see Henry Landsberger, "The Labor Elite: Is it Revolutionary?," in Lipset and Solari, *op. cit.,* pp. 256–300.

18. For a discussion of populism in the Latin American context see Torcuato Di Tella, "Populism and Reform in Latin America," in Claudio Véliz, ed., *Obstacles to Change in Latin America* (New York: Oxford University Press, 1966), pp. 47–74.

19. Germani's comparison of Argentina under Perón with the European fascist movements highlights the different social bases and results of "corporatist" ideologies which appear to be similar. See Gino Germani, "Mass Society, Social Class and the Emergence of Fascism," *Studies in Comparative International Development,* III, No. 10 (1967–68).

20. Hobsbawm, *op. cit.,* p. 47 *passim.*

21. Anibal Quijano, "Contemporary Peasant Movements," in Lipset and Solari, *op. cit.,* pp. 301–342.

22. Osvaldo Sunkel, "Change and Frustration in Chile," in Véliz, *Obstacles to Change in Latin America,* pp. 116–144. See also Espartaco (pseud.), "Crítica del modelo políticoeconómico de la izquierda oficial," *Trimestre Económico,* No. 121 (Marzo 1964), pp. 67–92.

23. On Cuba see Maurice Zeitlin, *Revolutionary Politics and the Cuban Working Class* (Princeton, N.J.: Princeton University Press, 1967). On Bolivia see Antonio García, "Los sindicatos en el esquema del revolución nacional," *Trimestre Económico* (Octubre–Diciembre 1966), pp. 597–629. On Argentina see Torcuato Di Tella, *El sistema político argentino y la clase obrera* (Buenos Aires: EUDEBA, 1964).

24. *The Process of Industrial Development in Latin America,* pp. 148–149.

25. James Petras and Maurice Zeitlin, "Miners and Agrarian Radicalism," *American Sociological Review,* XXXII, No. 4 (August 1967), pp. 578–586.

26. Robert Alexander, *Organized Labor in Latin America* (New York: The Free Press, 1965).

27. Quijano, "Contemporary Peasant Movements," p. 308.

28. José Antonio Moreno, "Sociological Aspects of the Dominican

Revolution" (unpublished Ph.D. dissertation, Department of Sociology, Cornell University, 1967).

29. The literature that argues that labor in Latin America is not revolutionary is summarized in Landsberger, *op. cit.*

30. On the APRA in Peru see Carlos Astiz, *Pressure Groups and Power Elites in Peruvian Politics* (Ithaca, N.Y.: Cornell University Press, 1969). On the Peronist leadership see Torcuato Di Tella, "Stalemate or Coexistence in Argentina," in Petras and Zeitlin, *op. cit.*, pp. 249–263.

31. Dale Johnson, "Industrialization, Social Mobility and Class Formation in Chile," *Studies in Comparative International Development*, III, No. 7 (1967–68).

32. For Argentina see Gustavo Polit, "The Argentinian Industrialists," in Petras and Zeitlin, *op. cit.*, pp. 399–430. Also, United Nations, Economic Commission on Latin America, *El empresario industrial en América Latina*, Vols. I–IV (E/CN. 12/642, 1962).

33. *The Process of Industrial Development in Latin America*, p. 147 *passim*.

34. Teotonio dos Santos, "Foreign Investment and the Large Enterprise in Latin America: The Brazilian Case," in Petras and Zeitlin, *op. cit.*, pp. 431–453. An excellent discussion of Latin America's dependence on the United States is found in a collection of essays edited by José Matos Mar, *La dominación de América Latina* (Lima: Moncloa, 1968). See especially Helio Jaguaribe, "La asistencia técnica extranjera y el desarrollo nacional"; Celso Furtado, "La hegemonía de los Estados Unidos y el futuro de América Latina"; Osvaldo Sunkel, "Política nacional de desarrollo y dependencia externa"; Fernando H. Cardoso and Enzo Faletto, "Dependencia y desarrollo en América Latina." See also Jorge Bravo Bresani, "Gran Empresa y pequeña nación," in José Matos Mar *et al.*, *Peru problema* (Lima: Moncloa, 1968), pp. 119–152; and "United States Business and Foreign Policy," below, pp. 229–248.

35. Ricardo Lagos, *La concentración del poder económico* (Santiago, Chile: Editorial del Pacífico, 1965); Albert Lauterbach, "Government and Development: Managerial Attitudes in Latin America," *Journal of Inter-American Studies*, VII, No. 2 (April 1965), pp. 201–225; Carlos Malpica, *Los duenos del Peru* (Lima: Fondo de Cultura Popular, n.d.).

36. For an extensive critical survey see Andre Gunder Frank, "So-

ciology of Development and Underdevelopment of Sociology," in *Latin America: Underdevelopment or Revolution* (New York and London: Monthly Review Press, 1969).

37. Data were kindly provided by Professor Maurice Zeitlin, who is preparing a study of the integration of economic elites in Chile.

38. *El empresario industrial en América Latina,* pp. 16–17.

39. *Ibid.,* pp. 42–44.

40. For a detailed discussion of the weakness of parties in Latin America see Douglas Chalmers, "Parties and Society in Latin America," paper presented at the American Political Science Association meetings in Washington, September 1968.

41. On the role of the state in Latin American politics see the introduction to Veliz, *Politics of Conformity*; Jacques Lambert, *Latin America* (Berkeley, Calif.: University of California Press, 1967), especially Part IV; and Marcos Kaplan, *Desarrollo económico y empresa pública* (Buenos Aires: Ediciones Macchi, 1966).

42. In this section I am drawing on some of the findings of my study of the Chilean bureaucracy. See *Politics and Social Forces in Chilean Development* (Berkeley, Calif.: University of California Press, 1969).

43. Landsberger, *op. cit.* See also Véliz, *Politics of Conformity*.

44. The divisions in Acción Democrática are discussed in "Venezuela Prepares for the December Elections," *Intercontinental Press,* VI, No. 29 (1968), pp. 716–719.

45. Moreno, *op. cit.,* especially Ch. 5.

46. For a discussion of the continuation of clientele politics under military-controlled civilian government see Norman Blume, "Pressure Groups and Decision-Making in Brazil," *Studies in Comparative International Development,* III, No. 11 (1967–68).

47. The April 1967 hemispheric summit meeting of chiefs of state made explicit the definitive shift from "social reform" to modernization from above. An excellent account of the proceedings is found in the *Christian Science Monitor,* April 27, 1967, p. 12.

48. On the negative effects of repression on political participation see Daniel Goldrich, Raymond Pratt, and C. R. Schuller, "The Political Integration of Lower-Class Urban Settlements in Chile and Peru," *Studies in Comparative International Development,* III, No. 12 (1967–68), pp. 3–22.

The Middle Class
in Latin America

The view that the middle class represents the vanguard of progress in Latin America is the single most influential current in U.S. and Latin American social thought: one of its best-known proponents is John J. Johnson, in *Political Change in Latin America*.[1] (It should be noted that this is also the thinking of the Latin American Communists, who are constantly discovering a "progressive bourgeoisie."[2]) Liberals may be expected to perceive the middle class as the primary agency of change. It is perhaps more useful, then, to discuss two authors who present themselves as socialists while defending the liberal viewpoint, and who thus compound erroneous and confused thinking. But, while dealing specifically with Victor Alba's and Robert Alexander's approach to the middle class,[3] the critique that follows is more generally directed at the great majority of liberal scholars and journalists who analyze and interpret Latin American politics today.

Victor Alba sees the middle class as the vanguard of a new modernizing, industrializing, and democratic force capable of restraining the extremes of Right and Left and, in the process, developing a nonfeudal, non-Marxist, democratic welfare state. Alba and his U.S. counterpart, Robert Alexander, proclaim that a "revolution" is now taking place in Latin America; that the middle class is the agency of this revolution; and that this revolution is effecting a "social and economic transformation." Alba presents a messianic vision of the Latin American middle class: "Rather in Latin America it is the interests of the middle class that coincide with the interests of all of Latin America (and in our context with the interests of mankind)." He rejects the Marxist view of the middle class and finds the working class degenerate, "full of vices. a condition for which it has only itself to blame."

He finds hope for the workers, however; the middle class may "re-generate the labor movement." This dogma about the middle class is encountered in one form or another in a number of writers who style themselves the "democratic left."

The middle class's political role, in fact, has little in common with the "mission" that Alba and Alexander prescribe for it. The emergence of the middle class, historically and in the present period, has not led to reform of land tenure, to sustained economic growth, or to the development of citizenship among the working class: the middle-class ascendance which Alba and his "demo-cratic left" celebrate has not resulted in the development of ef-ficient agriculture based on the medium-sized farm; nor has it resulted in the expansion of industry through savings and invest-ment, with rational economic decisions in the productive sectors; least of all has middle-class domination introduced the rural or urban working class to the civic virtues through meaningful social welfare measures, greater participation in industry and political life, and opportunities for social, political, and economic advance-ment.

The Alba thesis can best be tested by considering the role of the middle class in Chile, which experienced middle-class-led gov-ernments from 1938 to 1952, and where old and new middle classes have functioned over a long period of time in an Alba-type "liberal democracy," with little or no military intervention. The country is relatively stable and the middle class is "mature," i.e., permeated with contemporary Western values. The Communists and Socialists for the most part followed Alba's and Alexander's advice: they subordinated the workers' independent class interests to those of the "democratic" middle class.

The fundamental fact which stands out at the end of this period is the power of the traditional Right and its unshaken control of the rural area of Chile. The 1955 *censo agricola* confirmed this continuing concentration of rural property: 9.7 percent of the landowners owned 86 percent of the arable land, while at the other end of the scale 74.6 percent of the landholders owned 5.3 percent of the land. In the provinces of Santiago, Valparaíso, and Acon-cagua 7 percent of the landowners possessed 92 percent of the

machine-gunned while the middle-class reformist Radical Party approved the government's conduct and entered into a *tregua doctrinaria* (doctrinal truce) with the parties of the landowners and business, the Conservatives and Liberals. The Chilean middle class, either because it lacked property or because the property it possessed was insignificant, depended on and was subordinate to large landowning groups and large foreign concerns. The development of privately accumulated wealth and of capitalist enterprise depended on securing government office. State intervention, sometimes referred to as "economic nationalism" (or, as Alba views it, liberalism inclining toward socialism), became the dominant theme of the articulate middle class.

Charles Wagley, in his *An Introduction to Brazil,* noted the conservative bias of the middle class: "The Brazilian middle class can hardly be said to have a distinctive ideology comparable to that of its European and North American counterparts . . . in fact they identify with and share the aristocratic social values of the traditional upper class. . . ." He adds: "In a sense middle-class families are culturally the most conservative sector of Brazilian society." Finally, Wagley notes that the new industrial capitalists are "in fact fusing with the old traditional upper class to form a new dominant segment of Brazilian society." [4] Similarly, in his study of Chile, Fredrick Pike rejected the stereotype view of an agrarian-reform-minded middle class. He wrote: "Almost the only clear middle class trait has been the tendency to shun the lower mass and to embrace the aristocracy." [5]

The political problem facing the middle-class politicians was that, by themselves, the middle-class parties could not attain the political power necessary to create the economic opportunities for their own social advancement. The growth of a militant working-class movement, inchoate but seeking representation, presented itself to middle-class politicians as a formidable instrument for increasing opportunity and mobility for the middle class within the existing society. In order to challenge the oligarchy a new style of politics was introduced: mobilization politics based on middle-class demagoguery. But this political mobilization was distinctly limited. In the first place, only a small fraction of the populace was mobilized. To this day the middle-class parties in Brazil, Chile, Peru, and other countries prevent large numbers of the working class from exercising their democratic right to vote by maintaining literacy tests. Secondly, the middle-class parties were reconciled from the start to the maintenance of the traditional socioeconomic structure. Partial mobilization was sufficient to bring the middle-class parties to political office, but once there they generally shared power with traditional groups. Through government intervention the new middle-class political leaders created a national industrial complex and a national entrepreneurial group.

This development took place without modification of existing land tenure; many of Alba's new middle class are big landowners themselves—since 1925, 60 percent of the large landholdings in the rich valley of Chile has passed from the traditional oligarchy to affluent members of the new middle class. As Claudio Véliz notes: "No apparent contradictions developed between the aristocratic landowners and the wealthy radical leaders: on the contrary, they became fast friends and political colleagues once the rising bureaucrat had bought land and racehorses, joined the local country club, and taken his first golf lesson." [6] And there was no substantial expansion of the internal market based on effective mass demand. One result of this process was that the government bureaucracy and the middle class proliferated faster than the economy itself was growing. With their high consumption demands and their hostility to the laboring population, this nonproductive middle class joined forces with the middle-class capitalists-turned-landowners in imposing the costs of stagnation on the lower class— through "nontotalitarian" means, of course.

In contrast to the mythology of the "democratic left," the real historical role of the middle class in Latin America can be summarized as follows: the newly developed middle class and its parties were eager to achieve social recognition and willing to challenge the traditional oligarchy, but primarily within the basic structure created in the nineteenth century. Urban middle-class politics were characterized by partial mobilization of the population, and directed toward integrating the middle class into society. As the middle class emerged as a dominant force the country was transformed into a capitalist society, but without dynamic growth, a basic shift in landholding, or a marked rise in lower-class living standards. The principal vehicle for attaining political power was alliance with the working class. The principal instrument for creation of the industrial base was government financing through a development corporation. While the middle-class parties satisfied in large part the desires of important sectors of *their* social base, the working-class parties have notably failed in this area. The working-class/middle-class alliance worked almost wholly to the advantage of the latter. The working class sits at the bottom of the social hierarchy. It is unable to follow the traditional middle-class path of social ascent which usually begins with the acquisition of wealth, continues with the achievement of political power, and ends in the search for social prestige. Unlike the middle class, for the working class the attainment of political power is the necessary first step toward economic affluence and social status.

When one places the Alba-Alexander assertions about the middle class alongside contemporary survey findings, they appear even further divorced from reality. While Alba asserts that agrarian reform "rests upon the new, rapidly growing middle class," survey findings in Chile show that it is precisely a large majority from all sectors of the middle class which is *opposed* to land reform:[7]

Question: Do you favor helping current landowners rather than dividing the land?

	Yes	
	Percent	Number
1. Owners	69	(29)
2. Private employees and professionals	66	(29)
3. Public employees	60	(60)
4. Self-employed	57	(95)
5. Working class	27	(84)

It is interesting to note that it is the working class which offers the greatest support for agrarian reform; that the new middle class, i.e., the owner-capitalists, is least in favor, while the "petty-bourgeois" self-employed (the "old middle class") shows a higher propensity for reform. In a word, every statement that Alba makes is the opposite of the real situation. On the question of democratic rights, a similar pattern is revealed. A substantial sector of the Chilean working class is represented by the Communist Party, yet large sectors of the middle class would deny the working class representation, which would be tantamount to disenfranchisement:

Question: Should the Communist Party be outlawed?

	Yes	
	Percent	Number
1. Owners	57	(28)
2. Self-employed	43	(95)
3. Private employees and professionals	33	(67)
4. Public employees	21	(67)
5. Working class	31	(85)

It is also worth noting that the "new" entrepreneurial middle class is the strongest group opposing civil liberties: this new middle class is the most authoritarian sector of the middle class—again contrary to the Alba-Alexander dogma.

The most decisive cleavage to be found in the "middle class" is between those who consider themselves "lower" and "upper" middle class. Differences in income and status are more significant in defining the modernizing and the traditional sectors of the middle class than Alba's ambiguous terms "new" or "old," since, as we pointed out above, there is no "pure" bourgeois, i.e., the affluent middle class partakes of the traditional behavior and patterns of landownership:

Question: Do you favor helping current landowners rather than dividing the land?

	Lower Middle Class (287 responses)	Upper Middle Class (183 responses)
Divide the land	47 percent	32 percent
Aid the landowner	53 percent	68 percent

An important characteristic which emerges from these findings is that contrary to Alba there are profound cleavages within the middle class, indicating a vacillating and temporizing orientation: the middle class is split on whether to support the "order" of the traditional Right or the reforms of the workers' movement. On the basis of a survey of attitudes one has to conclude that, given the cleavages existing within the middle class and given the large percentages in most sectors opposed to major changes, especially in such vital areas as agrarian reform, the middle class does not appear to be the social basis upon which a political movement can depend in developing a dynamic force for modernization and democracy. Nor can the middle class be relied on as the guardian of democratic values. A working-class-based movement (despite the "defects" which Alba finds) offers the greatest potential support for industrializing and developing a viable modern nation, since the requirements for these processes coincide to a higher degree with working-class attitudes toward structure and policy.

Leaving aside its hostility toward democracy and reform, the middle class scarcely exhibits a "trust in industrialization"; rather the middle class in Latin America is overwhelmingly oriented toward present consumption.[8] In Chile personal consumption represented 81.1 percent of the Gross National Product during 1955–1957. This high rate of consumption was taking place while the distribution of income factor shares was increasingly skewed toward big property owners:

Distribution of Income Factor Shares (in percents)

	1950	1954	1958
Property income	53.9	57.3	58.9
Wages	19.0	16.9	14.4

It is not surprising that the countries with the largest Alba-style middle class—Argentina, Chile, Uruguay, and now even Brazil— have experienced little or no growth and actual disinvestment in railways, ports, and most utilities. The position of sectors of the middle class comes out just as clearly in individual responses as it does in aggregate economic behavior:

Question: Do you favor higher salaries over increased investments?

	Yes	
	Percent	Numbers
1. Public employees	81	(58)
2. Private employees and professionals	73	(62)
3. Self-employed	65	(96)
4. Owners	50	(26)

This finding contradicts the messianic function which Alba's "democratic left" assigns to the middle class. The same middle sectors which are opposed to agrarian and other reforms but at the same time are interested in higher standards of living indicate quite clearly that they are intent on improving their own condition without doing anything to improve the condition of the groups below them. Given the present slow growth rates in the middle-class countries of Latin America and in the agricultural sectors in particular, the added burden of middle-class demand for present consumption over investment indicates that there will be few financial and physical resources for future growth. If the middle class acted in accord with its conservative view of society and if it were seriously interested in economic development, it would be willing to sacrifice its salary demands in favor of capital investment. That this is not so presents serious problems for bourgeois ideologists who see "efficiency" and a "trust in industrialization" as the major characteristics of the middle class. Recent events in Brazil, where the predominantly middle-class-supported military dictatorship has jailed thousands, tortured hundreds, and murdered scores of trade unionists, peasant leaders, and students, underline the fact that a large number of the middle class who do not want reform and yet who are equally insistent on a higher standard of living are willing to suppress the demands of the laboring class with violence if necessary.

A related phenomenon is the tendency for middle-class groups in pursuit of higher living standards to join with landowners in squeezing the lower class. Frequently this behavior expresses itself in political support of and/or political alliances with conservative political parties, rooted in their common agreement on basic issues and structure. It is no accident that the "democratic left" of Peru's Alianza Popular Revolucionaria Americana (APRA) joined with the Right to oppose Belaúnde's very modest agrarian reform measures and supported the army's attack on starving Indian squatters. Belaúnde's middle-class liberal reform government failed to provide land for more than 2 percent of the landless peasantry. Similarly, the "democratic left" of Bolivia in the person of former President Paz Estenssoro was responsible for the shooting down of scores of Bolivian tin miners demonstrating for their subsistence allowances. In Chile, middle-class reformer Eduardo Frei promised the landless peasants that there would be 100,000 peasant proprietors in six years. Barely 20,000 received land, leaving 350,000 peasants still landless. Finally, the Betancourt regime in Venezuela frequently resorted to military and police terror and violence in suppressing its student sector for protesting the failure of the governing party, Acción Democrática, to implement its own agrarian reform and other social reforms. At his inauguration President Betancourt stated that land parcels would be distributed to 100,000 families during his administration. A Venezuelan Subcommission on Land Reform decided that 350,000 families needed land, though many thought that this was far too conservative an estimate. Ramon Quijada, a peasant leader in Acción Democrática who split from the "old guard," stated that as of 1963 only 10,000 families had received lands and substantial government aid. Quijada charged that the government was dragging its feet in the implementation of the agrarian reform. The ex-director of the Instituto Agraria Nacional (IAN), Rafael Silva Guillén, a member of the Social Christian COPEI Party, noted at the time of his retirement in 1963 that IAN's ability to purchase lands was seriously weakened by its lack of funds. Government aid was also drying up and many resettled peasants were unable to develop their newly acquired lands. Venezuela has 29.6 million hectares of arable land. (A hectare = 2.47 acres.) Before "distribution," 22 million hectares were occupied by large estates of over 1,000 hectares. Three years later, with the end of the four-year plan in view, the official figure dropped only to 21.5 million— 2 percent of the big estates had been redistributed. But even these meager figures do not tell the whole story. The official tabulations do not take account of the fact that some of the "reformed" areas, like the Yumare Project where 20 million bolivares was spent, did not produce anything. The Leoni and Caldera governments made few significant changes despite their campaign rhetoric. The *latifundia* in its modernized and commercialized form is still the dominant institution in the Venezuelan countryside.[9]

The profound cleavage between the middle class and the working class, the unwillingness of middle-class parties to develop a social reform program directed toward the needs of the urban and rural laboring populace, leads them to rely on the military and on force to maintain their economic position and social status. The rash of military takeovers can only be understood in the context of the middle class's failure to institute continuous and balanced economic growth which could provide meaningful benefits for the lower class.

There is a tendency among Latin Americanists in the United States to make a virtue of this alleged necessity. John J. Johnson and Edwin Lieuwen, for example, previously put great faith in the middle class; as this decade began to unfold and it became abundantly clear that the Latin American middle class could not develop the area or contain the discontent of the lower class, and as the military came more and more to combine the roles of undertaker to revolution and caretaker of the status quo, these writers saw the military as the new modernizing oligarchy. Alba has only partially accepted this new formula: he sees a partnership between one sector of the military (the "technicians") and the middle class. As the working class increases its pressure for basic change, perhaps a "democratic left" will be discovered in the military and renewed suppression of the working class will be justified as necessary to stem "totalitarianism" or "negative nationalism."

Alba is ambiguous about the social function of the "technocratic army." On the one hand, he speaks of the need to "dissolve old-fashioned armies and replace them by technical units (without arms) . . . ," and yet he follows this with the statement that these "technicians" would be "preparing for combat. . . ." To add to the confusion Alba proposes "disarmament" in Latin America "under the protection of the Organization of American States."

Presumably the member states would have armies to contribute to the OAS—or would the United States, which dominates the OAS, supply the "protection"? Alba's ambiguity on the question of the military reflects his need to pay lip service to the antimilitarism associated with democratic principles while recognizing, at least dimly, the real need of the middle class to maintain its social position through military force.

One of the more recent U.S.-supported coups, in the largest country in Latin America, Brazil, had the direct support and cooperation of the urban educated middle class, which feared the extension of the suffrage to the mass of starving illiterate rural workers (income under $100 per year). The nationalism of the Latin American middle class which Alba and Alexander always vaunt was proved a myth, as the following testimony by U.S. officials on the Brazilian military takeover indicates:

General O'Meara:	If we can make so much progress every year as we made (security deletion) we will be doing pretty well.
Congressman Gross:	Did we do this?
General O'Meara:	(Security deletion)
Congressman Gross:	We haven't the slightest idea whether these reforms are ever going to be made, have we?
General O'Meara:	They passed an agrarian reform law since Goulart was thrown out.[10]

This exchange clearly shows that "we," the U.S., were thoroughly involved in the Brazilian coup.

Needless to say, the "agrarian reform" to which General O'Meara refers is a farce. Thanks to the coup, the landlords are in firmer control than ever, now that peasant leaders and militants have been jailed or liquidated. Latin "negative nationalism"— Alba's phrase for Latin American anti-imperialism—flows from the fact that U.S. policy today is based on the fundamental premise that "the most promising way to foster disciplined responsibility in a free people is to hold democracy in military tutelage." [11] To that end over half of the aid to Latin America under the Alliance for Progress is now going to military regimes. It is Alba's unacknowledged pro-imperialism which prevents his understanding this phenomenon. The point of the matter, however, is that the middle class in Brazil, as elsewhere, prefers foreign intervention to social reform beneficial to the lower class. Whatever "nationalism" the Brazilian bourgeoisie feels is carefully buried under its wallet.

While social scientists of the developing countries frequently mention the need to foster a Westernized middle class, the benefits to society that are supposed to be forthcoming are notable by their absence. It is precisely the imitation by the Latin American middle class of U.S. and Western middle-class values which is responsible for stalling the developmental process and preventing incipient democratic movements from taking hold in the structure of the society. As Riesman and many others have pointed out, in the United States the ethic of the new middle class is predominantly oriented toward consumption; the period of saving and investment and the style of life accompanying it are no more. The Latin middle class has taken over the "consumptionist" attitude of the latter-day United States middle class—and, like typical converts, they have frequently accentuated this attitude in their behavior. Scarce credit is used to finance consumption, i.e., installment-buying and other U.S. practices. To make the imitation "real," many of the Latin American middle class prefer imported items, thus using up already short foreign exchange which could be turned toward investment. While the subjective factor of imitative behavior is important, there are also certain historical factors which shape the behavior of the emerging middle class, ultimately frustrating attempts to develop a modern industrial democracy. In an earlier period the Western middle class could invest in industry and export products without fearing competition from other industrializing countries. In this process the Western middle class developed "cumulative advantages" over their now-emerging brethren: markets (including overseas colonies not available to the Latin middle class), large-scale development of plant and equipment, technology, and, above all, concentrations of capital sufficient to modernize whole sectors of an industry in a short period.

The Latin middle class emerging in the present period, facing the highly developed industrial complexes which have both access to resources on the world market and influence on price-decisions, is at a competitive disadvantage. The profits from newly developed

industrial exports are lower and riskier than profits from investment in real estate, commodity speculation, or production for a
limited but protected home market. The contemporary significance
of the combined historical factors of Western "cumulative advantage" and Latin "competitive disadvantage" is that the Latin
middle class is neither saving nor investing in productive sectors.
As a result the Latin middle class, in a different historical context,
with different aspirations and opportunities, has not played, and
apparently cannot play, the role that was played several centuries
ago by the Western middle class.

The salient fact is that there is a profound "crisis of the middle
class" in Latin America despite its political hegemony, privilege,
and wealth. What creates the crisis is that its consumptionist outlook
was not *preceded* by a period of saving, investment, abstinence—
behavior expressive of the "Protestant Ethic." This is probably
related to the lateness of the middle class's arrival to political
power, which could also be related to the retarded social differentiation in Latin America whereby a significant urban middle class
developed only after the turn of the present century. Hence the
combined features of industrial underdevelopment and a large,
vocal middle class demanding more and more consumer goods
telescopes two different stages of Western capitalist development:
the stage of primitive accumulation and that of high effective consumer demand. The almost inevitable choking off of economic
development by the diversion of potential investment capital toward the achievement of Western middle-class standards of living
raises serious doubts about the viability of Western political,
economic, and social models for the underdeveloped countries. In
addition to the perpetuation of economic backwardness, the social
effects of following such models include widespread malnutrition
and hunger, disease and illiteracy, greater class differences and
sharper social conflict. The "new class" must increasingly rely on
the military, on one-party structures, on U.S. military force, and
other military-authoritarian devices to maintain stability; and these
in turn only exacerbate the instability, the growing conflict between
the "new class" and the mass, and the lack of economic dynamism
characteristic of contemporary Latin societies.

In Latin America, only the interests and outlook of the working class coincide with the interests of democracy, economic development, and national independence, i.e., freedom from U.S. imperialism. For the working-class parties, economic and social progress must be preceded by the attainment of political power, which can enable this group to establish an agrarian reform and increase agricultural production. Through nationalization of monopoly industry the necessary capital can be channeled into productive investment. Under government control, funds can be allocated for the construction of houses, hospitals, and schools rather than mansions, racetracks, and resorts. Piecemeal legislation within the present stagnant economies is barely sufficient to maintain a work force at subsistence levels. Chronic inflation undermines whatever gains have been made in the past, and alternating cycles of inflation, strikes, repression, and decline in standard of living form the real pattern of development as far as the working class is concerned. To break this cycle, a social group committed to structural reform must have access to political power. In the absence of a revolutionary middle class, the working class becomes a potential source of radical innovation.

The inability of the Latin American middle class to rule politically and its dependence on the military to maintain "order" and "stability" is a problem which many commentators have not considered. The ease with which the Castro forces took power and the absence of any effective opposition by the middle class indicate the degree to which the Latin American middle class is dependent on the traditional military. More basically, however, it indicates its inability to fashion a political program capable of appealing to the laboring classes and an organization and leadership capable of carrying out that program. The middle-class parties seem reform-minded only when the old order remains intact: once the intermediary institutions (church, state bureaucracy, army) are temporarily removed and the middle-class parties are directly confronted with a mass movement from below, they attempt to resurrect the old institutions and to contain the movement before it can produce profound social changes. It is because of this failure of the middle class, not because Castro mesmerized the masses or the Communist Party manipulated them, that the "democratic left" of Cuba is now in exile.

NOTES

1. (Stanford, Calif.: Stanford University Press, 1958).
2. See Luis Corvalan, "The Struggle for a People's Government," *World Marxist Review,* December 1962.
3. Victor Alba, "Latin America: The Middle Class Revolution," *New Politics,* Winter 1962; Charles Porter and Robert Alexander, *The Struggle for Democracy in Latin America* (New York: Macmillan, 1961).
4. (New York: Columbia University Press, 1963), p. 126.
5. "Aspects of Class Relations in Chile 1850–1960," *Hispanic American Historical Review,* XLIII, No. 1 (February 1963), pp. 14–33.
6. Claudio Véliz, "Obstacles to Reform in Latin America," *The World Today,* XIX (January 1963), pp. 18–19.
7. The survey data used in this unpublished study were collected by Professor Eduardo Hamuy and his assistants at the University of Chile in Santiago before the presidential election of November 1958.
8. Amanda Labarca Hubertson, "Apuntes para estudiar la clase media en Chile," in *Materiales para el estudio de la América Latina* (Washington, D.C.: Pan-American Union, 1951), pp. 71–89.
9. See my essay on Venezuela, pp. 92–107 below, for a more thorough treatment of agrarian reform.
10. Quoted in *Hanson's Latin American Letter,* November 7, 1964.
11. *Ibid.*

Peasant Politics in Chile:
A Case Study*

The farm "Culipran" is located in the municipality of Melipilla, Santiago Province, in the fertile Central Valley of Chile. It lies less than two hours from the capital. In October 1965, after a series of encounters with the landowner and fruitless attempts to have their problems rectified by the public authorities, peasants seized control of the farm, armed themselves, and prepared to resist forcible removal.

Under pressure from the peasants and the left-wing opposition, the Christian Democratic government expropriated the farm and established a land colony (*asentamiento*) within which the peasants would work collectively for three years. At the end of this period they would vote for either individual ownership, collective ownership, or a combination of the two.

This illegal violent action by the peasants and its effect on their behavior and political and social attitudes is the subject of this study. Our major concern here is to describe and analyze a case of political development, the formation of a new structure of authority, and the process of change from capitalist oligarchy to pluralistic collectivism.

Data was collected in January–June 1966 through taped interviews with twelve peasants: four leaders of the revolt, six followers, and two peasants (employees) who opposed the action. The interviews, which consisted of open-ended questions, varied from one to three hours in length, the average being two hours.

---

* Written with Hugo Zemelman.

Political Change:
The Formation of a New Structure of Authority

The process of change at Culipran was irregular, uneven, yet cumulative and complex. Long-established norms were challenged indirectly and through devious means. Protest was repressed: the protesters were deprived of their livelihood and expelled from the community. New movements began and old leaders went into other activities or were coopted. The old structure continued, bearing within it members whose memories of previous struggles lay dormant. Discontent quietly gathered, awaiting propitious moments to express itself. Yet minor changes in the structure of agriculture at Culipran accumulated over time and isolation lessened; mass communications expanded and penetrated the farm; external political agencies looking for means of gaining power fanned the desire for land and justice; a new literate generation of young peasants emerged, nourished on the ideas of equality and not yet having experienced the defeats and humiliations of their fathers. These periods of slow change were characterized by informal political discussions and interchange of ideas on how changes in their class position might take place; stories told by relatives, friends, or those on the farm who had visited "outside" were passed on by word of mouth.

Traditional relations based on deference and obedience had met with popular resistance in the past, though repression and sanctions usually limited it to desperate moments or times when external forces appeared capable of neutralizing the weight of official violence. Interviewee 5 recalled the peasant mobilization of an earlier period. He described the emerging resistance, the subsequent defeat, and the recent resurgence:

> Politics here ended some years ago, at the period of Pedro Aguirre Cerda, when there was a revolution in the farm leaving us in conditions in which we couldn't make politics. In these times, I am speaking of the year 1940–1941, a Socialist Party was organized here and since that time the idea has remained, the fighting idea, of taking advantage of the right time to take the land. Between ourselves, we always have had the intention of searching for a

better life, of ameliorating life a little bit. Pedro Aguirre Cerda was the presidential candidate supported by the Socialist Party; how many were there, some 150 more or less were found throughout the farm—it [the results of socialist agitation] was the Socialist "product." When the party was organized we began to go to Santiago, to San Antonio, and to Noviciado also in order to propagandize for Don Pedro. We went to several places. I became head of the militia—because there were militias in all the socialist parties —it was a separate group that had to protect order in case there was some question. In Melipilla there was not much propagandizing because there were many rightists, so they came looking for us, the peasant comrades. Isn't that a joke? If in Melipilla they were smaller than a match light, here in the farm we had three truckloads of people. When we arrived in Melipilla they had everything set from billy clubs to rubber stamps; we divided up the work: some stood guard while the others wrote and others handed out the propaganda. . . . By the time we were finished the whole town, the whole plaza, all the major streets were covered with slogans. It was then that the Socialist Party was organized here on the farm and that three comrades were kicked into the street, the owner booted them out because they never would quit the Party. The owner came around and advised them and he offered them a thousand and one things in order to see if they would quit but since they didn't want to he came and threw them into the street. And wasn't my father-in-law one of those that was thrown out also? . . . Yes, the owner threw them into the street over there in Puerta, he fired two, and others in Bajo. And they had to leave, nothing more to be done, because he kicked them all out. What happened afterwards . . . There was a change of president. We began to take heart when Mr., how is he called, that . . . Mr. Eduardo Frei came forth, that had to help us . . . "Now Mr. Frei will help us," we told each other. At the same time in this period the leaders of the Socialist Party didn't come around any more. Only the Christian Democratic and Communist parties came around, they came around propagandizing for the election of deputies and senators. Thus we took further courage and we said: "Now we have to organize ourselves anew again." [1]

The tradition and history of deference was thus marked by inarticulate and inchoate attempts by peasants to better their lot. Socialized as they were into acceptance of paternalistic and authoritarian control, they nevertheless recognized the means by which traditional relationships were imposed and maintained, particularly the periodic use of selective violence and the absolute power of the landowner over their everyday lives. Repressive social relations, that is to say, rested on a structure of political authority whose beneficiaries generally had the means to enforce their will through violence, with or without the sanction of constitutions and laws. Usually, in fact, the state itself assumed the duty and obligation of enforcing the authority of the owner. In some cases the owner himself was the lawmaker.

The peasants did not merely passively accept the "law of the lord," but formed their own ideas of right and wrong, and perceived a discrepancy between what they did receive and what they should receive in exchange for their labor. The earlier conception of "moral economy," the semireligious idea that each man should earn enough to maintain his family, still survived against the "modern" idea of individual profit maximization. Traditional relations were honored, though often perfunctorily, as part of the price of being able to secure a livelihood. Alongside this "traditional" attitude there also sprang up from time to time the desire to work for oneself rather than be exploited by the owner, a desire that turned the peasant's eyes toward the land itself which he tilled for another's benefit.

Because of the intricate interconnections among the obligations and responsibilities binding peasant and owner, changes in one constituent of the complex were liable to set in motion a whole series of other changes. These might eventually result in basic shifts in values and perception of status, and in some cases lead to revolutionary activity. The disintegration of the traditional structure of authority in Culipran was thus neither a cataclysmic event nor the effect of purely autonomous, impersonal social and economic factors.[2]

Uneven Development and Social Change

The process of modernization has been uneven in Chile, largely bypassing rural society, but in recent years deep inroads have been made in certain areas previously governed by traditional modes of behavior. Agriculture has been commercialized and oriented toward the market; owners are oriented toward maximizing profits. Traditional social relations were kept alive, however, since they served as a convenient means of controlling the labor force and preventing disruption of the productive process. Thus, while the landowners frequently calculated their production and marketed their goods in terms of a money economy, they continued using payments in kind and other devices of the earlier "natural economy" when dealing with the peasants. Within the farm, traditional deference patterns and paternalism persisted; externally the owner sought to maximize his gains like any other modern capitalist. The owner was able to maintain the traditional social relations and his modern commercial activity by isolating his labor force from the outside world; experience showed that external contacts led the peasants to make comparisons which reflected unfavorably on their own social situation.

For a long time the owners were successful in maintaining their authority, largely because of support from official governmental agencies and policies. In recent years, however, modernity has been introduced by a combination of several processes, all of them tending to undermine the traditional pattern of political authority and social relations. These processes are (1) increased communication among peasants, and between the peasants and forces promoting agrarian reform; (2) growth of corporate ownership in agriculture; (3) mechanization of production and specialization of labor; (4) replacement of payments in kind by cash payments; (5) rural-urban migration; and (6) commercialization of agriculture.

In Chile today, as in the past, the *fundo* is the predominant social and economic unit of the countryside. Its internal relations conform rather closely to the typical model of the traditional and patriarchal hacienda society. Managed either by the owner (*patrón*) himself or by an administrator fulfilling a similar social role, the *fundo* tends to be a particularistic world within which the *patrón* exercises quasi-absolute authority.

Foreign economic investment in agriculture has never been predominant in Chile, nor even of major importance until recently, so that the Chilean landlords were not weakened or displaced by a foreign absentee-owner class (as was true of Cuba, for instance, where no genuinely landed elite could exist because of U.S. capital's penetration of agriculture). The pattern of economic development in Chile was also such that the agrarian social structure and, therefore, the *terrateniente* (landlord) class were left largely intact. Isolated, localized, and few in number within the *fundos* themselves, the peasants formed a secure base for the power of the *terratenientes*.

The *fundo*'s major work force is composed of *inquilinos*—peasants who work the landlord's fields and contribute other types of labor in return for a house for themselves and their families, a ration of land, usually from a fourth- to a half-acre, and the right to graze their animals on the *patrón*'s land. Until recently the peasants seldom left the *fundo*, and their lives centered within the world bounded by its walls. They were more or less completely under the rule of the owner, who constituted the law in his own domain, rarely if ever challenged from within or without. Their values, their ideas about the world, even their sense of individual worth, were intimately tied to the values and preferences of the *patrón*. He, in turn, regarded his peasants and the peasantry in general as children in his charge, to be disciplined, guided, and occasionally indulged. Under the rule of the landlords as a class and the domination of the owner as an individual, the *inquilino* has been the crux of Chilean stability in the countryside, his ideology essentially the reflected image of the *patrón*'s. When the *inquilino* voted—if he voted at all—he did not find it incongruous to vote as his *patrón* told him; if he did find it so, the power of the owner over his life did not encourage him to protest.

The introduction in 1958 of a new voting system, pushed through parliament by an alliance of the center and the Left (the FRAP, an alliance largely of Socialists and Communists) made it easier for the *inquilinos* and other peasants to vote for the party of their choice, while the emergence of the Christian Democratic movement as a major political force brought issues to their attention that had not been legitimate subjects of public discussion and debate even a short time before. These factors in turn helped the Socialists and Communists gain political access to the *inquilinos* and the peasantry in general. More important, however, in the emerging political support for the *frapistas* among the peasants, are the small but cumulative changes that have been occurring in the Chilean countryside. Electrification, the transistor radio, and improved roads and other means of transportation have facilitated communication between the peasants in different areas of the country and have made it possible to reach many of them simultaneously with new interpretations of their conditions of existence and with exhortations to change them. The large *fundos* have apparently become increasingly devoted to production for the market, and new economic forms of agricultural enterprise are also beginning to change the face of the countryside. Agricultural corporations have gained in importance relative to the large individual landowner, and these corporations now own a significant (though unknown) proportion of the arable land, especially that held in large *fundos*.[3]

The production of crops for industrial purposes, the growth of lumber and sugar milling into important though still small industries, and increasing mechanization have all contributed to changes in the external environment and internal social relations of the *fundos*, tending to undermine their traditional structures. A great many children of the *inquilinos*, as well as of other peasants, have left the countryside for the cities to find work in industry and construction;[4] the possibility of such migration increases the *inquilino*'s independence vis-à-vis the owners. Moreover, even those peasants who stay on the land can now visit the city and have direct experience of a different way of life. To their friends and relatives still in the countryside, the migrants and visitors have described experiences which have become part of the cumulative pressures for change in the peasants' ideas.

Social Change, Political Development, and Authority

The attempt to understand the nature of political life in a rural setting involves a number of key questions. Is grass-roots political activity among peasants possible? What circumstances impel peasants to action? Is popular rule possible? What are the experiences that produce citizens with a high level of interest and participation, and a sense of political efficacy, confidence, and optimism about the future? Are peasants merely passive instruments of manipulative external elites or are they capable under certain circumstances of manipulating politicians to serve their own ends? How effective are negotiation and bargaining in producing change, and in what circumstances are mass mobilization, illegal activity, and the willingness to practice violence prerequisites for producing necessary changes? What is the relationship between civility and revolution—is the latter a prerequisite for the former? Is a civic culture a postrevolutionary phenomenon? Several aspects of the Culipran situation throw some light on these questions. One aspect is the pattern of decision-making and the mode by which problems are resolved; another is the process by which traditional political authority is displaced; a third is the forms of authority which can replace it.

Political development in Culipran was a process in which representative organizations and peasant leaders emerged who articulated the interests of previous undifferentiated social forces. Political *experience* was important in shaping responses of emerging citizens; this fact suggests that the historical continuity of grievances and the presence of participants in previous struggles were important agencies of change. To these historical factors was added the influence of the younger members of the community whose frame of reference and alternatives were derived from outside the farm through contacts with the "modern world." The interaction of the traditions and experiences carried by the few older peasants and the new modern values and notions of legitimacy expressed in the younger groups produced the dynamic fusion that led to conflict with the traditional mechanisms of social control.

Conflict and development must be seen in relational terms; the growth of class consciousness was the outcome of interclass relationships. In Culipran, political awareness among the peasantry developed in direct response to the negative policies adopted by the traditional authority figures toward the peasants' demands. The rigidity and inflexibility of traditional authority, the unresponsiveness and ineffectiveness of the official bureaucracy in the face of new demands, were an important determinant of the direction and development of radical political consciousness among peasants. In addition, the relationship of the peasants to urban-based political

groups contributed to the development of peasant political skills—
the ability to formulate, articulate, and publicize issues and problems.

Traditional Authority and Class Struggle

The structure of authority of the *fundo* exhibited many of the
characteristics of paternalistic rulership: the decisions were made
by the owner, or by administrators whose decision-making power
was delegated by the owner to whom they were solely responsible.
Interviewee 1 recalled that "before the takeover, my problems were
taken care of by the administrator, Don Ligualdo; we met with
him, and if something was going wrong for an *inquilino,* if it was
more serious like a crime, it went before a judge. But he [the ad-
ministrator] took care of each individual's problem. If it was a
problem that necessitated money, one went and spoke to the
owner to see what he would do."

Nevertheless, the history of paternalistic rule was punctured by
social conflict. Our peasant informants in Culipran revealed that
intense social strife and political mobilization occurred in 1920,
1935–1940, and again in 1946–1947, prior to the present upsurge
(1962 to the present). Interviewee 1 recalled: "I was ten years
old when Arturo Alessandri was elected [1920] and this hacienda
was the first to rise to strike; it was called by the Chilean Workers
Federation and we followed with a march in Melipilla." He pointed
to the gains achieved through struggle: "At the end of the struggle
my father's earnings increased from 80 cobres to 120, an increase
of 40 cobres."

Contact with the outside through military conscription and the
political experience of registering to vote may have prepared some
of the Culipran peasants for social struggle and political leadership
during the 1930's. "Later I grew older, was drafted into military
service and later registered to vote. Then with the election of
Pedro Aguirre Cerda the Peasant League was formed and I
became its leader. We gained an increase [in salary] . . . But later
the owner threw several peasants out into the street for being
involved in the union."

The cyclic character of these earlier peasant movements relates to events occurring beyond the borders of Culipran. Conflict and mobilization within the farm coincided with national political mobilizations organized by insurgent, urban-based, leftist movements seeking public office. The long periods of quiescence coincided largely with periods during which the urban insurgents were holding ministerial offices, or parliamentary activity predominated, or the laws proscribed radical political groups. Popular mobilization during the 1920 presidential election of the middle-class insurgent Arturo Alessandri produced no significant departures from the agricultural policies followed by traditional rulers. After his election the President and his party demobilized the peasantry. Repression and isolation of the peasants returned. Contacts with urban political forces were broken; their external support vanished. The administrative authorities continued to pursue policies buttressing the quasi-absolute power of the landowners. This pattern of rural mobilization and demobilization was repeated with little variation in the 1930's and 1940's.

Because of these reversals, little if any change occurred in the status of the peasant and in the structure of authority on the farm. However, marginal gains within the farm's basic system were obtained. More important, the class struggle created a tradition which was passed on by word of mouth; experiences were shared with the younger generation; repressed demands were related to future action. This cumulative process eroded established authority. Because all the individuals involved were not eliminated, they were able to pass onto the next generation the quest for change through struggle as an alternative to the paternalistic way of problem-solving. The older peasant rebels became the "experimental storehouse." Their experiences and the traditions they established legitimated the officially illegitimate activity of the young militants. The later eruptions of violent activity for "illegal ends" rested on the experience of self-mobilization and the "expertise" of older peasants who were active earlier.

Contract in an Authoritarian Setting

A built-in instability accompanied each settlement of grievances that occurred within the system of owner domination. The contract agreed to between owners and peasants in the years of peasant up-surge, whether verbal or written, was binding on the owner only so long as the peasant movement itself was alive. Later, with the isolation of the peasantry and the reestablishment of official sanctions of paternal authority, the rights of the peasants and obligations of the owners were annulled. Collective bargaining resulted at particular moments in history when urban forces supported peasant initiatives and movements: sustained self-mobilization depended on external support. Effective collective bargaining of local units, such as existed at Culipran at certain times, appeared only when external political support countered the strength of the Right, i.e., the administrative regulations and traditional authority of the landowners. The short duration of collective bargaining rights and the limited gains which they brought did not promote peasant confidence in organizations and channels for problem-solving within the traditional structure. The failure of pragmatic reformist methods prepared the ground for attempts at more basic changes.

Culipran's inability to create stable mechanisms for gradual change and the accumulation of experiences of class struggle within the structure of traditional authority were two major factors that led to the seizure of the farm.

Communication and Political Development

Contact with the outside world reinforced and accentuated existing motives to revolt, it did not create them. Communication with outsiders played an important role in shaping the perspective of the peasants and heightening their sense of exploitation. For example, a peasant who was a veteran of earlier struggles read in a newspaper that the government proposed an agrarian reform. He informed the other peasants. The agrarian reform project stimulated his desires and hopes for change. Interviewee 1 recalled one incident:

> In the recent period it was five years ago when we first began to organize again. It was when I read in a newspaper of the agrarian reform of Alessandri. Then I began to meet with the *compañeros* [comrades] and they didn't believe me; they never believed me. I called them to meetings and told them, "This is happening,

compañeros, and we are going to have to do this"; and we came together slowly, and I went on telling them; thus some came to believe in what I was saying and others didn't believe.[5]

While the peasants were skeptical of the report that the government would actually take a hand in affairs on the farm on which they worked, the news nevertheless activated them. It encouraged them to organize, to implement what they perceived as government-sanctioned activity. In Culipran the mass media's penetration of the farm served to stimulate latent feelings. The media encouraged the peasants to go beyond subpolitical desires for change; they shaped a political perspective. The mass media and the information it introduced did not create new desires so much as arouse and reinforce existing desires, products of earlier experiences. Mass communications were one input in the process of political change, dependent on the existence of traditions and experiences which facilitated acceptance or rejection of change.

Modernization and Political Change

The peasants of Culipran made contact with the outside world through the small-scale commercialization of crops which they raised to supplement their meager earnings as wage laborers for the landowner. The revolt of the peasants against the owner resulted partly from the fact that the growth of small-scale commercial agriculture activated desires for individual self-improvement. The unused land and the speculative practices of the owner aggravated a situation in which the peasants, as aspiring market-farmers, were confined to tiny plots, unable to fulfill their entrepreneurial desires. The seeds of revolt were present in the form of the nascent individual capitalist producers who had arisen within the *fundo*. The peasants' desire for economic expansion conflicted with the restrictive structure of social relations on the farm. These latent values are revealed in the comments of Interviewee 1:

> I have always been an *inquilino*, but all the time I have been thinking; I have had other desires: it appeared to me that I could do something more. My desire was to make money and live a better life; and to have a little plot of land that would be one's own, for one to run with its eight *cuadros* [blocks] that one

could work with his sons and to have some money in order to work the land. I already have some possibilities, because a *compañero* who is also a close friend told me he would . . . open a bank account for me.

The peasant's interest in commercial exploitation of agriculture was evident in his wish to obtain machinery to assist him: "If I had a little tractor and it worked five *cuadros,* I can assure you that with five *cuadros,* if it is good land, they will soon earn something like fifteen million pesos and figuring expenses at five that leaves ten for me." [6]

Contact with the outside world was somewhat restricted. Transportation and visiting were generally limited. Those peasants who became local leaders were usually among the minority who had more frequent interaction with the outside world. The fact that most peasants were isolated was less important than that there existed a significant minority who carried the experiences of commercial and urban society back to their brethren in the closed system of social control.

The high proportion of peasants in Culipran who were literate and the high percentage of eligible voters who actually cast ballots indicated the existence of an available audience for the mass media and for the mobile political organizations.[7] The transistor radio and less frequently the newspaper were the means through which the generally literate peasantry became aware of current events. The peasants responded to the news according to their own perceived needs, chiefly remembering items of particular relevance to their immediate local situation. The absence of many personal contacts with the outside world was no great obstacle to political mobilization.

The existence of mass rural literacy and mass political participation even on the minimum level of voting suggests that the passivity which sustained the traditional structure of authority was already being undermined. The mass media were effective in weakening further a system of authority which already contained the seeds of its own destruction in the growth of mass literacy and voting.

The modernization favored by the owner class itself became a key instrument in awakening the peasantry from traditional passivity, in activating struggles that destroyed the owners' authority. The owners' decision to change from payments in kind (*regalias*) to payments in cash contributed to the politicization of the peasantry. The withdrawal of traditional payments in kind was perceived by all the peasants as a threat to their daily existence. Interviewee 3 underlined the importance of the loss of these perquisites in producing the peasant revolt:

> Now I am going to tell you how it came about that the land was taken over. . . . The owner, May 1 [1965], took away the traditional *regalias*. He gave us a hectare and a half to be rented, the rest was taken away. He charged us. Nine thousand pesos were to be discounted from our salary. Three thousand for a carload of firewood. And for bread we had to pay 600 pesos. Then we remained to starve. We said: What are we going to do with the family? Here we are twelve in the house, two grownups. We would have to starve. What were we to do with a fourth of land to clothe and sustain the family? It was not sufficient to eat. This was on payday—Saturday. Then we came together around here: This is going to happen. It's going to happen that we are going to starve. What are we going to do? Are we going to stop work on Monday? Well, we did it. All of us joined the stoppage; and we asked him that he should give us more payments and that he shouldn't deduct these interest payments. Nothing was done. Nothing. Nothing. So he left us on the same old terms.

The alienation of the peasant from his ancient moorings on his tiny plot of land, the attempt by the owners to rationalize one dimension of social relations at the expense of traditional benefits, brought forth a series of counterresponses that went far beyond the original issues. Payments in cash and the charges imposed by the owner for traditional benefits depersonalized the relations between owner and peasants, and rendered the system of mutual obligations inoperative. The peasant-owner relation became more strictly instrumental. Affective, particularistic relations which served as a buffer and which tended to undermine the formulation of collective demands were eliminated. Capitalist modernization and rationalization served to alienate the peasants and to activate them toward collective action.

The Traditional Basis of a Modern Revolt

What began as a protest against the violation of traditional norms became a challenge to the traditional structure of social control. Once the struggle broke out, the goals of the peasants changed. They were not oriented toward restoration of the old obligations but toward taking over the profit-maximizing position of the owner and establishing themselves as individual capitalist farmers. The expropriation and division of the land was the revolutionary means of extending and deepening the process of modernization and individuation.

The owner's practice of manipulating the marketing of produce in order to maximize profits contrasted sharply with the traditional norms which he held up to the peasants as ideals, and the peasants were aware of this contradiction. They mentioned that the owner stored crops and meats in order to obtain higher prices even while the peasants were hungry. Yet for many peasants, the contrast between the individual gain of the owner and their own social needs served to highlight only the personal vice of the owner. For the peasant leaders, on the other hand, this contrast was instrumental in creating an awareness of the different class interests of the peasants and owners. As the peasants pursued their self-interest in conflict with that of the owner, the farm became further polarized. Conflict no longer revolved around a return to traditional obligation and rights, but around interest politics.

Alienation and Revolt

The instability of contractual relations, the violation of traditional norms, and the covert collaboration of public officials with traditional authorities created a discontented mass ready for and interested in radical change. Support from an active radical opposition outside the farm created the necessary external counterweight to the official support for traditional authority. Interviewee 3 expressed the growing frustration of the peasants:

> Then we went to Melipilla to seek a settlement; we went to the Labor Inspector, to the Governor, but we didn't get results there

either. Because he has bought all of them, he bought all the authorities; afterwards we went to court, more of the same; we stayed in the same way, because the judge didn't rule in our favor. . . . And those who were supposed to be looking after us, the democrats [the Christian Democrats], it must be made clear, didn't do anything, they did nothing for us. One could say that it was then that the local leadership from this *fundo* went and spoke with a Socialist municipal councilman, Matis Nuñez [of Melipilla].

Within the farm the relationship of forces was affected by sheer weight of numbers: an active and organized peasantry easily overcame the owner and his formal and informal allies on the farm. The structure of authority was topheavy, insofar as final authority was concentrated in the owner; in practice, however, considerable day-to-day decision-making power was delegated among the "employees"—the general manager, administrators, the foreman, and others. The social differences between the employees and the rest of the peasants were accentuated by the higher incomes and better *regalias* that the former received. The quasi-absolutist structure of authority then had as its major internal support a stratum of employee clients.

Their relatively privileged position bound the employees to the system which subjugated the peasants. Self-interest encouraged them to espouse the traditional paternal outlook; higher pay and social status were their rewards. By defending the prerogatives of the owner, the employees were defending their own status and its privileges against the peasantry.

The values articulated by the employees were largely traditional: security, dependence, obedience, "natural" inequality, and trust in the economically powerful. In practice these values were not incompatible with those of modern capitalism; in fact, they served as a mechanism of social control for the profitable exploitation of labor. Interviewee 6, an employee, expressed the dual attitude:

. . . the past year, during this month, I sold two truckloads of potatoes in the capital . . . and I sold 200 bags in February. For this reason I am not in disagreement with the owner regarding *regalias*. The others don't have the same, they can't reach the same position because as you know . . . everything goes by hierarchy; in a farm not everybody can be equal. There are privates, first corporal, second corporal, sergeants, brigade colonels, and a number of other ranks.

The employees' political allegiance to the owner showed during the peasant takeover, which they opposed, although they dared not express their opposition in the face of the overwhelming number of peasants mobilized against them. Even after the takeover the employees expressed their sympathy and support for the land-owner. They continued to share his conservative political outlook and linked their superior status with the maintenance of quasi-absolutist authority. The employees had improved their material position through their loyalty to traditional authority, and the owner had never withheld his favors from these upholders of the system. Nor did his termination of the traditional *regalias* affect them. The differential treatment sharpened the cleavage between the employees and the rest of the peasantry.

The peasants viewed employees as an alien privileged stratum. During the period when peasant insurgents were planning their takeover of the farm, they refused to take the employees into their confidence. The employees defended the concentration of authority vested in the owner, and stressed his importance in maintaining security and material benefits. An employee (Interviewee 6) noted: "From my point of view, the owner has been good to me because I was raised with him; he has always given me all the food; everything that I have is because of him; why should I speak bad of him? If some rebel it is because they have some vice, no? and others because they don't think and don't work, that is the other reason."

The employees condemned the decentralized democratic politics which evolved after the owner was evicted, and stressed the "disorder" of democratic politics in comparison to the authoritarian "peace" of the previous period. Debate and discussion at public meetings were characterized by Interviewee 6 as "worse than a dogfight." He went on to lament the loss of discipline and respect. While he grudgingly acknowledged the skill of government agronomists, he criticized them for not commanding more "respect." The employees were hostile to most changes on the farm: they attacked independent voluntary associations like the trade union as well as the independence and politicization of women. One employee boasted of the continuance of authoritarian patterns in his own household.

The employees explained peasant political activity as an outgrowth of their unwillingness to work. Interviewee 6 contrasted his own personal virtues which had led to "success" with the vices and lowly position of the other peasants in the following manner: "I am a democrat and I voted for Frei and before I voted for Jorge Alessandri and before that for Carlos Ibañez del Campo.[8] I have worked with the twenty-five in my family. We give our votes to the Right. And you ask why? Because that is the way to live a more orderly, more peaceful life; if you get along well with the owner, he will appreciate it. The future will be much easier for one. . . ."

It is interesting to contrast the employees' confidence in the benignity of the owner to the peasants' distrust and hostility; the employees' attitude is based on the granting of substantial rewards, the peasants' on the violation of rights. Moreover, because the employee was relatively satisfied with his previous position, his view of possible alternative modes of organizing society was narrow: "I have all my life been for the conservatives because if one does not live with the people who have money with whom is one going to live? It is evident that one must live with them."

Political alignments thus largely coincided with class divisions within the farm. The socioeconomic differences among the peasants—between the skilled workers and the poorest peasants—were less influential in shaping their political attitudes than were their common grievances against the owner. The deprivation they suffered at the hands of the owner more than offset the particular rivalries that existed among them. The peasants perceived the transformation of social relations into cash relations as producing a general deterioration of their common situation. The change of peasants into salaried workers, i.e., the loss of property status, was a key element in producing a general radicalization and providing a common basis for collective action.

In the earlier period, exploitation and inequality had at times produced overt resistance to privilege and struggle for incremental improvements. Later, the withdrawal of payments in kind was a catalytic agent that propelled the peasants toward modern ideas of self-interest and group action. Once social action was proposed the peasants became open to the ideas of self-government and representative institutions such as trade unions which could articulate their interest. Collective self-expression was embodied in their slogan at the time of the takeover: "The land for those who work it." Personal desires became social principles. Justice, formerly identified with the fulfillment of the mutual obligations between peasant and *patrón,* was redefined in terms of the peasants' own interests.

The Politics of Escalation: From Restoration to Revolution

The initial immediate causes of the disequilibrium of the social system provoked a series of related actions and reactions, each in turn escalating the level of conflict, leading from a strike to the expulsion of the owner from the farm. The intervention of external forces, the Left, hastened this process of escalation. Interviewee 7 noted:

> Before, the owner here was one of the worst possible, he didn't comply with his obligations to us. Of *regalias* he didn't give us more than a hectare of land and I had the right to one hectare and a half, as a master carpenter on this farm . . . we were working just one hectare and the salaries were small . . . We began to raise demands once Don Eduardo [the owner, Eduardo Marín] began charging us money here, charging us for keeping our animals; it was then that the people put themselves in motion and began to demand; that a strike was called here against him. We didn't want to work . . . Thus he had to return all that money to us. Manuel Muñoz [a Socialist peasant leader] came from Santíago to organize that movement. Could we have done this alone? No. Later the comrades from the Socialist Party came from Melipilla.

For most rank-and-file peasants the breakdown of paternalism was an important event in the chain that led to the revolt; most peasants had lacked a clear idea of alternatives to the existing structure of authority. Once the revolt was under way and, in the course of seizing the farm, an alternative began to crystallize, peasants began to articulate and value their independence and to form ideas of individual proprietorship. For most peasants the values of peace and security were connected with owning their own plot of land. Agreements, because they were breached more often than not, and the owner's bad faith in bargaining and negotiating, produced great anxiety among the peasants. The peasants did not feel secure and repeatedly expressed their irritation with the untrustworthiness of the owner. The growth of social solidarity among the previously atomized peasants was an important outcome of their political activities. Solidarity in turn contributed to their success in achieving their goals. Those members of the work force whose actions tended to undermine solidarity were isolated and referred to in a derogatory fashion as *amarillos,* scabs.

The Civic Culture: A Postrevolutionary Phenomenon

After the peasants seized the land and the government expropriated it from the owner, there were a number of significant changes. Traditional subservience among the peasants was replaced by confidence in their ability to direct their economic and social activities. Interviewee 12, for example, was indignant with the government agrarian reform agency (CORA) because it considered retaining the former employees of the owner. He was insistent on keeping them out:

> According to stories and nothing more, they told me that it [CORA] wants the foremen and all the employees that were here previously to remain; that CORA wants to direct them as its employees. We are not going to permit this under any conditions. We have struggled for this, we want people that work on the farm and we don't want to be pushed by anyone, we will get ourselves used to working for ourselves, to run the farm now; so we are not going to accept it . . .

The peasants supported the idea of a new democratic authority based on the solidarity of the peasants and their involvement in directing the farm. Interviewee 12 noted:

I know now that the peasant has to be organized, because unity is the only force that the peasant has, he has no other force [*fuerza*]. And the trade unions are what are very important in a farm, because that is the workers' defense. Political parties also have importance evidently, because through the political parties comes the help of parliament. We here have had it [aid] and we are grateful to the parliamentarians of the Socialist Party, the Communist Party, and also some parliamentarians of the Christian Democratic Party . . . I am here chairman of the union and now I am vice-president of the peasant committee . . . . We were elected by secret ballot by all the heads of family on the farm. All the offices do not yet function well because we are just beginning but until now we have not had trouble with the peasant committee, the problems have not been serious but I believe we will have problems from now on like this business with the employees . . . People come from other areas, as chiefs, and we have to accept them because of agreements* and the agreements are laws, we all agree on that, all the people are united and we know we all have rights.

Despite their militant solidarity and sympathy for the Socialists and Communists, most of the peasants were eager to divide the land. Justice was equated with each individual proving his worth in the marketplace. Interviewee 12 stated: "Sure we are better off now after taking the land. If we had a good owner like the one in San Manuel with good *regalias,* I would have liked it. But it is better to have a parcel of land, because on a parcel of land he who is lazy doesn't get any of the rewards, but he who had a plot of land and is not lazy can work it even at night. Each one has to work their own land." [9]

The peasantry in Culipran combined militancy, revolutionary activity, and pragmatic support for Socialist politicians with the goal of establishing a private capitalist enterprise. Thus peasant political activity in this case defied the dichotomous categories of conservative and radical.

---

* The peasants sign an agreement to work for one-year periods with government-appointed officials who handle the expropriation proceedings.

NOTES

1. The political leaders referred to in the interview are: Pedro Aguirre Cerda, a member of the Radical Party supported by the Popular Front Coalition which included the Socialist and Communist parties; he was president from 1938 until his death in 1941; and Eduardo Frei, a leader in the Christian Democratic Party, who was elected president in 1964 for a six-year period. Parenthetically, the peasants appear unaware that one of the key reasons for the repression and containment of peasant insurgency in the late 1930's and early 1940's was the acceptance by the Socialist and Communist parties of ministerial and parliamentary responsibility for a Radical Party government committed to the status quo in the countryside.

2. This study focuses on relations between human beings: the patterns of social control and deference and the process by which individuals undertook to change their situation.

    Impersonal processes do play a significant role in facilitating changes in the structure of authority. What we mean to point up, however, is that such processes must be analyzed in terms of how they affect, how they filter through, human beings. The agency of change is living individuals; the activity of individuals is oriented and informed by their awareness of their particular situation and the larger environment which surrounds them. Human consciousness, more specifically political consciousness, itself becomes an important variable in the process of change.

3. For instance, a still incomplete study by Maurice Zeitlin of economic concentration in Chile shows the following: of the twenty largest *fundos* (measured in hectares of first-class land) in the ten agricultural provinces from Aconcagua to Ñuble, six, with 29 percent of the land held by the top twenty, belong to corporations; another two, with 9 percent of the land, belong to limited partnerships by inheritance (*comunidades*); two more, with 10 percent of the land, belong to government institutions; the Catholic Church has one with 4 percent of the land; and nine individuals own the remaining nine *fundos*, comprising 49 percent of the land held by the top twenty. Raw data from Agrarian Reform Training Institute (ICIRA), Santiago.

4. The trend toward urbanization in Chile is marked. The 1940 census was the first to note a greater urban than rural population;

in 1940, the urban population was estimated at 52.5 percent; in 1952, at 60.2 percent; and in 1960, at 68.9 percent, according to the population censuses of those years. This urban growth, however, "has not been accompanied by a proportional increment in industrialization." CORFO, *Geografía económica de Chile* (Santiago, Chile: Editorial Universitaria, 1965), pp. 376 ff. Merwin Bohan and Morton Pomeranz, authors of *Investment in Chile: Basic Information for United States Businessmen* (Washington, D.C.: Government Printing Office, 1960), comment: "The growth of cities in every section of the country gives evidence that the rural worker and his family are no longer satisfied to remain in an environment that gives little hope for advancement or improvement" (p. 40).

Our own investigation indicates an *absolute* drop in the number of landless workers (*inquilinos* and wage laborers), between 1935 and 1955. Taking the raw census figures presented for provinces, and adding them, we arrive at the following:

All Provinces			Provinces: Aconcagua-Ñuble		
Inquilinos	Wage Laborers	Total	Inquilinos	Wage Laborers	Total
1935					
107,906	201,418	309,324	58,701	119,914	178,615
1955					
82,367	176,612	258,979	48,986	101,492	150,478

These figures, to the extent that comparison between them is valid, indicate the vast migration of the rural workers to the city. Thus the indirect contacts that the rural workers who remain are having with the life of the city and of a politicized working class are obviously extensive.

5. Jorge Alessandri, an independent conservative, was elected in 1958, and served until 1964 when Frei was elected.
6. Five thousand pesos were roughly equivalent to one dollar.
7. Most political parties confined their visits to the rural areas to pre-electoral periods, a practice which did have some effect in slowing down the pace of political mobilization.
8. Carlos Ibañez del Campo, supported by a coalition of the Right and the Left, was president from 1952 to 1958. His policies gen-

erally favored the Right and there was considerable repression of popular movements, especially after his first year in office.

9. San Manuel is a nearby farm. The owner maintained a very paternalistic system and had the general reputation of being quite generous with his peasants.

II
Political
Movements

Peronism:
An Argentine Phenomenon

Behind the complex shifts in Argentine politics, the struggle of factions and personalities, the bitter-end feuds of small left-wing groups, stands the Peronist Presence: the powerful four-million-strong CGT (General Workers Confederation), the ten years (1945–1955) of "Popular Government," the multiple clubs and informal associations, the sense of being a "part of the nation" with all that implies in terms of personal independence, aggressiveness, and self-confidence among the working classes. The fact is that fourteen years after the overthrow of Perón, the Peronist myth still holds sway over the majority of the working class, and probably a majority of the voters. In the 1965 elections, despite government restrictions, Peronism obtained about 43 percent of the total vote, which equaled the combined total vote of the next three highest parties. That is why the military and its parliamentary allies do not permit a plebiscite calling for the return of Perón.

The strength of the carryover from the past is rooted in the material and psychological benefits gained by a high percentage of the Argentine masses. The Peronist movement retains its vigor because it is not simply against the status quo (it is not a protest movement) but has had the experience of power and realized many of its fruits. This difference from almost all other Latin American national-popular movements is important for understanding the persistence of the Peronist mystique. Unlike those analysts who focus attention on the personal aspects of the movement, many workers feel that Peronism means jobs, stability, security, status, organization, and economic improvement. Perón's charismatic effect on workers is largely a result of his ability to

81

publicize effectively his positive achievements. There is nothing mysterious about that.

The contradictory elements of Peronism—a mix of conservative paternalism and an aggressive popular mass base—have been noted by some observers. To be sure, the contradiction is due partly to the fact that the revolution of 1945 was carried out largely, though not totally, from above. But more important for its long-term effect was the internal transformation within the Peronist mass organizations: what started above took hold below. The post-1955 Peronist movement has been, *par excellence,* a movement from below, marked by the occupation of factories and political strikes against repressive military governments or military-controlled civilian governments. The continued strength of the trade unions and of Perón's appeal suggests that what occurred (whatever Perón's intentions) was not just government imposition of organizational forms to control the workers, but the creation of organizations comprising the majority of industrial workers and capable of defending their interests after the Popular Government fell. The years following the overthrow did not see the disappearance of Peronism. The viability of the trade unions and the movement did not depend exclusively on the *patrón* or the state. On the contrary, Peronist organizations withstood military persecution and emerged stronger than ever since they provided benefits and protection to their members which other organized forces were unwilling or unable to provide. At least in the short run, they served the interests of the working class.

But if one cannot equate a national-popular movement like Peronism with fascism, neither can one disregard the abrupt and sometimes brutal methods used by Perón to deal with his opponents. The corporative elements in the Peronist ideology (*justicialismo*) have certain similarities to Italian fascism. Even today, trade-union differences are occasionally settled by bullets rather than through discussion and voting. And the remnants of corporative ideology are still discernible among the trade unionists who advocate a direct link between trade unions and political institutions. Nevertheless, it can be said that during the 1945–1955 period, Peronism was an essentially national-popular movement, with authoritarian trappings.

A major factor conditioning attitudes toward Peronism in Argentina was a double failure of the traditional Left. First, it failed to organize the majority of unskilled industrial workers and therefore was unable to provide tangible benefits to the great mass of the working class. The Communist and Socialist parties were based on craft unions and isolated plant unions, highly fragmented and generally ineffective, leaving the mass of workers out of the range of their organizations. This undercut any ideological appeal based on class analysis. Second, the traditional Left could not relate to the basic social conflicts within the country since it sought alliances with traditional parliamentary groups and tied itself to the foreign policy needs of other countries—the Socialist Party to those of the United States, the Communist Party to those of Russia.

These tendencies were accentuated during World War II when the Communist and Socialist parties joined the "Democratic Union" and, in the name of antifascism, set aside all pretense of defending working-class interests. The traditional Left finally severed itself completely from the working class when it joined other groups and the United States in denouncing the emerging national-popular movement as "fascist" precisely when the workers were being initiated into citizenship *en masse*. A consequence of the Left's declining prestige was a contempt for ideology, which was identified with tortured abstractions defending authoritarian national institutions in the name of a mythical internationalism. This facilitated the growth of the national-popular movement, illustrated, symbolically, on October 17, 1945, by the raising of Argentine flags and the downing of red ones—an assertion of national independence against Stalinism and U.S. imperialist domination.

There are three sources for Peronism's continuing strength: (1) its symbolic importance as a movement which succeeded in creating an identity for the average worker, raising morale, and impelling the self-organization of the working class; (2) its organizational legacy of clubs, unions, hospitals and credit unions; (3) its national-popular ideology which provided, in however loose a fashion, the basis for working-class solidarity.

The heterogeneous organizations, leadership groups, and ideologies gathered under the Peronist umbrella preclude a definition of "the" Peronist. Nor is there a single style of politics; the range of Peronist politicians runs from typical parliamentary gentry, through militant trade unionists, to gun-carrying commandos.

While there are frequent nonideological power struggles, there are also small, militant activist groups which seek to further polarize Argentine society around the question of *el retorno,* the return of Perón. Some trade-union leaders have expressed their growing independence from Perón and point to their strength without him. It is doubtful that they would accept such state direction as existed during the 1945–1955 period. Other Argentines denounce *el retorno* as mystification of the masses. Nevertheless no decisive social changes can occur without the masses who support the Peronist movement.

Peronism has two basic organizational characteristics: the parliamentary-electoral and the trade-union structure. The trade unions maintain their independence from the parliamentarians, which has both advantages and disadvantages. On the one hand, it allows freedom of action for a militant rank and file. On the other, the parliamentarians are not held responsible to their constituents and frequently wander over to conservative ranks.[1]

Unlike trade-union practice in other countries in Latin America, but similar to that in the United States, union contracts are usually made on an industry-wide basis, since the unions themselves are so organized. This is decisive in explaining both the strength of the union movement and the nation's political instability. A well-organized labor movement has the power to back the demands it makes on the system. In countries like Chile where the divisions and fragmentation of the labor movement are nurtured and exploited by the ruling class, stability and parliamentarianism flourish and military coups such as occur in Argentina are unnecessary.

Peronism, however, cannot be described in strictly formal organizational terms. It is manifested also by working-class solidarity, self-respect, consciousness, and independence, evident in such significant details as the workers' style of dress and their mode of address to members of the upper class, which would be considered insolent in countries like Chile but which in Argentina reflect the pervasive presence of the Peronist political culture.

The divisions within the CGT are between the followers of

Augusto Vandor, the leader of the metallurgical workers' union who was assassinated in the summer of 1969, and those of Raimundo José Ongaro, the leader of the more militant unions. These divisions reveal attempts by various leadership groups to accommodate to existing political forces (which means sacrificing Perón's return) while working to capture the Peronist popularity and organizational heritage. Trying to undercut conservative trade-union effort at accommodation, the militants have aligned themselves with the Ongaro leadership group and sought to focus the discussion around issues which can polarize political life: the class struggle and nationalism.

Attempts by the leadership groups to negotiate with the military and the middle-class Radicals reflect the basic political problem in Argentine government. The post-Peronist governments have lacked popular support, hence authority, while the Peronists have a majority but are barred from government. A settlement could be achieved if the Peronists were willing to accept partial recognition and some political power in exchange for giving their moral authority to the existing government. The growing independence from Perón of sections of the trade-union leadership enhanced the possibility of such a settlement. The rub here is that an independent and militant mass working-class movement is not acceptable to the ruling military elites.

Peronist leaders are quick to say that they are revolutionaries opposed to the oligarchy, imperialism, and the military.[2] But the Peronist will add that "the oligarchy" does not refer to all the big landowners, even less the industrial capitalists.[3] Nor is he concerned with expropriating their holdings. He is in favor of directing the oligarchs toward nationalist goals, through controls, and integrating them into the process of economic development. Furthermore, even foreign investors are not to be expropriated; they must merely put a healthy part of their profits back into the country. Finally, the military is not to be destroyed but negotiated with, so that terms for coexistence can be defined. The policy of the Peronist elite toward these enemies can be defined in general terms as integration of the oligarchy into the Argentine system, allowing them limited participation, and maintaining the status and salary of the military, in exchange for political nonintervention.

The militant Peronists, on the other hand, look toward the class struggle as a means of uprooting the oligarchy and its industrial allies. This attitude is manifest, for example, in the pro-Peronist weeklies *Socialismo de Vanguardia* and *Lucha Obrera,* both of which relate the class struggle to the return of Perón. Against these "insider" tactics, other militant groups like the Movement of National Liberation (MLN) operate as "outsiders" on the assumption that the Peronist bases are more concerned with tangible bread-and-butter issues than with the actual return of Perón. They further argue that if the "return" came about it would be a disaster for the Left, especially for those groups supporting it. Neither the insiders nor the outsiders have as yet shown that they can muster any significant numbers apart from the established leadership groups.

Peronist militants favor confronting the military through political warfare (general strikes, factory occupation), and seek to develop the potential for popular mobilization around the taking of power. For them, the national-popular movement should not be allowed to stultify around electoral machines and a few, select, well-financed trade unions. It is rather a means of completing the unfinished revolution, especially in regard to the *villas de miseria* which surround Buenos Aires and are found in the interior around the socially explosive sugar area, Tucumán.

Until May 1969 the moderate Peronists like Vandor who collaborated with the Onganía military government seemed to have the upper hand within the Peronist trade-union movement. But the wide appeal among the rank and file for basic change is manifest in the totally effective general strike which took place in May 1969 and in the revolutionary declarations of the Córdoba workers. However, the meaning of that revolutionary rhetoric is, at bottom, still ambiguous. In an interview, one trade-union militant expressed a strong desire for "structural changes"; yet he was vague about what specific changes he had in mind, and preferred to speak in terms of "the social function of the enterprise," "man, the integral being," and "solutions" with "a markedly American stamp and spirit and a style profoundly Argentine."

The possibility that Peronism in the 1970's will develop as it did in the 1945–1955 period is very slight. The heterogeneous alliance of the bourgeois-church-military with the working class which Perón forged was underwritten by the enormous funds accumulated by Argentina during World War II. Those funds no longer exist. The working class now has a degree of class consciousness, organization, and therefore independence, which it lacked in the late forties, and is less susceptible to control from above. The possibilities for easy development based on import substitution, which was Perón's bait for the national bourgeoisie, have been practically exhausted. The income cake cannot be redistributed to the masses without seriously affecting one or more partners in the "national front." In fact, the sharp conflict that pits the workers against the "national industrialists" today indicates that the old coalition is no longer viable.[4] The economic and social reality of contemporary Argentina makes the former Peronist coalition very unstable and, in practical terms, unworkable. A realignment of forces would appear inevitable the moment after a national-popular government came into existence.

The defeat of Presidents Frondizi and Illia was the first, not the last, blow against reconstituting a society of middle-class dominance. The Argentine middle class fears both coming to grips with a stagnant economy and the consequence thereof—a majoritarian working-class-based movement. Thus, one finds military *golpes* alternating with frustrated efforts at middle-class governments, both reflecting the same reality.

The June 28, 1966, military overthrow of the Illia government and the assumption by General Onganía of supreme powers is the latest example of this cycle. The major purpose of the military was to control the Peronists in the labor movement, who were seen as a distinct threat in the coming elections. The attempt by the middle-class Illia to permit the "accommodationist" wing of the Peronists some representation in exchange for trade-union support was thus frustrated by the intransigent military, for whom Peronism is not a negotiable issue. It is interesting to note that Illia did not mobilize the working class against his overthrow since this might have led to opposition from entrepreneurial groups that backed him. Rather, he attempted to maneuver among the military and when he lost, he went into exile. Though unhappy about losing the presidency, Illia left the social structure intact, hoping that a new bourgeois parliamentary government would emerge once the military "restabilized" the political situation.

This was not to be the case: four years after the military coup the generals show no inclination to abandon power. The increasing social polarization of Argentine society has led to increasing military control, not the reestablishment of the parliamentary facade; military tribunals and maximum sentences followed the massive strikes of workers in mid-1969. Increased social conflict and political polarization may transform the vague populist ideas current in the workers movement to a class-based socialist ideology.

A central characteristic of Peronism up to this point, however, has been its lack of ideology: "the answers come from the people." This pragmatic approach was useful in forming coalitions with such diverse groups as the military, the church, the industrialists, and the trade unions. This muddling-through, moreover, was encouraged by the availability of sufficient resources and funds to permit flexible relations between institutions and the social forces they represented. Pragmatic alliances even in today's Argentina may have short-run success, but they offer few assurances of a stable coalition because the economy is not growing fast enough to satisfy each of the major social groups. Thus, revolutionary politics and class struggle are increasingly replacing the pragmatism and bargaining politics which have been unable to meet the demands of substantial sectors of the Argentine working class.

The Peronist movement itself, however, is still largely pursuing a pragmatic path. Although leadership conflicts have allegedly pitted "reformists" against "revolutionaries," a glance at the antecedents of each combatant will reveal that today's revolutionaries were yesterday's reformists and may easily revert back tomorrow. Their positions have to be understood not in terms of ideology, nor even simply power, but as differing responses to a situation in which the Peronist movement cannot find its place in existing society: the existing elites cannot accept Peronism until it is transformed into a bureaucratic shell under strong government supervision, a position which even collaborationists like Vandor found hard to sell to the rank and file. The power struggles of Peronist elites are attempts to establish their authority within the movement in order to deal with a hostile government. The shifts in ideology and in selection of leaders by Perón himself are likewise attempts to balance off one group against another in order to maintain his personal authority over the movement.

The predominant ideology of the Peronist labor movement generally goes by the name *communidad gremial* or trade-union communitarianism. The credo of the affluent and powerful Light and Power Union, a strong advocate of this doctrine, reads as follows: "Two great banners, 'Trade-Union Discipline,' in order to consolidate the trade-union community, and 'Labor Discipline,' in order to strengthen our participation in industry, with respect to all of the national community for which we labor." Claiming to support neither socialism nor capitalism, this doctrine holds that the trade unions can become the base on which to build institutions that serve the worker and his family, from cooperative housing, clubs, and summer hotels, to schools for general education and technical training. The trade union and its appendages become a "community within a community." Militancy functions as a defensive instrument for maintaining that community. This doctrine falls far short of developing the struggle for power in the larger society. While in the past the *communidad gremial* functioned as a strong veto group in affairs dealing directly with the trade unions, under Onganía's military regime even the better organized and affluent unions have had their prerogatives sharply limited. Critics of the concept have noted that only a very select few wealthy unions could build such a community within a community and that Argentine society is not generating enough of a surplus to satisfy the demands of both the trade unions and the entrepreneurs.[5]

Since the 1966 military coup the Peronist movement appears to be divided between those who collaborated with the junta and those who went into opposition. In the first category the old-line Peronist leaders search for ways to defend their prerogatives and privileges. Their battle for survival does, however, engender a certain militancy, especially on the level of trade-union action. The mass base, largely formed during the Peronist period, is increasingly restive and seeks a temporary way out through the fight for limited gains. Hemmed in by the army on one side, the Radicals and old-line Peronists on the other, this mass base is still capable of battling when aroused, as was seen by the occupation of most major industrial plants in 1964, the general strike of June 1966, and the massive struggle of May 1969. On the other hand, the oppositionists are a mixed group, all gathered under the national-popular banner, searching for new modes of struggle beyond Peronism, but with the Peronist masses.

Following the fall of Perón, the Peronist labor movement consolidated its position and has become, in its own right, a powerful social force. This independence produced a strong current in the labor movement seeking a complete break with the Peronist past. Moreover, the unions created from above by Perón for his own purposes have shed most of their earlier authoritarian ideas and organizational structures. Although the use of violence and pressure persists, political life and competition do exist in the Peronist unions; Communists, Trotskyists, and Socialists vie for allegiance separately or in coalition with various dissident neo-Peronist groups. Not yet resolved is the relationship between a mass popular democratic movement and its most prestigious figure, the authoritarian Juan Perón.

Peronism of the pre-1955 period and today are distinctly different. The principal difference is the growth of autonomous centers of working-class power and a new sense of working-class solidarity. The result is that the labor movement can impose its will with or without Perón and, in the case of his return, against Perón, if he should attack the basic interests of the class.

If the average Peronist worker lacks a clear ideology, he shows a willingness to fight for short-term changes; if he lacks a strategy for power, he does have a defensive strategy; if the "trade-union community" is under the present circumstances a utopia for most workers, there is sufficient organizational strength in the labor movement to sustain a direct struggle with the government.

NOTES

1. Since the Onganía military coup of 1966, all parliamentarians have played a very marginal role in Argentine politics.

2. Remarks of this general nature were sprinkled throughout lengthy interviews with Alonso of the Garment Workers Union and Juan José Taccone, secretary-general of the Light and Power Union.

3. Not all Peronists maintain this "dual position." Raúl Pedro Scalabrini, a leading Peronist writer, for example, indicated a strong desire to have large landed estates expropriated. (Interview with Scalabrini.)

4. The supposed conflict between rural landowners and industrial capitalists is largely a myth. See, for example, Hugo Berlatzky, "Relaciones entre el sector agropecuario," *Fichas,* No. 1 (April 1964), pp. 56–60. A "national-popular alliance" of workers and business groups against the traditional landowner is highly unlikely; the social conflicts within the urban industrial sectors are quite pervasive and open, as the 1969 strike movement indicated. Likewise, the thesis that the Argentine ruling class, especially the industrial sector, "necessarily" comes into conflict with foreign capital is disputed in a well-documented article by Alfredo Parera Dennis, "Naturaleza de las relaciones entre las clases dominantes argentinas y las metropolises," *Fichas,* No. 4 (December 1964), pp. 3–25.

5. To avoid the charge that the Power and Light workers are a privileged group, the union has developed a series of aid programs for the shanty-town dwellers called *Labor de Solidaridad,* through which the union donates money and members' time and skill in building and providing facilities. Whatever the political value of such a contribution, it does little in the way of integrating the slum dwellers into that "community" to which the members of the Power and Light Union feel they themselves belong.

Venezuela:
A Decade of Capitalist Democracy

According to most U.S. writers on Latin American affairs, Venezuela has, since 1959, been experiencing a "democratic revolution." [1] Under the auspices of the Acción Democrática party (AD), it is argued, a number of far-reaching changes have been brought about which have fundamentally restructured Venezuelan society. The policies of the current President, Rafael Caldera, a member of the Christian Democratic Party (COPEI), are viewed largely as a continuation of the "democratic" revolution initiated by AD. A decade's development is sufficient basis for analysis and evaluation of the claims made on behalf of the Venezuelan democratic-capitalist alternative to social revolution. By determining what changes have been brought about, we can see whether Venezuela is a viable model for the rest of the hemisphere.

The Political Economy of Stagnation

The main defect of most accounts of Venezuelan politics is the serious understatement both of the long-term social and economic problems that have emerged from the past decade or more of development, and of their impact on politics.

The economy stagnated throughout the 1960's, while inequalities between classes accentuated. The per-capita growth rate for 1961–1966 was 1 percent—*less* than the minimum growth rate set forth by the Alliance for Progress (2.5 percent). [2] In 1968 it rose slightly, to 1.6 percent. After ten years Venezuela continues to be extremely dependent on the petroleum industry, 90 percent of which is owned by U.S. corporations. [3] Petroleum accounts for 30 percent of the Gross National Product, 90 percent of export earnings, and

65 percent of government revenue.[4] U.S. enterprises operating in Venezuela are largely multinational corporations with investments in other oil-rich areas, especially in the Middle East. When Venezuela's democratic-capitalist government increased the country's share of the earnings to 48 percent, the multinational corporations began to increase production in their Middle Eastern and Canadian holdings. As a result, beginning in 1958 there was an abrupt decline in new investments in the petroleum sector. U.S. petroleum companies reduced their capital expenses in Venezuela so that in 1960 gross fixed investment declined by 22 percent.[5] Not radical enough to nationalize the oil industry and promote expansion under public auspices, nor conservative enough to provide the right kind of incentives for foreign investors, AD's policies encouraged stagnation. The lack of dynamic expansion in the petroleum sector affected other economic activity related to it, like the steel industry that supplies tubing. It is important to note that the stagnation of the 1960's follows forty years during which Venezuela has been experiencing the development of underdevelopment, i.e., increasing penetration and control by external investors, increasing dependence on foreign-owned economic sectors, and greater vulnerability to external decision-makers. The contrast between past and present is suggestive. In 1920 oil constituted 2 percent of the value of exports; in the 1960's U.S.-owned oil accounted for over 90 percent of the value of exports (together with U.S.-owned iron ore, 97 percent), and there is no reason to think that this dependent relationship will change under Caldera. The main sector of the economy, the petroleum industry, has been declining. The value of petroleum exports in 1961 was 11 percent lower than in 1957. Between 1962 and 1966 total oil exports declined from $2.5 to $2.3 billion.[6] There has been a sharp drop of new investments and stagnation in exports, few new wells have been put into operation, and exploration has practically ceased. In the decade since 1960 the Venezuelan economy has suffered a net outflow of capital.

The industrialization effort shows definite signs of slowing down: an 11.1 percent rate of growth for 1950–1959 dropped below 7.5 percent in 1960–1966. (The National Plan called for a 13.5 percent rate of growth.)[7] There are indications that Venezuela may be at the point of exhausting the easy opportunities for development based on import-substitution. Traditional consumer industries still account for the bulk of manufacturing output (52 percent) while heavy industry is still very much a marginal factor, accounting for only 10 percent of output.[8] The persistently low purchasing power of the majority of Venezuelans requires industry to seek new export markets abroad, a task that it appears singularly unequipped to accomplish, given the inefficient nature of industrial activity. Industrial development has been based on government "welfare" programs: credits, low taxes, high tariffs, and heavy investment in infrastructure financed by oil revenues. Behind the protective wall established by Venezuela's "democratic revolutionaries," large monopoly enterprises have emerged which produce high-priced shoddy merchandise. An industrial survey in the 1960's found that 196 units of big industry produced 60 percent of the total industrial output.[9]

Venezuela's democratic-capitalist development strategy has not been directed toward maximum utilization of existing human resources. By focusing on the development of capital-intensive industry—a policy largely in accord with the profit-maximizing needs of foreign and domestic investors—the emerging industrial enterprises have not absorbed the growing urban labor force. The benefits of industrial growth are reaped by the investors, managers, professionals, and to a much lesser degree by employees and a thin stratum of unionized industrial workers. The great majority of the urban labor force which is not directly integrated into factory production is excluded from the benefits of industrial expansion. It is precisely through state-subsidized capitalist development that inequalities have been accentuated. Unemployment, ranging from 10 to 17 percent of the economically active population in urban centers,[10] and disguised unemployment, found largely in the expansion of penny capitalism and subsistence occupations associated with the service sector, are the results of the migration of rural laborers. Both are products of the profit-oriented, capital-intensive development strategy chosen by Venezuela's democratic-capitalist politicians.

In their efforts to create a favorable climate for private investors, AD and COPEI political leaders have created an unfavorable climate for social and economic reforms. The conservatization of the AD leadership, which dominated the government until 1969, contributed substantially to the establishment of probusiness policies and priorities. The hostility of the AD "old guard" to the younger nationalist-populist groups within the party, and to the *fidelistas* and Communists in the trade unions and universities, was complemented by a rapprochement with the military and investor groups. AD's acceptance and encouragement of large-scale foreign and domestic private investment required it to maintain rigid controls over labor and the students, and to reject mass mobilization politics in favor of clientele politics. Many of the constraints imposed on political and economic debate, and the inability of AD to deal with a number of key socioeconomic issues, can be traced to its initial choice of political allies and enemies. The subsequent exclusion of the Left from open political action in turn limited the ability of the remaining moderate reformers within AD to effectively mobilize support for more energetic redistributive policies. The linkages that emerged between the "old guard" in AD and the business and financial community were expressed through (1) tacit understanding with the military, involving continued allocation to them of a substantial share of the budget and the decision to forego any reorganization of the army or reduction in arms spending; (2) agreement with the oil companies not to nationalize their holdings; (3) formal political alliance with the business-dominated COPEI, and later with the right-wing National Democratic Front led by Arturo Uslar Pietri. In exchange for control over government office and an opportunity to promote the interests of the managerial and domestic industrial class, the old-guard AD leadership agreed to drop its populist, anti-imperialist program. For the socially mobile members of the middle class, AD provided opportunities for advancement as well as employment through the expansion of industry, commerce, and government offices (administrative expenses increased 9 percent in 1966 alone). Social welfare programs, largely products of revenue from the oil industry, benefited middle- and upper-middle-income groups—those with fixed employment, professional status, access to AD political bosses or trade-union functionaries. Public investment declined but operating expenses increased because of excess bureaucratic personnel, i.e., AD party stalwarts on government payrolls.

Public policy and economic development continued to be excessively dependent on foreign capital, since tax laws are full of loopholes and most of the affluent Venezuelans are experts in tax evasion. Between 1960 and 1966, the central government became increasingly dependent on petroleum for its income: in 1960, 58.2 percent of government income came from petroleum, in 1966, 62.6 percent.[11] The Venezuelan bourgeoisie has one of the lowest tax rates in the world; government tax revenues from nonpetroleum industry continue extremely low. Faced with the prospect of social-security and income-tax legislation, the Venezuelan bourgeoisie put the squeeze on by withdrawing capital—and the government capitulated.

Because the Venezuelan bourgeoisie is highly dependent on U.S. capital, when the petroleum industry is not expanding domestic investors easily lose confidence, and insecurity can cause a massive flight of capital in a short period of time, given the ease with which capital can be transferred. The flight of capital, or the threat of it, made AD's (and now COPEI's) public policy largely dependent on the good will of the domestic and foreign investor groups, rather than on the needs of lower-income groups or rational economic planning.

Agrarian Reform Under Democratic Capitalism

The Venezuelan experience with agrarian reform is a failure on three counts: (1) it has not substantially weakened the economic power of the large landholders and as a result technical aid and credit programs have largely benefited the large commercial farmers; (2) it has failed to provide land to about two-thirds of the *campesinos* in dire need; (3) it has failed to provide sufficient credit, technical assistance, and other means for promoting the development of those farms which the *campesinos* have received.

Venezuela's agrarian reform law, passed on March 5, 1960, was largely a compromise between the big-landowner interests and the original intention of the AD to carry out a "profound structural change." At the time, estimates of the number of potential recipients of land ranged up to 380,000 families, comprising 2.2 million individuals.[12] Landless laborers, the most numerous group, made up 58 percent of the total. Approximately 100,000 *campesino* families have received some plot of land since the inception of the program.[13] The Venezuelan agrarian reform has not been resisted by the *latifundistas*. The government paid very high prices for their land, allowing the landowners, who raised their prices to take advantage of "democratic" land reform, to earn very substantial profits, which in some cases were used to purchase new lands in outlying areas. Further, the agrarian reform law did not generally apply to large commercial plantations which were efficiently operated. Hence most of the early expropriations were of the most rundown farms and the undeveloped public lands, both requiring enormous investments to develop; hence the extremely high costs in carrying out the only limited changes that have occurred in Venezuela, costs no other country in Latin America can afford. Between 1963 and 1965 the bulk of the expropriated land (58 percent) came from public lands as the AD protected and stimulated the development of big efficient commercial farming.[14] All told, 45 percent of the land distributed has been public land, in many cases not the best land, nor in the best geographical location relative to markets. By 1964 the redistributive phase of agrarian reform was deemphasized. The Director of the National Agrarian Institute has noted: "The program was oriented toward the physical consolidation of farm settlements with increasing attention given to the economic factor." [15] A 1969 statement by the same official pointed to the fact that agrarian policy was a class policy oriented toward commercial agricultural capitalism: ". . . little significant progress has been made in the reduction of the concentration of land ownership in few hands, in the increase of peasants' production or income, or in the formation and strengthening of economic enterprises and organizations of small farmers." [16] The beneficiaries of agrarian reform account for less than 13 percent of agricultural production and only 5 percent of meat output.[17] In addition the big commercial farmers controlled the growth and production of the most profitable products. Because AD-COPEI chose to subsidize the *latifundio* class, financial limitations have placed enormous constraints on expanding the agrarian reform program even if they wished to pursue such a policy.

The great majority of the large landholdings have not been affected. The large landholders, while less important than formerly in the over-all economy, continue to control important economic and political resources which allow them to shape agrarian policy and the allocation of funds for agricultural development. As a result, many of the beneficiaries of land reform are operating on a subsistence basis or have abandoned their plots of land because of economic failure, largely the result of the lack of credit. Among the beneficiaries of the reform, 70 percent do not use chemical products, 62 percent do not purchase seeds, 80 percent do not purchase animals, and 61 percent do not buy machines.[18] Moreover, there has developed a new class differentiation among the beneficiaries: those who initially succeeded are becoming affluent while those who experienced difficulties have become ineligible for future credits; plots of land without credits result in the return of the subsistence *minifundio* and the indentured tenant farmer working for his more prosperous neighbor. One observer has noted that over 50 percent of the recipients of land were earning less than $250 a year from their agricultural activity, while less than 12 percent were earning $1,000 or more.[19] Despite the fact that large commercial farmers comprise only a fraction of the rural population, they accounted for over half of agricultural credits— 491,950,000 bolivares compared to 475,605,000 for the *campesinos*.[20]

The declining economic benefits of the peasants reflect the declining power of the peasantry in national politics, a trend which continues under Caldera and COPEI. Within the framework of agricultural politics, the big commercial farmers obtain an increasing share of the benefits through their connection with the processing and commercial distribution of agricultural products. Within the AD coalition the peasantry has become increasingly subordinated to both the urban and the rural capitalist. For the 280,000 *campesino* families which have not received any land, prospects under the rule of the bourgeois parties are bleak. Despite agriculture's barely adequate per-capita rate of growth, income for the majority of the rural population continues on the subsistence level.

Agricultural capitalists are an important component of the national ruling class despite the quantitative insignificance of agriculture's contribution to GNP. Representatives of the Federation of Farmers and of the Federation of Cattlemen have been elected to the top positions in Venezuela's major organization representing business interests, FEDECAMARAS.[21]

The bureaucratization of peasant organizations and trade unions, along with attempts to depoliticize economic decision-making (i.e., allow business elites and their political agencies to draw up and administer government plans) suggest that there is considerable direct integration of the political and economic spheres. Independent organizations representing the interests of the masses are less visible than institutions representing various phases of economic activity and dominated by elite economic interests. The corporate-state model of politics has become increasingly noticeable not only in Venezuela but in all of Latin America. Labeling Venezuelan politics democratic is thus highly misleading: bureaucratization, apoliticism, and technocratism fit in well with conservative business notions of class harmony and the traditional Catholic idea of an organic society. Traditional Catholic political and social values are linked to the needs of modern capitalist development. Current economic planning and development utilize democratic ideals as a facade for oligarchic or elitist decision-making. Key policy-makers continue to be drawn from big business and there is continuous interchange of personnel between politics and business. The elaborate web of interrelationships among private economic interests and dominant parties, administrative agencies, and executive bodies sharply limits the kinds of problems considered and the options and instruments available to public planners in shaping economic and social policy. Under the banner of promoting productivity, Venezuela's Christian Democratic "revolutionaries," elected in part with peasant votes, have utilized government resources to provide incentives to promote the productivity of the elite. Electoral politics in Venezuela are largely a means by which political brokers in government bargain with economic elites: they exchange government revenues and profit-oriented legislation for social advancement for themselves and their immediate clients, while maintaining the myth of a pluralistic democracy.

The Costs of Political Stability

The policies adopted by Venezuelan President Rómulo Betancourt during his term of office (1959–1964) were a direct repudiation of the nationalist-populist programs of AD. In a move to placate the fears of the U.S. and Venezuelan business community, Betancourt rejected the idea of nationalizing key industries like oil. As noted earlier, AD accepted Venezuela's dependence on U.S. capital and instead chose merely to increase its share of the earnings. Likewise, AD rejected the idea of rapid and thorough expropriation of the large landed estates in favor of colonization of government lands, costly payments for the private lands purchased, and subsidies to modernize production on the large landed estates. The civil administration and the police and military apparatus were left intact; the major change was the expansion of the bureaucracy to accommodate the patronage demands of AD supporters. The old administrative apparatus, largely a product of the earlier conservative governments, was hardly responsive to popular demands for social innovation. In order to rule, Betancourt chose to come to terms with the major institutions of the old order, the foreign and domestic investors, the military, and the large landholders. Based on a highly bureaucratized party and a trade-union apparatus closely linked to the government bureaucracy (the organizational apparatus and activities of the AD/COPEI-dominated Federación Campesina were financed by the Ministry of Labor), and drawing substantial financial support from the public treasury and physical support from the police and army, Betancourt, Raúl Leoni, and the extreme right wing of the AD were able to drive populists, nationalists, and moderate reformers outside of the party. The new political order envisioned by the purged and conservative AD involved a much narrower spectrum of parties and views. Political competition occurred within a consensus opposed to nationalization of oil, to rapid and extensive expropriation of large private landholdings, and to mobilization politics. As part of the process of converting Venezuela into a capitalist democracy, wholesale repression was launched to forestall mass mobilization of the nationalist students and of the underemployed and unemployed of Caracas. Simultaneously, conspiratorial attempts by supporters of Pérez Jiménez to seize power were frustrated. The new political order was forcibly established despite the serious revolutionary challenge of nationalist-populist forces throughout the 1959–1963 period. Student revolts and popular demonstrations were followed by guerrilla action and military uprisings.[22] The defeat of the revolutionary Left and of the Jiménez antiparliamentary Right was largely the result of the cooperation and support Betancourt received from the Venezuelan military and police and from U.S. government officials, investors, and military missions. The relative political stability achieved since 1964 is based on the collaboration of AD and the business-oriented political parties of the Right, and on the ability of these parties to work out their political differences and to unite against their common social and political enemies. Legislation which challenged the privileges and prerogatives of any of the parties to this consensus was likely to result in political deadlock. Thus the political stability which has been achieved has been paid for by the inability of the political system to redistribute income, to pass a progressive income tax, and to deal with massive unemployment or with monopolistic and inefficient enterprises which produce consumer items at exorbitant prices. In the meantime AD has increasingly become a party devoid of reformist currents: in 1960 it rejected the position paper (*Documento de los jóvenes de Acción Democrática*) of its youth sector, who later formed the Movement of the Revolutionary Left (MIR); in 1962 it purged the national leader of the peasant unions, Ramón Quijado, for demanding a thorough agrarian reform; in 1968 it lost the moderate reformers led by Luis B. Prieto Figueroa (AD-elected President, 1964–1967) who formed the People's Electoral Movement (MEP). By 1970, AD was largely made up of party bureaucrats who share a general hostility to large-scale social change, a general acceptance of business values, and an obsession with the spoils of office.

Social Development and Urban Reform

Venezuela's democratic-capitalist political leaders faced many of the same acute social problems in urban areas that confront the rest of Latin America: unemployment, inadequate housing and education, and vast inequalities in income.

In the area of housing a number of institutions have spent considerable sums of money on urban construction. In almost forty years the Banco Obrero alone has invested 1.9 billion bolivares in housing, of which 60 percent went to Caracas.[23] Private construction reaches several hundred million bolivares. Yet 50 percent of Caracas' families cannot afford to purchase either public or private housing due to low income.[24] The democratic-capitalist revolutionaries not only have failed to deal with the housing problems of low-income groups but have observed the growing slumification of Caracas in silence. A Venezuelan urban planner has pointed out that while *barrios* (slums) covered 5 percent of the urbanized areas in 1938, they were 15 percent of the total by 1959 and up to 18 percent in 1966.[25] Slums are situated in flood-exposed areas, and suffer from an almost total lack of sanitary facilities. These slums contain 30 percent of the population of Caracas.[26] Most of the government and private financial resources which have produced the building boom in Caracas have benefited the middle and upper classes. A report by the Inter-American Committee of the Alliance for Progress noted: "With respect to housing . . . the lack of access of lesser income groups still constitutes a serious consideration within the Venezuelan social structure." [27]

In education, the picture is similar, despite the fact that the democratic-capitalist politicians and their supporters in the United States have publicized their educational accomplishments, along with agrarian reform, as their greatest achievements. Only one out of every five entering students completes six years of primary school in rural areas, and only one out of three in the nation as a whole.[28] While some progress was made in the early 1960's, since that period the situation has not improved and may have gotten worse. One observer notes that enrollment in rural schools has declined from 314,194 in 1959/60 to 291,537 in 1967/68.[29] In

Caracas the proportion of out-of-school children rose from 17 percent in 1961 to 25 percent in 1966.[30] As the public education situation deteriorates, the upper- and middle-income groups increasingly turn to private schools as a means of preparing their children for entrance into the better occupational slots. Education under the democratic-capitalist governments has not been a vehicle for opening up social opportunity for the lower classes but a means of reinforcing the vast socioeconomic inequalities which already exist. The quantitative expansion of educational facilities and spending had little or no effect in democratizing Venezuelan society.

Rural unemployment and underemployment, amounting to 55 percent of the economically active population, have caused a large-scale exodus to Caracas and other cities.[31] Many of the rural refugees are found in the low-paid jobs in the service sector. While petroleum and mining provide 600 new jobs per year and industry 10,500, commerce and services provide 26,800.[32] The tertiary sector now contains 43 percent of the economically active population compared to 18 percent in the secondary sector; in other words, for every one industrial worker there are 2.3 service workers. More specifically, for each industrial worker there are almost two workers in domestic services.[33]

In terms of income distribution the vast inequalities which were present during the 1950's persisted during the years of democratic-capitalist rule. The lowest 30 percent of the population receives 6 percent of national income while the top 10 percent of the population receives 38 percent.[34] The gap is probably much higher because of the large amounts of unreported income collected by upper-class investors and financiers.[35]

Conclusion

The democratic-capitalist parties have played an important role in stabilizing capitalist property relations and defending the prerogatives of the business elite in Venezuelan society. As one student of Venezuelan politics has perceptively noted: "The real power in the economic sector is in the hands of the . . . conglomerates which have no need for an interest group intermediary in dealing with the government." [36] Venezuelan politics has permitted free discussion and competition only among the parties supporting different strategies for capitalist development. AD-COPEI were instrumental in defeating a nationalist-populist challenge which threatened the property underpinnings of Venezuelan society; they successfully rebuffed the challenge from the Right which sought to abolish the parliament in favor of a centralized authoritarian regime. In social terms AD created a new middle-class farmer group in the countryside, its agrarian reform substantially benefiting approximately 15 percent of the previously landless *campesinos*.

Through the expansion of the educational system and government agencies AD has increased opportunities for the middle and lower-middle class. It has promoted government agencies concerned with development and provided financial assistance to urban and rural businessmen. At the same time the AD organizational network has effectively isolated the mass of urban slum dwellers and landless *campesinos* from left-wing political parties and groups which could articulate their grievances. In the absence of the Left, the right-wing COPEI and the antiparliamentary Right have seized upon the discontent of the excluded mass, especially in Caracas, to displace AD influence. The election of Caldera to the presidency and the resounding electoral victory of Pérez Jiménez in the 1969 senatorial election in Caracas are indications of the rejection by the populace of the integration of AD with the bureaucratic and propertied middle strata.

Acción Democrática has followed a strategy of socioeconomic development mainly oriented toward the promotion of the middle class within the political and economic framework established by U.S. and Venezuelan propertied interests. In this it has to a substantial degree succeeded. However, the democratic-capitalists have not changed Venezuela's semicolonial economic structure. Venezuela's economic development remains dependent on the decisions of U.S. petroleum interests. Furthermore, Venezuela's new "national" capitalists are highly dependent on U.S. corporate interests. For example, one writer notes that "Many of the ostensibly independent parts manufacturers are in fact 'captives' of a given foreign-owned automotive assembler since their production goes almost exclusively into the assembly of this make car." [37] The drain of capital from Venezuela through remission of earnings of U.S.-owned enterprises has been an important factor in Venezuela's over-all economic stagnation. Average annual profits and interest amount to $650 million.[38] For every new investment dollar, U.S. investors earn a return of three.[39]

The social and political aspirations and economic appetites of middle-class businessmen, bureaucrats, and professionals (especially lawyers) have been satisfied largely through the participation and activity of their party representatives in Congress and in the Executive. The political representatives of these same middle strata have largely been responsible for transforming the state into an instrument for capitalist industrial development—to the limited extent that development has in fact occurred. In order to achieve the political stability necessary for urban economic goals, middle-class politicians organized peasant support and created a new commercial agricultural class. However, Venezuela's agrarian reform was limited by AD's foremost consideration: achieving a political base of support for urban and rural capitalist development. Once a firm political base was created among commercial agriculturalists AD turned from reform to "modernization." AD and COPEI have been successful only in initiating capitalist development and then in representing the interests of the successful propertied and administrative middle strata. To accomplish this AD was willing to sacrifice the socioeconomic needs of the great majority of the Venezuelan population, the independence of the Venezuelan economy from U.S. domination, and the political freedom (and lives) of the young generation of Venezuelan nationalists and revolutionaries. The outcome of Venezuela's democratic-capitalist effort is hardly attractive to the impoverished masses of Latin America, to the new nationalist-populists in the church and the army, or to the revolutionary students and intellectuals in the universities.

NOTES

1. See, for example, Robert J. Alexander, *The Venezuelan Democratic Revolution* (New Brunswick, N.J.: Rutgers University

Press, 1964); John Friedman, *Venezuela: From Doctrine to Dialogue* (Syracuse, N.Y.: Syracuse University Press, 1965); Edwin Lieuwen, *Venezuela*, 2nd ed. (London: Oxford University Press, 1964); John D. Martz, *Acción Democrática: Evolution of a Modern Political Party in Venezuela* (Princeton, N.J.: Princeton University Press, 1965).

2. Consejo Interamericano de la Alianza para el Progreso (CIAP), *El esfuerzo interno y las necesidades de Venezuela*, OEA/Ser.H/XIV, CIAP/178 (Washington, D.C.: Pan American Union, 1967), p. 3. (Hereafter referred to as *CIAP Report on Venezuela.*)

3. Arturo Sosa, "Structural Factors in Venezuelan Economic Development" (mimeographed paper presented at Johns Hopkins School of Advanced International Studies Conference on Venezuela, November 1969), p. 3.

4. Guillermo Morón, "Venezuela," in Claudio Véliz, ed., *Latin America and the Caribbean* (New York: Praeger, 1968), p. 144.

5. *CIAP Report on Venezuela*, p. 5.

6. *Ibid.*, p. 94.

7. *Ibid.*, pp. 50–51.

8. *El desarrollo industrial de Venezuela*, CORDIPLAN, 1968.

9. *Encuesta industrial de 1961*, CORDIPLAN, 1963.

10. *CIAP Report on Venezuela*, p. 114.

11. *Ibid.*, p. 75.

12. J. Raúl Alegrett R., "Venezuelan Agrarian Reform: Its Impact and Outlook" (mimeographed paper presented at Johns Hopkins School of Advanced International Studies Conference on Venezuela, November 1969), p. 3.

13. *Ibid.*, p. 7.

14. Raúl Dominquez Capdevielle, "El camino para una reforma agraria de tipo nacionalista," *Ruedo Ibérico*, No. 22–24 (Diciembre 1968–Mayo 1969), p. 255.

15. Alegrett, *op. cit.*, p. 6.

16. *Ibid.*, p. 6.

17. *Ibid.*, pp. 7–9.

18. *Ibid.*, p. 9.

19. *Ibid.*, p. 11.

20. *CIAP Report on Venezuela*, p. 45. In 1966 4.5 bolivares equaled one dollar.

21. Alegrett, *op. cit.*, pp. 13–14.

22. This is discussed in more detail in my earlier essay, "Revolution

and Guerrilla Movements in Latin America: Venezuela, Guatemala, Colombia, and Peru," in James Petras and Maurice Zeitlin, eds., *Latin America: Reform or Revolution?* (New York: Fawcett, 1968), pp. 329–369.

23. Alberto Morales Tucker, "The Urban Dilemma of Venezuela: The Case of Caracas" (mimeographed paper presented at Johns Hopkins School of Advanced International Studies Conference on Venezuela, November 1969), p. 8.
24. *Ibid.*, p. 21.
25. *Ibid.*
26. *Ibid.*
27. *CIAP Report on Venezuela*, p. 17.
28. José Rafael Revenga, "The Efficacy of Education in Venezuela" (mimeographed paper presented at Johns Hopkins School of Advanced International Studies Conference on Venezuela, November 1969), p. 3.
29. *Ibid.*
30. *Ibid.*
31. Tucker, *op. cit.*, p. 32.
32. Yearly figures extrapolated from Revenga, *op. cit.*, Table 1.
33. José Augustin Silva Michelena, "El Siglo XX," *Ruedo Ibérico*, No. 22–24 (Diciembre 1968–Mayo 1969), p. 99.
34. United Nations, Economic Commission for Latin America, *Estudios sobre la distribución del ingreso en América Latina: Annexo Venezuela* (E/CN. 12/770, October 1966).
35. *Ibid.*
36. David Blank, "Political Conflict and Industrial Planning in Venezuela" (mimeographed paper presented at Johns Hopkins School of Advanced International Studies Conference on Venezuela, November 1969), p. 16.
37. *Ibid.*, p. 32.
38. D. F. Marcos Zavala, "Problemas principales y situación actual," *Ruedo Ibérico*, No. 22–24 (Diciembre 1968–Mayo 1969), p. 58.
39. Rodolfo Quintero, "Las Tres conquistas de America Latina," *Ruedo Ibérico*, No. 22–24 (Diciembre 1968–Mayo 1969), p. 44.

The Cuban Revolution in Historical Perspective

Cuban-U.S. relations at the end of the last century marked a turning point in U.S. policy toward Latin America. In contrast to the early nineteenth century, when U.S. policy-makers and business interests welcomed and supported Latin American independence struggles, at the turn of the century U.S. military forces intervened and aborted the Cuban struggle for national independence, imposing the Platt Amendment which gave the United States license to decide Cuba's political future.

Cuba was the last Latin country to overthrow Spanish colonialism—and the first to encounter U.S. imperial aspirations. In the early 1930's, Cuba became the first country in the Western Hemisphere in which workers temporarily established soviets. It was also the first country under the Good Neighbor Policy to have its government overthrown by U.S. policy-makers without the direct use of U.S. military force, during the first term of President Franklin D. Roosevelt. Cuba thus came into the modern period with two political experiences which profoundly shaped its political development: an aborted national revolution and an aborted social revolution, both induced by U.S. policy-makers, both contributing to the development of a strongly anti-imperialist undercurrent. The Cuban Revolution of 1959 telescoped both phases of Cuban history: the national and social revolution merged and, under the conditions of twentieth-century capitalism, produced a socialist revolution. Failing to complete a struggle against nineteenth-century colonialism, Cuba was the first Latin American country to succeed in overthrowing twentieth-century imperialism. Lacking a bourgeois revolution led by an entrepreneurial puritan elite, Cuba experienced a social revolution which prepared the way for realizing the goals of a highly productive developing society, guided by a collectivist ethic.

Prior to the 1959 Revolution Cuban politics and government policy were influenced primarily by the pattern of landownership and the semicolonial nature of its economy: the issue of elite control of the plantations and sugar mills was outside the pale of political debate—it was the "given" of the political system. Politics, as a result, was largely the struggle for patronage and graft, a means of social mobility and personal enrichment, both for the conservative and reformist parties. Because the economic system offered so few opportunities for advancement, controlled as it was mainly by foreign corporations and a small number of Cuban families, the political arena became the center of violent competition: assassination and gunplay frequently accompanied political changes, which had few if any consequences in redistributing benefits to society at large.

Ideologies and political labels meant little: political gangsters and conservatives referred to themselves by such titles as the Revolutionary Insurrectional Union, the Revolutionary Socialist Movement, etc. In the late 1940's a leading middle-class liberal "reformer" was charged with misappropriating $174 million in public funds.

The emergence and growth of Fidel Castro's 26th of July Movement were in part a response to the corruption and fragmentation, the vacuous rhetoric and mindless violence that characterized Cuban political life and its liberal middle-class parties. Fidel Castro and his followers drew their inspiration from an earlier period in Cuban history: from the struggles and writings of José Martí during the Spanish-Cuban war and from the example of the martyrs of the abortive social revolution of the early 1930's. The roots of Castro's thought and action can be traced back to these earlier struggles: his populist emphasis, his reliance on mass movements to defend the Revolution, and his distrust of the middle class stem from the earlier Cuban experience. Castro's affirmation of Cuba's sovereignty and right to bargain from a position of equality reflects the determination to avoid the humiliating conditions under which U.S. policy-makers dictated their terms to previous Cuban governments.

Thus, side by side with exploitation and corruption there existed in Cuban political history social struggle and personal heroism. Some of the individuals who played an important role in the Cuban Revolution of the 1950's embodied this mixed background, and were violent men of limited purpose. And it was many of these same individuals who later turned against the Revolution when it began to transform the socioeconomic basis of society and not merely to change the holders of government posts.

The civil war that led to the overthrow of Batista's regime was short and costly. Eight thousand lives, excluding Batista's torture victims, were lost in two years of civil war. The decisive battle, the victory of the guerrillas at Santa Clara, led to the defection of large numbers of army units while mass popular demonstrations broke out in Havana and the rest of Cuba. A general strike lasting four days insured the victory of the Castro-led July 26th Movement and its allies: "Industry, commerce, and transport in Havana remained at a standstill until January 4 [1959] when workers were urged to return to their jobs." [1] The strike effectively prevented the formation of any government other than that proposed by the guerrilla leadership. The initial indication that the revolutionary leadership was serious about its commitments occurred during the first month of revolution: agrarian reform was undertaken in Oriente Province. It was announced that unused lands were to be divided and parcels handed over to peasants.

Two events were important in defining the nature and future course of the Cuban Revolution: the Revolution was consummated with the active support and involvement of the majority of the Cuban working class; the revolutionary government began to implement its social commitments to the peasantry. For both reasons the Cuban Revolution from the beginning took shape as a mass social revolution; it was not, as some journalists and commentators have assumed, a "middle-class revolution" that would later be "betrayed." In February 1959, the agrarian reform was extended: 22,500 families in eastern Cuba each acquired sixty-seven-acre plots.[2] The size of the army was reduced: 1,066 officers and enlisted men were dismissed.[3] The coercive arm of the old regime was being dismantled, preparing the way for basic changes.

On June 3, 1959, agrarian reform became law. Property was limited to 999 acres (except for efficient farmers), all land in excess was to be expropriated and paid for with twenty-year bonds.[4] By the end of 1959 the National Institute of Agrarian Reform (INRA) had confiscated or "intervened" 2.2 million acres. Over $300 million of U.S. money invested in sugar was affected by the Agrarian Reform Law. The reaction of the U.S. government, reflecting its concern for private investors, was swift and unfavorable. The State Department sent a note to the Cuban government reminding Cuba that "this right [to expropriate] is coupled with the corresponding obligation for prompt, adequate, and effective compensation." [5] In translation, this diplomatic formula meant: since Cuba cannot pay cash in dollars immediately under terms acceptable to U.S. investors, it must not expropriate.

It was during the first six months of the Revolution, as the Castro leadership defined its social-revolutionary direction, that the basic socio-political alignments and divisions manifested themselves. The National Association of Cattlemen of Cuba, the Tobacco Growers Association, U.S. investors, the Bishop of Santiago de Cuba, the Partido Auténtico all joined in the attack on Castro and the measures taken to fulfill the social revolution.[6] Defections occurred among those politicians and interested groups who had hoped for a return to the negotiations and transactions of the pre-Batista period: five cabinet ministers resigned, twenty-six air force officers were replaced, and Provisional President Urrutia, raising the issue of communism, refused to sign revolutionary laws. The Cuban Confederation of Labor (CTC) called a general strike to support Castro: 400,000 to 500,000 *guajiros* poured into Havana; Cuba came to a standstill and the social revolutionaries defeated the middle-class liberals. The latter moved from opposition to exile and some to armed resistance. Armed groups were reported a few miles from Pinar del Río as early as July 1959. Air flights from Florida began supplying arms and leaflets to the opponents of the social revolution. Spurred on by the U.S. government's hostility to the agrarian reform and other revolutionary measures of the Castro government, the fragmented and disorganized Cuban middle-class politicians turned to terrorist activities. In October 1959, forty-seven Cubans were killed or wounded. The Cuban government responded to the defection of the middle class by forming people's militias, arming workers and peasants and reducing the regular army by 50 percent.[7]

Along with the agrarian reform the Castro government initiated the second major program to modernize Cuban society: educational reform. The underdeveloped educational system was thoroughly transformed: new schools were built (many army barracks were transformed into schools), teaching techniques were modernized, a massive teacher-training program was begun, students were given free texts and classroom materials, a massive scholarship program for the poor was established, and there was a nationwide mobilization to eliminate illiteracy.

The first year of the Revolution established the pattern for future development. Cuba was undergoing a profound social revolution that would come into conflict with the basic interests of U.S. and domestic investors. The measures taken by the Castro government to insure the success of the social revolution and the countermeasures adopted by the old Cuban politicians and U.S. policy-makers reflected the profound cleavage in Cuban society.

The Castro leadership at first attempted to modernize society by adopting nationalist measures designed to integrate foreign and domestic investors into the national development effort. It was after the failure of these policies that the pragmatic revolutionaries turned toward public ownership and socialist policies as the only available alternative. This transitional period, between prerevolutionary private enterprise and public ownership, was characterized by a series of measures by which the government hoped to regulate and control private corporations. For example, in 1960 a central planning board was established to supervise economic activity and to set forth regulations for private firms. In February of the same year, INRA began setting up cooperatives rather than dividing the land into small plots.

Along with the nationalist-populist domestic policy, Cuba initially adopted an independent neutralist position in foreign policy. As this approach became ineffective in counteracting U.S. attempts to blockade Cuba, it was changed toward an independent Communist foreign policy, thus obtaining Communist-bloc support as a counterweight to unrelenting U.S. military, economic, and political pressure.

In the beginning Cuba attempted to encourage reforms within the existing institutions in the hemisphere. For example, early in 1959, in an address before the Venezuelan Congress, Castro criticized the Organization of American States (OAS) and called for the formation of a democratic bloc to function within it, to expel dictatorial governments.[8] In April 1959, in a speech in New York's Central Park, Castro suggested a Marshall Plan for all of Latin America, "in order to avoid the danger of communism." A month earlier Castro had declared his neutrality in the Cold War between the Soviet Union and the United States; at the same time he made a point of criticizing the U.S. government for allowing exiles publicly to buy arms.[9]

The United States began seriously to lay the groundwork for Castro's overthrow when the Cuban government announced its plans for agrarian reform and the expropriation of large plantations. U.S. policy-makers refused to aid Cuba's social revolution, and U.S. trade with Cuba declined from $1.75 billion during the last year of the Batista dictatorship to $907 million during the first year of the Revolution. On the other hand, the Cubans were interested in diversifying their commercial relations, to gain greater political independence and lessen their economic dependence on the United States. In February 1960, during a visit by the Soviet leader Mikoyan, Cuba signed an economic agreement with the Soviet Union involving twelve-year credits of $100 million at 2.5 percent. The Soviet Union agreed to buy five million tons of Cuban sugar at world-market prices over five years and in exchange to provide Cuba with refined petroleum, pig iron, aluminum, fertilizer, and technical assistance for building factories. Cuba initiated a drive toward greater industrialization involving chemicals, metallurgical industries, iron, and steel. However, by the mid-1960's, Cuban policy changed and agriculture became the basis of development while industrialization was relegated to a secondary position.

As a result of Cuba's new economic relations, U.S.-Cuban affairs continued to deteriorate. The United States did not prevent

Cuban exiles from using its territory for incendiary raids on Cuban sugar fields, attacks that were reported as early as January 1960. Castro responded by pointing out that U.S. business was responsible for Cuba's history of "stealing, killing, and subjugation of the national interest." [10] As was to be the case repeatedly, Washington officially denied that Cuban exiles and their U.S. supporters were operating from Florida, even when U.S. news media reported them. By early 1960, almost 13 percent of Cuba's cane fields had been bombed.[11] The Castro leadership began to import arms, brilliantly anticipating U.S. policy moves. At the time liberal commentators looked upon this as a move Cuba could ill afford. Castro was better informed about the problems facing Latin American attempts at nationalist revolution. In Bolivia, the National Revolutionary Movement refused to diversify its sources of external support (including an offer by the Soviet Union to build a tin smelter). Bolivia, totally dependent on U.S. loans, was forced to accept U.S. policy on economic development and was in no position to resist the reconstitution of the army. In contrast with the failure of U.S. counterrevolutionary strategy against Cuba, in Bolivia in 1964 a pro-U.S. army faction led by General René Barrientos overthrew the nationalist government of Paz Estenssoro and began an intensive program of undermining the organizations of the revolutionary mining workers. In Guatemala during the early 1950's President Arbenz attempted to implement a moderate agrarian reform program through existing institutional channels. Lacking arms and relying on the traditional armed forces, Arbenz was easily overthrown by a small CIA-organized military force. The Guatemalan agrarian reform was reversed. Aware of the failures of previous nationalists, Castro was also cognizant of the reasons for the abortiveness of the reforms. Cuba's importation of arms from the Communist countries and Castro's establishment of the popular militias proved to be the necessary conditions for the survival of the revolutionary social changes. Castro's arms policies were clearly aimed at preventing the restorationist forces from recouping their fortune.

The major thesis propagated by U.S. policy-makers to justify their campaign to defeat the Cuban Revolution was set forth in April 1960 by Secretary of State Herter: ". . . many long-time friends of Cuba in the U.S. and elsewhere in the hemisphere who were heartened by the ideals expressed by the present leaders of Cuba when they assumed control of the government have been gravely disillusioned by what is coming to be considered a betrayal of these ideals. . . ." [12] Anti-communism and charges of betrayal became the leitmotif for the CIA-organized invasion the following year led by army officers who had served during Batista's bloody dictatorship.[13] In response to the charge of betrayal Castro pointed out that he was loyal to the social revolution but not to the needs of the private investors: "As prime minister I have been faithful to the revolution. Cuba is going through a profound and genuine revolution and that is the main reason for the misunderstanding which is due to many interests which will never be in agreement with a genuine and just social revolution." [14]

The increasing polarization between Cuba and the United States had three direct effects on Cuban politics: (1) it increased the number of defections of embassy and military personnel, wealthy and affluent members of society, and owners of the mass media; (2) it led to further expropriation of U.S. investments, including 272,472 acres of United Fruit land; (3) it further radicalized Cuban politics. In a clear break with the parliamentary politics of Cuba's past, on May 1960, before a half-million supporters, Castro denounced elections as incompatible with social revolution.[15]

U.S. policy-makers mounted a multiple offensive against the Cuban Revolution, violating Cuban sea and air space, cutting the sugar quota (July 6, 1960), holding Congressional hearings in which former Batista officials were given the national spotlight, etc. With a unanimity characteristic of totalitarian countries Congress voted 394 to 0 to approve a measure authorizing the President to cut the foreign sugar quota. The lines were drawn. Cuba, determined to carry through its social revolution, enacted a law which allowed the expropriation of all enterprises and properties wholly or partially owned by U.S. corporations (amounting at the time to $500–$600 million). President Eisenhower rejected any modus vivendi. He stated that the United States would not "permit" the establishment of a regime dominated by international communism in the Western Hemisphere.[16] The United States moved to extend its embargo against the Cuban Revolution by pressuring client states throughout the hemisphere and the rest of the world. The U.S. Senate approved an amendment to the mutual security appropriations bill which would cut off foreign aid to any nation supplying military or economic assistance to Cuba.[17] But U.S. plans to have Cuba condemned at the OAS meeting of August 1960 were defeated. A few years later, however, after military coups led by pro-U.S. generals had occurred in Bolivia, Brazil, Honduras, and Argentina, the United States had no problem in diplomatically isolating the Cuban Revolution in the hemisphere.[18]

In addition to official policies, private U.S. groups played an important part in creating a climate of opinion leading to military action. The AFL-CIO supported terrorist exiles who attempted to undermine Cuba's economic efforts—unsuccessfully, largely because peasants turned in the would-be revolutionaries to the Castro militiamen.[19] When Castro publicly exposed the Retalhuleu training base in Guatemala from which Cuban exiles were being prepared by U.S. officials to attack Cuba, the mass media as well as the U.S. government greeted his charges as proof of the persecution mania of a deranged mind.[20] Political journals, spokesmen of student groups and cultural associations—later revealed to have been subsidized by the CIA—repeated the themes of betrayal of the Revolution and Communist subversion put forth by Herter and later published in a White Paper by the State Department.

On January 3, 1961, the U.S. government broke relations with Cuba, where only a fraction of U.S. investment had not yet been nationalized. Newly elected President John F. Kennedy (who during his election campaign had called for stepped-up U.S. assistance to the armed exile groups) reaffirmed the Monroe Doctrine and gave no indication of wanting to negotiate U.S.-Cuban differences. Castro (perhaps influenced by Khrushchev) expressed what appears in retrospect to have been wishful thinking concerning the possibilities of reaching a peaceful accord with the Kennedy government, stating: ". . . we are going to begin anew. Our attitude will not be one of resentment." [21] Cuba offered to negotiate its differences with the United States and accepted Argentina as a mediator. The Kennedy Administration refused mediation. In his State of the Union message Kennedy set forth in the blunt language of the true believers in private enterprise the intransigent hostility which was to characterize U.S. policy toward Cuba: "Questions of economic and trade policy can always be negotiated. But Communist domination in the hemisphere can never be negotiated." [22]

Cuban foreign policy increasingly aligned itself with the Communist bloc not only because of U.S. intransigence but because the United Nations failed to provide adequate safeguards against U.S.-supported military action. In fact, in the years and months prior to the U.S.-sponsored invasion, the General Assembly as well as the Security Council four times refused to condemn the United States as an aggressor.[23]

The psychological and military buildup prior to the invasion of Cuba was intensified. In early April 1961, the State Department issued its White Paper, prepared by Arthur Schlesinger, Jr., which presented U.S. charges against the Cuban government, discussing such themes as the betrayal of the revolution, the delivery of the revolution to the Sino-Soviet bloc, etc. Past and present U.S. aggression was glossed over in one sentence by the Harvard historian: "We acknowledge past omissions and errors in our relationship to them." [24] The major purpose of the White Paper was to prepare U.S. public opinion for the participation of the U.S. government in the invasion of Cuba.

Terror and destruction by the CIA-financed forces in Cuba increased. The Hershey sugar mill was burned, causing $5 million damage. The El Encanto department store was burned, causing $7–$8 million damage. B-26 bombers attacked Cuban air bases and then returned to Miami. Cuban representative to the United Nations Raúl Roa pointed out that the raid was a prelude to invasion. The U.S. Ambassador to the United Nations, Adlai Stevenson, rejected the charges, stating categorically that they were "without any foundation." As subsequent events soon revealed, the Cubans were right and Stevenson had not been telling the truth. On April 17, 1961, the invasion took place; two U.S. destroyers conveyed 1,500 Cuban exiles to the island. The internal uprising which the CIA expected never occurred. At the end of the third day of fighting the invasion force was defeated. It is worthwhile to note a key section in the program of the U.S.-directed invasion force: "Those who had been unjustly dispossessed would have their assets returned." [25] The peasant and worker militiamen were not in sympathy.

The relationship between the Castro leadership and the pre-revolutionary Cuban communist party, which called itself the Popular Socialist Party (PSP), was complex and shifting, except for one basic factor: the Castro leadership always played an independent and dominant role before and after taking power, down to the present day. The Cuban Revolution was successful despite the fact that the majority of the PSP opposed the insurgents up until the last few months before Batista was overthrown. Throughout the post-Batista period when the Cuban government was implementing the social reforms it had promised, the PSP leadership formed the rearguard, opposing further changes until Castro announced them, then falling into line.

Early in 1959 Castro attacked the PSP as "divisionists" and "antirevolutionaries" for agitating over wage demands while the government was attempting to carry out its agrarian program.[26] *New York Times* reporter Tad Szulc, in discussing the Cuban road to socialism, noted Castro's insistence on the fact that in accepting socialism, Cuba did not deny itself the right to work out its own variation on the basic theme.[27]

On May 1, 1961, following fourteen hours of demonstrations by all sectors of the populace, Castro declared the Revolution socialist. Following the successful defeat of the invasion forces, the Cuban leadership no longer attempted to maintain a middle position between capitalism and socialism; it no longer sought legitimacy in the welfare-state provisions of the 1940 Constitution. The cumulative changes (nationalization of industry and public ownership of land), pragmatically arrived at, defined Cuba as a collectivist society. The defeat of the counterrevolution at the Bay of Pigs undermined the internal opposition. The Cuban leadership sought to consolidate the new institutions on a fresh basis. On July 26, 1961, Castro announced the single revolutionary party, Partido de la Revolución Socialista (PRS). The groundwork for the PRS had been established in the preceding months by another body, Organizaciones Revolucionarias Integradas (ORI). ORI supposedly brought together members from the old communist party (PSP) and Castro's own 26th of July Movement. The key coordinator of ORI, Anibal Escalante, had been PSP executive secretary. The first major conflict between the Castro leadership and the old Communists concerned the manner in which Escalante was organizing the new political formation. In March 1962, Castro accused Escalante of assigning members of the PSP to ORI leadership posts, excluding representatives of the July 26th Movement and of the Student Directorate, and trying to make a PSP-dominated ORI into a privileged ruling clique. Escalante left Cuba for a trip to Eastern Europe. He later returned, and in 1966 began to organize a secret opposition. Escalante and his supporters allegedly handed over confidential Cuban documents to Soviet and Eastern European agents and urged the Soviet Union to use its economic aid as a means of pressuring the Cuban government to accept Escalante's leadership. This group of pro-Soviet Communists, referred to in the Cuban press as the "microfaction," was arrested, tried, and given long prison sentences.

In the period of tension between the old-line Communists and the *fidelista* Communists inside Cuba, external relations between the Cuban revolutionaries and the Soviet Union were far from smooth. The differences centered on the policy toward the struggles in Latin America. The Soviet Union advocated the policy of peaceful coexistence, which translated itself into a strategy of collaboration with middle-class liberal forces interested in incremental changes. At first the Cubans attempted to adapt to the Soviet approach, giving support to the Soviet position on all major issues.[28] On October 10, 1961, Raúl Roa reiterated Cuba's desire for peaceful coexistence within the hemisphere and mediation of its differences with the United States. In response, on October 12, Dean Rusk, in a speech to the National Association of United Church Women in Miami, said that there was absolutely no prospect for coexistence between the United States and the Castro government.[29]

While the Cubans, perhaps somewhat under Soviet influence, attempted to negotiate, the United States intensified its opposition. In January 1962, at the OAS foreign ministers conference, the United States (with the purchase of Haiti's vote in exchange for a $15-million airfield) was able to muster the necessary two-thirds vote to exclude Cuba from the OAS, although the legality of the procedure was highly questionable and the countries voting against or abstaining represented 70 percent of the population of Latin America.[30] President Kennedy imposed a new trade embargo designed to deprive Cuba of its remaining dollar earnings in the United States.

To the pressure of the U.S. embargo and of Cuba's diplomatic isolation in the hemisphere, Castro's answer was the Second Declaration of Havana, a document that supported armed revolutionary struggles in Latin America. The political orientation of the Declaration was in direct conflict with the Soviet line of peaceful coexistence and further rejected the Soviet assertion that the Latin American bourgeoisie was capable of leading the revolutionary struggle.

Military forces in Ecuador, Brazil, and Argentina soon convinced Presidents Arosemena, Goulart, and Frondizi to follow U.S. policy and to break relations with Cuba. The differences between Cuba and the Soviet Union over the issue of peaceful coexistence vs. revolution sharpened as the United States continued to intensify its political and economic warfare. From the Cuban point of view the choice was quite limited: either encourage revolutions on the mainland and break the U.S. blockade, or the Cuban Revolution would have to submit to U.S. policy-makers. These alternatives were the real choices imposed by the United States, though the Russians pretended that it was otherwise. During the U.S. military blockade, the Soviet Union quickly accepted U.S. terms without any substantial concessions. When President Dorticós of Cuba pressed Stevenson at the United Nations—"Give us guarantees that the U.S. government does not intend to attack Cuba"—Stevenson, sounding like Lyndon Johnson, responded, "the maintenance of Communism is not negotiable." [31]

Castro himself publicly admitted that "during the development of the crises [the U.S. military blockade] there arose certain discrepancies between the Soviet government and the Cuban government." The Soviet Union supported the U.S. demand of unilateral U.N. inspection of Cuban territory to oversee the dismantling of the missiles. Castro rejected this infringement of Cuban sovereignty and proposed mutual inspection: the U.N. inspection team would visit Cuba *and* the bases in the U.S. from which attacks were launched on Cuba. The United States rejected this proposal and the matter was dropped. These latent differences between Cuba and the Russians became public in 1966 when the Soviet Union began developing economic relations with and offering aid to Latin American governments which supported the U.S. economic blockade and political quarantine of Cuba. At the same time, the pro-Russian Communist parties in Latin America began to attack the strategy of armed revolution and the revolutionaries struggling to bring about a social revolution. In Brazil, Venezuela, Colombia, Guatemala, and Peru, the supporters of Russian foreign policy denounced the revolutionaries and in some cases sided with the government, thus easing the way for the Russians to establish diplomatic and commercial relations. The Cubans publicly criticized the Russians, attacked their political followers in Latin America, and affirmed Cuba's support for the armed-struggle road to social revolution. The external strains between the Cubans and the Communist-bloc countries were also evident in the increasing emphasis that Castro placed on the need for Cubans to depend only on themselves to carry through their developmental tasks.

The assertions by Castro of the independence of the Cuban Revolution and his call for greater self-reliance were thinly veiled responses to Soviet economic pressures to force Cuba to accept the Soviet line. The dependence of Cuba on moral over material incentives was another aspect of the Castro leadership's attempt to develop a different type of socialism from that found in the Communist bloc. In a speech on March 13, 1968, at the University of Havana, Fidel Castro touched on themes related to the Cuban road to socialism:

> But, of course, with its standard of living arising from a developed economy whose income is incomparably higher than that of any underdeveloped country, imperialism can offer material incentives of many types, and, in the face of this, what are we to do? What is the duty of the Revolution if not to strengthen its determination, to exalt all types of moral values among the people? Feelings of internationalist solidarity, justice, equality, love of country, love for the people, for the struggle; the satisfaction of

having a giant task, a historic task, to carry out, and accomplishing it, facing up to it, overcoming obstacles. That is the kind of people we have to create. Anything else is ridiculous. And the results of having gone too far along that [other] road are already beginning to be observed elsewhere.

We will continue along our road; we will build our Revolution, and we will do so fundamentally through our own efforts. Great is the task that faces us! A people that is not willing to make the effort has no right even to utter the word "independence," no right even to utter the word "sovereignty"! Let us struggle bravely, among other reasons, to minimize our dependence on everything from abroad. Let us fight as hard as possible, because we have known the bitterness of having to depend to a considerable extent on what we can get from abroad and have seen how this can be turned into a weapon, how at the very least, there is a temptation to use it against our country. Let us fight for the greatest independence possible, whatever the price!

Of course, that offended the "principles" of the microfaction; that was a crime: dignity was a crime, honor was a crime, the Revolution was a crime! [32]

Despite the pressures from the United States and the Soviet Union, Cuba has seriously committed itself to three goals: social equality, economic and social development, and political independence. Early in the revolution the Cuban government fixed the highest income at 6,000 pesos a year.[33] The salary differentials between workers employed in the different branches of the economy are substantially smaller than those in any other Latin country. The average wage in the highest-paid industry in Cuba is only 40 percent higher than the lowest. In the other major Latin countries it is 100 percent or more, with the exception of Brazil where it is 80 percent higher.[34] The inequalities between workers and other occupational groups in Cuba is probably even less than in other Latin countries. In order to provide equal opportunity in education, the Cuban government finances 150,000 scholarships for the sons and daughters of workers and peasants so that they can complete their studies—a program that has yet to be undertaken in any other Latin country.

The literacy campaign that the Cuban government launched

in 1961 is said to have reduced illiteracy from 23.6 percent to 3.9 percent, largely due to the extensive mobilization of high school and university students.[35] The Cuban government's yearly expenditures for education average about 10 percent of the budget, about twice as much as is spent by the Costa Rican government and almost four times as much as by the Guatemalan government.

At the beginning of the revolutionary process Cuba's economic policy was influenced by the traditional association between development and a growing degree of industrialization.[36] The attempt to shift Cuba from a sugar-exporting country to an industrial country overnight was not successful. In August 1963, Castro outlined a shift in Cuba's development policy. Reversing the pattern taken by Stalin and his supporters in Eastern Europe, Castro stressed the need for balanced growth rather than a headlong rush toward industrialization. Cuba is delaying development of a steel industry until after 1970 and in the meantime is expanding agriculture and investing in a chemical industry based on sugar cane byproducts. Sugar and cattle are the basis of Cuban development until 1970 (the sugar goal for 1970 is ten million tons). In a speech to the National Association of Small Farmers (ANAP) Castro assured the small private farmers that they would not be driven out by the development of large-scale state agriculture. Castro stated that the proportion of state lands to small farms would be 70 percent to 30 percent, but made clear that there was no place in Cuba for large private landowners or the rural bourgeoisie (anyone owning more than 168 acres).[37] The Cuban government has tolerated the small farmers largely because it controls sufficient state lands so that the economy does not depend on individual plots.

Cuba turned to specialization in sugar production, taking advantage of the comparative advantages that it possessed in this respect in order to make "the sugar industry the fundamental pivot of a new type of economic development within the international division of labor associated to the world socialist system." [38] The urban and rural reforms resulted in redistribution of income, but between 1961 and 1963 a decline in sugar production resulted in stagnation of per-capita wealth. The shift from industrialization to agricultural development began in 1964. The government's plans gave agriculture priority, establishing a Ministry of Sugar Industry and providing additional financial resources.

The tremendous disproportions in Cuba's prerevolutionary industrial structure contributed to the decision to forego immediate plans for industrial development. Only 5.4 percent of the gross value of industrial production was accounted for by the metallurgical and machine industries, compared to 25 percent in Argentina, Brazil, and Mexico, and 14 percent for Chile, Colombia, Peru, Uruguay, and Venezuela.[39] The source of this distortion is associated with Cuba's total dependence on the United States during the previous half-century, during which Cuba produced raw materials and absorbed all types of manufactured goods. In order to redirect the economy the revolutionary government nationalized most enterprises. The state sector of industry now includes 95 percent of production; the remaining 5 percent belongs to marginal economic activity. Within the state sector, industrial production is concentrated in 172 plants which account for 70 percent of production and employ 49 percent of the workers.[40] Because Cuban industry is concentrated basically in processes that constitute the final stages in the production of consumer goods it shows a great dependence on foreign trade. The revolutionary government's import policy has been to expand the importation of intermediary goods (from 36 percent in 1954–1958 to 51 percent in 1963–1964) and to reduce the importation of consumer goods (imports declined from 39 percent in 1954–1958 to 24 percent in 1963–1964).[41] Sugar is Cuba's major export, accounting for 86 percent of the export total, followed by nickel, 4.5 percent, and tobacco, 4.1 percent.

Today Castro's development perspective for Cuban socialism rejects the Communist-bloc theory which ties development to rapid industrial growth. Cuban economists argue that there is no need to industrialize rapidly in the Communist bloc—unlike the situation in the capitalist world—because relations between states are different. These economists accept an international division of labor within the Communist bloc, with the proviso that the prices of exchange be equitable and stable. They argue that specialization is functional because the social structure of a postrevolutionary society permits it to utilize the surplus as a motor of development. In exchange for providing the industrial socialist societies with agricultural goods at lower costs than they can produce them, such a division of labor would also allow the underdeveloped socialist societies the opportunity to purchase manufactured goods at fixed lower prices. In this framework, industrial growth in Cuba would function to promote and service the production of agricultural goods and by-products. Putting it in somewhat different terms, the Cubans argue that the shift from industrial to agricultural development stems from the higher relative cost of importing industrial goods as against that for agricultural inputs and the resultant adverse trade balances. Agricultural specialization is perceived as compatible with the optimal use of national resources and with optimal international economic efficiency. Thus, the principal economic effort in Cuba will remain concentrated on raising sugar production to ten million tons in 1970, by which time they hope to begin to diversify the economy.

Castro and the Cubans are building socialism by adopting, on an experimental basis, an approach substantially different from that utilized in the other Communist countries—the use of moral incentives. In contrast to the formative years in the Soviet Union and Eastern Europe, as Che Guevara once said, Cuba "always stresses the ideological aspect, the education of the minds of people and the call to duty." [42] Castro appeals to the Cuban masses to work harder and produce more not in order to enrich oneself, but to realize the values of equality, community, and brotherhood, and, by enhancing social solidarity, to enrich the life of the collectivity. Castro summed up the Cuban approach to building a socialist society when he said: "We cannot encourage or even permit selfish attitudes among men if we don't want man to be guided by the instinct of selfishness."

Conclusion

The success of the social revolution in Cuba and the hostile U.S. response leaves little doubt (except in the minds of capitalist true believers) of the essentially counterrevolutionary and antidevelopment role of the United States in Latin America. It was the overbearing presence of the United States which accounted for the political and economic underdevelopment of the island. Textbook writers and journalists who call for more concern and involvement by the United States in Latin America are actually working against the possibility of Latin development despite their protestations to the contrary. As the first successful socialist society in the hemisphere, Cuba proved that social revolution not only was possible but could maintain itself in power only ninety miles from the shores of the United States. In its first ten years the Cuban Revolution has moved from political to social to economic goals: from the overthrow of Batista, to the socialization of the economy and redistribution of goods, to the latest phase, social mobilization to develop the economy. During the 1970's Cuba faces many difficult choices and problems in its drive for economic development; whatever the decisions that are taken, the ten-year experience of the most far-reaching social, cultural, and political changes will shape the context in which those choices will occur. Regardless of the policies adopted in Washington, the social and economic achievements of the Cuban Revolution are irreversible. The only question that remains is how long U.S. policy can prevent the rest of Latin America from also taking the path of social revolution.

NOTES

1. *Hispanic-American Report* (*HAR*), XII, No. 1 (March 1959), p. 21.
2. *HAR,* XII, No. 2 (April 1959), p. 89.
3. *Ibid.*
4. In October 1963 the Second Agrarian Reform was passed. The law limited landholdings to a maximum of 168 acres per landowner. The Second Agrarian Reform gave the state sector approximately 70 percent of the nation's total land, with the private sector holding the remaining 30 percent.
5. *HAR,* XII, No. 6 (August 1959), p. 319.
6. *Ibid.*
7. *HAR,* XII, No. 10 (December 1959), p. 543.
8. *HAR,* XII No. 1 (March 1959), p. 26.
9. *HAR,* XII, No. 3 (May 1959), p. 147.

10. *HAR*, XIII, No. 1 (March 1960), p. 25.

11. *HAR*, XIII, No. 1 (April 1960), p. 101.

12. *HAR*, XIII, No. 4 (June 1960), p. 238.

13. About 200 of the 1,113 captured invaders had been Batista soldiers and police. They were the core of the invasion leadership. Approximately 125 had owned large estates, few had been workers or farmers. *HAR*, XIII, No. 12 (February 1963), p. 1101.

14. *HAR*, XIII, No. 4 (June 1960), p. 238.

15. *HAR*, XIII, No. 5 (July 1960), p. 307. In a poll conducted by the Cuban magazine *Bohemia,* it was reported that 80 percent of the people supported Castro completely. *HAR,* XIII, No. 6 (August 1960), p. 382.

16. *HAR*, XIII, No. 7 (September 1960).

17. *HAR*, XIII, No. 8 (October 1960), p. 552.

18. The State Department announced in January 1963 that noncommunist shipping to Cuba had fallen 75 percent from 1961 levels as a result of continuing U.S. pressure. *HAR*, XVI, No. 1 (March 1963), p. 33.

19. In 1962 the AFL-CIO set up a program under which Latin American union officials received training in new methods of fighting communists. The program was integrated with the U.S. government's programs and was openly supported by the U.S. Agency for International Development, which put up $250,000 to help finance it. The program was administered by another AFL-CIO creation, the American Institute for Free Labor Development (AIFLD), which, as later revealed, was subsidized by the CIA. Concerning the AIFLD, the *Hispanic-American Report* noted: "Besides instruction in the rudiments of trade unionism, such as collective bargaining and organization, the heart of the program was a two-week course on the 'dangers and safeguards for democratic labor' consisting of antirevolutionary indoctrination using Cuba as a test case. The Institute had a 24-man board of trustees including 12 U.S. labor leaders and 12 businessmen from the United States and Latin America. J. Peter Grace, president of W. R. Grace and Company and president and chairman of the Institute's board, and George Meany, vice-president of the Institute, joined in a declaration stating that the essential point which inspired the Institute was that 'the workers, the owners and the government have united in an effort' to strengthen 'free and independent' workers movements throughout the world." Not surprisingly many of the graduates of the Institute have col-

laborated with pro-U.S. military dictators and businessmen at the expense of the workers. *HAR*, XV, No. 7 (September 1962), p. 666.

20. *The Hispanic-American Report* was an exception. It reported at the time: "Reliable observers in Guatemala say that without doubt there is in Retalhuleu a large and well-fortified base where Cuban exiles are being trained to invade Castro's fortress. . . . Reliable reports from Cuba say that Fidel Castro is informed about the base. . . ." *HAR*, XIII, No. 9 (November 1960), p. 583.

21. *HAR*, XIV, No. 1 (March 1961), p. 32. The United States responded by instituting a travel ban prohibiting its citizens from traveling to Cuba.

22. *HAR*, XIV, No. 3 (May 1961), p. 214.

23. The neutral nations, plus so-called "socialist" countries like the UAR, Mali, Guinea, Ghana, failed to even *vote* against the United States in February 1962 on a Czech-Rumanian resolution calling on the United States to cease interference; the vote was 50 to 11 with 39 abstentions. The same countries failed to support even a milder proposal recommending a settlement according to the U.N. charter. *HAR*, XV, No. 2 (April 1962), p. 129. With support like that it is not surprising that the Cubans turned to the Communist bloc, which at least was willing to publicly oppose U.S. intervention.

24. For a detailed account of the falsifications, distortions, and omissions in the White Paper, see Maurice Zeitlin and Robert Scheer, *Cuba: Tragedy in Our Hemisphere* (New York: Grove Press, 1963).

25. Testifying before the Senate Foreign Relations Subcommittee on Inter-American Affairs, General Lemnitzer reportedly testified that the CIA had spent some $45 million on the venture. *HAR*, XIV, No. 5 (July 1961), p. 406.

26. *HAR*, XII, No. 5 (July 1959), p. 266.

27. *HAR*, XIV, No. 6 (August 1961), p. 499.

28. Cuba's pro-Soviet foreign policy was most clearly seen in the September 1961 Belgrade meeting where the Cuban delegation supported the Soviet resumption of nuclear tests, as well as the Soviet position on Berlin, disarmament, and reorganization of the United Nations.

29. *HAR*, XIV, No. 10 (December 1961), p. 891.

30. *HAR*, XV, No. 1 (March 1962), pp. 80–81.

31. *HAR*, XV, No. 10 (December 1962), p. 902.
32. *Granma* (Havana), English Weekly Review, March 24, 1968, p. 7.
33. *HAR*, XIII, No. 8 (October 1960), p. 526.
34. United Nations, Economic and Social Council, *El proceso de industrializacion en América Latina*, Vols. I–III (E/CN./2/716, Santiago, Chile, 1965). United Nations Economic and Social Council, *El desarrollo industrial de Cuba* (ST/ECLA Conf. 23/ L.63, March 1966).
35. Paul Sweezy and Leo Huberman, *Socialism in Cuba* (New York: Monthly Review Press, 1969), p. 27. About 34 percent of the teacher trainees in 1960–1961 were children of workers and peasants in contrast with the 2 percent prior to 1959. This is just one indicator that suggests the greater mobility and opportunity for the lower class in postrevolutionary Cuba. *HAR*, XV, No. 6 (August 1962), p. 508.
36. It has been said that Che Guevara, who was then Minister of Industry and responsible for all the state-owned industries and for the four-year industrialization plan (1962–1966), was to blame for Cuba's overcommitment to industry at the expense of agriculture. This argument is wrong on two counts: most Cubans supported rapid industrialization, largely in reaction to Cuba's historical experience as a one-crop, raw-material-exporting nation; secondly, Guevara was quite cautious in his approach. As early as February 1961, Guevara was reconsidering the plan to construct a steel mill and modified the optimistic estimates of Cuba's ability to industrialize. *HAR*, XIII, No. 2 (April 1961), p. 129. In December 1962, Guevara insisted that sugar not be neglected as other industries developed. He called for 100 percent mechanization of sugar. *HAR*, XV, No. 12 (February 1963), p. 104.
37. *HAR*, 16, No. 8 (October 1963), p. 765.
38. *El desarrollo industrial de Cuba*, p. 17.
39. *Ibid.*, Part II, p. 3.
40. *Ibid.*, p. 10.
41. *Ibid.*
42. *HAR*, XV, No. 12 (February 1963), p. 1104.

The Military and the Modernization of Peru*

For the first time in Peruvian history a serious effort to develop a modern industrial capitalist society is being undertaken. A military government closely linked to nationalist professional groups has promulgated a broad program which includes substantive changes in the system of land tenure and indicates target areas for public and private investments.

The military government has set itself a number of strategic economic goals:

(1) The establishment of a dynamic capitalist industrial society in which public and private Peruvian entrepreneurs will play a dominant role.

(2) The incorporation of the peasantry into the market economy through the expropriation of the large traditional haciendas of the sierras and the distribution of land to the peasants.

(3) The exclusion of those foreign firms whose behavior violates the political rules and economic guidelines established to foster national industrial development.

(4) The transfer of private capital from agriculture to non-agricultural pursuits, especially in the secondary sector.

The military government is clearly *developmental* in its orientation. The earnest effort at redistributive policies such as the agrarian reform are subordinated to the over-all effort to provide inducements for future industrial growth. Likewise, *nationalist* policies such as the expropriation of the International Petroleum Company (IPC), a subsidiary of Standard Oil of New Jersey,

---

* Written with Nelson Rimensnyder.

130

have largely served to provide the junta with issues attracting great popular support. Policies regarding concessions to foreign investors both in the exploitation of minerals and in manufacturing suggest that the junta is largely concerned with integrating foreign-owned resources and enterprises into a broader national development perspective. The *populist* concerns of the junta are mainly directed toward socioeconomic improvement of the peasantry without permitting its effective mobilization. Land reform will be carried out and administered largely by government-appointed agrarian officials (*técnicos*).[1] Independent actions which the peasants might take on their own behalf will not meet with the approval of the junta. Activities of the industrial working class which revolve around traditional class organizations and issues are treated as threats to the industrial-development orientation of the junta.[2] Paternalistic projects involving profit-sharing and "co-participation" in management are counterposed to the politics of class struggle. The junta has moved to depoliticize the universities and create a professional, technically oriented university.

In sum, the horses of populism and nationalism are tied to the carriage of developmentalism. The politics of capitalist modernization-from-above[3] in the framework of a colonial economy require the junta to place restrictions and controls on the economic activities of both the traditional Peruvian elite and the foreign investors established in their mineral-based economic enclaves. At the same time the junta must curb the opportunities of the Left in order to maintain control of the process and extent of social change, especially the transfer of property. While resisting pressures from the advanced capitalist countries that would distort development priorities, the junta must also provide incentives and a favorable investment climate in the urban industrial areas: hence the need to maintain a docile and "managed" labor force. Paradoxically, in carrying out policies designed to produce a modern capitalist industrial society, the military must overcome the opposition of the center of world capitalism and the reservations of its own entrepreneurial elite.

Internationally it is the Communist countries, including the Soviet Union and Cuba, and domestically the Peruvian Communist Party, which have shown the greatest enthusiasm for the policies of capitalist modernization-from-above.[4] The policies of the military junta can best be understood by examining the interplay between recent Peruvian political history and the process of political socialization of the officer corps—the strategic policy-making elite in Peru today.

Social Background

The policies of the military aimed at carrying out a bourgeois modernization are products of their class background and the position of the military in Peruvian society. With few exceptions the members of the junta are from provincial middle-class families; they were not members of the urban industrial bourgeoisie, which is largely linked to and dependent on foreign investors and which tends to subordinate its policy preferences to those of their foreign partners. Likewise the officers did not originate from commercial families with strong links to the large landowning families. From the economic and geographic point of view, the members of the junta have their roots in the marginal middle class of the provinces and since they do not identify completely with the large domestic propertied interests, they are not wholly subject to the pressures and influences emanating from these classes. Their marginality allowed them to evolve developmental and agrarian reform policies which other middle-class political elites have shunned because of their integration in the international-agricultural-banking economic power structure.

At the same time, however, the middle-class origins of the junta and their political socialization through the military produced a strong antipathy toward working-class or revolutionary socialist politics. Moreover, most of these officers have received instruction and political indoctrination in the United States, and some have made as many as six visits. Though the political courses they took there were partially geared to indoctrinating them with anti-communism and the virtues of Western-style private enterprise, the Peruvian military has apparently been selective in what it chooses to learn. Their animosity to communist revolution has been matched by attempts to modify Peru's current dependence on the United States, suggesting that the overseas students are not the docile, loyal, and obedient products that the educational program is supposed to turn out.

The fact that military officers originate from and lead middle-class styles of life should not obscure the fact that they have to a certain degree an independent base of power outside of the existing property structure which allows them political autonomy. Not linked to the existing "mutual support societies" characteristic of the other middle-class propertied groups, they are less susceptible to the logrolling politics which undermines the formulation of a systematic development strategy. In the final analysis the military share the same long-term ideals as many of the propertied groups who are opposing their reform measures today. However, what is crucial in the immediate situation is the fact that the military lacks the support of precisely those propertied groups which it needs in order to modernize society and which would be the final beneficiaries of the current policies.[5]

Recent Political History

The first indications that Peru's military men differed from traditional Latin American military *caudillos* appeared during the military government of 1962–1963. Most commentators believed that the assumption of power was precipitated by fear of an imminent APRA (Alianza Popular Revolucionaria Americana) victory in the 1962 presidential elections,[6] the military being portrayed as the defender of the old order against the "populist" APRA. This account fails to deal with two facts: APRA had several years earlier come to terms with the traditional ruling class, and—as we shall see—the military had changed both in its ideas and social composition.

Reasons much deeper and more complex than that of the old military-*aprista* hatreds account for the military coup. The younger military men in Peru's armed forces were becoming impatient with the policies and actions of the ruling civilian elites. Development-oriented, and well aware of Peru's extreme inequalities of wealth and income, they were increasingly apprehensive over the possibility of a violent revolution emanating from the country's economically depressed and politically excluded rural and urban poor.

The main purpose of Peru's military government of 1962–1963 was to assure the election of a civilian president who would develop unused resources, alleviate some of the inequities of Peru's socioeconomic structure, and restrain the growing revolutionary movement centered in the rural areas.[7] Radical structural changes affecting the prerogatives and privileges of the elites were not the objective of the officers who ruled in that short-lived (ten months) government. The men who headed the military junta of 1962–1963 were close to retirement and were acting to some degree under the influence of junior staff officers (majors, lieutenant colonels, and colonels) who were largely the products of different social and educational experiences. Many of these younger officers would later surface as the generals who are influential in the present junta.

The military coup of July 18, 1962, occurred during large-scale rural insurgency and while traditional conservative and *aprista* politicians were busy maneuvering to obtain political office. In 1962 the conservative Prado Administration, elected with *aprista* backing in return for legal recognition in 1956, returned the favor by supporting *aprista* leader Haya de la Torre for the presidency. The other two major candidates were ex-dictator Manuel Odría and Fernando Belaúnde Terry. No candidate received a majority in the balloting and Congress was constitutionally charged with selecting the candidate. In order to exclude Belaúnde from the new government, APRA allied itself with the right-wing former military dictator Odría and concluded a deal by which Odría was to become president while APRA dominated the Congress. The military, apparently provoked by both the politicking and the rural insurgency, intervened to prevent the deal from being consummated. Ten months after the coup, in June 1963, the military held new elections and Belaúnde became president. -

Politics and social policy during the Belaúnde years served to reinforce the feeling among the socially mobile officer corps that Peru needed structural changes to generate dynamic development if the capitalist order was to prevent a massive and uncontrollable revolution from below.

The Inter-American Committee for Agricultural Development (CIDA) estimated in 1966 that approximately one million *cam-*

pesino families in Peru did not have access to or own sufficient land to maintain an above-subsistence living.[8] At a conservative average of five members per family, this means that approximately five million persons (or 40 percent of Peru's population) did not have sufficient land to subsist on. These landless families were highly concentrated in the sierra where per-capita income averages around $15–$20 a year.

According to the National Office of Agrarian Reform, under the Belaúnde-sponsored Agrarian Reform Law of 1964, 11,760 rural families received 380,000 hectares, about thirty hectares per family (1 hectare = 2.47 acres).[9] This distribution took place over a four-and-one-half-year period. CIDA census estimates reveal that Peru adds 11,000 landless or near landless rural families to the population yearly.[10] Thus, under Belaúnde a total of some 40,000 more families needing land was added to Peru's economically depressed rural poor. His agrarian reform law failed even to keep pace with population growth.[11] Belaúnde favored measures to attract foreign private investment in Peru's extractive industries without limiting their profits or specifying their relationship to Peruvian development needs. He contracted large external loans under unfavorable terms (short-term repayment and high interest rates) to develop a highway and to open the eastern jungle areas to settlement and exploitation. The highway program was not linked either to agrarian reform or to specific industrial projects designed to develop the interior. The development of needed services and facilities on the local level was to be achieved through Cooperación Popular—the mobilization of volunteer labor. After an initial spurt of activity, Belaúnde's Cooperación Popular turned into a government patronage machine unrelated to social development. In addition, his financial policies caused rampant inflation and forced a devaluation in the currency. Massive corruption and speculation were routinized among high-ranking government officials.[12] During the IPC negotiations in late September 1968, Belaúnde agreed to grant new concessions to the oil companies. In addition, when the agreement was to be signed, the last page was discovered to be missing, touching off a nationwide outcry. The accumulation of numerous short- and long-term grievances contributed to the overthrow of Belaúnde on October 3, 1968.

The assumption of total executive and legislative power by the present military junta signaled a shift from an impotent middle-class government to a military regime which is also rooted in the middle class but which is committed to breaking the stalemates in the political system that had blocked the emergence of a new and dynamic approach to economic development.

The social mobility and relatively high educational level of members of the Revolutionary Military Government, as it is officially styled, are important factors in understanding its policy orientation. The Peruvian military resemble armed intellectuals rather than the stereotype image of the Latin American *gorila*. The President, General Juan Velasco Alvarado, comes from a middle-class family of modest means.[13] He enlisted in the army as a private in 1929, as did at least one other member of the government, was selected the following year by competitive examinations to attend the Chorrillos Military School near Lima, and graduated first in his class in 1934. All of the fourteen Cabinet Ministers graduated from one of the three Peruvian military academies during the late 1930's or early 1940's. Several members of the government were contemporaries at Chorrillos, and two were roommates for a time. Many returned to Chorrillos as administrators or instructors sometime during their subsequent military careers. Only two members of the government came from upper-class families, and few married outside their social background, which was almost exclusively middle class. All of this suggests that we are dealing with a homogeneous, close-knit "generational group."

More important from the point of view of intellectual influences was the common experience shared by the more than half of the fifteen junta members who attended special courses in the 1950's at the Center for Advanced Military Studies (CAEM).[14] Both the subject matter and the instructors had a profound effect on the evolution of their political consciousness. From their course work came their commitment to developing and changing Peruvian society. Together with their middle-class status this experience moved them in the direction of a bourgeois revolution-from-above. For it was at CAEM that the future rulers of Peru were exposed to courses on Peru's socioeconomic structures, the dependent nature of its economy, and the vulnerability of internal development to external fluctuations. For the most part these courses were taught by left-wing nationalist academics who were well informed about the problems of Peruvian socioeconomic development. Many members of the current military government maintain their links with their former professors. More recent graduates of CAEM continue to receive the same education and to keep up the pressure for change. President Velasco has often sought legal advice from left-wing nationalist elements, of whom the best known is the president of the bar association, Alberto Ruiz Eldredge.[15]

Politics and Development Strategy

Possessing an awareness of the historical processes which produced the present social structure and the attendant impediments to industrial development, the military has come to view the traditional political institutions as incapable of carrying out the necessary changes; they are unwilling to entrust leadership of this revolution-from-above to the civilian politicians, legislature, or elected government. In early August 1969, the military government announced that it would remain in power "until at least 1975" in order to guarantee that Peru will be well on the way to accomplishing the goals of the twenty-year development plan which the government unveiled in November 1968, one month after assuming power.[16]

The twenty-year plan, known as "The Strategy for Peru's Long-Range National Development," reflects the government's major preoccupation: rapid industrial development and the prerequisite social reforms necessary to assure such development. The plan enumerates five basic reforms: (1) expropriation of all large landed estates; (2) a new mining policy to include more public participation, regulation, and control in integrating Peru's mineral resources into the national economy, and to insure that these resources are used for internal industrial development, not merely extracted for export; (3) an industrialization policy designed to reduce Peru's imports and increase exports, especially in the growing South American regional market; (4) reorganization of public administration, recruiting personnel on the basis of technical competence, to create a more efficient instrument for implementing development policies; (5) fiscal reform. The plan, subdivided into five zonal plans, does not envision wholesale nationalization but rather selective takeovers by the state and inducements to existing entrepreneurs to expand their activities. Over a twenty-year period the junta hopes to realize the following objectives: a greatly enlarged and expanding internal market; a more balanced geographical distribution of population; structural changes that will eliminate present institutional obstacles to development; expanded infrastructure; a more equitable distribution of national income and a doubling of per-capita income; subordination of external investment to national development policies; less economic dependence and vulnerability to external forces.[17]

The language of the plan suggests that the military government is not going to preside over a development strategy limited by rigid guidelines or to be accomplished in the space of a few years. An examination of the government's rhetoric, goals, and accomplishments over the past year provides us with some basis for determining what the future holds in terms of radical social change and significant economic development.

One week after coming to power the military government expropriated the International Petroleum Company,[18] announcing that no compensation would be granted and charging IPC with extracting oil from Peru since 1924 under illegal agreements. The expropriation had two immediate results. It created instant popular support for the military government and it incurred the hostility of the United States. A U.S.-Peruvian confrontation developed over the threatened implementation of the Hickenlooper Amendment, under the terms of which all U.S. government economic aid to Peru—Alliance for Progress, AID, and similar programs—would be cut off if IPC was not compensated.[19] Additional pressure existed in the threat to cancel Peru's sugar quota, a move which would have serious repercussions on the country's economy.

The popular support generated by the nationalist action gave the government an opportunity to consolidate its power, purge itself of conservative dissidents, and inaugurate its program of development from above in a tranquil and favorable internal environment. The Nixon Administration, seeking to avoid a confrontation that might radicalize the junta, decided not to apply the economic sanctions; instead it chose to negotiate, hoping to utilize indirect pressures to obtain a settlement of the IPC compensation demands. Since April 1969 when negotiations began, the Peruvian military has remained adamant—no compensation. Nor have there been any overt indications that Peru would consider compensation in exchange for increased U.S. economic aid or private investment pledges. Apparently the military government is confident that the Hickenlooper threat is past. In early August 1969 the Peruvian press reported that the whole affair has been a "meaningless bluff and a most unhappy example of political blackmail." [20] The IPC expropriation is a good indication of the military government's intention of making foreign capital subordinate to Peruvian law and economic development needs. In his Independence Day speech on July 28, 1969, President Velasco said that his government considered the case closed and that future decrees affecting the conduct of foreign capital in Peru could be expected.[21] He spoke of the negative role which unrestrained foreign capital had played in Latin American development, pointing out that Peru and the rest of Latin America are net exporters of capital and that income earned in Latin America finances the development of the highly industrialized nations. Velasco defined his government's attitude as follows:

> This unacceptable situation must be overcome. Latin American development needs foreign capital. But this capital does not come for philanthropic reasons. It is worthwhile for it to come here. There is, therefore, a mutual convenience which must be clearly and justly normalized for benefit of both parties. So foreign capital must act within the legal bounds of our countries under rules which guarantee the just participation of our countries in the wealth which they and their men produce.[22]

The Petroleum Decree (Law 17440, issued in February 1969) gives some indication of what the military government aims to achieve in the area of extractive industry. New concessions will no longer be permitted under old laws: all new contracts are to be negotiated on "fixed profit" terms; all concessions are to include provisions for state participation and profit sharing.[23] In addition, all existing foreign- and domestic-controlled concessions are subject to renegotiation for terms more favorable to the government.

But the act of the government to date that could, if fully implemented, have the most profound effect on Peru's social structure and economic development is the agrarian reform measure (Law 17716). Since this law was decreed on June 24, 1969, 66,000 hectares of the coastal sugar lands have been placed under government administration pending the completion of expropriation procedures and the formation of cooperatives.[24] The cooperatives will be under government supervision and will function as state enterprises. The large sugar estates along the coast and in the sierra affected by the law include those owned by wealthy Peruvian families and private foreign interests such as W. R. Grace & Co. of the United States.[25] All associated sugar-processing facilities and installations on the plantations are marked for expropriation. The agrarian reform is being carried out "without prejudice or favor," as promised by President Velasco, at least along the coast, in order to "end once and for all the unfair social order that has kept peasants in poverty and inequity." [26] If the military government fully implements the agrarian reform, the large cotton plantations and sierra cattle and sheep operations will also be affected. The one major nonsugar-growing sierra estate expropriated by the government was the 247,000-hectare cattle and sheep ranch operated by the U.S.-owned Cerro de Pasco mining company.[27] The Cerro Corporation received $490,000 in cash compensation for the installations on the land. The sum of $1,800,000 has been paid for 90,000 head of livestock. Twenty-year bonds were issued as payment for the land. This expropriation, however, was officially carried out in January 1969, prior to the present law, under the authority and provisions of the 1964 Agrarian Reform Law. The property is to be divided among the peasants working the land, who are to operate the farms cooperatively. This was the first expropriation activity in the agrarian sector undertaken by the military government and it had wide national support. It may have been a pilot project designed to test the response of antagonists and protagonists in the public at large toward a radical agrarian reform.

Subsequently the government decided to expropriate the large, efficient, modern sugar plantations on the coast, an economically powerful and politically influential sector of the Peruvian power structure.[28] The Agrarian Reform Law was applied there immediately, but application was slower in the sierra. So far little or no defiant opposition has materialized from the large sugar growers of the coast. The reason may be that for some time sugar interests have been transferring their investments to other sectors of the economy. Implementation of the agrarian reform on the coast allows for a smooth and rapid channeling of compensation bond payments into the more modern private sectors of the economy. Records show that forty-four major *latifundistas* of the coast now have substantial investments in Peruvian mutual stock funds, the construction industry, insurance and savings companies, mining, public utilities, transportation, and the mass media.[29] The government is counting on the demonstration effect of the successful and peaceful coastal expropriations to make things easier when the sierra is hit with expropriations. In any case this strategy will effectively isolate the landed elite and inhibit a united opposition from acting in concert. The clear intention of the junta's agrarian reform law is to encourage capital investment in industry and mining. Under arrangements for compensation payment, most bonds can be readily converted to cash if they are immediately invested in Peruvian enterprises designated by the government, thus preventing capital outflow and encouraging industrialization. The exact manner in which this important provision of the law will be carried out remains to be seen.

Along with the agrarian reform, changes occurred in ministerial personnel. On June 13, 1969, President Velasco demanded the resignation of the conservative Minister of Agriculture, General José Benavides. The initial appointment of Benavides was viewed by many in Peru, including high officials in the Office of Agrarian Reform (ONRA), as an indication that the military government was not seriously concerned with agrarian change.[30] Benavides was closely associated with members of the National Agrarian Society, the association of large landowners, and expressed strong opposition to large-scale expropriation of land.[31] He was a continuous source of irritation to other members of the government, including General Jorge Fernández Maldonado, the Minister of Energy and Mining, who soon after his appointment became the spokesman of the "radical" sector within the government. Benavides was replaced by another of the "radicals," General Jorge Barandiaran Pagador.[32]

Other measures instituted to implement economic and social goals included reform of the banking system, water rights, and public administration.[33] Banks incorporated in Peru must now be controlled by Peruvian citizens. The Water Code Decree (Law 17752) of July 1969 makes all water, no matter what its source, state property, and establishes a water-control authority to coordinate water-resource utilization with the agrarian reform program and general economic development policies. The administrative changes have been most noticeable at the ministry level. In early April 1969 the Ministry of Development, which had become a catchall for a myriad of functions, was eliminated and its responsibilities divided among four new ministries: Industry and Commerce, Energy and Mines, Transport and Communications, and Housing. The Ministries of War, Navy, and Aviation are to be consolidated under a new Ministry of Defense. In June 1969 the Ministry of Finance was reorganized and is now responsible for coordinating national economic activity with the general development policies of the government. In addition, the National Planning Institute is now to be under the Finance Ministry and its plans are to be forwarded to the appropriate ministries and agencies for implementation. Formerly the Institute functioned apart from the government and its plans were usually ignored; now it has become a central agency in designating government priorities and in allocating government funds, and hence will play a much more important role in shaping the direction of economic development.

A number of other changes geared toward modernizing Peruvian society are projected. In his Independence Day speech of July 28, 1969, Velasco said that business, fishery, credit, and tax reforms were also being planned.[34] Business reform will reportedly involve profit-sharing by employees in accordance with productivity, and cooperative ventures with labor participating to some degree in management. Tax reform would include control of evasion, reduction of indirect taxes, and an effective progressive income tax.

Reform of the fishing industry would involve protection of small operators and heavier taxation of larger enterprises.

All of these decrees reflect the military government's dual policy of initiating modernization, yet remaining firmly in control of the political situation. One of their strategies to insure such control is to reduce the effectiveness of the old party machines and to begin to build a new power base of their own among the peasantry and agrarian workers through some of the measures mentioned above. Moreover, government leaders have occasionally hinted that a new constitution might for the first time give the vote to all those over twenty-one without regard to literacy or property ownership. The government's stated intention of remaining in power for at least six years further undermines the patronage-based electoral parties.

The effort to maintain political control can best be seen in the new University Law. Issued in early March, during the annual university summer break, its purpose is twofold: to make higher education relevant to the development needs of the country, and to eliminate political activity on the campuses. Professors have been divided on the law, some supporting it and others publicly and privately denouncing it. Student leaders have been highly critical, yet efforts to organize effective protest have been quickly suppressed by police and university administrative action.

Under the University Law, all universities are to maintain their autonomy in administrative, financial, and academic matters, but will no longer have the right of "extra-territoriality" in matters concerning "threats to public order." [35] This means that police and military personnel may now freely enter the university grounds and buildings, make arrests, and intervene in "riotous and mutinous situations." The law in effect destroys all semblance of university autonomy. In addition, university administrations have the authority to expel students who engage in or organize political activities. Prior to this law the university administration had to request and receive permission from the University Council, composed of administration, faculty, and students, before expelling a student for nonacademic reasons. The clear intention of the junta is to depoliticize the university and thereby remove a possible source of left-wing opposition to continued military-directed modernization programs.

External Obstacles to Development

In implementing its plan to modernize and industrialize Peru within a capitalist economic system under domestic and not foreign control, the military government has been confronted by numerous external obstacles. The government has been expending considerable time and effort to overcome or remove these impediments to the execution of its development policies. One of the most crippling obstacles concerns repayment of Peru's massive foreign debt.

Under Belaúnde, Peru's foreign debt climbed to $847 million, 70 percent of which must be payed off over a four-year period beginning in 1970. The principal creditors are the United States ($200 million), West Germany ($157 million), Italy ($87 million), France ($52 million), followed by Great Britain, Spain, and Japan.[36]

Peru's Treasury Minister, General Morales Bermúdez, has made two trips to the United States and Europe in an attempt to obtain extension of the payment period. During July–August 1969 he visited various European capitals trying to win support for his plan to refinance Peru's payment schedule over a ten-year period. The principal reason for seeking an extension appears to be the long-range development plans of the government rather than the country's short-range financial situation. As of August the reserves of the Banco Central exceeded $110 million and the balance of payments has shifted from a deficit of $17 million in the year ending June 30, 1968, to a surplus of $30 million in the period ending June 30, 1969.[37]

So far, however, the Treasury Minister has failed to secure agreements allowing for the refinancing of the debt because of the fears of the international financial community. Despite some offers from foreign investors primarily interested in obtaining concessions in the mining sector, little positive aid was forthcoming from the capitalist world. U.S., German, French, and Italian financial and investor groups refused to consider refinancing current debts or further investments in existing companies until agreements are reached guaranteeing the security of present and future investments. And the government's capitalist modernization effort was further delayed by the reluctance of U.S. mining companies to sign agreements to expand production and to develop facilities for refining ore in Peru. The military's dependence on foreign investment is based on the assumption that tax revenue from profits, wages, and export duties would alleviate the country's foreign-debt payment problems and thereby free more capital for industrialization and government social welfare programs.[38]

Negotiations with the U.S. companies about expansion began during the Belaúnde period. They recommenced after his overthrow, with the Minister of Economy and Finance, General Jorge Fernández Maldonado (who is considered by the international business community to have "Nasserist political tendencies") as the chief negotiator for the junta. He assured General Velasco that a $345-million expansion agreement with the U.S.-owned Southern Peru Copper Corporation would be completed in time for Velasco's Independence Day speech on July 28, 1969. The speech was to include a detailed account of the agreement to demonstrate that the military government sought and welcomed foreign capital, but simply wanted to integrate it into the development of Peru's entire economy. The agreement, it was thought, would help to allay some of the international financial community's fears concerning the military government's motives and attitudes toward foreign capital, and would also prompt other major U.S. mining companies operating in Peru to expand their investments. Besides Southern Peru Copper, the military government has been negotiating with the Homestake Mining Company for a $10-million expansion of its operations near Arequipa, with Anaconda for a $70-million expansion of its Cerro Verde operations in the same area, with the Cerro Corporation for a $115-million expansion of its Junín-Ancash operations, with American Smelting and Refining for $250 million and with Kaiser for $91 million. The military modernizers argued that if all investment expansions were begun this year, Peru could double its copper exports to $400 million by 1973 and reach $650 million by 1975.[39] The government is also anxious to grant lucrative exploration, exploitation, and domestic marketing concessions to major petroleum companies in an effort to develop what are considered to be rich petroleum reserves in the northern continental shelf and the northeastern jungle areas of Peru. The government hopes that if mining agreements can be established, similar terms can be secured for petroleum. Recent history suggests that the military's hope of modernizing through massive foreign investment is in fact overly optimistic. U.S. copper mining companies in Peru have invested very little in new capital or equipment for expansion since 1955.[40]

Peru is currently seventh in world production of copper, fourth in zinc and lead, and third in silver. The military government views these assets as crucial sources of the revenue needed to modernize the agrarian sector, and to provide the social and economic infrastructure required for industrialization. The choice facing the military modernizers is whether to sacrifice their plans for national development by making further concessions to the U.S. companies, or turn to public enterprises as the instrument for developing the mineral resources—in which case the modernization-from-above strategy would tend to shift toward a revolutionary collectivist approach.

There is evidence, however, that the military is seeking a way out of the impasse by "internationalizing" the sources of new capital for mineral exploitation. In September 1969 Southern Peru Copper Corporation was warned that if it was not disposed to sign an expansion contract, the military government would "act to protect Peruvian economic interests." [41] The Minister of Economy and Finance has said on various occasions that the government would offer Southern's concession at Cuajone for sale on the international market if the company didn't sign the expansion agreements. Belgian and Japanese mining concerns have expressed interest in this and other copper concessions.

It is clear that U.S. policy-makers in association with U.S. business interests are applying pressure to weaken the nationalist aspects of the Peruvian development program. The U.S.-controlled Export-Import Bank is under orders not to approve any new loans involving Peru, thus providing Southern Peru Copper with a convenient pretext for delay in initiating its expansion program.[42] The chief objections of U.S. investors go to the very heart of the junta's program. Resentful of exchange controls that could effectively keep profits in Peru, U.S. investors demand a guarantee on remission of profits to foreign accounts over a "tolerable" period of time.[43] The Peruvian government considers these objections to national controls as serious obstacles to their over-all development plans. The junta is attempting to overcome the opposition of U.S. policy-makers and established interests by appealing, over their heads, directly to the U.S. investment community as a whole. A full-page advertisement entitled "Peru Today: Highlights of Achievements in the Last 12 Months, Financial Summary and Investment Opportunities," appeared in the *New York Times* in the fall of 1969.[44] The text emphasized the potential for profitable exploitation of minerals, especially copper and phosphate, and specified the advantageous features of a recent decree guaranteeing new investors reduced tax rates, accelerated depreciation allowances, adequate foreign exchange for profits and services, deduction of any losses incurred over a previous five-year period from future profits, and a dispensation permitting up to 50 percent of profits to be reinvested tax free in refineries and/or in plants for treating metallurgic products, for five years after a mining contract expires. Investment incentives were offered to potential investors in the petrochemical, carbochemical, and fertilizer industries. Tax holidays and other incentives lasting up to 1983 were offered to attract investors in industries producing for the export and domestic market. The military government offers to provide the infrastructure for outside capital if it comes into the growth areas designated by the government for development.

The brand of nationalism advocated by the military government is not incompatible with strong doses of foreign capital, and while the junta would no doubt prefer to diversify its sources of investment among the capitalists, Velasco has declared that Peru would seek economic support from "any country in the world." [45]

The commitment to economic development over ideological considerations can be seen in the new commercial, economic, and diplomatic relations established with the Soviet Union and other Eastern European countries.[46] Although this policy has allowed the junta to counter the threat of economic sanction from the United States with the possibility of closer economic and political relations with the Communist world, it may be weakening their appeal for new foreign investment from capitalist countries. So far, Communist trade and aid have been somewhat limited, since current Peruvian exports are not in great demand in the Soviet Union and Eastern European countries.[47] The Soviet Union has offered $100 million in trade credits for heavy machinery. Czechoslovakia has offered $6 million in credits for capital goods as well as technical assistance for the development of zinc, copper, and petroleum facilities. Poland has offered $25 million in credits for machinery, food, medicine, and toys. Hungary has offered $5 million and Rumania an undisclosed amount. Until now, however, the junta has been unable to persuade the Soviet Union to finance the Olmos Irrigation Project in northern Peru's Lambayeque Department. The project when completed would bring 247,000 acres of land under cultivation for the first time. The project plans include hydroelectric plants to generate 350,000 kilowatts of power for the industrialization of the Piura, Lambayeque, and La Libertad departments. A U.N. study estimated the cost of the project at $325 million.

The junta is also seeking financial support from South Africa's General Mining and Finance Corporation for construction of a $22-million tunnel under the Andes as part of the Majes-Siguas Irrigation Project in the desert foothills fifty miles west of Arequipa. This project would bring 140,000 acres of previously uncultivable land under production.[48]

Peru's relations with the United States, meanwhile, remain in suspense, largely because of the IPC compensation issue. In addition to the Hickenlooper threat, U.S. policy-makers wield power over the Peruvian economy via the sugar quota. The United States buys half (450,000 tons) of Peru's annual production at seven cents a pound, as against the two or three cents per pound which generally prevails in the world market. The price differential amounts to about $50 million yearly. If alternative markets could not be located quickly, cancellation of the sugar quota would mean not only loss of this income but unemployment for about 50,000 sugar workers (mostly concentrated on the north coast), thus creating further internal burdens for the junta.[49]

Another problem which has complicated U.S.-Peruvian relations is Peru's claim to a 200-mile coastal fishing limit. Section 3(b) of the U.S. Foreign Military Sales Act (Pelly Amendment), October 22, 1968, provides for suspension of arms sales to a country if a U.S. fishing vessel is captured more than twelve miles off a coastline and fined. In addition, the amount of the fines is to be deducted from foreign aid commitments to that country.[50] After a couple of vessels were seized, Washington began to apply the pressure: on April 3, 1969, the Peruvian Ambassador in Washington was informed that military aid was suspended. The Peruvians responded by seizing another ship. More important, the U.S. MAAG (Military Advisory and Assistance Group) Mission of about fifty officers was ordered out of the country by the military government.[51] The arms-sale ban was lifted on July 3, 1969, but its imposition increased tension between the two countries.

By fall 1969, then, the terms of the dilemma facing the junta were clear: Should they sacrifice their national development plan to meet the demands of foreign investors? Or should they attempt to locate alternative sources of capital through internal savings, creation of public enterprises, and closer relations with Communist countries?

During the fall months the Velasco government took a series of actions that seem to reflect the pressures emanating from the more radical wing of the junta.[52] Foreign investors in the mining sector were told to put unexploited concessions into operation within seven months or the government would repossess them. A suburban law was put into effect, providing for the rapid expropriation of suburban plots of land in order to eradicate the *barriadas* and to build private houses. If seriously applied, this program could signify a hard blow at banking and real estate interests. In addition, Vice-Admiral Enrique Carbonell, considered a radical, recently joined the junta. He was the one responsible for exposing IPC's illegal remission of several million dollars shortly after the company's expropriation by the junta, resulting in the fall of two of the junta "moderates."

In September 1969 the government severely restricted imports, virtually prohibiting all luxury items and goods which compete with domestic production. And it established a state monopoly over the importation of meat and dairy products to end speculation in the market for foodstuffs. The agrarian reform had been extended to all the coastal sugar plantations and was beginning to be applied in the cattle ranches of Cuzco for the first time.

At about the same time the government announced that an important Soviet mission, headed by a vice-minister, would be arriving in Peru to study the possibility of a vast program of irrigation in the northern desert plains. Moreover, the government appears to be relaxing its authoritarian posture regarding popular demands, decreeing, for example, that striking workers of Cerro de Pasco be awarded a raise 23 percent higher than that offered by the company—an action strongly denounced by the business community as "demogogic."

Although the ideology of the military continues to reflect a developmentalist perspective, cumulative social changes resulting from piecemeal legislation to further specific economic goals may begin to develop their own dynamic. The tension between Peru and the United States and the opening of new commercial relations with both Communist and non-Communist nations in Europe and Asia may allow the junta to increase the state's role in organizing and directing economic institutions. Already the original developmentalist perspective has been modified to take account of the intransigent opposition of foreign and domestic investors, and the receptivity of the populace to socioeconomic changes and nationalist policies. Whether the military chooses to continue operating on a pragmatic basis in response to specific pressures, or whether they will formulate a radically new political strategy will depend on their ability to work out a modus vivendi with U.S. corporate capitalism.

Postscript, February 1970

The policies of the junta have zig-zagged from populist-nationalist to conservative over the first two years. These shifts in policies reflect the push and pull of the different factions within the junta as well as the pressures of the outside world. The hostility of the United States has tended to strengthen the position of the nationalists. During the fall of 1969 the nationalist faction appeared to be gaining ascendance, helped significantly by the intransigent posture adopted by U.S. businessmen and policy-makers.

In the event, however, the signs and symptoms of radicalization turned out to be misleading. Behind the scenes a struggle was taking place within the junta. Minister of Development Maldonado represented the political wing which favored the promotion of economic development through heavy state intervention, largely via public corporations and public loans. Minister of Economy and Finance Francisco Morales Bermúdez belonged to that wing most anxious to promote development through agreement with U.S. investors. These differences apparently came to a head in the discussions surrounding the exploitation of Peru's rich copper deposits in Cuajone (a reserve estimated at 450 million tons). As already noted, an agreement with the Southern Peru Copper Corporation (a consortium comprising American Smelting and Refining, Cerro, Phelps Dodge, and Newmont Mining) had been under negotiation for months, with the outcome being held up pending the settlement of the struggle inside the junta. The denouement finally came in late December 1969, with a victory for Francisco Morales Bermúdez and the pro-imperialist sector of the junta. Under the terms of this agreement, Southern Peru contracted to invest $355 million in expanding copper production.

But more important, the new agreement signaled a definitive rapprochement with the U.S. government and brought to an end the nationalist phase of the junta's activity. Coincidental with the copper agreement, the agrarian reform has slowed down. The political rapprochement with the U.S. and the signing of the copper agreement serve as a guarantee for the rest of the international investment community that Peru is, after all, safe for capitalist exploitation.

It thus appears that the hopes aroused by the expropriation of IPC and the rhetoric surrounding the agrarian reform were premature if not altogether ill-founded. In the month prior to the copper agreement nine members of the Movement of the Revolutionary Left (MIR) were arrested for "subversion," and a revolutionary socialist leader, Ricardo Gadea, was sentenced to five years in prison.

The military junta has clearly taken the path of development through subordination to foreign investment; in the next period it will probably sacrifice development for external support to stay

Table I
Biographical Data on the Junta

Name	Rank, Date of Rank	Position	Age
Juan Velasco Alvarado	Division General, 1965 (Army)	President	60
Edgardo Mercado Jarrin	Brig. General, 1966 (Air Force)	Minister of Foreign Affairs	54
Alfredo Avunseno Cornejo	Brig. General, 1967 (Army)	Minister of Education	54
Jorge Barandiarán Pagador	Brig. General, NA (Army)	Minister of Agriculture	50
Armando Artola Azarate	Brig. General, 1967 (Army)	Minister of Interior	50
Ernesto Montagne Sánchez	Division General, 1968 (Army)	Minister of Defense	53
Jorge Chamot Biggs	Major General, NA (Air Force)	Minister of Labor	50
Francisco Morales Bermúdez	Brig. General, NA (Army)	Minister of Economy and Finance	48
Jorge Maldonado Solari	Brig. General, NA (Army)	Minister of Development	47
Eduardo Montero Rojas	Major General, 1963 (Air Force)	Minister of Public Health	51
Jorge Camino	Rear Admiral, NA (Navy)	Minister of Industry and Commerce	56
Alfonso Navarro***	Vice-Admiral, 1968 (Navy)	Minister of Navy	58
Aníbal Meza Cuadra Cardenas	Brig. General, NA (Army)	Minister of Transportation and Communications	49
Rolando Gilardi Rodríguez	Lt. General, NA (Air Force)	Minister of Aeronautics	49
José Graham Hurtado	Brig. General, 1968 (Army)	Chief, Presidential Advisory Committee	51

* Chorrillos Military Academy

** Center for Advanced Military Studies. Many Junta members attended, graduated, and later returned as administrators or instructors.

*** Considered moderate-conservative and often differed openly with more radical elements in junta. Was replaced in September 1969 by Vice-Admiral Enrique Carbonell, a nationalist.

NA: Information not available.

Table I (*Continued*)

Birthplace	Family Social Origin	Year Graduated from Military Academy	CAEM** Assoc.	U.S. Training or Assignment
Piura	Middle Class	*1934	x	x
Lima	Middle Class	1941	x	x
Arequipa	Middle Class	*1939	x	x
Chiclayo	NA	*1941	x	x
Moquegua	Upper Class	*1940	x	x
Lima	Middle Class	*1938	x	x
Lima	NA	1942	NA	x
Lima	Grandson of former president	*1943	x	x
Ilo	Middle Class	*1941	x	NA
Yurimaguas	Middle Class	1941	NA	x
Iquitos	NA	1936	NA	x
Lima	Middle Class	1934	NA	x
Bolívar	NA	*1942	NA	x
Arequipa	Middle Class	1941	NA	x
Arequipa	Middle Class	*1941	x	NA

in power. Splits among the military may occur; national-populists will have the choice of capitulating before the rightist course chosen by Velasco or of breaking discipline, turning to the people, and struggling to reverse the policy of development through subordination.

NOTES

1. On the appointment of government officials to supervise the administration of expropriated estates see interviews in *Caretas* (Lima), XIX, No. 400 (August 14, 1969), pp. 16–19, 48–50. In addition, imprisoned peasant leader Hugo Blanco has said that "government bureaucrats and soldiers will bungle successful implementation of the new Agrarian Reform Law." Blanco thinks that men like himself who have exceptional ability to organize the sierra peasantry should have major roles in the agrarian reform. See interview in *Intercontinental Press* (New York), VII, No. 31 (September 29, 1969), pp. 848–849.

2. The junta has demonstrated that it intends to keep unions under effective government control. See *Front* (Paris), "Un An de Pouvoir Militaire," I, No. 3 (September 1969), pp. 38–41.

3. For an excellent discussion of capitalist modernization from above see Barrington Moore, *Social Origins of Democracy and Dictatorship* (Boston: Beacon Press, 1966).

4. On Cuba's favorable response see Fidel Castro's speech of July 14, 1969, in *Granma,* July 15, 1969.

5. On the first anniversary, October 3, 1969, of the junta's seizure of power, President Velasco accused an unnamed group of industrialists and landowners of plotting against him through their "economic apparatus and the reactionary press." In his speech he said that "oligarchs" were in collusion with foreign elements and were creating an investment crisis in the nation. For further discussion of Velasco's anniversary speech see *Marcha* (Montevideo), October 10, 1969, p. 19; *Washington Post,* October 5, 1969; and *The Economist para América Latina* (London), III, No. 21 (October 15, 1969), p. 31.

6. For background information concerning this period in Peruvian politics see Fredrick B. Pike, *The Modern History of Peru* (New York: Praeger, 1967), pp. 282–320; and Lewis Hanke, *Contem-*

porary Latin America (Princeton, N.J.: Van Nostrand, 1968), pp. 128–132.

7. For an account of the motives at work in the 1962 military coup see Peter Nehemkis, *Latin America: Myth and Reality* (New York: New American Library, 1966), pp. 93–104.

8. See CIDA report, *Una evaluación de la reforma agraria en el Peru,* (Washington, D.C.: Pan American Union, 1966), p. 1.

9. Oficina National de la Reforma Agraria, *Boletin Informativo* (Lima), September 1968. For additional information see *Peruvian Times* (Lima), June 27, 1969, pp. 1–2.

10. CIDA report, p. 5.

11. While Balaúnde was failing to carry out promised reforms, the military was busily engaged in suppressing what might have been the beginning of the revolution from below. Between 1960–1965 mass peasant radicalism, especially in the south, was becoming a major concern of many military personnel. It is interesting to note that although the military killed and jailed hundreds of peasants during the repression of 1962–1964, it nevertheless accepted the *de facto* seizure of land that had occurred—the first indication of a new attitude. See my "Revolution and Guerrilla Movements in Latin America: Venezuela, Guatemala, Colombia, and Peru," in James Petras and Maurice Zeitlin, eds., *Latin America: Reform or Revolution?* (New York: Fawcett, 1968), pp. 329–369.

12. Foreknowledge of the 1967 currency devaluation enabled many high government officials to make substantial sums in the money markets. For IPC-related corruption see *The Economist para América Latina,* III, No. 6 (March 19, 1969), pp. 11–12.

13. Biographical data on the junta members was kindly provided by the Peruvian Embassy, Washington, D.C. We would also like to thank U.S. Congressman Dante Fascell and Senator Frank Church for their aid in attaining supporting data.

14. See Table. For a brief background sketch on CAEM and its activities see Pike, *op. cit.,* p. 315.

15. *Visión* (Mexico City), XXXVII, No. 5 (August 29, 1969), pp. 12–16. This issue of *Visión* was not permitted to circulate freely in Peru because of its critical observations regarding the junta's lack of wide national support.

16. *Peruvian Times,* August 8, 1969, p. 1.

17. *Orientaciones para la transformación de nuestra dinamica social dentro de una estrategia de desarrollo nacional a largo plazo*

(Lima: Institute of National Planning, November 1968). The Institute was one of the developmental institutions established by the military government of 1962–1963.

18. For a discussion of the history of petroleum politics in Peru see *Marcha,* No. 26 (June 1969), pp. 7–29.

19. On the Hickenlooper Amendment see U.S., Senate, *Congressional Record,* 87th Cong., 2nd Sess., 108, Part 16, October 2, 1962, pp. 21615–21620. For a historical perspective, see Marvin D. Bernstein, ed., *Foreign Investment in Latin America: Cases and Attitudes* (New York: Knopf, 1966). General Valdivia, a member of the junta, declared that the Peruvian government had been threatened by the International Monetary Fund with cancellation of credits amounting to $75 million if Peru did not restore the property of IPC. Other agencies alleged to be applying financial pressure include AID, IDB (Inter-American Development Bank), and the World Bank. See the *New York Times,* December 8, 1968.

20. *Peruvian Times,* August 1, 1969, p. 1.

21. For summary of Velasco's speech see *ibid.*

22. *Ibid.*

23. *Peruvian Times,* February 28, 1969, pp. 1–2.

24. The coastal plantations, including the sugar plantations, were exempt from expropriation under Belaúnde's Agrarian Reform Law of 1964. Article 25 of that law allowed individual members of agricultural corporations to declare single expropriation exemptions. The collective declaration of these exemptions would effectively exclude the large estates from judicial or administrative action under the Belaúnde law. On expropriations under the junta's 1969 agrarian reform law see *Peruvian Times,* July 4, 1969, p. 2.

25. W. R. Grace & Co. lost 12,000 hectares. See *ibid.*

26. *New York Times,* June 26, 1969, p. 4.

27. On the expropriation of the Cerro de Pasco lands, see *Peruvian Times,* January 3 and 17, and May 9, 1969.

28. "La reforma agraria y los empresarios," *Caretas* (Lima), XIX, No. 399 (July 24, 1969), p. 25.

29. *Ibid.*

30. The previous director of ONRA, Lander Pacora, resigned six months after the military took power and expressed surprise when the new agrarian reform law was decreed. In a private interview in Washington, D.C., on June 25, 1969, he openly admitted that

he had not thought the military government would decree such an effective, thorough, and radical law.

31. In an interview printed in *Correo* (Lima), May 10, 1969, p. 4, Benavides was quoted as saying that expropriation was too costly to be feasible. Arguing that the land-tenure system was not a major cause of Peru's agrarian problems, Benavides favored incentives to the current landowners to increase production as a way of reducing the country's high imports of food.

32. Apart from the traditional economic elite, other vested interests have voiced their opposition to the agrarian reform. The sugar worker unions of the coast, given legal recognition and permitted to organize by the military government of 1962–1963, have gained pay raises and many fringe benefits as well. Their principal concern now is whether in becoming employees of state enterprises they will lose their right to strike and bargain effectively. Several labor leaders and sugar workers interviewed in early 1969 on the Hacienda Pomalca, a large Peruvian-owned sugar-growing and processing operation on the north coast, have also questioned the government's political motives, suspecting that the agrarian reform law was being applied in a way to destroy the *aprista*-controlled unions that dominate the sugar industry and thus further undermine APRA power and influence among the working class. See *Caretas*, XIX, No. 400 (August 14, 1969), pp. 16–19, 48–50.

33. *Peruvian Times*, August 1, 1969, p. 1.

34. *Ibid*.

35. For a copy of the University Law see *Marcha*, June 26, 1969, pp. 85–96. For additional information and commentary on the law see *Visión*, XXXVI, No. 7 (March 28, 1969), p. 14.

36. *The Economist para América Latina*, III, No. 16 (August 6, 1969), p. 14.

37. *Ibid*.

38. *The Economist para América Latina*, III, No. 17 (August 20, 1969), p. 32.

39. *Peruvian Times*, February 28, 1969, p. 1.

40. *Ibid*.

41. *The Economist para América Latina*, III, No. 17 (August 20, 1969), p. 32.

42. *Ibid*.

43. *Ibid*.

44. *New York Times*, September 28, 1969, p. E5.

45. Statement of December 16, 1968, reprinted in *Peruvian Times,* January 10, 1969, p. 1.
46. For details on the establishment of diplomatic relations and the signing of trade agreements with the Soviet Union and the Eastern European bloc see *Peruvian Times,* April 25, 1969, p. 1.
47. See Pearson Commission Report of the Commission on International Development, October 1, 1969, portions of which are quoted in the *New York Times,* October 2, 1969, p. 74.
48. *Peruvian Times,* April 18, 1969, p. 1.
49. Peru's sugar workers are unionized and among the better paid workers in the country. For a discussion of Peru's sugar industry and its labor elite see *Visión,* XXXVI, No. 7 (March 28, 1969), pp. 30–31.
50. Under the Fisherman's Act all captains are reimbursed by the U.S. government for fines resulting from fishing within the extraordinary limits (200 miles) set by numerous Latin American countries. Fines, based on ship tonnage, have varied from $5,000 to $20,000.
51. *Washington Post,* May 25, 1969, p. A1.
52. *Marcha,* October 3, 1969, p. 18.

Guerrilla Movements
in Latin America

The 1960's were years of intense social and political warfare in Latin America: mass peasant movements, large-scale mobilizations, a revitalized nationalism, and, most important, the development of guerrilla warfare in many countries. The years immediately following the success of the Cuban Revolution were a time of revolutionary euphoria: from Mexico to Argentina revolutionary detachments went to the mountains to begin the struggles to liberate their countries from the domination of the foreign investors, large landholders, and oligarchic governments. In three countries, Colombia, Venezuela, and Guatemala, the guerrilla movements were at one time significant political forces capable of challenging the power of the ruling elites. In other countries, such as Peru, guerrilla warfare followed large-scale mobilization of the centuries-long-oppressed Indian to retake the land stolen from their ancestors. The peasants, organized in peasant unions, initiated scores of land invasions. The old collectivist ethic was rejuvenated. In Colombia a growing number of revolutionary priests began to challenge the medieval inquisitorial Church which dominates the society: they openly called for the overthrow of Colombia's social and economic establishment. The peak of the radical revolutionary movement was reached at different times in different countries during the early and middle 1960's. By 1966, however, the tide began to shift: the counterrevolution headed by the United States and its elite allies in Latin America was increasingly in ascendance. Between 1966 and 1969 the counterrevolution appeared invincible: revolution appeared remote. In 1969 a new upsurge occurred, involving new forms of struggle; the older *fidelista* rural guerrilla strategies were modified or discarded. This chapter is an attempt to analyze four revolutionary movements of the 1960's,

159

their emergence, and their impact on political developments. Similarity in methods of struggle disguises the fact that each guerrilla movement has gone through its own particular historical experience, reflecting, and shaping, the specific form which the "crisis of authority" has taken.

Revolution and Counterrevolution

A social revolution is not imminent in Latin America. The defeat of the revolutionary upsurge of 1958–1960, the failure of the middle-class governments of 1960–1963, and the emergence of new military dictatorships, sometimes supported or organized by the United States, have stabilized U.S. tutelage and Latin oligarchical control while exacerbating the underlying social and economic problems of these diverse societies. Throughout the 1960's conflict was most evident in the fractures which developed in traditional Latin institutions (church, army, university), and evident also in the mass involvement of previously passive peasants and Indians in social struggles. The breakdown of authority on different levels was typified by widespread banditry (Colombia, for example, has had numerous kidnapings), and for a time by development of "autonomous republics" within Colombia, and local self-government in Peru and Guatemala. But it was in the challenge for power launched by the guerrilla movements that the "crisis of authority" manifested itself most tellingly.

The Revolutionary Movement of November 13 (MR-13) is one of the guerrilla movements in Guatemala. Its leader, Comandante Marco Antonio Yon Sosa, a strong supporter of the Chinese Revolution and the armed struggle for socialism, proposed an alliance of workers, peasants, and students to fight for a "worker-peasant government." The Guatemalan Communist Party (PGT) called for a coalition with the progressive bourgeosie leading to a "national-democratic government" and denounced MR-13 as "adventuristic." In 1965, Luis Augusto Turcios left MR-13 and formed an armed group called the FAR (Rebel Armed Forces) which was independent and yet supported the position of the PGT. The FAR functioned, at first, as a pressure group on the military to achieve the election of a national-democratic government, which the PGT advocates.

Unlike MR-13, the PGT subordinated the armed struggle to the electoral road to power. In line with this position, the PGT said of the March 1966 elections, "In synthesis, the elections will develop under the climate of popular advance toward liberation." [1] Before the elections, the PGT called for a vote for Menéndez Montenegro; *after* the elections the FAR characterized his party as an "oligarchical and pro-imperialist clique . . . answering to the North American Embassy." [2]

By the summer of 1966, the FAR appeared to have grown considerably larger than MR-13, and to have a more effective organization. This was probably due to (1) the recognition and support that Turcios received as the official Guatemalan delegate to the Tri-Continental Congress held in Havana in January 1966; (2) the expulsion from MR-13 of several influential members, leaders of an ex-Trotskyist grouping (Posadista) who openly admitted using MR-13 funds to finance their "international"; and (3) the more "activist" orientation of FAR which was highlighted by mass peasant organizing and the dramatic kidnaping of high government officials.

In late 1966, there was an informal pact between the two guerrilla groups which eventually led to their formal merger in 1968. The political basis of such a unification was largely the socialist perspective of MR-13; the electoral position of the PGT was completely repudiated. Prior to the merger, FAR, while not supporting the government, had focused on the military, which they distinguished as the major institution blocking peaceful democratic reforms. MR-13 continued to demand a "worker-peasant government"—something which the Menéndez government was not. What caused the change in the FAR's position was the government's large-scale offensive in 1967: this attempt to wipe out the insurgents pushed the FAR to the position of MR-13 and caused it to break its ties with the Communist Party. Unfortunately, Luis Turcios died in an auto accident precisely when the guerrillas were under greatest pressure.

However, the defeats suffered by the guerrillas during the government's offensive and their different backgrounds and experiences led to new internal conflicts. By mid-1969 the guerrilla group had fragmented into four distinct groups. The two fractions which still appear to be active, though not on the same scale as before, are those led by César Montes and Yon Sosa. In comparison with their mass following and influence in 1966, the guerrillas of 1970 are largely confined to defensive operations in isolated regions.

In the initial revolt the Guatemalan military officers-turned-guerrillas were mainly concerned with vaguely nationalistic goals and lacked the ideological sophistication of their Venezuelan counterparts. But these cadres gave the Guatemalan MR-13 the important advantage of being militarily well prepared, which is one reason why the activity of MR-13, though less publicized and less dramatic than that of other guerrilla movements, has had the virtue of being more sustained; Yon Sosa has avoided head-on collisions with the military and has concentrated on slowly building support among the Indian villagers around La Sierra de las Minas. Between 1961 and 1965, MR-13 moved in a Marxist direction. The January 1966 issue of the journal *Revolución Socialista* revealed that MR-13 had gone beyond the national anti-imperialist character of other guerrilla movements and explicitly defined its program and organization as Marxist-Leninist.

MR-13, with its nationalistic ex-military officers promoting an armed struggle for a socialist program within a largely rural Indian milieu, provides an unusual contrast to an urban-based communist party which declares the need for a liberal parliamentary government. The reasons for this anomalous situation are to be found in the recent political history of Guatemala and Cuba. Arbenz's fall from power in 1954 and the subsequent establishment by the CIA of a military dictatorship produced a strong nationalist sentiment against U.S. intervention and made clear that the armed forces are a decisive force in determining the fate of a popular government; there has been little in recent Guatemalan history to recommend the electoral route to social change. In addition to this national sentiment, and linked to the necessity for armed struggle, there existed the example of Cuba's reorientation from a nationalist to a socialist goal.

The leaderships of MR-13 and the FAR are, by social origin, a reflection of the crisis in the old traditional authority structure:

the leaders, as ex-army men, are largely from the traditional middle class which has provided many of the officers in the military. (Despite the differing programs of a number of guerrilla movements, they share in common the fact that their leaderships are largely composed of defectors from traditional institutions and elites.[3])

In Colombia, guerrilla warfare, civil war banditry, "independent republics," and "red republics" have been fixed features of national life for decades, at times extending over half the country. The death toll from civil war, banditry, and government violence during the last fifteen years is conservatively estimated to exceed 300,000. Here old-fashioned peasant communists, together with idealistic students, uprooted peasants, and university alumni form the backbone of the Colombian leadership. One of the more successful guerrilla raids was led by an ex-student leader, a young woman called Mariela Amaya o Paulina González who, after graduating from the university, packed a rifle and led a group of guerrillas in an attack on a government outpost in Santander Province.

Unlike the relative novelty of guerrilla warfare in Guatemala and Venezuela, the contemporary guerrilla movement in Colombia has a long tradition. As early as 1930–1931, armed groups demanding agrarian reform were emerging. The Colombian Communist Party (CCP), under the sway of the heady doctrines of the "Third Period," decided to create socialism in one province. The CCP established a peasant zone under its control in a remote area of southern Colombia which became known as "Red Viota" or the "Red Republic." Surrounded by jungles and virtually inaccessible to government forays, "Red Viota" could not be defeated from outside, but the hard-working peasants and Communists became so successful in their farming that they virtually lost all interest in extending their practice to other areas, thus in a sense defeating their own original goals in seeking agrarian reform. Nevertheless, the independent self-governing tradition of Viota became a rallying cry in the more recent period when similar areas of Colombia were occupied by peasants fleeing from both social and governmental violence. The development in the mid-1960's of the "independent republic" of Marquetalia reflected both the earlier attempt of peasants to establish a stable society, uncorrupted and based on local control, and a new approach to counter the repressive central government by extending the movement to other areas. This independent republic was not able to withstand encirclement by the government. In 1964 a drive by the U.S.-advised, 16,000-man Colombian Army effectively destroyed it.

Out of the conflicts in the Colombian Church came one of the most dynamic and gifted revolutionary leaders in recent Latin American history, Camilo Torres. Son of one of the oldest aristocratic families in Colombia, educated in Louvain, he found his calling in the armed revolutionary struggle. Like others before him, Torres came to this decision after trying many other means.

In early 1965, Camilo Torres achieved what few other recent Latin revolutionary leaders have been able to do: he built an enormous popular urban following which included significant sectors of the trade-union movement in addition to student and peasant support. From May to September of 1965, wherever Torres spoke, the major plazas were crowded to overflowing. *Frente Unido,* the weekly newspaper which Torres directed, was avidly read. His message was profoundly revolutionary: expropriation of all landed estates without indemnification, nationalization of all natural resources, urban reform, egalitarian wage scales, and popular control of government. The sources cited by Camilo and his mode of expression were distinctly Christian. This combination of a modern revolutionary social message with a Christian rhetoric presented the greatest single challenge the Colombian elite had faced. Because Camilo Torres' own defection symbolized the break between the authoritarian elitist past and the revolutionary future, the legal political roads were closed, and he was finally shot and killed in guerrilla combat. Against orders from the hierarchy, forty priests held a high mass for him.

What proved decisive in Camilo Torres' political evolution was his turn away from the elite centers of power (the university where he taught, the church where he preached) to the people, the street and, finally, the countryside. Explicitly rejecting "permeationist" or traditional formulas of the Communist Party calling for coalition with the "progressive" wing of the Liberal Party, Camilo turned to the task of rallying popular revolutionary opposition through direct contact with the masses, leading to the formation of a new political organization, Frente Unido.

Camilo Torres' decision to turn to guerrilla warfare was based on a realistic appraisal of Colombian politics and a profound commitment to his radical ideals.[4] The suppression of legal political meetings, blocking of peaceful mass mobilization, the constitutional provision confining the electoral process to competition between the two major parties, reduced the choice to either accommodation to the legal system (hence, to the social system) or armed struggle. He chose to live by the revolution, and he died fighting for it.

The experience of Camilo Torres, who originally thought in terms of building an urban-rural political mass party based on the trade unions and peasants' associations, reveals the difficulties in applying classical European patterns of struggle to Latin America. Nonetheless, Camilo Torres continued to maintain that the guerrilla struggle was always subordinate to the need to develop a mass urban and rural revolutionary organization. His constant references to his own personal insignificance were not only an expression of personal modesty, but dictated by his political vision: the guerrilla movement was not a substitute for but an instrument of the larger mass movement of opposition. The impact of Camilo Torres may be greater in the long run than in his own lifetime, as he has come to be looked upon by Catholics as the Che Guevara of the Church. Most of the growing number of revolutionary groups among Catholic clerics and laymen have been greatly influenced by Camilo's writings and example.

The Venezuelan guerrilla movement, perhaps the most publicized movement of its kind in the world, is the one least understood by its friends as well as its detractors. Until recently, both the U.S. government and the Left throughout the world were predicting either an imminent "communist takeover" or a "popular revolution" which would demolish the old order. Obviously, neither has occurred, nor do they appear likely for some time; the guerrillas continue to exist, and are apparently wiser and perhaps more firmly established. The fact remains that the Venezuelan guerrilla movement has been subject to erratic shifts in personnel and strategy. Partly this is the result of functioning in a country which has very substantial oil revenues, the largest U.S. military mission in Latin America, and a sophisticated political leadership. This leadership has perpetrated sufficient violence to prevent the revolutionaries from functioning openly in politics, and at the same time, has handed out a sufficient number of doles, jobs, and promises to neutralize a discontented populace.

The Venezuelan guerrilla movement began as a response to the government's violence and its denial of the constitutional rights which the "Venezuelan Democratic Revolution" was ostensibly upholding. Though there were frequent incidents of violent conflict between students, unemployed workers, and police prior to 1960, the turning point in Venezuelan political life and the emergence of a guerrilla movement date from October of that year. The official U.S. version of events appears in *Venezuela: U.S. Army Area Handbook for Venezuela,* prepared by American University's Foreign Area Studies Division Special Operations Research Office (SORO).[5] The *Army Handbook's* falsified version of the Betancourt government's resort to violence is that it was a defensive measure, to protect democracy against Castroite terror: "The radical Left came out overtly for the overthrow of the Betancourt government . . . because of the government's anti-Castro stand. In an October 1960 issue, the MIR [Movement of the Revolutionary Left] weekly newspaper *Izquierda* published an editorial advocating the overthrow of the government by violent means. *When as a result of this editorial, three MIR leaders were arrested, 2,000 students of the Central University rioted.*" As a consequence of these events, there were triggered off "riots . . . throughout the country and the national guard and police took severe measures to put down the disorders."[6] It was during this period that the cycle of violence and counterviolence began to develop in a serious fashion and resulted in the students finally taking to the hills. The editorial in *Izquierda* of October 14, 1960, on which the *Army Handbook* bases its argument justifying Betancourt's violence, actually stated the opposite of what the *Handbook* claimed. In fact Domingo Alberto Rangel, who wrote this editorial, said that a popular insurrection could not succeed and even argued that the Betancourt government itself might, if it took the proper actions, avoid a revolution. The evidence presented by the government was so obviously contrived that the Chamber of Deputies in

July 1961 (then still controlled by the pro-Betancourt AD-COPEI government coalition) turned down the Supreme Court's request to waive Congressman Rangel's immunity in order that he might be tried. On October 22, 1960, Movement of the Revolutionary Left (MIR) spokesman Saez Merida made perfectly clear that the Left preferred the ballot to the bullet, and that they were preparing for the 1963 elections. He went so far as to reaffirm his group's nonsubversive nature and continued to make positive references to Betancourt's regime: ". . . the MIR does not pursue popular subversion against the constitutional regime." [7] Unfortunately for the Left, their professions of faith in the constitutional regime saved neither their persons nor their party from persecution. Following the arrest of three MIR editors, the political secret police (DIGEPOL) raided the buildings of all the left-wing parties, while on the day of the arrests National Guardsmen opened fire on students inside the Central University, thus violating the autonomy of the University, an action which was condemned even by conservative Catholic (COPEI) leader Rafael Caldera. On October 22, Minister of Education Rafael Pizani, a moderate liberal who believed in civil liberties, obtained the release of the arrested students and resigned in protest over the wave of government repression.

It must be recognized that under these circumstances the student protests were not riots or part of a Communist plot to overthrow the government by violence, but an attempt to regain the constitutional rights and democratic liberties of the MIR editors who were being framed. By denying the Left its freedom of expression, by repressing legitimate opposition and forcing it to utilize "illegal means," then retrospectively rewriting history in order to prove that the outlawed opposition was acting illegally all along, the Betancourt government's own authoritarian violence provoked a counterviolence, the guerrilla movement.

The Venezuelan guerrilla movement began primarily as a predominantly student group. While there were only about 150 students attending the eleven junior and four senior seminaries in 1961, the guerrilla movement has had no problem enrolling hundreds of idealistic students. Most of the latter are Venezuelans, concerned with the poor, unlike the majority of the Catholic clergy in Venezuela who are Spaniards and concerned with attending to the superficial piety of their predominantly upper- and middle-class clientele. Estimates of the size of a guerrilla force are difficult to make, but this writer's guess is that in 1965/66 there were 200–300 in Venezuela (and about 200 in Colombia and 100–200 in Guatemala). This is a fairly stable figure, as the turnover was not so high as when the movement first began and young students had a romantic view of life in the hills.

The Venezuelan guerrilla movement went through essentially three phases: (1) the "student vanguardist" period, 1960–1962; (2) the period of intense urban warfare, 1962–1964, involving a variety of urban actions ostensibly intended to electrify the masses; (3) the "agrarian reform" phase, 1964 to 1968. In 1969, while still operating in the countryside, the guerrilla group led by Douglas Bravo was again attempting to build urban bases of support. The strategy appears to be one of combining urban popular struggles with rural guerrilla action.

During the vanguardist period, the students engaged in gun battles with the police either from the Central University or from buildings in the city. The dramatic episode called "The Battle of Stalingrad" typifies both the character and nature of the guerrilla movement in the early period: several hundred students barricaded a school building and exchanged shots with the police, finally being surrounded and forced to surrender after suffering heavy casualties. In this period, a strong current among these guerrillas believed that the students were the agents of social revolution. These were the days when young nationalistic military officers conceived of a "left" coup and in 1962, at Carúpano and Puerto Cabello, unsuccessfully attempted to realize it. During the second phase, from mid-1962 to the end of 1963, the still predominantly urban-based guerrillas attempted desperate measures and sensational acts to dramatize the struggle, hoping in this way to galvanize the masses. Famous art works were stolen, soccer players were kidnaped, pipelines were blown up, etc. The substitution of this type of individual action for mass mobilization proved as ineffective as the previous armed confrontations with the police. Concomitant with the failure of the urban guerrilla movement, however, a number of guerrillas began to coalesce in the countryside. The rural guerrilla force included a heterogeneous mixture of army officers fleeing from the defeats at Puerto Cabello, students turned guerrilla fighters, a small number of peasants, and a number of older political leaders who were being sought by the government. On February 20, 1963, all the diverse groups met and formed the FALN (Armed Forces of National Liberation).

The third phase came following the failure of the electoral boycott called by the urban guerrillas during the 1963 elections. Now the rural areas became the center of guerrilla activities; the urban movement continued as an auxiliary activity. More fundamental was the discussion that ensued over the basic question of armed struggle vs. "legal means." Following the electoral defeat, the "legalists" got the upper hand and a six-month truce was declared. Between January and June 1964 the guerrillas waited to see if the legal channels would open as their moderate colleagues had argued. Instead, in May of that year, the new president, Leoni, simultaneously inaugurated a full-scale antiguerrilla military campaign and in an interview with a French correspondent declared that the guerrillas were finished. He interpreted the truce as a sign of weakness, not as a period of good will in which democracy could be restored.

The "legalists" were defeated and some of the older leaders of the MIR like Alberto Rangel split and formed a new group. The armed guerrilla struggle was begun once more, this time in the countryside. Initially, the FALN claimed to have established four major fronts and to be gaining support among the peasants. In fact, the guerrillas have been badly hit by defections and now operate in remote rural areas. Lacking much of a rural base and cut off from possible sources of support in the urban areas, the guerrilla movement went through a severe crisis throughout 1968–1969. A contributing factor was the policy of the Venezuelan Communist Party.

In the fall of 1965, while the FALN was once again involved in combat, the Venezuelan Communist Party issued a call for a "democratic peace." It stated the willingness of the VCP to renounce the armed struggle in exchange for assurances that it would be granted legal recognition, that political prisoners would be released, and that there would be no reprisals. Early in 1966 a serious division occurred within the ranks of the FALN between those who sought in some manner to reach an understanding with Leoni and those who wanted to continue the revolutionary struggle. The old-line leadership of the VCP, including the Machado brothers and Pompeyo Márquez, took the former position, while the left-wing MIR became the advocate of continuing the struggle. Within the Leoni government two trends developed: one sought to come to some understanding with the VCP, while the hard-liners viewed the renunciation of armed struggle by certain VCP leaders as proof of the successful application of the government's all-out war tactics. By 1969 the Communist Party was participating in electoral activity, was openly denouncing the guerrillas, and had expelled all those who supported armed struggle. Shifts in the position of the VCP and the temporary setbacks have had their effects, but it would be a mistake to believe that despite the decline of guerrilla action, the revolutionary struggle will disappear or be rendered harmless, as Betancourt, Leoni, and Caldera have rediscovered each time they announced a "decisive" defeat. It is possible that new forms of struggle in the cities and in the *barrios* will emerge that combine mass action with revolutionary politics.

While the Communists move toward the right, a growing sector of radicalized Social-Christian students and workers are looking less to reactionary Christian Democratic Party leader Rafael Caldera and more to the ideas of social revolutionary Camilo Torres. Small splinter groups have already formed, and more discontent within the trade unions is likely. The Venezuelan "national revolution," far from being a romantic illusion motivating the gunplay of a few young people, is a profound force radicalizing one student generation after another. Each in its turn has sought to break out of the political confines set by an economy totally subordinate to the United States and rigidly defended by one of the best equipped and highly disciplined armed forces in Latin America.

In Peru the revolutionary struggle has centered around two types of movements: mass rural organizations and, later, guerrilla units. At first, unlike the other countries, there was massive peasant and Indian involvement in revolutionary unions and land invasions, in some cases associated with urban revolutionary parties. In his monograph, *El movimiento campesino del Peru y sus líderes,* Aníbal Quijano, a Peruvian sociologist, wrote: "In the last ten years the Peruvian peasantry has developed an attitude which completely rejects the traditional order . . . and has become an active force for changing it in a rapid and if necessary violent way. Sectors of increasing breadth are incorporating this new attitude and conduct despite the repressions and massacres on the part of successive governments and landowners and they are seeking to coordinate themselves on a national scale and to enlarge their capability and goals." [8] Unlike traditional peasant agitation, which was always sporadic, ephemeral, and isolated in limited regions of the country, the movement involved the greater part of the Peruvian Sierra and the greater part of the coast, and was not handicapped by regional or communal isolation.

The peasant movement reached its peak in 1963. It secured total control in numerous regions, especially the valleys of La Convención and Lares in the Department of Cuzco, where autonomous, peasant-based nuclei of power were established. Peasant activity was developed through three principal channels: unionization, land invasions, and incorporation into militant urban political groups. In contrast to the armed detachments—the "vanguard" strategy—of the guerrillas in Venezuela, Colombia, and Guatemala, the emphasis in Peru was on mass mobilization, large-scale participation around immediate demands—"those who till the land shall own it"—and the use of relatively nonviolent direct action, e.g., occupation of a hacienda. Where armed detachments existed they were an integral but subordinate part of the larger movement and their functions were primarily to defend the squatters. While the guerrillas functioned on a hit-and-run basis (exhorting peasants to revolt during a raid on the local military barracks and then leaving), the Peruvian peasant organizers lived and worked in the areas, spoke the language of the Indians (Quechua or one of the other dialects), and were integrated with and subject to the control of their constituents.

This type of movement was less elitist in conception and more democratic in practice; it directly involved those whom the revolution ostensibly concerned rather than having an urban elite substitute itself and make the revolution "for" the peasant. Significant within this new Indian uprising was the revitalization of the collectivist traditions which had been eroded by the commercialization of life and values in recent years. Quijano, observing this "rebirth of community," noted: ". . . one of the consequences of the land invasion is the revitalization of communal property, which was in an advanced state of disintegration . . . instead of the present big-landholding/tiny-plot complex, there is substituted collective and communal ownership." [9] Interestingly, the need for cooperation in carrying off "land invasions" resulted in the lessening of violence among the disparate and often previously conflicting Indian communities. The new unions, organized as part of the present peasant movement, principally in the mountains, were made up of a heterogeneous population both from the socioeconomic and the cultural point of view. They brought together serfs from the traditional hacienda, semiserfs, tiny-landowning peasants, landless agricultural laborers, and also diverse groups such as small traders, etc.

From the cultural viewpoint, the constituent population of a peasant union varied from the strictly Indian and the *cholos* (mixed Indian-Creole) to elements belonging totally to the western Creole culture. These peasant unions were revolutionary; they were not oriented toward improving themselves within the master-serf system, but toward transforming the whole social order by organizing a basis of power in opposition to the official and traditional authorities. It was the mountainous zones where the peasant unions' action was widest and most intense, and these were the zones with the greatest density of Indian and *cholo* population.

The land invasion stage of the peasant movement was an outgrowth of the unionization of the peasants in the valleys of La Convención and Lares in Cuzco under the leadership of Hugo Blanco in 1960. There was a general strike of serfs and semiserfs in the zone near the northern coast in Convención and Lares that lasted two months. Lacking "strike benefits," parents sent their children to neighboring towns to avoid starvation, and husband and wife tightened their belts until they won. The successful outcome encouraged Blanco and the regional federation to begin the land invasions, early in 1961, taking over land in more than one hundred haciendas in the Convención and Lares valleys in a relatively peaceful and gradual manner.

As a result of massive repression by army units and the arrest of Hugo Blanco in 1963 (he is now serving a twenty-five-year sentence), the movement faltered. However, unlike the other more publicized revolutionary movements such as the Venezuelan FALN, the Colombian ELN (Army of National Liberation), and the Guatemalan MR-13, which tend to be predominantly urban in composition, the National Federation of Peruvian Peasants (FENCAP) represented, and still represents, a mass, rural challenge for power.

Unremitting pressure by the Belaúnde government and the military, and the violent attacks by *búfalos* (professional gunmen) from APRA (Alianza Popular Revolucionaria Americana, former nationalist party in Peru) seriously weakened the mass movement and caused a rethinking of the direction of the Peruvian revolutionary road. Since the mass peasant movement could not defend itself and was an easy target, guerrilla forms of struggle emerged.

In October 1959, a group of militants expelled from APRA founded the Comité de Defensa de los Principios y de la Democracia Interna. Opposed to the APRA line of collaboration with U.S. imperialism and traditional landowners, this group was composed primarily of students and young radicals. At the beginning of 1960, they took the name of APRA Rebelde, and in October 1960 declared their revolutionary principles in Chiclayo.

Coinciding with the 1959 struggle of the young APRA militants for internal democracy and a principled position was the development of the Cuban Revolution, which further radicalized these young rebels. In contrast to the stagnation, corruption, and authoritarianism of APRA stood the self-sacrificing struggle of the Cuban revolutionaries. The adherence of APRA Rebelde to *fidelismo* definitively separated the old APRA from the new national-popular revolutionaries. While the rebels moved in the direction of social revolution, APRA joined forces with the ultra-right Odría military-landowning group.

In 1961, APRA Rebelde adopted its present name, Movement of the Revolutionary Left (MIR), and in March 1964, they approved a resolution which attempted to reorient their previously university-urban base: *Todos al campo*—everyone to the country-side. On June 7, 1965, under the leadership of their secretary-general, Luis de la Puente, and Guillermo Lobatón, the MIR carried out its first armed action. MIR strategy, while not excluding other means of struggle, underlines the principle that "the armed struggle is the principal element of the Peruvian revolutionary process." [10] De la Puente, a young lawyer from a provincial lower-aristocratic family, first became active as a student leader in APRA. Later he led the rebels toward the formation of the MIR. During 1964–1965, he lived among the peasants of Cuzco, shar-ing their life and preparing for the armed struggle. Along with de la Puente and others, Guillermo Lobatón was one of the signers of the leaflet announcing the initiation of the war of national lib-eration. Later, Lobatón, who was the most active guerrilla leader, functioned mainly in the central part of Peru. Lobatón was one of several Peruvian students who had been studying abroad and who had returned to form the nuclei of de la Puente's guerrillas.

These guerrilla leaders expressed the discontent found among university-educated individuals from the elite who are totally dis-affected from a society in which a few thousand individuals satisfy every whim while millions suffer hunger pangs. As members of the educated elite, they were able to develop a global vision of society and to perceive the futility of confining their activities to the university or to their professions. They perceived the limits of operating within the legal system in order to effect basic changes; hence they tended to regard the traditional left (first APRA and then the Communist Party) and legal political activity as useless at best, and as a deception of the masses at worst.[11]

The seven-point program of the MIR identifies the reforms con-sidered necessary for the realization of the national-popular revo-lution:

1) Immediate dissolution of parliament as an instrument of the oligarchy and imperialism.
2) General amnesty for political prisoners and punishment for all government and military officials responsible for massacres.
3) Authentic agrarian reform involving complete liquidation of the *latifundios* and the free transfer of the land to the peas-

ants; middle farmers who work their own land and who are
efficient producers not to be expropriated; preferential treatment
by the state of all aspects of peasant life and work.

4) Sliding scale of family wages for workers, public and private employees, professionals, and technicians.

5) Urban reform expropriating large real estate interests, i.e.,
excepting middle and small property owners, to make present
tenants owners of their dwellings.

6) Immediate recovery of Peruvian petroleum.

7) Recovery of broad national sovereignty; elimination of treaties and agreements that compromise national independence;
establishment of diplomatic and commercial relations with all
countries.

The MIR identifies three main groups as opposed to this "national-popular revolution": the North American imperialists, the
big bourgeoisie, and the big landowners. On the other hand, the
MIR estimates that the revolution will be the work of the peasants,
workers, and the patriotic and progressive sectors of the petty
bourgeoisie and the national bourgeoisie under the leadership of
a revolutionary party to be constituted in the course of the struggle in which the MIR is considered a factor.[12]

While the official organ of the pro-Soviet Peruvian Communist
Party, *Unidad,* presented a formal program which appeared similar, the PCP differs from the MIR in three vital respects: (1) in
practice, if not always in theory, it rejects guerrilla struggle; (2)
it is almost exclusively an urban grouping; (3) it does not reject
coalitions led by the traditional parties. The pro-Peking Communist group, whose newspaper, *Bandera Roja,* probably has a
wider circulation than *Unidad,* has two tendencies. One, led by
José Sotomayor, is considered similar in approach to that of
Unidad. The other, led by Saturnino Paredes, supports the insurrectional line.[13]

The rapid rise to public notice of the guerrilla leaders de la
Puente and Lobatón was determined by their tactical decisions to
confront the Peruvian Army directly. However, lacking significant
organized urban support and intending to base their movement
among the peasantry, they seriously underestimated the capability
and mobility of the army. Peruvian rangers, trained and equipped

by the United States specifically to deal with guerrilla movements, aided by several thousand Peruvian soldiers and by napalm bombing of peasant areas sympathetic to the guerrillas, succeeded in killing most of the guerrillas under the command of de la Puente and Lobatón. Upwards of a thousand peasants were killed in napalm and firebomb attacks.

The early guerrilla struggles have a larger significance. The students at the University of San Marcos, Lima, have become more committed than ever to the revolutionary struggle. Along with Camilo Torres, de la Puente is viewed as a symbol of courage and commitment in the midst of general social decay and personal opportunism. Values which determine career choices, the collective consciousness which becomes the reservoir for seemingly "spontaneous" popular outbursts are shaped by the legendary example of the lives of men like de la Puente. In creating a new sense of moral authority as a spring for action against the old society, the fallen guerrillas can be looked upon as a source of sustenance for a new generation of revolutionaries.

By the end of the 1950's, a number of former radical parties which had monopolized the national-popular movements were completing a decade-long retrogressive process of reconciliation with the dominant elites. In Peru, for example, the once insurgent APRA was sapped of its militancy by the slow process of social change which broadened, without basically altering, Peruvian society. New commercial and industrial groups fused with the old landowning oligarchy, and U.S. investors forged further alliances with the new middle class. The modernization of Peruvian society, although limited and haphazard, was sufficient to inspire the retreat of APRA's middle-class leadership from a sharp confrontation with the oligarchy and North American capitalists. Having won political legitimacy and social recognition for the urban middle strata it represented, the old, radical-sounding APRA leadership now gave its blessing to the existing order.

While organizations such as APRA were in the process of accommodating to the status quo, there also emerged, in the 1950's, new militant radical groups and tendencies which were uncompromising in their opposition to native oligarchs and U.S. economic-political penetration. However, at the time they found no alternative to working within the existing framework of such parties as APRA, which retained the allegiance of large numbers. While the left-wingers were ready to press their views within the existing mass parties, the leadership of these parties, fearful of the challenge, successfully sought to preserve their power through a variety of expediencies ranging from bureaucratic expulsions to physical violence.

In the eyes of militant dissidents, therefore, these parties were no longer useful as vehicles of revolutionary change; and the illusion that they were susceptible to democratic internal reform was abandoned. Forced to operate and seek popular support outside this framework, the revolutionary left wing found it inordinately difficult to make contact with the large sectors of the urban working class rigidly controlled by the APRA in Peru, or Acción Democrática in Venezuela, the Partido Revolucionario in Guatemala, the Liberal or Conservative parties in Colombia. As a result left-wingers sought constituencies among students, who were not tightly reined by party bureaucracies, and among the previously unorganized peasants and Indians. In Venezuela the radicals turned to the unemployed urban workers, slum dwellers and non-unionized workers of Caracas, where 80 percent of the working class was anti-Betancourt.

For the above broadly outlined reasons, the conflicts between revolutionaries and moderates that took place within the mass parties which were out of power in the 1950's evolved into actual battles between revolutionary-led guerrillas and the forces led by these same mass parties which were now in power (or in a position to win power) in the 1960's.

In addition, the policies pursued by the Communist parties also obliged the new popular revolutionaries to concentrate on the countryside and to take the path of guerrilla struggle. These parties could not attract the militants if for no other reason than that the Communists pursued policies which were similar in practice to those of the ex-national-populists: marginal reforms for their organized constituents, coalitions with legal parties, and authoritarian organization and discipline to hold their bases intact. Neither the Communist programs nor methods were consistent with the structural changes sought by the militants. But more relevant here to understanding the rural guerrilla orientation of the radicals is that the Communists, too, denied the Left access to urban working-class areas under Communist control.

Illegal politics was an attempt to break out of the stagnation of the totally urban-based, traditional leftist and ex-leftist opposition. To open up politics meant to open up rural society. In the final analysis armed struggle, as a technique, was the logical extension of an attempt to extend the conception of citizenship and nation-hood beyond the confines of organized interest groups, beyond the scope of the major cities. In the context of the semicolonial societies of Latin America, revolutionary guerrilla warfare can be seen as an instrument fostering the development of citizenship to the extent that it weakens existing authoritarian institutions and creates the conditions for self-mobilizing, autonomous social organizations in the countryside. By focusing on the foreign de-pendence of the existing government and by creating a larger iden-tity based on indigenous control of national resources, the guerrilla movement contributes to the formation of a collective conscious-ness that later may become a decisive element in the process of "nation-building."

Why didn't any of the Latin American Communist parties initiate guerrilla struggle during and after the period of the Cuban Revolution? And why have the Communist parties failed to at-tract the new generation of revolutionary leaders? There are cer-tainly sufficient examples of successfully organized military-political warfare in Latin America—in Mexico, Bolivia, and Cuba. Iron-ically, the early Communist movement (or at least part of it), prior to the worldwide popular front, supported guerrilla-military warfare in Brazil (the famous Prestes Column) and in Colombia. This course was abandoned in Brazil, and in Colombia the rural guerrilla movement of the early 1930's, which occupied certain areas, was discontinued in favor of supporting the "progressive" oligarch Alfonso López. This striking lack of revolutionary initia-tive in the Latin American Communist parties was epitomized by the Cuban Communists, whose failure to resist the Batista coup was a key factor propelling the formation of the independent July 26th Movement in Cuba.

According to the Communists, Latin America is in the throes of a "democratic revolution" led by the progressive bourgeoisie and its parties against U.S. imperialism and the "feudal" landowners. This "national-democratic" revolution is allegedly in the first of two stages, to be followed at some undisclosed date by the "socialist" revolution. The immediate task is the formation of middle-class-led popular front governments. In practical terms, this means supporting the electoral aspirations of middle-class parties.

This strategy is based on two unsound premises: (1) that the urban bourgeoisie is in conflict with the landowners (frequently they have close commercial and family connections), and (2) that the major conflicts are between national capitalists and imperialists, not between workers on the one hand and native and foreign capitalists on the other. The convergence of interests of these supposedly antagonistic groups is indicated by the fact that not one of the middle-class-led governments in the postwar period has either carried out an agrarian reform or consistently resisted U.S. economic or military penetration. Middle-class governments which made even a first step toward reform have been singularly incapable of maintaining their power. Those which retained power retreated and became agencies for the repression of popular movements (for example, the governments of Frei, Belaúnde and Betancourt).

Committed to a strategy which requires an electoral orientation and therefore a modicum of legality, the Communists eschew all actions which might alienate the middle-class political leaders. Beyond that, they frequently denounce as "adventurers," "putschists," etc., those revolutionaries seeking a radical restructuring of society through nonelectoral means. This quiescent character of Communist politics makes it attractive primarily to the less dynamic elements of the new generation who tend to reinforce the reformist nature of Latin American Communist parties.

In contrast to the popular-revolutionary position of Camilo Torres, the Colombian Communist Party supported the middle-class liberal candidate, Alfonso López Michelson, in the March 1966 elections, in which over 65 percent of the Colombian populace abstained from voting to manifest its repudiation of the two-party dictatorship. In fact, the most decisive political struggle waged by

Camilo Torres was against the Liberal-Conservative two-party system. He appealed to all revolutionaries—peasants who had previously voted Conservative and Communist workers who had been instructed to vote Liberal—to join the Frente Unido against the two-party system and the oligarchs who control it.[14] The broad support which Camilo Torres received from all sectors of the popular classes was a direct repudiation of the Communist position of coalition behind the candidate of the left-liberal bourgeoisie, who received about 10 percent of the vote.

As a response to Communist conservatism, a large part of the revolutionary opposition, the major guerrilla movements—the Guatemalan FAR and MR-13, the Venezuelan FALN and the Colombian FARC (Coordinated Revolutionary Armed Forces) and ELN—are becoming increasingly independent and critical of the local Communist parties and less subject to top-level manipulation.

A broad range of revolutionary strategies can be found outside of official Communist parties. Those members of OLAS (Organization of Latin American Solidarity) outside of the CP and the Trotskyists view Latin society as polarized between the workers, peasants, and students, on the one hand, and the landowners, U.S. imperialism, and native capitalists, on the other. They perceive the anti-imperialist struggle as inseparable from the class struggle: the defeat of foreign imperialism requires the defeat of its allied national bourgeoisie.

In most Latin American countries, the Trotskyist groups are quite small, isolated, and fragmented. In Peru, however, the leader of the mass organization of the peasantry in the early 1960's, Hugo Blanco, was a Trotskyist. The Bolivian miners' unions and militias were influenced by Trotskyist cadres. More significant than their physical presence is the Trotskyist critique of the Communist strategy of collaboration with the "national bourgeoisie" and of the conception of revolution in stages. Diverse revolutionary organizations have accepted this critique without accepting the sectarian attitudes of these isolated groups.

The real weakness of the guerrilla movements is not that they are "premature" or that electoral alliances of a popular front variety are viable alternatives. The degree of U.S. military and political involvement in Latin America and the closed nature of the political system based on the existing fragile social structure in fact make legal, nonviolent politics highly ineffective. Rather the political weakness of the guerrilla movements has been their lack of a revolutionary political organization with mass peasant and urban working-class support to provide material and political aid to the guerrillas and to counter repression by the state. The guerrillas have attempted to build *focos* of armed resistance as a means of mobilizing the masses. They have substituted the *foco* for mass mobilization of the rural peasantry and urban workers. They failed to develop the guerrillas as armed detachments, putting themselves at the vanguard of a mass movement and defending it against the inevitable government repression. One of the reasons for the failure of the early guerrillas was their lack of a mass peasant organization which would have permitted them to fuse with the population. The frequent problem of "security" resulted from a lack of trained cadre and disciplined organization.

The Latin American revolution and its direction are not being debated in terms of armed struggle vs. popular fronts, but of how to combine the armed struggle with the mass mobilization of the countryside and the organization of the advanced sectors of the working class. This perspective excludes the popular front strategy of the old national-popular and Communist parties. It also means that the revolutionary movements, in their political thinking, are going beyond the pragmatic-empirical level of basing revolutionary strategy on armed struggle alone. The new revolutionary synthesis, sometimes called the *brazo armado,* appears to encompass the mass political organization that Hugo Blanco was so successful in organizing among the peasantry, with the audacious armed detachments employed by de la Puente and Lobatón. Recènt history appears to indicate that mass movements without armed detachments simply invite official terror and repression; guerrilla detachments without mass movements are isolated, easily surrounded and overwhelmed by the armed forces. The new strategy seems to call for multiple fronts and combined action; urban working-class and student cadre organization capable of mobilization; mass rural organization around concrete and immediate issues such as land occupation; and mobile guerrilla movements coordinated with the urban-rural mass movements.[15]

NOTES

1. *El Popular,* Uruguayan Communist Party daily, March 5, 1966.
2. *El Siglo,* Chilean Communist Party daily, April 4, 1966.
3. Data on the Brazilian revolutionary leadership tends to substantiate this thesis. Two key leaders of the Brazilian revolutionary movement, Father Francisco Lage and Francisco Juliao, both came from traditional large landholding families. Father Lage, an avowed revolutionary socialist, was instrumental in organizing the *favelados* (slum dwellers) in Belo Horizonte, capital of Minas Gerais. Working with him were five Brazilian bishops led by José Tavora, Archbishop of Aracaju, who edited a manual to teach illiterates, entitled *Vivir es luchar,* "To Live Is to Struggle." Father Lage supported the armed-struggle road to socialism, rejecting the position of the Brazilian Communist Party which supported the theory that capitalism was the next stage of development and that hence the Brazilian bourgeoisie had to be supported. The split in traditional institutions like the Catholic Church was never more evident than in Brazil after the U.S.-supported military coup of 1964. While Father Lage was jailed and tortured for eight months, the majority of the high ecclesiastics were giving their blessing to the new anti-communist savior, the military dictator Castelo Branco. See Michel Bosquet, "Con Juliao y Francisco Lage," *Marcha* (Montevideo), March 18, 1966.
4. Before his entry into politics, Camilo was one of the leading sociologists in Colombia and was a visiting fellow at the University of Minnesota (1961). In one monograph, "The Proletarianization of Bogotá," he presents substantial evidence on the differential calorie intake of the working class and middle class of Bogotá, pointing to the tremendous social gap between them. In addition to being an outstanding example of a committed revolutionary, Camilo Torres showed how modern sociological research could be applied to examining politically relevant problems from a popular democratic standpoint.

5. SORO is only one among a number of U.S. Army agencies and activities sponsored by American University, which also operates a Counter-Insurgency Information Analysis Center. The direct working relation between American University and the military establishment is spelled out clearly in the *Bibliography of Research Studies and Related Writings on the Political Influence of Latin American Students* published by SORO. This is prefaced by the statement: "The Special Operations Research Office (SORO) of the American University, operating under contract with the Department of the Army, conducts research on military problems in support of the requirements stated by the Department of the Army. As an added service SORO operates the Counter-Insurgency Information Analysis Center (CINFAC) to provide rapid response replies, in its field of competence, to queries from Department of Defense agencies, their contractors, and as directed, to other governmental departments and agencies." The interlock between a sector of the academic world, American University, and the U.S. military in Latin America is only one manifestation of a more general phenomenon. A more recent example is the exposure of the involvement of U.S. professors in the Pentagon-financed Camelot Project in Chile, whose purpose was to discover the Chilean military's attitude toward a U.S. military invasion in case of communist subversion.

6. *Handbook,* p. 529. (Emphasis added.)

7. *El Nacional,* October 22, 1960.

8. Santiago, Chile, 1966 (mimeo).

9. *Ibid.*

10. *Voz Rebelde,* organ of the Peruvian MIR.

11. Héctor Béjar is one of the examples of a guerrilla leader, a former Communist student leader who left the Party to form the Army of National Liberation (ELN). For a critical discussion of the guerrilla experience, see Héctor Béjar Rivera, *Peru 1965: Notes on a Guerrilla Experience* (New York: Monthy Review Press, 1970).

12. "Llamado de los guerrilleros del MIR peruano," reprinted in *Revolución,* publication of the University MIR of Chile, 1966.

13. Edgardo Da Mommio, "Reportaje al Peru: Guerrilla," *El Mundo* (Buenos Aires), March 3, 1966.

14. There is a significant division between the rural-based Communists led by Manuel Marulanda, head of FARC, who have

espoused the road of armed struggle, and the urban-based Communists who have opted for the electoral road and support of progressive sectors of the Liberal Party.

15. See "Revolutionary Movements in Latin America," below, pp. 185–190, for an updating of this discussion.

Revolutionary Movements in Latin America

Two factors stand out in analyzing Latin American revolutionary politics: (1) the cyclical nature of revolutionary struggle: periods of fragmentation and quiescence alternate with periods during which there is crystallization of a leadership, a notion of revolutionary action, and heightened socio-political conflict that threatens or eventually leads to the overthrow of the existing ruling class; (2) the existence of two approaches to revolutionary political action: (a) movements which develop through the mobilization of large numbers and whose leaders owe their influence to support from this revolutionary force; (b) vanguard groups composed of a select, politicized, and militarized cadre which aims strategic blows at the enemy, hoping to undermine its authority in order to enable popular support to emerge at a later date.

During the 1960's these approaches were manifested in the conflict between *fidelista* guerrilla-oriented groups and the traditional "orthodox" Communist parties. The vanguard approach has been formalized into a theory, most notably by Debray and Guevara, though polemical articles over the years have been numerous. By the late 1960's, however, the dichotomies between guerrillas/mass movement or *fidelista*/Communist Party were no longer the most useful ones in analyzing revolutionary politics in Latin America.

One reason is that both the *fidelista* and the Soviet-oriented Communist parties were increasingly irrelevant to the emerging patterns of socio-political warfare emerging in Latin America. The revolutionary struggles of the late 1960's were post-*fidelista* and post-Stalinist: the rural guerrilla movements had virtually disappeared; the Communists were less and less important in the mass struggles developing in many of the urban centers. Cuban support for *fidelista* groups has increasingly dropped off; Cuban policy has been more and more oriented toward moves by established forces in the direction of nationalist policies which might contribute to breaking the economic blockade imposed by U.S. imperialism, thus facilitating Cuba's own internal economic development. The Soviet Union has increasingly turned toward diplomatic and economic cooperation with Latin regimes without any regard to their internal or external policies. Aid and credits have been extended not only to Peru and Chile but to the right-wing dictatorships in Bolivia and Argentina and to the totalitarian Brazilian military junta. Soviet economic aid reinforces U.S. programs geared toward stabilizing the status quo, while Soviet ideological influence and ties with the indigenous CP's weaken the latter's ability to relate to the sharpening internal struggles developing within Latin America. Hence the growth of new forms of mass struggle and vanguard groups should not be seen as a direct continuation of the older *fidelista* or Communist movements. Both the Organization of Latin American Solidarity and the Third International are minor factors in the major socio-political battles of recent years. Outside of Chilean politics and possibly among the Uruguayan trade-union movement the CP has been a marginal participant in mass struggles; guerrillas are active in Guatemala (notably the forces led by Yon Sosa, which are not of *fidelista* inspiration), Venezuela (though relations between Douglas Bravo of the FALN and Cuba are on the verge of breaking down), and Colombia (where the guerrillas are divided into two factions, neither of which has made much progress in recent years).

The present lines of conflict are blurred: vertical and horizontal divisions and coalitions have appeared, suggesting that masses and elites can be bound together, for a time at least, in common nationalist-populist movements. The military-peasant alliances in Peru and Bolivia are cases in point. The issue which has been the key cohesive factor in the past and which is reemerging now is the presence of U.S. imperialism in Latin America.

The murder of Che Guevara in Bolivia was not the end of revolutionary struggle in Latin America but of a particular revolutionary approach—the strategy of rural *focos*. Between 1960 and 1968 the thought of the vanguardist groups was dominated by the theory of the revolutionary *focos*. There was considerable difference of opinion as to the correct application of the *foco* theory. In addition, several attempts were made to organize outside of the *foco* framework; for example, the mass peasant unionization strategy of Hugo Blanco projected the idea of dual power through the creation of a structure of authority in the countryside parallel to that of the central government, which would lead to a national revolution. Rural guerrilla movements were organized in a number of countries; political organization and activity in urban areas were relegated to a marginal position. With strong support from the United States, the Latin American ruling classes were able to isolate and suppress the guerrilla movements and protect the property and privileges of foreign and domestic investors. In their quest for security and control, U.S. policy-makers and Latin American elites installed a series of military governments which achieved not only suppression of armed groups but elimination of the emerging mass movements. For the five-year period 1963–1968, U.S. policy-makers appeared to enjoy great success: pro-U.S. governments were established and nationalist revolutionary forces were squelched.

In this same period during which the CP and *fidelista* groups were being defeated, new social and political forces were emerging. Some of the leaders were graduates of the older movements, shaken by the recent defeats and searching for new forms of struggle. The continued need for revolutionary action was based on the fact that U.S. political-military success was not based on any significant change in the structural factors underlying social and political conflicts. In fact, U.S.-supported regimes proceeded to exacerbate all the socioeconomic problems while closing off the political escape valves that had previously existed for airing grievances.

The post-*fidelista* revolutionary Left is primarily urban and combines armed vanguard actions with mass struggles. The massive protest demonstrations that greeted Rockefeller in every Latin American country he entered in 1969 were signs of the new urban insurgency. The May 1969 general strike in Argentina and the barricade fighting in Córdoba, Santa Fe, Tucumán, Rosario, etc., were further evidence that the Argentine working class was capable of carrying the struggle beyond bread-and-butter issues.

In Uruguay the urban guerrillas, the Tupamaros, were increasingly effective. They repeatedly discredited the government and gained popular support through selective direct action. In Brazil the military government's policies, aimed at eliminating all legal opposition, have helped to crystallize an underground armed resistance which is increasingly moving beyond the university to embrace professionals, clergy, soldiers, and trade unionists. The Brazilian old Left, lacking a political arena in the parliamentary-electoral sense, has become largely irrelevant. Denationalization of Brazilian industries, decapitation of mass movements, wage and salary freezes, credit squeezes, and inflation have accentuated existing inequalities. As the impoverishment of the people and the proletarianization of the nation have increased, so has the corps of urban guerrillas. In Argentina urban guerrillas have improved their techniques and sharpened their focus: twenty U.S. firms were blown up in one evening. The new revolutionary Left is not only resourceful but independent and self-reliant, largely owing to a number of successful bank robberies.

The overbearing presence of the United States, the closed political systems, the persisting socioeconomic problems and the reemerging popular movements in the cities have in certain instances forced a sympathetic political response even within such traditional institutions of control as the church and the army. As the initial impact of repressive policies has worn off, new popular pressures have begun to press on existing elites. While in no sense representing a revolutionary alternative, sectors of the church and the army have begun to search for ways of heading off revolutionary changes from below. They seek to bring about specific reforms without alienating U.S. and domestic investors. These limited changes by reformist clergy and soldiers, however, are unsatisfactory to the militants, who are thinking of more basic changes. The elites alternate between using coercion and reformist measures to ease popular pressure for change. Nevertheless, the problems and forces outside of the traditional institutions have increasingly become linked to those within them. In Guatemala, Colombia, Brazil, Bolivia, and Peru small numbers of clergy and soldiers have disengaged in varying degrees from the dominant ruling elites and have joined the popular struggles. The growth of oppositionist forces within the major ideological and coercive institutions of Latin America can only contribute to undermining the current authoritarian socio-political order and to strengthening the revolutionary movement.

In Latin America today there is a new upturn in revolutionary activity, as indicated by the growing importance in three major countries of urban guerrillas and mass popular movements (Brazil, Argentina, Uruguay). The growth of revolutionary politics has the effect of encouraging divisions in traditional institutions that further increase the opportunities for politicizing new strata of the population. Rooted in anti-imperialist, populist, and democratic ideas, these new revolutionary movements project a set of changes that will carry them over into a socialist society.

In geopolitical terms we can state that in the countries on the Caribbean rim, especially those which still possess a large peasant population, modified versions of the rural guerrilla strategy will continue, along with greater preoccupation with urban political organizing. The rural-based guerrilla strategy continues to be influential, especially in Colombia, Guatemala, and Nicaragua, but may decline in Venezuela. On the east coast of South America, the revolutionary movement is overwhelmingly based in the cities, though it may spread to the rural areas. The intense syndicalist activity in Argentina and Uruguay is now complemented by military actions by commando sections of vanguard groups. In Brazil the burden of the struggle lies with the vanguard groups which have been able to draw elements of the army and church into the struggle. On the west coast of Latin America, specifically Chile and Peru, the tendency is for largely institutionalized groups to take the lead in pushing for moderate change. In Chile a broad coalition of the Left could provoke an institutional crisis if it won the elections. Increased polarization and an institutional crisis, unlikely outcomes, could provide vanguard groups like the Movement of the Revolutionary Left (MIR) with a chance to grow. In the present circumstances the Communist Party stands as a watchdog to prevent mass movements from exceeding the bounds of legality. In Peru the military junta has moved toward accommodation with

U.S. investors; the decision to sacrifice a militant nationalist course has led to internal divisions which could generate an opening for the Left.

The problems in making a revolution have thus far exceeded the ability of the Latin American revolutionaries to overcome them; but the ability of the U.S. and Latin American ruling classes to create an independent developing democratic society which would obviate the need for revolutions is even less apparent.

III

The United States and Latin America

The United States
and the New Equilibrium
in Latin America

In recent years, there has been considerable ferment in a number of Latin American countries. Social conflict in the form of violent confrontations between the populace and the police has been especially intense in the more developed nations—Uruguay, Mexico, Argentina—and in the more industrialized regions of Brazil, Chile, and Peru. Yet despite this ferment, and despite the example of Cuba, social revolution is not imminent anywhere in Latin America. To the contrary: a new political equilibrium has been established on the continent, the outcome of (1) the policies of the U.S. government in the period after the Cuban Revolution; (2) the policies and orientation of Latin American decision-makers; and (3) the policies of the Moscow-oriented Communist parties of Latin America. We propose here to examine these policies and their influence on the prospect for social and economic reform, and to discuss the viability of the "new equilibrium." [1]

United States Policy: Ideology and Practice

The overwhelming presence of the United States in Latin American economic, political, military, and social institutions on all levels of policy-making is both cause and consequence of the absence of social revolution.[2] Rather than a period of Latin American initiative in a revolutionary upsurge following the Cuban Revolution, the years after 1962 were a period of counterrevolution. The United States was on the offensive to forestall revolution, supporting military regimes, organizing counterinsurgency forces, and, in the case of the Dominican Republic, carrying out a military occupation. Yet the U.S. counterrevolutionary offensive had the positive result of destroying the foundations of the major assumption supporting U.S. hegemony in Latin America—that of a hemispheric "harmony of interests." [3]

This idea, the basis of Franklin D. Roosevelt's "Good Neighbor Policy" and of cognate conceptions like "Pan-Americanism" and the "Inter-American System," began to be clearly articulated by scholars and journalists in the field of U.S.-Latin relations shortly before the beginning of World War II, and persisted through the Cold War years, emerging finally in the "Alliance for Progress" in the 1960's. As the dominant power in the hemisphere, the United States has everything to gain from an ideology which harmonizes the interests of a highly developed, expansionist, industrial society with those of underdeveloped, dependent, export nations, and which justifies U.S. military interventions against the threat of radical social change as defense of the common good.

Never more than liberal rhetoric in the first place, the notion of a harmony of interests finally lost its intellectual legitimacy in the invasion of the Dominican Republic in 1965, which demonstrated explicitly the U.S. rejection of coexistence with social revolution.[4] Such coexistence had already been rejected implicitly in Guatemala and Cuba, and in the series of U.S. policies which opposed middle-class democratic regimes because of their alleged instability, supported the military as the agency of development and security, and provided military aid and advisers to a considerable number of Latin countries.[5] The open confrontation between the military force of the United States and the Dominican people brought to the surface the long-existing division within the hemisphere as a whole, a cleavage shown earlier by U.S. attitudes and subsequent policy toward the Cuban Revolution. The language of harmony in the recent emphasis on an "Inter-American Peace Force" merely serves to stress the opposing reality of conflict, arising from the mass discontent produced by the negative effects of U.S. influence in Latin America.[6] The indicators of disharmony can of course only be taken into account within a framework which does not rest on the assumption that the dominant and the subordinate nations have common interests. On the other hand, the evidence of conflict does not deny that certain Latin American elites have supported and benefited from U.S. policies.

An examination of U.S. policy toward Latin America—that is, of the Alliance for Progress and its failure—reveals that central to it was (1) the conflict between Cuba and the United States over such basic issues as control of internal resources and approach toward development;[7] and (2) the assumption that the Cuban Revolution would exacerbate the latent and manifest conflicts between the United States and Latin America.[8] The shifts and adjustments in U.S. policy between 1960 and 1965 reflected changes in the level of conflict between the United States, Cuba, and the rest of Latin America and in the internal relationships of forces within the southern continent. In the initial period, when Washington considered the possibility of other Cuban-type revolutions as imminent, it did tolerate or accept limited conflicts with U.S. interests (as in Brazil, where a projected development program ran counter to U.S. aims) and was willing to concede a certain independence to its allies to prevent a thwarted nationalism from nourishing genuinely radical tendencies. Up until 1962, U.S. policy can be defined in terms of two levels of conflict. The first and basic level is that of structural conflicts, as with Cuba. Secondary conflicts, such as those with Brazil during the Quadros or Goulart governments concerning the nationalization of a particular firm, or commerce and relations with the Communist bloc, were handled tactically because U.S. policy-makers gave priority to containing the impact of the Cuban Revolution in Latin America.[9]

The major flaw of the harmony-of-interest approach is that it is unable to account for this data. In contrast, a conflict model of U.S.-Latin American relations would account for the shifts in U.S. policy toward Latin America in the period after the Cuban Revolution in the following manner. In response to the Cuban Revolution, U.S. policy-makers devised a dual strategy: an Alliance for Progress which was ostensibly to promote social reform and economic development, and a buildup of Latin American military forces to insure that Castroism was defeated. Most of the Alliance funds were applied to refinancing loans and balancing budgets, and only a small percentage was ever applied to concrete reform projects.[10] More important, the funds were directed toward maintaining a social structure whose dominant elites were not interested in any kind of agrarian reform or economic development that would conflict with their (and U.S. investors') property holdings.[11] Hence the "aid" funds became a means of bracing up the old elites against the winds of change rather than a stimulus for reform. Simultaneously, U.S. military aid to Latin America during the early 1960's jumped more than 50 percent per year over that granted during the Eisenhower years.[12] Originally the United States banked on the middle class to carry out socioeconomic reforms compatible with U.S. economic interests and foreign policy.[13] But as long as the military served as a safeguard to existing conservative elites and U.S. interests, such moderately liberal governments as those of Quadros, Goulart, Bosch, Arosemena, Morales, Frondizi, Estenssoro, were unable to carry out liberal reforms. Popular expectations, however, aroused by the promises of the Alliance for Progress and native middle-class demagoguery, became a source of instability. The mobilized populace came into conflict with U.S. interests within the country; at the same time large-scale popular mobilizations were increasingly led by new nationalist-populist leaders who sought to realign Latin America's foreign policy. Late in 1962 these factors led in turn to a shift in U.S. policy. Rather than turn to popular revolutionary forces as the alternative to the "democratic" but impotent middle-class-led forces, U.S. policy-makers opted for stability and the military, and began speaking of the military in Rostow's terms, as the new, vital, "modernizing" force.[14] Priority was placed on preserving rather than reforming, on "security" rather than change. In part this was probably due to the political success achieved through military means during the Cuban blockade. The "military" definition of Latin reality, and the ease with which the use of force was being accepted, soon led to U.S. support of Latin military *golpes* and later facilitated the sending of U.S. Marines to the Dominican Republic.

It is interesting to note the practical consequences of the harmony-of-interest doctrine for the groups in Latin America who hold this viewpoint. Calling themselves the "democratic left," they collaborated with the United States and the military in isolating Castro and defeating revolutionary insurgents in the name of democratic reforms. But as the political axis shifted rightward, the reformists discovered that they themselves became the targets of the Right; thus their defeat of revolution undermined their own efforts to carry out reforms. In this context, U.S. policy-makers, aware of the cleavages and instability in hemispheric relations, allocated over two-thirds of Alliance for Progress funds to military dictators or to military-controlled civilian governments, despite earlier injunctions against supporting such regimes: Alliance funds were supposed to promote democracy.[15]

The Latin American Ruling Class

On more than one occasion Latin American diplomats have sharply criticized U.S. policy and then proceeded to cooperate in implementing it. The seemingly ambiguous attitudes of some Latin American governments toward U.S. practices and policies in Latin America must be understood in relationship to three inter-related factors: (1) the dependence of the Latin American governments and elites on U.S. economic-military support;[16] (2) the fear of internal popular revolts; and (3) the desire to emulate Western socio-political patterns of behavior, i.e., a degree of political independence, high level of consumption, etc.

The occasional "ambiguity" of Latin American ruling-class policy flows from two contradictory imperatives: on the one hand, the need to keep political and economic power out of the hands of the masses, and on the other, the desire to assert national independence and to promote a relatively comfortable standard of living. The former pushes the elite toward the United States and in the direction of alliances to safeguard their current position; the latter pulls the elite away from subordination to U.S. authority in order to maximize commercial and development opportunities. The criticism of the United States which has occasionally been aired by Latin diplomats at hemispheric conferences reflects discordant impulses, the internal relationship of forces and the external opportunities and debilities which each decision-making group confronts.

The dependence of Latin American elites on external factors reflects their internal weakness, their inability to mobilize domestic human and material resources. At the same time, to attempt to mobilize these internal resources for national development would engender various conflicts with both private and public U.S.

interests.[17] Moreover, a really effective mobilization would cut into the privileged positions of established social groups. Mass mobilization politics would likely weaken the ability of the elites to resist popular social pressures without sacrificing some part or all of their privileges. The policy of maintaining the status quo entails the immobilization of the populace. Underlying this "immobilism" and lack of national effort are the facts of social conflict based on sharp social cleavages. The perpetuation of the unequal distribution of goods and services which underlies societal divisions is the *sine qua non* of policy-makers' existence. as political men. The more enlightened segments of the elite seek to create a larger income cake to provide marginal changes as the most effective means for perpetuating the current social stratification. The differences within society not only undermine serious efforts at "national mobilization" but, by presenting a threat to the established order, force the elites into dual dependency: (1) on foreign "economic aid" to compensate for their inability to mobilize internal resources; (2) on U.S. military assistance as a counterweight to mass popular pressures.

In the grip of this double dependence, political leaders from the elite emerge who adopt a populist rhetoric and seek to promote "limited popular mobilizations" as a way of creating spheres of independence for trade and bargaining with the United States.[18] However, this is hardly a viable or effective policy. The cautious attitude which the "populist" elite adopts toward mass movements sets distinct limits on these mobilizations-from-above. The mobilized mass is made to conform to the short-range desires of the elites and, above all, is prevented from "getting out of control," i.e., formulating action around specific class interests. The bureaucratization of the mass movement, the cooptation of rank-and-file leaders, the isolation of "extremists" (those who formulate a program for comprehensive and more egalitarian change), the use of physical coercion are some of the means by which the elite creates a mass movement around specific issues for a limited time, then lays it to rest.[19]

The practical goal of some of Latin America's enlightened policy-making elites is an institutionalized revolution based on a quasi-one-party system such as Mexico's.[20] The opposition would be ineffective and the major social sectors "integrated" into corporate bodies which would make marginal demands on the system and which would be managed by bargaining elites.

What makes it highly unlikely that other Latin American countries can take the "Mexican road" is the fact that the Mexican Revolution *began* as a peasant populist revolution and *ended* with a dominant capitalist class directing a bureaucratized revolution with the help of a revolutionary myth.[21] The forces which dominated the revolutionary stage are not the forces which are ruling Mexico today. The Mexican bourgeoisie was the product of the Mexican Revolution, not its maker.

In Latin America today, on the other hand, all the cumulated forces of a prolonged capitalist development are present in key decision-making positions.[22] The presence of modern corporate directors in the policy-making centers and their links with the landowning elites, foreign investors, and U.S.-influenced international financial institutions, make it highly unlikely that a Mexican-style revolution will be repeated. The strategically situated Latin middle strata oppose, neutralize, or contain popular insurgent forces which could provide the necessary levers for opening society —as partially happened in Mexico. As a result, populist forces in Latin America have increasingly turned toward the Cuban rather than the Mexican Revolution as a model. The social forces which made possible a nationalist-capitalist revolution in Mexico are increasingly looking toward revolutionary collectivist solutions.

In brief, the second factor decisive for the creation of the new equilibrium in Latin America is the accession to power of decision-makers who articulate the policies and interests of commercial, industrial and agricultural corporate elites. These groups share with U.S. policy-makers a profound distrust of mass mobilization politics while remaining dependent on Washington for financial and military aid. Despite aspirations toward independence, their greater desire to hold on to their class privileges favors the maintenance of U.S. hegemony.

Communist Parties: The Politics of Coexistence

Mass movements from above generally have enjoyed the participation and support of Communist parties in Latin America.

While these parties are frequently militant on the mass level in trade unions and, to a much lesser extent, in peasant movements, at the upper levels the leaders continually subordinate the party to "progressive forces," i.e., middle-class regimes or parties.[23] The Communist parties are thus militant pressure groups, not groups oriented toward taking power. Frequently, however, this is enough to put them outside the law—and they join the armed struggle. But again, this is not, at least at the leadership level, an attempt to "seize power" but a means of regaining legality and parliamentary rights. The armed struggle itself is an element to be used in bargaining with the government, bargaining frequently carried on through intermediaries.

Moreover, these policies and tactics usually put the Communists into conflict with revolutionary forces which are oriented toward power.[24] Before the Cuban Revolution the Cuban Communists denounced Fidel Castro as a "petty-bourgeois adventurer." [25] Peruvian peasant leader Hugo Blanco was attacked in the *World Marxist Review* as a "hireling of the CIA" by the Peruvian Communist Party, which was informally supporting the government of Belaúnde.[26] Since 1965 the Communist Party of Venezuela has been calling for a "democratic peace"—a return to legality in exchange for ending the armed struggle.[27] Although the government has yet to agree formally, the Communists have withdrawn all their members from armed opposition and have sided with the government on a number of occasions—policies which have been bitterly resisted by the guerrillas organized in the Armed Forces of National Liberation (FALN).

The Communist Party of Bolivia rejected a revolutionary strategy even after the Barrientos military coup and refused to support Guevara and the guerrilla forces.[28] Thus the Bolivian Communists contributed to the isolation of the guerrillas and facilitated the task of the Bolivian and U.S. military forces. The conflict between the pro-Moscow Bolivian Communist Party and Guevara symbolizes the conflict between the coexistence policies of the Soviet Union and Latin American revolutionary politics. The Soviet Union generally views Latin America as lying within the sphere of influence of the United States. At the maximum, therefore, the Soviets would like to see Latin governments which are independent enough from State Department policy to establish diplomatic and commercial ties with Russia and perhaps offer some resistance to U.S. military intervention. At the same time, Soviet policy-makers want to keep these "independent" governments sufficiently distant to avoid incurring heavy economic and political obligations toward them.[29] The Soviets are not interested in becoming involved in another Cuban situation.

The over-all effect of Communist Party activities, reflecting the influence of Soviet policy interests, has been seriously to undermine the efforts at social revolution in Latin America. Combined with the U.S. commitment to military and repressive solutions, Communist "pragmatism" has extracted a heavy toll among the post-Cuban revolutionary generation in almost every country in Latin America. While U.S. policy has fostered a new equilibrium through increasing reliance on nonliberal regimes, the Communist parties have strengthened that equilibrium by opposing the use of more disruptive methods of political warfare.

The major obstacle to the creation of the new equilibrium has not been pro-Moscow Communism but Castroism. The relationship between the Cuban Revolution and Latin American political development has been complex.[30] Between 1959 and 1962 the Cuban leadership supported a broad spectrum of Latin political groups, ranging from left-wing to moderate nationalist and including persons like Quadros of Brazil. In the period following the missile crisis and Cuba's closer relations with the Soviet Union, Cuban policy was contradictory, giving increasing support both to the official Communist parties and to the left-wing nationalists (MIR of Venezuela and Peru) who supported armed revolution. The Guatemalan guerrilla leader Yon Sosa was denounced, and the first Tri-Continental Conference (1966) contained a preponderance of "official" Communists.[31] Nevertheless, a shift in Cuban policy was evident in the conference's emphasis on armed revolutionary struggle and in the considerable opposition to policies of the pro-Moscow parties. By the latter part of 1966 the Cuban revolutionary leadership had definitely moved away from the "official" Communists toward the militants (nationalist, Communist, or other) conducting armed guerrilla warfare. In March 1967 Castro openly denounced the official Venezuelan Communist Party and the Soviet Union, and defended the guerrillas in Venezuela and elsewhere; the next month Che Guevara's call for revolution was released by the Cuban news service.[32]

The April 1968 issue of the Cuban theoretical journal *Pensamiento Crítico* was wholly devoted to a discussion and analysis of revolutionary political developments in Guatemala, and included articles by the guerrilla groups condemning the pro-Moscow Guatemalan Labor Party (PGT) for its unwillingness to support revolutionary struggle. In 1969 the Cuban leadership strongly favored the unified guerrilla movement which has emerged in Guatemala—including former "Trotskyite" outcast Yon Sosa, who is the current undisputed leader; all formal and informal ties between the PGT and the guerrillas appear to have been broken off.

The U.S. escalation of the war in Vietnam, its military intervention in the Dominican Republic, and the subsequent development of a rationale for U.S. military intervention throughout Latin America may have influenced Cuba's shift to the left. The efforts of *fidelista* movements to overcome the hegemony of the pro-Moscow Left among the more radicalized sectors of the population have had mixed results.[33] Whatever their future success, the continued influence of the pro-Moscow Communists has helped to consolidate the new equilibrium for the present.

The New Equilibrium and Post-Alliance Politics

The new equilibrium in Latin America has developed simultaneously with a more conservative approach by U.S. policymakers to Latin America's long-standing political, social, and economic problems. This conservatism is apparent in the downgrading of agrarian and structural reform in favor of technocratic changes and economic integration; the promotion of agriculture and deemphasizing of rapid industrialization; the support of and aid to military dictatorships as recognized political agencies at the expense of freely elected governments; the organization of a hemispheric military force; the enunciation of the doctrine of unilateral intervention and the renunciation of the principles of sovereignty expounded and implied in the Good Neighbor Policy.

The discussions at the April 1967 hemispheric summit meeting in Punta del Este, Uruguay, made explicit some of the new directions of U.S. policy. One of the outstanding analysts of U.S.-Latin American affairs, James Nelson Goodsell of the *Christian Science Monitor,* noted:

> Economic integration has replaced social reform as the major goal of the Alliance for Progress. . . .
>
> Although not a part of the plan, the United States strongly favors the integration theme—and President Johnson pushed it strongly at the recent Punta del Este meeting. . . .
>
> A corollary to the economic-integration theme replacing the theme of social reform is one of agriculture taking over from industry as the key sector in economic growth in the next decade. Under the original Alliance for Progress concept, drafted here in August, 1961, industrial growth and its effect on urban life were seen as the key element in economic thinking.
>
> But this now is changing—and it is likely that agriculture will become the key element in the decade of the 1970's.
>
> Yet it is a new concept of agriculture: downplaying agrarian reform and emphasizing instead increased production, export diversification, improved credit and incentives, better marketing, and promotion of farm machinery and fertilizer production. All of these features fit neatly into the pattern of economic integration.[34]

The new orientation toward agriculture is a euphemism for an alliance with the current *latifundistas* who dominate agricultural activity through their ownership of land and control over the labor of peasants. The current orientation of U.S. policy toward the big landowners contravenes the guidelines and principles of the Alliance for Progress, one of whose objectives was:

> To encourage, in accordance with the characteristics of each country, programs of comprehensive agrarian reform leading to the effective transformation, where required, of unjust structures and systems of land tenure and use, with a view to replacing latifundia and dwarf holdings by an equitable system of land tenure so that, with the help of timely and adequate credit, technical assistance and facilities for the marketing and distribution of products, the land will become for the man who works it the basis of his economic stability, the foundation of his increasing welfare, and the guarantee of his freedom and dignity.[35]

The reversion to a traditional policy and the forsaking of the revolutionary rhetoric of the early Alliance years has been accompanied by greater reliance on dictatorial forms of political rule, a decreased reliance on economic aid in comparison with the early 1960's, and increasing use of economic resources merely to expedite favorable commercial relations with the United States.[36] Reliance on the military appears to assure U.S. policy-makers that every government on the southern continent is secure; the fear that, without political and economic concessions, the region might be lost to communism, seems to have faded.[37]

The new U.S. approach to fostering "democracy" involves a three-stage process: (1) open support of a military dictatorship to eliminate "subversion"; (2) elimination of popular opponents of U.S. hegemony; (3) "modernization" of the dictatorship, establishing procedures and formal structures that limit or curtail mass mobilization politics, to produce a government which conforms with U.S. global policies and investor interests. Lincoln Gordon, Ambassador to Brazil during the period of the U.S.-supported dictatorial takeover in 1964, explained this process of transition from military dictatorship to democracy just after taking office as Johnson's new Assistant Secretary of State for Latin American Affairs: "Constitutional democracy is the desirable norm everywhere, but there are only approximations of it around the world. . . . It is more realistic to view democracy as a process in time and place. I'm more interested in purpose and direction than in the status at any given moment." [38] According to this viewpoint, a military dictatorship is the midwife of constitutional democracy. Gordon's statement and others in a similar vein clearly depart from traditional views of constitutional democracy and are more akin to rationalizations for authoritarianism.

The strategy of the United States toward Latin America in the post-Alliance period has shifted toward the creation of new regional organizations. A key element in this new strategy is the promotion by U.S. policy-makers of an Inter-American Peace Force.

The issues raised by an inter-American army and military intervention have been discussed by the U.S. Secretary of State and the foreign ministers of the Latin states. In practice, the questions have, to a large extent, already been resolved. U.S. fighting forces have been or are presently active in a number of Latin countries at the request of some of the very governments which are ostensibly raising "principled" objections to interventionism—for example, in Peru, Bolivia, Guatemala, Venezuela, Colombia, and the Dominican Republic. U.S. military officials have for some time planned and helped to carry out military strategy against national revolutionary movements.[39] High State Department officials and the President have stated at inter-American conferences and on numerous other occasions their support for intervention against leftist regimes.[40]

The Latin governments presently prefer to operate on a pragmatic basis, accepting *de facto* intervention while arguing publicly against their dependence on U.S. military force, for domestic political reasons. The United States, however, both by tradition and for international and domestic reasons, prefers a legal basis for its interventions, hence its efforts to promote an inter-American army backed by the Organization of American States. Because of Latin opposition, U.S. policy-makers have allowed this project to lie dormant, though they have certainly not dropped the matter. In Central America, the United States has succeeded in creating an integrated regional military force to suppress insurgency, the Central American Defense Council (CONDECA), which may foreshadow future U.S. policy efforts in the rest of Latin America.

The increased involvement of the United States in Latin America's internal struggles was underlined by former Secretary of Defense Robert McNamara in testimony before Congress:

> During the past year, serious insurgency and terrorist attacks have been successfully countered in several Latin American countries. In others, political threats have been contained. Venezuela has been able to improve substantially its control of guerrilla and terrorist elements during recent months. U.S. trained units of their armed forces and police have spearheaded a government campaign both in the cities and in the countryside. In Peru the government has already made good progress against guerrilla concentrations, and U.S. trained and supported Peruvian army and air force units

have played prominent roles in this counter-guerrilla campaign. In Colombia, U.S. training, support and equipment, including several medium helicopters, have materially aided the Colombia armed forces to establish government control in the rural insurgent areas.

Violence in the mining areas and in the cities of Bolivia has continued to occur intermittently, and we are assisting this country to improve the training and equipping of its military forces.

Pressure on the government of Guatemala resulting from Communist terroristic tactics has increased markedly during the past year. We are supporting a small Guatemalan counter-insurgency force with weapons, vehicles, communications, equipment and training.

In Uruguay, protracted economic stagnation has contributed to popular unrest which recently culminated in a serious wave of strikes throughout the country. Our military assistance to Uruguay is oriented toward improving the small arms, ammunition, communications and transportation equipment of its security forces.[41]

The former Secretary's account of U.S. policy in Latin America is a mixture of euphemism and evasion. McNamara's reference to the repression of popular movements ("control of guerrilla and terrorist elements") is matched by a discreet silence over the exploitative social systems in Latin America to which Washington is supplying "weapons, vehicles, communications, equipment and training." McNamara's admission that U.S. policy in Uruguay was directed against "popular unrest" caused by "protracted economic stagnation" is perhaps the clearest indication that U.S. efforts are not oriented toward achieving popular social reforms. In this period of popular awakening and mass politics, the defense of North and South American business interests depends on Washington's ability to strengthen and influence the repressive apparatus in Latin America, while preserving a facade of representative government. After the military-supported regime has established policies and institutions acceptable to the United States, elections are held with handpicked candidates equally acceptable to the United States. Needless to say, the results of competitive elections in such a context are predetermined. The elections thus arranged are then utilized as propaganda weapons by the U.S. and Latin elites for legitimizing their hegemony. One likely consequence of this strategy is the accumulation of popular resentments which at a propitious moment will explode anew. U.S. policy thus prolongs the Latin political cycle of violence-instability-repression, which in turn helps to postpone structural changes.

The most serious effort to institutionalize U.S. hegemony in the hemisphere and to protect the Latin social systems is found in the proposed inter-American military force.[42] Former Secretary of Defense McNamara set forth the rationale behind this strategy in the following fashion:

> We think that all of the OAS countries have an obligation to encourage the development of democracy and to help keep internal situations from spilling over and disrupting the peace of the Hemisphere. We think that some kind of peace-keeping force might be useful; that the system should have some more effective and responsive arrangement for dealing collectively with a clear and present danger to the peace and security of the Hemisphere. Such an arrangement, supported by a peace-keeping force, would represent a real sharing of responsibility and would also give pause to those elements which might seek to disrupt the peace. We believe the problem is being increasingly better understood now, and we shall continue to search for a formula acceptable to our Alliance partners.[43]

McNamara's appeal is to the existing Latin governing classes; his fears are explicitly of national-popular revolutionaries, not "international Communism" (*"internal* situations . . . disrupting the peace of the Hemisphere"—my emphasis).

From the U.S. government's point of view, the necessity and value of an inter-American force is clear: it generalizes responsibility and legitimizes the use of force to defend U.S. corporate domination of the hemisphere.[44] Secondly, it permits the United States to continue reaping the benefits of control while minimizing such external costs as U.S. casualties which might be resented at home.

The establishment of hemispheric military training bases, the growing involvement of AID and of U.S. military officers and quasi-political figures in arranging Latin military-political affairs, the increase of military appropriations, the closer ties developed between U.S. and Latin military personnel through civic action programs—all these are features of the new, multinational version of U.S. interventionism.[45]

The first major success in securing hemispheric support for U.S. intervention in Latin America occurred at the time of the U.S. blockade of Cuba in 1962. This unilateral action by the United States, imposing decisions by force on Cuba with the acquiescence of the Soviet Union, created enormous pressures on the Latin governments to fall into line. When the United States tied the question of its dominance in the hemisphere (with the right to unilateral intervention) to the threat of total war, the Latin countries offered no resistance. Moreover, the "Cuban threat" which was the major U.S. justification for the intervention was considered a real one by the Latin governments, both as inspiration to national revolutionary forces in their own countries, and as an example of a successful, developing socialist society.

The convergence of these factors during the Cuban blockade—unilateral U.S. military action with global consequences, Soviet acquiescence, and the accelerated deterioration of social, economic, and political conditions within Latin countries—facilitated the acceptance of intervention in the hemisphere. From Latin support for U.S. unilateral action at the time of the Cuban blockade, it was a short distance to Latin acquiescence in the U.S. occupation of the Dominican Republic.

The moral fibers which sustained middle-class "nationalism" for half a century have weakened considerably. For many Latin governments it is preferable to adjust to U.S. sovereignty in the hemisphere than to risk popular mobilization that might undermine precarious social structures. For domestic political reasons, Latin diplomats continue to express formal opposition to U.S. intervention, but in practice they do not reject the presence of U.S. military personnel in Latin America. This "double-bookkeeping" on the question of sovereignty may finally be resolved. In the meantime, Latin and U.S. elites confronted with popular revolutionary movements are not overly concerned with the language spoken by the military guardians. By 1968 the military had moved closer toward total control of political life in Latin America. "Dual power" situations, in which civilian governments tried to maneuver between popular and military power centers, were gradually but decisively resolved in favor of the military. This is what happened to Frondizi in Argentina, Estenssoro in Bolivia, Bosch in the Dominican Republic, Goulart in Brazil, Menéndez in Guatemala, among others.

The intimate connection between (1) the progressive militarization of political life in Latin America; (2) the acceptance of U.S. hegemony as the price of maintaining elite control; and (3) the development of an inter-American military force is fully revealed in the character and consequences of the Brazilian military coup of 1964. The largest country in Latin America, Brazil could have become either the center of autonomous revolutionary movements or an important though subordinate ally in the advancement of U.S. policy. The overthrow of Goulart and the establishment of the military dictatorship was prepared and organized by the Brazilian military high command and supported by U.S. officials and military staff.[46] The continent-wide significance of the events in Brazil was little realized at the time, but the policy of multilateral military intervention against a leftist political regime in the largest country of Latin America was to bear fruit in the course of a single year. The presence of the Brazilian army alongside of U.S. troops in the Dominican Republic was the first concrete manifestation of this policy. The military coup which subsequently took place in Argentina was assured of U.S. support.[47] The Latin American countries now ruled by a military junta, or by governments established with the direct intervention of the military, include Argentina, Bolivia, Brazil, Dominican Republic, Ecuador, El Salvador, Guatemala, Haiti, Honduras, Nicaragua, Paraguay and Peru.[48]

President Johnson pointed to the importance of Brazil and highlighted the long-range significance of the inter-American army for U.S. strategy in his address at Baylor University, May 29, 1965. Discussing U.S. military success in suppressing popular revolutionary movements, Johnson said:

> Today those achievements are guaranteed—guaranteed by the troops of five nations, representing this hemisphere. They are under the command of the able Brazilian general, General [Hugo Panasco] Alvin, and for the first time in the history of the Organi-

zation of American States [it] has created and it has sent to the soil of an American nation an international peace-keeping military force.[49]

He then went on to present his political manifesto, an open declaration of war against all popular national revolutions, which he equated with "international wars."

Out of the Dominican crucible the twenty American nations must now forge a stronger shield against disaster. The opportunity is here now for a new thrust forward to show the world the way to true international cooperation in the cause of peace and in the struggle to win a better life for all of us.

We believe that the new world may most wisely approach this task guided by new realities.

The first reality is that old concepts and old labels are largely obsolete.

In today's world, with the enemies of freedom talking about wars of national liberation, the old distinction between the civil war and international war has already lost much of its meaning.

Second is the reality that when forces of freedom move slowly, whether on political or economic or military fronts, the forces of slavery and subversion move rapidly and they move rapidly [sic] and they move decisively.

Third, we know that when a Communist group seeks to exploit misery the entire free American system is put in deadly danger. We also know that these dangers can be found today in many of our lands.

There is no trouble anywhere these evil forces will not try to turn to their advantage and we can expect more efforts at triumph by terror and conquest through chaos.

Fourth, we have learned in the Dominican Republic that we can act decisively and we can act together.

Fifth, it is clear that we need new international machinery geared to meet the fast-moving events. When hours can decide the fate of generations, the moment of decision must become the moment of action.[50]

The actual creation of an inter-American army would accelerate the entrenchment of U.S. hegemony in the hemisphere, with the Latin American countries losing even the quasi-sovereign status which they have maintained until now. Recognizing that nationalist feelings are an obstacle to U.S. aims, U.S. policy-makers have sponsored meetings of high military personnel to break down parochial attitudes and implant a hemispheric perspective. The major theme of these conferences is that the Latin American general staffs have a common political role to play on a continent-wide scale, and that they face a common enemy—communism and popular revolution. The fact that popular revolutions directly threaten the privileged groups in Latin America, of which they are one, makes them quite open to this message, as does their dependence on U.S. support. The military elite is thus willing to lend legitimacy to U.S. hegemony in the hemisphere. The achievement of this goal, however, will not be immediate. Some civilian governments with somewhat different social and political bases and structures either are not in a position, or are unwilling, to sign away national sovereignty in such a fashion.[51]

The inability of liberal regimes to cope with rising popular demands and severe economic problems, and their overeagerness to accommodate foreign investors has resulted in numerous military coups whose claim to legitimacy was defense of national sovereignty. The military takeover in Peru and the subsequent expropriation of the International Petroleum Corporation, as well as increasing commercial relations with the Soviet bloc, suggest the possibility of a new-style right-wing nationalism that may try to take a Gaullist approach in foreign affairs, while maintaining the status quo at home. However, in the past, right-wing nationalist rhetoric has rarely been matched by substantive measures against foreign interests, serving rather to undermine efforts at internal reform.

The New Equilibrium and the New Revolutionary Left

Peaceful coexistence is a new name for the old sphere-of-influence politics: the two power blocs attempt to stabilize world politics through agreements which satisfy "national interests." But what suits the Soviet national interest, at least as defined by current leaders—allowing the United States to rule the Western Hemisphere—ill suits Latin America. The policy of peaceful coexistence pursued by the Soviet Union and its fraternal parties in Latin

America conflicts with the social and economic needs of the vast majority of the Latin American people. In an underdeveloped continent whose social inequalities are maintained or deepened by the presence of U.S. economic enterprises and externally supported military regimes, the strategies dictated by the Soviet policy of "peaceful coexistence" present additional obstacles to any social and political changes that conflict with U.S. interests.[52]

The successful alliance between U.S. policy-makers and Latin American military governments has forced reformist-leftist forces to employ revolutionary means to achieve reformist ends; electoral methods are ineffective. Thus, to the long-term destabilizing effects of U.S. policies on Latin America's economic and social development, we must add the radicalizing effects on its political development. U.S. success is achieved at the price of the growing disenfranchisement and opposition of nongovernmental personnel. As the United States seeks control through military means, it is creating mass anti-U.S. feeling that could lead to popular support for the emerging armed guerrilla movements. In a word, the present equilibrium could generate revolutionary alternatives; it is not a locked box. Parliamentary political channels are being closed to Latin American reformers like Bosch, Goulart, Arbenz, and Morales, and the appeal of the traditional Communist parties has been weakened. And international revolutionary movements such as those proposed at the 1967 meetings of the Organization for Latin American Solidarity (OLAS) in Havana are developing.

The Communist parties of Latin America have entered a crisis phase, attempting to relate to the U.S.-Soviet détente while confronting a new revolutionary challenge. The command relations between the Soviet Union and the Latin American parties have apparently been replaced by more collaborative arrangements. Nevertheless, the leadership of the Latin American parties, nurtured for years on Soviet modes of thinking, accustomed to dependence, and operating in a highly bureaucratized political situation, find it difficult, if not impossible, to reorient themselves.[53] They have produced no new analysis or strategy relevant to the socio-political changes which have occurred in Latin America in recent years. Despite the emergence throughout Latin America of capitalist landowning and industrial elites, the Communist parties write and speak of the "antifeudal" revolution as if they were living in the seventeenth century.[54] Despite the emergence of military dictators or military-controlled civilian governments, the Communist parties still propose parliamentary electoral activity (*via pacifica electoral*) as if Latin America were Scandinavia.[55]

Where the Communist Party is legal, its main effort is in organizing popular fronts—under middle-class party hegemony. In exchange, the Communists negotiate for marginal favors, bargain for economic gains for their trade-union constituents, and hope that relations will be established with the Soviet Union.[56] The popular front's policy toward Cuba is a secondary consideration, not important enough to disrupt friendly relations between the Communists and their middle-class "partners." More significantly, structural change is relegated to the distant future.

When the Communist Party is illegal, it searches for a legal party to support, and thus the framework within which it makes political choices depends upon the repressiveness of the regime. Even under the Castelo Branco dictatorship, the Brazilian Communist leader Luis Prestes proposed a legal strategy, neglecting to indicate to his followers how it should be implemented.[57] Parallel and complementary to the legal approach of the Brazilian Communist Party, the Soviet Union negotiated a series of trade and aid agreements with the Brazilian regime. The Soviet Union and its ideological supporters have defended the economic agreements with the Latin American oligarchies by pointing to Cuba's trade with Spain. The position of each country and the nature of the economic relations are, however, somewhat different. Cuba is an underdeveloped country under enormous pressure from the United States. Its relation with Spain is purely commercial. The Soviet Union, on the other hand, does not need the trade with Brazil, Colombia, or Venezuela. More important, the Soviets have offered credits and aid, not merely trade, to these governments, thus helping to stabilize the regimes.

Just as "late-developing" nations face the problem of industrializing in competition with already established, highly industrialized countries, today in Latin America revolutionary groups face the problem of establishing revolutionary organizations in competition with already established Communist parties and

former national-populist parties, as well as with the bureaucratically controlled trade unions, all groups whose leaders are
committed to bargaining within the status quo and whose followers enter into "client" relations with those in power. Yet despite
organizational competition on the Left and repression from the
Right, significant nuclei of left-wing revolutionaries have emerged
in a number of countries, almost exclusively outside the Communist and former nationalist parties.

The major effort at the July 1967 OLAS Conference in Havana
was the attempt to deal with the problems of uniting a Left which
includes both social revolutionaries struggling to overthrow middle-
class regimes and Communist upholders of middle-class hegemony.[58] The OLAS Conference was an attempt to organize a
new Latin American international revolutionary organization. The
Conference decided that the only revolutionary organizations
which could be accepted were those willing both to support the
thesis of armed revolutionary struggle and to differentiate themselves from parties not following that course.[59] This was for all
practical purposes a repudiation of the position of the Soviet Union
and its supporters in Latin America. Like the "twenty-one conditions" that Lenin and the early Bolsheviks set forth for membership in the Third International, Fidel Castro and the Latin revolutionaries put forth the thesis that support of armed revolutionary
struggle was a precondition for membership in the new international. The new strategy emphasized the conservative and dependent position of the Latin American bourgeoisie and thus
rejected the tactic of a "popular front." Analyzing the growing
class differentiation and polarization in the rural areas, the OLAS
resolution identified the peasantry as the principal historical agency
of revolution. The current parties and organizations being inadequate to the tasks of revolutionary struggle, the Conference called
for new organizational forms capable of combining political activity and military struggle, under a unified politico-military leadership. Since the locus of struggle is in the countryside, the new
revolutionaries argued that the rural-based leadership directly engaged in the struggle should devise the appropriate strategy. This
analysis and strategy was at variance with the pro-Moscow Communist approach on every major issue. Armed struggle based on

the peasantry and led by politico-military units (guerrillas) against the native bourgeoisie and imperialism was counterposed to the pro-Moscow Communist strategy of urban-based parties engaged in electoral collaboration with the "progressive bourgeoisie." [60] For countries like Uruguay, Argentina, and Chile, which contain large industrial working classes and a relatively small peasantry, neither OLAS nor the traditional Communists offered any insights for radical action. Starting from different premises on the level of international politics (revolution vs. coexistence) the new revolutionary Left and the pro-Moscow Communists have set out on two clearly divergent paths: the former intent on destroying the new equilibrium in Latin America, the other seeking changes through adapting to it.

Conclusion

Reacting vigorously to the opportunities opened by the détente with the Soviet Union, the United States has seized the political initiative in Latin America. U.S. policy has been geared toward stability in order to maintain hegemony over the region. Ideological spokesmen fostered the idea of the harmony of interests of the two regions, suggesting that the development of one area was compatible with the other. Cutting across this ideology, a series of violent internal struggles (Cuba, Dominican Republic) quickly became "internationalized," revealing the profound stake that the United States has in maintaining the status quo not only within the hemisphere as a whole but within each country. U.S. policymakers thus attempted to shift attention from bilateral conflicts through hemispheric internationalism. While the Alliance for Progress was ostensibly set up to promote reform, its real function was to restabilize the region. This development of a multinational strategy is related to the growing importance of the multinational corporation in U.S. overseas expansion.[61]

The Nixon Administration, though calling for new policies and severely criticizing the Alliance for Progress, will generally follow the policies of the Johnson Administration, with some qualifications. It is expected that in terms of development policy Nixon will deemphasize U.S. government loans and will place greater reliance on private enterprise and international banking agencies. Nixon's appointees in charge of Latin American policy reflect his preference for private businessmen. Charles Meyer, Nixon's choice for the post of Assistant Secretary of State for Inter-American Affairs, was in charge of Sears, Roebuck's East Coast operations, and previously its vice-president in charge of Latin American operations. He was also a director of the United Fruit Company. John Irwin, Nixon's personal envoy to Peru, has directorships in IBM and the U.S. Trust Company.

Nixon's handling of the Peruvian expropriation of IPC suggests he will follow a flexible, cautious approach. Rather than rash confrontations leading to mutual escalation, he tends to favor negotiations and maneuvers that lead to realignments within the junta, isolation of the nationalists, and an eventual settlement on terms acceptable to U.S. investor interests.

The new equilibrium reasserting U.S. hegemony in the hemisphere is presently only slightly threatened by the emergence of a new revolutionary Left. However, if the new revolutionary groups are able to detonate mass insurgency, which presently does not exist, the new equilibrium in Latin America may be undermined. U.S. hegemony in the hemisphere, which was restabilized after the challenge of the Cuban Revolution, could break down if and when the radicalized intellectuals join forces with the currents of nationalism and populism. The great mass of people who have effectively been excluded from politics within the new equilibrium may, in the not too distant future, redefine not only their position in society but relations between the nations of the hemisphere.

NOTES

1. For a more detailed discussion of the prospects for revolutionary change see my earlier article, "Revolution and Guerrilla Movements in Latin America: Venezuela, Guatemala, Colombia, and Peru," in James Petras and Maurice Zeitlin, eds., *Latin America: Reform or Revolution?* (New York: Fawcett, 1968), pp. 329–369. For a superficial and ill-informed account see Norman Gall, "The Legacy of Che Guevara," *Commentary*, December 1967, pp. 21–44.

2. For an account of U.S. involvement in Latin American politics through counterinsurgency and civic action programs, see Willard F. Barber and C. Neale Ronning, *Internal Security and Military Power* (Columbus, O.: Ohio State University Press, 1966). (Reviewed below, pp. 366–371.) In 1968, in connection with the death of Che Guevara, former Bolivian Minister of Interior Antonio Argüedas testified to the important role that the Central Intelligence Agency played in the political affairs of his country: see *New York Times,* August 25, 1968; *La Presencia* (La Paz), August 18, 1968; *Granma* (Havana), August 25, 1968, p. 12. On the economic and political influence that the United States wields in a Caribbean country, the Dominican Republic, see Fred Goff and Michael Locker, *The Violence of Domination: U.S. Power and the Dominican Republic* (pamphlet published by the North American Congress on Latin America, 1967). For a discussion of U.S. influence in Brazil see Carl Oglesby and Richard Shaull, *Containment and Change* (New York: Macmillan, 1967), especially pp. 83–97, and Teotonio dos Santos, "Foreign Investment and the Large Enterprise in Latin America: The Brazilian Case," in Petras and Zeitlin, *op. cit.,* pp. 431–453. *Ramparts* magazine (March, April 1967) has documented the CIA infiltration of the National Students Association, the AFL-CIO, and CIA-influenced use of these organizations in Latin America. On the use by the U.S. government of cultural organizations active in Latin America as propaganda fronts, see Christopher Lasch, "The Cultural Cold War: A Short History of The Congress for Cultural Freedom," in Barton Bernstein, ed., *Towards a New Past: Dissenting Essays in American History* (New York: Random House, 1968), pp. 322–359.

3. For a more extensive discussion of the "harmony of interests" ideology, see "Latin American Studies in the United States: A Critical Assessment," below, pp. 327–344.

4. The best-documented account of the popular basis of the Dominican revolt and resistance to the U.S. invasion is found in José Antonio Moreno, "Sociological Aspects of the Dominican Revolution" (unpublished Ph.D. dissertation, Department of Sociology, Cornell University, 1967). A detailed refutation of the Johnson Administration's justification for the invasion of the Dominican Republic is in Theodore Draper, "The Dominican Crisis: A Case Study in American Policy," *Commentary,* December 1965, pp. 33–68.

5. There was some mild opposition, especially in the Senate, to the new policy being put forth by the Executive. Speaking in defense of the promilitary stance and chastising her critical colleagues, Senator Margaret Chase Smith boldly stated: "Some respected Members of the U.S. Senate frown upon our having any military ties with South American countries. They would have us stop all our military assistance to South American countries. With this I am in basic disagreement. I am because, in my opinion, the greatest friends that the United States has in South America are the members of the military forces—and the greatest enemies of communism are the members of the military forces." (U.S., Senate *Congressional Record,* 87th Cong., 2nd Sess., 108, Part 4, March 24, 1962, p. 4957.)

   In the concluding chapter of their study of U.S. policy and the Latin American military, Barber and Ronning note that ". . . there are signs of an increasing reliance on military solutions to . . . threats of communist subversion while at the same time, the Kennedy policy of giving all-out moral and economic support to the so-called democratic governments has been dropped" (*op. cit.,* p. 242).

6. For a discussion of the manipulation of the terminology of international relations to suit the power needs of a nation see A. F. Organski, *World Politics* (New York: Knopf, 1968), pp. 272–299. An interesting discussion of strategies of the status quo appears in Vernon Aspaturian, "Revolutionary Change and the Strategy of the Status Quo," in Lawrence W. Martin, ed., *Neutralism and Nonalignment* (New York: Praeger, 1962), pp. 165–195.

7. See Robert F. Smith, *The United States and Cuba: Business and Diplomacy, 1917–1960* (New Haven, Conn.: Yale University Press, 1960); Maurice Zeitlin and Robert Scheer, *Cuba: Tragedy in Our Hemisphere* (New York: Grove Press, 1963); James O'Connor, "On Cuban Political Economy," in Petras and Zeitlin, *op. cit.,* pp. 486–500. A month-by-month account of the U.S.-Cuban conflict can be found in the *Hispanic-American Report* between 1959 and 1964.

8. Robert F. Smith, "Decline of the Alliance for Progress," in Marvin E. Gettleman and David Mermelstein, eds., *The Great Society Reader* (New York: Random House, 1967), pp. 372–382; J. P. Morray, "The United States and Latin America," in Petras and Zeitlin, *op. cit.,* pp. 99–119. The policy the United States followed in expectation of growing conflict and polarization was seen by

many social scientists as auguring a new era of friendliness and cooperation between the U.S. and Latin America. This point of view was expressed in, among others, Edwin Lieuwen, *U.S. Policy in Latin America: A Short History* (New York: Praeger, 1965), especially pp. 111–125; and Lincoln Gordon, *A New Deal for Latin America: The Alliance for Progress* (Cambridge, Mass.: Harvard University Press, 1963).

9. In 1962, regarding the conflict between Brazilian Governor Brizola and the International Telephone and Telegraph Company, Secretary of State Rusk noted: "I don't believe the United States can afford to stake its interests in other countries on a particular private investment in a particular situation. We have to keep working at these things." Quoted in John Hickey, "The First Year: Business," *Inter-American Economic Affairs,* XVI (Summer 1962), p. 63.

10. Simon Hanson, "The Fourth Year: The Fatal Barrier to Growth and Reform: Latin America's Economic Philosophy," *Inter-American Economic Affairs,* XX (Autumn 1966), p. 63.

11. John Moors Cabot, former Assistant Secretary for Inter-American Affairs, stated: ". . . the need to protect our large economic stake inevitably injects a conservative note into our policies [toward Latin America]." *New York Times,* November 7, 1963. On the conservative bias of U.S. policy see Robert F. Smith, "Social Revolution in Latin America: The Role of U.S. Policy," *International Affairs* (London), October 1965, p. 644.

12. The average U.S. military assistance to Latin America for the fiscal years 1959–1960 (the later Eisenhower years) was $31,-460,000. The average military assistance for the 1961–1965 fiscal years was $50,260,000. U.S., House, *Foreign Assistance and Related Agencies Appropriations for 1967,* Hearings Before a Subcommittee of the Committee on Appropriations, 89th Cong., 2nd Sess. (Washington, D.C.: Government Printing Office, 1966), pp. 772–773.

13. Barber and Ronning, *op. cit.,* pp. 22–27.

14. W. W. Rostow, *View from the Seventh Floor* (New York: Harper and Row, 1964).

15. The opening statement of purpose of the official document of the Alliance for Progress, the "Declaration to the Peoples of America," categorically stated: "This Alliance is established on the basic principle that free men working through the institution of representative democracy can best satisfy man's aspirations, including

those for work, home and land, health and schools. No system can guarantee true progress unless it affirms the dignity of the individual which is the foundation of our civilization." *Alliance for Progress* (Official Documents of the Meeting of the Inter-American Economic and Social Council at the Ministerial Level held in Punta del Este, Uruguay, August 5–17, 1961) (Washington, D.C.: Pan American Union, 1961).

16. For a detailed account of Latin America's dependence on the United States for training, supplying, and financing its military, see Barber and Ronning, *op. cit.*, Chs. 4–6. The United States is by far the dominant exporter of manufactured goods to and importer of raw materials from this region, in addition to controlling most of Latin America's strategic resources. See "United States Business and Foreign Policy in Latin America," below, pp. 229–248.

17. For a more detailed discussion of this point see Andre Gunder Frank, *Capitalism and Underdevelopment in Latin America* (New York: Monthly Review Press, 1967).

18. Perón in Argentina and Vargas in Brazil were examples of this type of authoritarian-populist political leader. See Torcuato Di Tella, "Populism and Reform in Latin America," in Claudio Véliz, ed., *Obstacles to Change in Latin America* (London: Oxford University Press, 1966), pp. 47–74; and Helio Jaguaribe, "The Dynamics of Brazilian Nationalism," *ibid.*, pp. 162–187.

19. There are several examples of once revolutionary or innovative political movements which have been transformed into relatively conservative bureaucratic machines. The Revolutionary Institutional Party (PRI) in Mexico, the Democratic Action Party (AD) in Venezuela, the National Revolutionary Movement (MNR) in Bolivia all began as movements of national mobilization and ended by alienating and purging the reformers from their ranks. On Mexico see Pablo González Casanova, *La democracia en Mexico* (Mexico City: Siglo XXI, 1964); on Bolivia, William Leons, "Revolution in the Hacienda" (unpublished manuscript); on Venezuela, James Cockcroft, *Venezuela's Fidelistas—Two Generations* (Stanford, Calif.: Stanford University Institute of Hispanic-American and Luso-Brazilian Studies, 1963).

20. An unsuccessful attempt to approximate the Mexican experience in Chile is discussed in my study, *Chilean Christian Democracy* (Berkeley, Calif.: University of California Institute of Interna-

tional Studies, 1967). On Argentina see Torcuato Di Tella, *El sistema político argentino y la clase obrera* (Buenos Aires: EUDEBA, 1964).

21. Casanova, *op. cit.*; Moises González Navarro, "Mexico: The Lopsided Revolution," in Véliz, *op. cit.,* pp. 206–229.

22. On the industrial elite and the middle class see Fernando H. Cardoso, "The Industrial Elite," and Luis Ratinoff, "The New Urban Groups: The Middle Classes," in S. M. Lipset and Aldo Solari, eds., *Elites in Latin America* (New York: Oxford University Press, 1967), pp. 61–93, 94–114. Also Fredrick B. Pike, "Aspects of Class Relations in Chile 1850–1960," and Gustavo Polit, "The Argentinian Industrialists," in Petras and Zeitlin, *op. cit.,* pp. 202–219, 399–430.

23. Because of the sharp attacks which Fidel Castro has launched against the Communist parties for their revisionism, they are less and less willing to make their alliances with the middle class explicit, preferring vague terms such as "nonproletariat forces." One of the most influential pro-Moscow Communist leaders in Latin America recently spelled out their policy in the following terms: "The problems of our temporary alliance with non-proletarian and non-communist forces call for a new approach. Our allies now have much greater opportunities for marching ahead, not of course without vacillation and difficulties. Whatever happens, it is farthest from our minds to use them at some specific stage only to discard them at another. On the contrary, we could wish for nothing better than to co-operate with them indefinitely. What we communists want is a progressive alignment of all champions of democracy and socialism, recognizing the right of every ally to participate in all stages of the revolutionary process and in all governments that the people's struggle may bring into being." Luis Corvalan, "Alliance of the Anti-Imperialist Forces in Latin America," *World Marxist Review,* X, No. 7 (July 1967), p. 50.

24. For a more detailed discussion see my "Revolution and Guerrilla Movements in Latin America," in Petras and Zeitlin, *op. cit.,* pp. 330–350.

25. On the relationship of the Cuban Communist Party and Fidel Castro see Zeitlin and Scheer, *op. cit.,* Ch. 6.

26. E.g.: "U.S. imperialism and the Peruvian oligarchy have been seeking a suitable pretext for consolidating the position of the [military] junta . . . [such a pretext] was obligingly given by the

Trotskyites of the Hugo Blanco group who killed a number of policemen for purposes of provocation. Besides having ample funds at its disposal the Blanco group has the backing of the North American press, which tries to depict it both at home and abroad as the 'champion' of the Peruvian people." "Atrocities Committed by Military Junta," *World Marxist Review,* VI, No. 7 (July 1963), p. 85.

27. Lengthy excerpts from a Venezuelan Communist Party policy statement defending the line of "democratic peace" appeared in a speech in which Fidel Castro attacked their position. "Their attitude toward the guerrilla struggle will define the communists in Latin America." *Granma,* March 13, 1967, p. 1.

28. References to the opposition of the Bolivian Communist Party to the guerrillas are found in "The Diary of Che Guevara," *Ramparts,* July 27, 1968. See also *Le Nouvel Observateur,* November 7, 1967; *Marcha* (Montevideo), November 24, 1967; *The Militant* (New York), November 24, 1967; *World Outlook* (New York), November 24, 1967.

29. In pursuit of its "national interest" the Soviet government in 1966 granted Chile $50 million in credits and aid after the Frei government concluded a twenty-five-year agreement which guaranteed and augmented U.S. private investment. More indicative of the low estimation in which the Soviet Union holds the Latin revolution, the Russians granted the Brazilian dictatorship $120 million in aid and credits and sent friendship and cultural missions to Venezuela and Colombia; those to Bogotá arrived on the day the Communist Party Central Committee was arrested. For further discussion of this point see Richard J. Barnet, *Intervention and Revolution* (New York: New American Library, 1968), and Herbert Dinerstein, *Intervention Against Communism* (Baltimore, Md.: Johns Hopkins University Press, 1967).

30. For a detailed account of Cuba's changing foreign policy see *Hispanic-American Report* between 1959 and 1962.

31. Castro's denunciation of Yon Sosa is found in his "Closing Speech to the Tri-Continental Conference in Havana," *Granma,* special supplement on the Tri-Continental Conference, English edition, January 16, 1966. On the composition of the conference see Adolfo Gilly, "A Conference Without Glory and Without a Program," *Monthly Review,* April 1966, p. 22.

32. Castro's speech, printed in *Granma,* March 13, 1967, is in English under the title, *Those Who Are Not Revolutionary Fighters Can-*

not Be Called Communists (New York: Merit Publishers, 1967). Guevaras' call, "Vietnam and the World Struggle for Freedom," was released by Prensa Latina on April 17, 1967, and was published in the Cuban-based magazine *Tricontinental,* June 1967.

33. See my "Revolution and Guerrilla Movements in Latin America," in Petras and Zeitlin, *op. cit.,* pp. 329–369; Gall, "The Legacy of Che Guevara," *op. cit.*

34. *Christian Science Monitor,* April 27, 1967, p. 12.

35. *Alliance for Progress,* Official Documents of the Meeting of the Inter-American Economic and Social Council at the Ministerial Level held in Punta del Este, Uruguay, August 5–17, 1961 (Washington, D.C., Pan American Union, 1961).

36. Carlos Sanz de Santamaría, Chairman of the Inter-American Committee on the Alliance for Progress (CIAP), stated in 1968 that Latin America's trade problems were assuming crisis proportions, and that any increased aid is "tied aid"—donor nations tie aid to exports of their goods and services and impose restrictions on imports from the very underdeveloped countries they are trying to help. *Alliance for Progress Weekly Newsletter,* VI, No. 38 (September 16, 1968), p.1. Ninety percent of all AID aid funds went for purchases from U.S. corporations. *U.S. Statistical Abstract,* 1967, p. 827.

37. President Kennedy speaking at the White House to Latin American diplomats and members of Congress in March 1962 noted: "Those who possess wealth and power in poor nations must accept their own responsibilities. They must lead the fight for those basic reforms which alone can preserve the fabric of their societies. Those who make peaceful revolution impossible will make violent revolution inevitable." *President Kennedy Speaks on The Alliance for Progress* (Washington, D.C.: Agency for International Development, 1962).

By the mid-sixties the fear of revolution was considerably diminished. U.S. policy-makers' new sense of security was voiced as far back as 1966 by President Johnson: ". . . what can they say? . . . we seem to be doing all right in the Dominican Republic. We've had no Bay of Pigs in Latin America. . . ." *Newsweek,* September 26, 1966, p. 27.

38. *Newsweek,* January 31, 1966, p. 54.

39. U.S. influence over Latin American armed forces has increased enormously in the past five years. Contrary to the assertions of some U.S. academicians that Latin armies would become less

political through contact with the U.S. military, their involvement in and control over political life has deepened, and political freedoms and social justice have become correspondingly attenuated in Latin countries. The evidence for U.S. influence on the Latin military is unmistakable: command and staff structure in each of the services are similar to those of the U.S.; in Venezuela, Colombia, and Guatemala, all the services use U.S. military doctrine —most texts used in the schools are direct translations of U.S. Army manuals; large numbers of officers of all services have attended service schools in the United States; others have received specialized counterinsurgency training in the Canal Zone. U.S. military assistance has consisted in training and advising, and in the three abovementioned countries U.S. officers have actually engaged in directing the fighting forces. The Venezuelan armed forces are under the closest "advice": the U.S. Army mission of several hundred is the largest in Latin America and is indispensable to even the procedural functioning of the Venezuelan Navy. The U.S. Air Force mission is stationed with each tactical unit in all schools except the cadet school, as well as at Air Force Headquarters. (See *The U.S. Army Handbook on Venezuela.*)

40. The House of Representatives on September 20, 1965, by a 312–52 roll call vote adopted a resolution (H Res 560) which in effect endorsed the unilateral use of force by any Western Hemisphere country. The resolution named no countries, but as the *Congressional Quarterly Weekly Report* (September 24, 1965) states, it "appeared tailored to give approval to situations such as the United States intervention in the Dominican Republic in April, 1965." H Res 560 stated that "the intervention of International Communism, directly or indirectly, however disguised, in any American State, conflicts with the established policy of the American Republics for the protection of the sovereignty of the peoples of such states and the political independence of their governments. . . ." It expressed the sense of the House that "in any such situation any one or more of the high contracting parties to the Inter-American Treaty of Reciprocal Assistance may take steps to forestall or combat intervention, domination, control and colonization in whatever form, by the subversive forces known as International Communism and its agencies in the Western Hemisphere."

41. U. S., House, *Department of Defense Appropriations for 1967,*

Hearings Before a Subcommittee of the Committee on Appropriations, 89th Cong., 2nd Sess., (Washington, D.C.: Government Printing Office, 1966), pp. 30–34.

42. The U.S. Government first officially introduced a resolution calling for the formation of an inter-American force in May 1965 at the Tenth Meeting of Consultation of the American Ministers of Foreign Affairs. Needless to say, the United States was able to gather the necessary votes to have the measure approved. See Barber and Ronning, *op. cit.,* Appendix I, pp. 299–305.

43. *Ibid.*

44. President Kennedy attempted to gloss over the historically regressive role which the military played in Latin America with the notion of "civic action." In his message to Congress on March 22, 1962, Kennedy stated: "Military assistance will in the future more actively emphasize internal security, civil works and economic growth of the nations aided." At least thirteen Latin American countries now have U.S.-supported military "civic action" programs. In Bolivia, the first to organize such a program on a substantial scale, the United States also reorganized the army; the traditional army was literally destroyed by the 1952 revolution and replaced by popular militias. It was with AID funds that the new U.S.-organized Bolivian Army built a few schools and then seized power and opened a frontal assault on the tin miners. A U.S. pamphlet for army commanders, *Civic Action,* describes politico-military civic action as a weapon against communist-inspired subversion, effective as both a preventive measure and a technique of guerrilla warfare and counterinsurgency.

45. See Barber and Ronning, *op. cit.,* Chs. 5–6.

46. In the first eighteen months after the Brazilian military seized power in 1964 at least seven of the twenty-three elected governors were removed from office. Those removed were replaced by military men loyal to the dictatorship. In some cases, governors who were just as conservative in their social and economic views as the military were removed to stress the military's role and power in the government. See *Correio de Manha* (Río de Janeiro), April 1, 1965.

47. Thomas Mann, former Assistant Secretary of State for Inter-American Affairs, clearly stated the U.S. position: "I am not one of those faced with the Communist Menace and who are anti-military in Latin America. I think the military is a force for stability." U.S., House, *Hearings Before the Committee on Foreign*

Affairs, 89th Cong., 1st Sess., February 16, 1965 (Washington, D.C.: Government Printing Office, 1966), p. 157. On U.S. military aid to the military government of Bolivia, see U.S., House, Foreign Assistance and Related Agencies, *Hearings on Appropriations, 1966,* pp. 1262–1264. On Argentina, see U.S., House, Foreign Assistance and Related Agencies, *Hearings on Appropriations, 1968,* pp. 739–740.

48. A chronological listing of military coups in Latin America between 1956 and 1966 can be found in U.S., House, *Foreign Assistance and Related Agencies Appropriations for 1967* (cited in note 12 above), pp. 629–630.

   Once the United States had approved the military as a modernizing and stabilizing force, a "military-coup multiplier" was started. The 1968 Peruvian military coup apparently was strongly influenced by the Argentine, which in turn was influenced by the U.S.-approved Brazilian coup. Malcolm Browne of the *New York Times* noted: "Qualified Peruvian sources feel that this time the military leaders have patterned their move on the 1966 coup in Argentina. . . . Peru's new rulers issued a manifesto strikingly similar in much of its wording to a similar document issued in Buenos Aires during the Argentine coup." *New York Times,* October 5, 1968, p. 19. In fact, the Peruvian military coup occurred shortly after the Seventh Conference of Military Chiefs at Río de Janeiro. The Conference stressed the leading role of the army in economic, political, and social development and in the fight against "Castro-Communism" in Latin America. See Maria Elena Ballantine, "Peru: El golpe del Oro Negro," *Marcha,* October 4, 1968, p. 20.

49. U.S., Senate, *Congressional Record,* 89th Cong., 1st Sess., 111, Part 9, June 1, 1965, pp. 12126–12127.

50. *Ibid.,* p. 12127.

51. Up to now, Mexico and Chile have opposed the idea of an inter-American army. Mexico has a history of interventions by the United States and a large sector of public opinion that vocally opposes them. Chile has a large Marxist-oriented working class and a substantial nationalistic middle class that would strongly oppose such a policy. These groups are represented in the Communist and Socialist parties and in the left wing of the Christian Democratic Party, which together would control a majority of the electorate.

52. See Frank, *op. cit.,* and for a more general discussion, James

O'Connor, "The Meaning of Economic Imperialism," a paper presented at the Center for the Study of Democratic Institutions, August 15, 1967, and part of a larger study which is forthcoming. For a discussion of the role of noneconomic institutions in U.S. expansion see Franz Schurmann, "On Imperialism," presented at the Center for the Study of Democratic Institutions, August 16, 1967, and Barnet, *op. cit.;* William Appleman Williams, "A Natural History of the American Empire," *Canadian Dimension,* IV, No. 3, pp. 12–17; Robert Smith, "The United States and Latin American Revolutions," *Journal of Inter-American Studies,* IV, No. 1 (January 1962), pp. 88–104.

53. An interesting critique of the sterile approach of the official Communist parties to Latin American politics is found in an article by Espartaco (pseud.), "Crítica del Modelo políticoeconómico de la Izquierda oficial," *Trimestre Económico,* No. 121 (Marzo 1964), pp. 67–92.

54. In recent years a number of outstanding Latin American social scientists have developed a sophisticated analysis of the nature and consequence of U.S. domination of Latin America and the new patterns of economic development. An excellent collection of essays is José Matos Mar, ed., *La dominación de América Latina* (Lima: Moncloa, 1968). Among the essays which effectively challenge the old dogmas are Fernando H. Cardoso and Enzo Faletto, "Dependencia y desarrollo en América Latina"; Osvaldo Sunkel, "Política nacional de desarrollo y dependencia externa"; and Celso Furtado, "La Hegemonía de los Estados Unidos y el Futuro de América Latina."

55. Probably the best known critique of Communist political strategy is Régis Debray, *Revolution in the Revolution?* (New York: Monthly Review Press, 1967). The discussion is continued in Paul Sweezy and Leo Huberman, eds., *Régis Debray and the Latin American Revolution* (New York: Monthly Review Press, 1968).

56. For a more detailed discussion of Communist policy as illustrated by the Chilean Party see my *Politics and Social Forces in Chilean Development* (Berkeley, Calif.: University of California Press, 1969), especially Ch. 4, "The Politics of the Popular Front."

57. As a result of the problems presented by the legal strategy, there have been a number of splits in the Brazilian Communist Party. A detailed critique of the internal party difficulties is in "Carta de Carlos Marighella al Ejecutivo del Partido Comunista

Brasileño Solicitando Su Renuncia," in *Pensamiento Crítico,* No. 7 (Agosto 1967), pp. 209–218.

58. See the OLAS documents in *Granma* (Weekly Review, English edition), August 27, 1967.

59. "OLAS: Resolutions of the Working Commissions of the First Conference," *ibid.* See especially the report of Committee One, "Armed Struggle Is the Fundamental Line," regarding the "national" bourgeoisie in Latin America.

60. The General Declaration of the First OLAS Conference noted:

"With the increase in economic growth during the years following independence, certain conditions favorable for the independent development of capitalism and a bourgeoisie in Latin America were created: but this development was paralyzed, deviated and deformed by imperialist penetrations. However, the organic weakness of the Latin American bourgeoisie, so far as breaking up the latifundia—which had to be done if agricultural production and the internal market were to be expanded—and the inter-connection of their class interests with the class interests of the landowners would force the bourgeoisie to form a closely united oligarchy with the landowners directly linked to the caste which controls the professional army—in whose hands the decisive levers of political power are concentrated.

The tremendous political gravitation that this imperialist penetration entails is self-evident. The same contradictions between the Latin American bourgeoisie and U.S. imperialism are developed under conditions of such subjection that they never take an antagonistic character. The impotence of the Latin American bourgeoisie is absolute."

61. For a detailed statistical breakdown of overseas U.S. economic expansion see Harry Magdoff, *The Age of Imperialism* (New York: Monthly Review Press, 1969).

United States Business
and Foreign Policy
in Latin America

An understanding of some aspects of U.S.-Latin American relations involves a discussion of (1) the argument of the neo-imperialist school, (2) U.S. capitalism's stake in Latin America, (3) the background of some important makers of U.S.-Latin American policy, (4) the interrelationship of U.S. policy and corporate capitalism, and (5) the impact of U.S. policy and business in Latin America.

The Argument of the Neo-Imperialist School [1]

In recent years the development of the multinational corporation has attracted increasing attention from economic analysts. The position of the neo-imperialist school of thought is that sooner or later the existence of multinational corporations will probably make the concept of national sovereignty irrelevant to underdeveloped countries, since U.S. corporations, by achieving economic hegemony within and through these multinational units, are increasingly shaping the over-all culture of the underdeveloped regions. Unlike the Marxists, the neo-imperialists regard such developments as advantageous; the multinational corporation is seen as the means of transmitting technology, know-how, modernization, etc.

Unfortunately, there is not much evidence to support the neo-imperialist thesis, either historically or in the contemporary world. In *Capitalism and Underdevelopment in Latin America,* Andre Gunder Frank has persuasively argued that historically Latin America's underdevelopment has been due to the advanced capitalist countries.[2] In brief, he points out that the imperialist countries have all along extracted wealth from the satellites for their

230 The United States and Latin America

own development, causing greater social and economic disparities despite changes in the nature of economic activity in the satellites. The result is that capitalism on a world scale produces a developing metropolis and an underdeveloped periphery, a process that is repeated on a national scale between the local metropolis and its domestic satellite regions and sectors. To test his hypothesis that it is the subordination of the satellites to the metropolis which causes underdevelopment, Frank presents evidence on the cases of "limited development" which have occurred in Latin America. Spurts of growth have occurred in those satellite regions that were less strongly tied to the metropolis and thus had the opportunity for greater autonomous development, especially industrial development (e.g., São Paulo and Minas Gerais). Likewise he argues effectively that it was in periods when the links between satellites and metropolis were weakest, during the First and Second World Wars and the Depression of the 1930's, that the greatest development occurred. Contrary to the neo-imperialist thesis, the history of Latin American development suggests that it has been independence from, not alliance or integration with, the metropolis which has permitted even such short-term development as has occurred.

In modern times the multinational corporation, far from being a positive element in dynamic and balanced economic growth, makes it difficult or impossible for national economic integration to take place within Latin American countries. U.S. corporations integrate the resources of Latin America—especially bauxite, oil, copper, etc. —into their own structures. The West Indian economist Lloyd Best, in his analysis of the role of the multinational corporation in the Caribbean, pointed out:

> . . . perhaps the most important characteristic of the regional economies is that they are dominated by a series of international corporations. Moreover these corporations form parts of wider international systems of resource allocation. This is true of the mining corporations, the sugar companies, the hotel chains, the banking, hire purchase and insurance houses, the advertising companies, the newspapers and the television and radio stations . . . in so far as there is harmonization among these concerns, it is for the most part achieved within the context of the metropolitan

economies where they are based, and not in the peripheral economies
of the countries where the companies actually operate. Moreover,
the policies of the corporations are determined by their parent
companies operating somewhere in the northern hemisphere and
not by the local need to integrate industries and to increase interdependence between different sectors of the economy. [The colonized
nation] is, therefore, hardly more than a locus of production made
up of a number of fragments held tenuously together largely by
government controls—themselves often borrowed from elsewhere.
In other words it is to be appreciated that it seems to be inherent
in the structure of the international corporations which operate in
the region that the Caribbean economies remain fragmented and
unintegrated. It is not merely a question of the flow of goods, though
that is important; it is principally that the corporations are the
channels through which metropolitan technology and forms of
organization are introduced into the economy with little reference
to the overall domestic factor market.[3]

A similar point is made by Glaucio Soares regarding what he refers
to as the "new industrialization" in Brazil.[4] Precisely because of
the growing importance of U.S.-owned corporations and because
of the transmission of modern capital-intensive technology, higher
levels of productivity are achieved without considerable expansion
of industrial employment. Soares, through detailed analysis and
comparison of census data, shows that the economy influenced by
externally integrated, modern corporations is able neither to ab-
sorb the growing urban populations in industrial production nor
to employ them in the administrative sector. The economy dominated by the multinational corporation becomes characterized by
chronic underemployment and unemployment.

The typical response of the neo-imperialist school to the problem of malintegration of the multinational corporations and the
underdeveloped economy is that taxation can perform the integrating function. In fact, however, where taxation has been tried, it
has not worked. In Chile taxation has been used to increase imports, not to integrate the companies into the local economy. In
addition, the tax mechanism does not work because, as Dudley
Seers has pointed out,[5] the large foreign-owned companies are
highly integrated and hence can choose to take their profits out

either at the branch plant or at the level of the home office. Thus if local taxes are high, the parent firm can charge the subsidiary high fees for managerial services, materials, and the like.

Corporation decisions are made with the aim of increasing the profits of the company as a whole, not to serve the interests of the country in which the branch plant is located. For example, U.S. subsidiaries are forced by the parent to buy materials from the parent corporation though in many cases it would be more profitable for the colonized country if these subsidiaries could purchase their supplies elsewhere. The dependent countries get only a small fraction of the total value added in the production and sales of the raw materials extracted by the giant U.S. corporations integrated into the U.S. industrial economy.

U.S. Capitalism's Stake in Latin America

Latin America has been and is now considered an important area for profit-making by U.S. corporations. Total U.S. assets and investments in Latin America amounted to $18.207 billion in 1965.[6] This represented approximately 17 percent of all U.S. assets and investments abroad. The great bulk of these investments and assets, $14.4 billion, or 79 percent, was accounted for by private investment.[7] Much more important from the point of view of U.S. businessmen and policy-makers are the annual *earnings* derived from their investments. Utopian liberals have on occasion argued that the U.S. government should finance the nationalization of U.S. enterprises, in the interests of both areas, by providing the capital for adequate compensation to U.S. investors. U.S. corporate executives and policy-makers have rejected the idea. The reason is obvious: the high earnings of investors more than make up for their initial outlay in a brief period of time. The U.S. government also prefers to have easy access to low-priced strategic materials; for example, the U.S. government saved, and Chile lost, $500 million on copper purchases during World War II through a price-fixing agreement. Between 1924 and 1951, one copper corporation, Braden, with an initial investment of $2.3 million, shipped over $324 million from Chile to help develop the United States.[8]

Between 1960 and 1965, income on U.S. investments in Latin

America totaled $6.4 billion. Of this amount, direct investments accounted for 73 percent of the income.[9] U.S. income from Latin America has risen considerably during this period. In 1960, U.S. income on investments in Latin America totaled $858 million. In 1965, it was $1.25 billion, a 45 percent rise in five years.[10] U.S. corporate capitalism's earnings are derived from a variety of economic sectors which it controls. For the years 1964 and 1965, direct investment earnings in smelting and mining accounted for $404 million; petroleum, $679 million; manufacturing, $875 million; other activities, $409 million.[11]

In countries like Brazil, Argentina, and Mexico, which have developed to a certain degree independently of the United States, U.S. investors are oriented toward capturing the existing market for manufactured goods (e.g., chemicals and transportation equipment). In the more underdeveloped countries, U.S. investment is oriented toward mining, petroleum, and raw materials. In neither case does U.S. investment create new dynamic enterprises that might compete with enterprises in the mother country.

Business Latin America cites current events in the auto industry to provide evidence of the trend toward capturing the market for manufactured goods:

> . . . Ford Motor Co. revealed last week that it is negotiating with Kaiser Industries to purchase the latter's interest in Willys Overland do Brasil. Ford is believed to have similar designs on Kaiser's holdings in Industrias Kaiser Argentina. IKA in turn acquired the automotive division of Siam di Tella two years ago. Volkswagen bought out Brazil's Vemag and has reportedly made a bid to acquire Automotriz Santa Fe in Argentina. . . .
>
> Ford, which now has about 14 percent of the Brazilian commercial vehicle market and has just entered the passenger car field by introducing its relatively high-priced Galaxie, would immediately obtain a strong position (about 33 percent of total sales) in the auto market if it succeeds in buying into Willys. IKA holds a similar attraction in Argentina, where such an acquisition would expand Ford's range to middle- and lower-price cars.[12]

The article explicitly notes that "In the main, these actions represent attempts to enlarge the companies' shares of the market and to consolidate resources, particularly production facilities." [13]

In 1965, to take a "typical year," U.S. earnings on direct investment in Latin America amounted to $1.17 billion. Of this, repatriated profits amounted to $888 million.[14]

In addition, for two years, 1964 and 1965, direct investment receipts of royalties and fees amounted to $319 million.[15] If we include such items as undistributed subsidiary earnings, we can add another half-billion dollars to the U.S. take.[16] Most of these earnings are returned to the U.S., at the expense of Latin American development, perpetuating backwardness and stagnation, depleting resources, and fostering concentration of wealth and great inequalities. We might consider this Latin America's "aid" to U.S. corporate development. Beyond this, a substantial proportion of funds used by U.S. capitalism to extract its profits originates in Latin America. In 1965, foreign funds borrowed by U.S. corporations through foreign affiliates amounted to $530 million.

Latin America has served the U.S. corporations equally well as a source of both raw and strategic materials, and as a profitable market for U.S. goods. Between 1960 and 1965, the United States amassed a favorable trade balance of $6.4 billion with Latin America,[17] the yearly figure doubling from $683 million in 1960 to $1.3 billion in 1965.[18] In this sense Latin America functions as a typical colony. Traditional commodities—raw materials, foodstuffs, and nonmanufactured goods—account for about three-fourths of total sales. Latin American dependence on trade of raw materials for manufactured goods has been one of the region's greatest problems, because of the decline in prices of primary goods and the deterioration of the terms of trade. From 1954 to 1960, the average price of Latin exports to the United States fell by some 20 percent, while the average price of Latin imports from the United States rose by more than 15 percent.[19] U.S. corporate capitalism pocketed the difference.

The colonial economies of Latin America, dependent on U.S. capitalism, continue to be highly vulnerable to sharp and sudden oscillations in commodity earnings: for example, the price of cocoa fell from 22.5 cents a pound in 1964, to 16.1 cents in 1965; sugar, 8.3 cents a pound in 1963, was worth only a fifth as much by 1966.[20]

Latin America ranks next to Western Europe as the largest market for U.S. goods. The category of "machinery and vehicles" has been accounting for about one-third of total U.S. exports, and in turn, 26 to 36 cents out of each dollar received from U.S. exports of commercial (nonmilitary) machinery and vehicles have come from Latin America.[21]

U.S. control over strategic raw materials in Latin America allows for the development of the United States as a world military and political power. Strategic raw materials are vital to the growth of numerous U.S. industries whose earnings and products have far-reaching effects in terms of the over-all performance of the U.S. economy. Copper production in Chile, over 90 percent of which is owned and controlled by U.S. corporations, is both an important component of U.S. expansionist war efforts, and a factor in the development of refineries, processing plants, electrical manufacturing, etc.

In short, we can say that U.S. business has an enormously important stake in Latin America. The region's underdeveloped, dependent, colonial economies are valuable sources of profit and materials to U.S. capitalism.

U.S. Policy-Makers

U.S. government policy toward Latin America has consistently favored corporate capital's interests over Latin American aspirations for economic development and social reform. But this is hardly surprising, given the business linkages of the makers of U.S. policy.

U.S. policy toward the Dominican Republic offers a well-known case in point. A study by two staff members of the North American Congress on Latin America research group points out that the key officials selected by President Johnson as advisers, and the key officials who made the actual decisions leading to the U.S. suppression of the popular revolution, were corporation lawyers and directors with a direct or indirect economic stake in the status quo ante:

> The powerful U.S. economic interests, with a stake in the outcome of Dominican events, most certainly had access to U.S. Administration officials and most likely expressed their deep concern. For example, prominent New Dealer Abe Fortas was a director of the Sucrest Corporation for 20 years, third largest East Coast

cane sugar refiner; Adolf A. Berle, Jr., known Latin American expert and advisor to several presidents, was Chairman of the Board of Sucrest for 18 years and is still a director and large stockholder; Ellsworth Bunker was Chairman, President, and 38-year Director of the second largest East Coast cane sugar refiner, National Sugar Refining Corporation (partially founded by his father), and one-time stockholder in a Dominican sugar mill; Roving Ambassador W. Averell Harriman is a "limited partner" in the banking house of Brown Brothers Harriman, which owns 5 percent of National Sugar's stock (his brother, E. Roland Harriman, sits on the board of National Sugar); J. M. Kaplan, molasses magnate, is a large con-tributor and influential advisor to many Democratic Party candi-dates and the ADA; Joseph S. Farland, State Department consultant and ex-U.S. Ambassador to the Dominican Republic, is a Director of South Puerto Rico Sugar Company; Roswell Gilpatrick, Deputy Secretary of Defense, is the managing executive partner of the Wall Street firm of Cravath, Swaine, and Moore, legal counsel to National Sugar; and Max Rabb, partner in the Wall Street firm of Strook, Strook, and Lavan, legal counsel for Sucrest, is an influential Johnson supporter. The above sugar refiners, plus the largest U.S. refiner, American Sugar, depend directly on the Dominican sugar and molasses supply for their operations. Any disruption in the supply would seriously hamper price stability. Even without these direct economic interests, it would be difficult for these gentlemen in their "neutral" decision making roles to escape the assumptions, inclinations, and priorities inculcated by their economic and social milieu.[22]

An analysis of key U.S. policy-makers in the Latin American area as a whole sheds further light on the relationship of U.S. policy and corporate capitalism. A recent study of the socioeconomic ca-reer patterns of thirty influential policy-makers who played a sub-stantial role in the development of U.S. policy between 1961 and 1965 suggests that their backgrounds hardly qualify them as sup-porters of nationalist popular revolution. Overwhelmingly edu-cated in private schools (the great majority from the Ivy League), half were either directly engaged in business or were corporation lawyers prior to entering policy-making positions. Over 70 percent of the policy-makers had been corporate directors or stockholders of major corporations or had served private corporations in a legal capacity.[23]

The key factors which influence political decision-makers have little to do with their "social origins." Much more important in determining an individual's politics are the values and outlooks which are shaped by career experiences. Social origins, family background and upbringing may *predispose* individuals toward a particular career; but it is the career and the concomitant political and social orientations and commitments that provide the frame of reference for political decisions. Institutional constraints pressure the individual to conform to the dominant values—with monetary incentives or by the threat of failure. Few if any career men escape these pressures. Corporate institutions politically socialize the upwardly mobile professionals, some of whom are later recruited into the politically elite. Hence when leading policy-makers carry out policies beneficial to the corporate ruling class, it is not due to some "secret conspiracy" or "cabal," but a direct outgrowth of the prior process of political socialization and selection. The result of this "filtering" process is that top public officials tend to share the outlook, values and interests of the corporate elite and make decisions accordingly.

U.S. Policy and Corporate Capitalism

A brief survey of actual policies which these corporate representatives have helped to shape will clearly illustrate their primary aim of protecting and enhancing the position of the U.S. corporate rich and maintaining over-all U.S. hegemony in the hemisphere. In particular, the Alliance for Progress and related legislative and administrative measures offer telling evidence on this point.

Amidst all of the reformist rhetoric of the Charter of Punta del Este, which established the Alliance, there is a significant clause pushed by U.S. policy-makers which committed the Latin governments to the promotion "of conditions that will encourage the flow of foreign investments." To secure these investments, Congress passed the Foreign Assistance Act in 1961, amended in 1963 to prohibit Congressional appropriations to benefit a state that fails to make "speedy compensation . . . in convertible foreign exchange . . . to the full value" of any property expropriated from U.S. citizens.[24] Any Latin country which did not guarantee U.S.

investments and the "rights" of U.S. investors both to convert their profits to dollars and to remit them was to be cut off from all aid as of December 31, 1966. According to the 1961 Foreign Assistance Act as amended in Section 620 (d), U.S. aid is not to be furnished to any enterprise that will compete with a U.S. business, unless the country concerned agrees to limit the export of the products to the United States to 20 percent of output.[25]

Most of the so-called aid does not go for development and reform. Speaking at a U.N. Development Program session, Paul Hoffman, its chief administrator, stated: "The gross flow of such [development] assistance in 1966 . . . was nearly $12 billion. However, deducting from the gross figure repayments on loans, interest payments, dividends, private investment, and other relevant items, we find . . . only about $3.2 billion." [26] On the question of trade, the U.N. Conference on Trade and Development (UNCTAD) agenda in 1968 took note that the "non-tariff barriers, of special importance to low income countries, have not been significantly reduced." [27] Regarding aid, UNCTAD noted, "Taking the developed countries as a whole, their aid—mostly in the form of loans—declined from 8.7 percent of GNP, to .72 percent in 1965 and the downward trend continues." [28]

The 1961 Foreign Assistance Act stipulated that U.S. aid be used to favor the U.S. economy. Latin Americans cannot even shop in other markets since virtually all U.S. loans are now tied to purchases of goods and services in the United States. Ninety-five percent of AID expenditures for machinery and vehicles, and 90 percent of all AID commodity expenditures, were made to U.S. corporations.[29] The same practice is followed by the Inter-American Development Bank. The Alliance goals of social reform and economic development were assumed to be compatible with the more fundamental aim of securing a primary role for U.S. investment; the latter purpose imposed the limits within which fulfillment of the other goals was discussed. Evaluating the Alliance for Progress from this vantage point, one could agree with one of the foremost international bankers, David Rockefeller, when he said in 1965, "The climate of investment is improving." [30]

In terms of its primary functions of protecting existing investment and its earning power, and creating new opportunities for profit-making, the Alliance for Progress amounted in short to a government-administered welfare program for U.S. investors. Increased U.S. government funds were used to subsidize weakly based Latin governments which were not capable of implementing internal changes. In return, Latin governments receiving Alliance funds contracted agreements with the U.S. government and U.S. firms which created a favorable climate for investment and increased their profit returns.

At the time the Alliance for Progress began operations, the Cuban Revolution had created a great fear among the international investment community. A sizable flight of capital (estimates ran as high as $1 billion per year) threatened to bring down the already bankrupt Latin economies. In the fiscal year preceding the inception of the Alliance, 1960–1961, private direct investment had been $214 million. In 1961–1962 (the year the Cubans defeated the U.S.-directed mercenaries at the Bay of Pigs, and Castro moved toward socialism), investment was minus $24 million; in 1962–1963, it was $11 million; in 1963–1964, $90 million; in 1964–1965, $207 million.[31]

Impact of U.S. Policy on Latin America

U.S. investment "recovery"—still less than 1960–1961—coincided with three interrelated developments which created a more encouraging climate for foreign investment: (1) the installation of military dictators who closely identified with the outlook of U.S. investors; (2) the repression and defeat of several reform and revolutionary movements in Latin America; (3) the introduction of measures designed to guarantee U.S. investments, increase profits, and liberalize profit-remittance opportunities.

It should be pointed out right from the beginning that there were divergencies among U.S. policy-makers, particularly between Congress and the State Department, over the best way to promote investor interests. Some Congressmen took a hard line, urging the issuance of ultimatums to Latin governments that either they proceed immediately according to a prescribed path or face severe sanctions. The State Department took a more strategic view, and urged the adoption of flexible tactics in the face of adverse circumstances, in order to gain time. In 1962, opposing the inflexible approach to defending U.S. investors abroad, Dean Rusk remarked: "I don't believe the United States can afford to stake its interests in other countries on a particular private investment in a particular situation. We have to keep working at these things." The Secretary of State took the long view: ". . . I would hope we would not use legislative mandates which in effect would cause us to break relations with important countries over particular points of policy, because in the longer run, it seems to me, that leads us into many blind alleys."[32] In other words, rather than promoting the interests of any particular business group, the strategy was to create stable satellites throughout the hemisphere. The State Department's mode of operation subsequently proved quite successful, as the Brazilian case illustrates. On February 16, 1962, Governor Leonel Brizola expropriated the property of the International Telephone and Telegraph Corporation. Congress clamored for economic sanctions in order to protect foreign investors. The State Department did better. It pressured Brizola to pay the companies the price they desired, in return for which the U.S. government agreed to reimburse the Brazilian government out of Alliance for Progress funds.[33]

U.S. corporations dictated State Department policy and substantially benefited. Rusk himself admitted that the policy adopted was the result of U.S. investor influence. The key to the paradox of U.S. corporations supporting the expropriation action of an apparently left-wing Latin nationalist was offered by Rusk: "A number of them [U.S. corporations] would prefer to sell out their utility holdings and then reinvest in industries in the same country that have access to a free market situation. This [nationalization with indemnification] is on the initiative of some of the companies." [34] Because U.S. corporations determined U.S. policy, Alliance for Progress funds were spent in expropriating unprofitable U.S. firms at above market prices. In turn, U.S. corporations invested the receipts in more profitable activities, and also gained special dispensations on profit remittance. The success of the flexible approach in this incident put the State Department in a position to pursue further its strategic goal, elimination of the Brazilian nationalist government. A sudden break in relations in 1962 as advocated by parochial Congressmen might have secured neither benefits to the utility investors nor a favorable situation for the rest of the U.S. corporate community. By maintaining relations and working within Brazil, the United States was able to participate in the overthrow of the Brazilian government and to influence the new military dictatorship. The outcome was a government that more than met the criteria of the U.S. Congressmen regarding the protection and encouragement of U.S. corporations.[35] An investment guarantee treaty was signed in which Brazil agreed to surrender its right to nationalize U.S. property. Controls on profit remittances and tax concessions were considerably loosened. Thus, within two years, flexibility (i.e., the manipulation of Alliance funds), had clearly proved its usefulness.

Another means by which the Alliance for Progress serves U.S. investors is by servicing past debts. In striving to maximize profits in Latin America, U.S. and other foreign creditors had overextended themselves. The external debt of the Latin countries had grown to the point where most of them were unable to meet their payments. The Alliance stepped in to rescue the financiers: estimates of the proportion of Alliance funds used to benefit foreign creditors run from 25 to 40 percent of disbursements during the first four years.[36] Alliance loans to cover external debts helped to maintain the appearance of solvency in Latin America—but, of course, involved new debts and additional loans. By 1964 Latin America's debt had increased to $11 billion; foreign debt service rose from 5.5 percent of balance of payments receipts in 1956 to 15.4 percent in 1964.[37] The effect of all this was to further limit the autonomy of Latin economic policy-makers and increase the leverage of U.S. policy-makers in promoting a favorable climate for U.S. investors. Between 1961 and 1965, profit remittances increased by some $200 million a year, and annual royalties and fees by some $60 million.[38] The over-all effect can be seen in the development of the Investment Guarantee Program between 1963 and 1966.[39]

In 1963, Argentina did not approve the program's sections regarding expropriation and war risk. By September 1966, the whole Investment Guarantee Program had been accepted.

In 1963, Brazil had not signed. By 1966, it had approved the whole program.

In 1963, Bolivia refused to sign sections guaranteeing investments against revolution and insurrection. In 1966, it agreed to these guarantees.

In 1963, Guyana had not signed. By 1966, the whole program had been accepted.

In 1963, Chile refused to sign sections dealing with investment guarantees against expropriation, revolution, insurrection, etc. In 1966, under President Frei and the Christian Democrats, it approved the whole program. Frei not only guaranteed the giant U.S. copper companies against nationalization, but significantly lowered their tax rate, overpaid for Chile's share of one of the least profitable and smaller mines, and has used the national armed forces to guarantee that the copper workers' wage demands do not cut too deeply into earnings.[40]

Similar changes occurred for Ecuador, Honduras, and Paraguay.

The installation or promotion of friendly governments by U.S. policy-makers was instrumental in increasing the number of signatories. The military dictators of Brazil, Argentina, Bolivia, Honduras, and Ecuador proved to be such staunch defenders of U.S. investors and upholders of U.S. investment guarantees that AID has been able to reduce its insurance rate in the Investment Guarantee Program.

As of September 1966, the AID Specific Risk Investment Guarantee Program covered seventy-five countries, including almost all of the Latin American countries. Under its terms, the President of the United States assures U.S. investors protection in whole or part against any or all of the following risks: (1) inability to convert into U.S. dollars other currencies, or credits in such currencies, received as earnings or profits from the approved project, as repayment or return of the investment therein, in whole or in part, or as compensation for the sale or disposition of all or any part thereof; (2) loss of approved project investment, in whole or in part, due to expropriation or confiscation by a foreign government; (3) loss due to war, revolution, or insurrection.[41] In addition, there exist "extended risks guarantees which protect investors against losses occurring from any normal business risk in certain situations." [42] The Guaranteed Investment treaties thus provide, for all intents and purposes, a guaranteed annual profit for investors. The supposed risk which investors take and for which they earn their profits is nonexistent.

Specific clauses of the Investment Guarantee Program have larger implications; for example, in order for a corporation to be eligible, U.S. citizens must own over 50 percent of the stock— thus ensuring U.S. ownership and control of new investment.[43] Under another section of the program (Section 231 of the Foreign Assistance Act of 1961), in accord with its major goals of promoting capitalist expansion and corporate profits, AID has authority to pay up to 50 percent of the costs of a survey of profit-making opportunities in the less developed countries.[44] Among the criteria governing AID investment guarantee policy is the stipulation that "The investment must benefit the economy of the foreign country, with emphasis on the private sector." The judge in this matter of benefits is the same private investor: "In evaluating the effect of each investment upon the economy of the underdeveloped country, heavy reliance will be placed upon the representations of the investor and upon views of the AID mission." [45]

The link between the U.S. government and U.S. investors vis-à-vis the Latin American governments (and all the rest of the colonial "third world") is explicit and concrete. Any attempt by these governments to exercise their sovereignty by expropriating private U.S. investors immediately puts them in confrontation with the U.S. government; such internal acts of state automatically take on a supranational character. In this specific concrete sense, the United States has escalated the class struggle to the international plane.

Official governmental agencies are not the only means of implementing U.S. corporate capitalism's policies. The U.S. trade-union leadership, AFL-CIO, in cooperation with the CIA and U.S. corporations in Latin America, has played a complementary role. Together, they have trained and financed an apparatus to subvert and destroy militant unions that defend their national and members' interests and to collaborate with dictators and pro-U.S. business interests. The National Student Association, financed by, and in association with, U.S. governmental agencies, served as a transmission belt for propaganda and as a means of subverting Latin organizations and their leaders. The Congress for Cultural Freedom, partially financed by the CIA, operated on the intellectual front, its intellectuals in uniform driving home the "lessons" of anti-communism. The Institute of International Education and U.S. universities have instituted programs to depoliticize Latin American universities, attempting to reduce opposition to repressive governments and robbing the downtrodden populace of one of its important tribunes.

From the Latin side, the most successful transmission belts of U.S. policy are military dictators, like the late René Barrientos and Castelo Branco, and in general, the status-quo-oriented politicians and social forces, whose installation and/or maintenance in power has been strongly encouraged by the government and corporate policy-makers of the United States. Over two-thirds of the Latin countries are ruled by military dictators or military-controlled civilian governments. Political terror and assassination are prominent features in two countries in which direct U.S. intervention took place, Guatemala and the Dominican Republic.[46] U.S. intervention resulted in the establishment of unpopular governments which increasingly relied on the police, army, and the U.S. to maintain "order"—and the status quo. Little has been done in the way of agrarian reform: 5 percent of the landholders still own over 70 percent of the land. In Chile, supposedly a showcase for U.S. development efforts, only 20,000 families have received land in the first five years of the Alliance for Progress—leaving 342,000 families still waiting for Frei's "revolution in liberty" to mature.[47] Despite all the State Department's propaganda and guarantees to "free enterprise," the figures on the Latin economies indicate continuing stagnation: over-all per-capita GNP growth for Latin America for 1966 and 1967 was 1.6 percent, well below the minimum goal of 2.5 percent per-capita growth called for in the Charter of Punta del Este.[48] Of the eighteen countries, only five reached the minimum goal, while several (Venezuela, Argentina, Uruguay, Paraguay, Haiti) had negative growth rates for the two-year period.[49] The flourishing of U.S. corporate capital's interests has curtailed the constriction of Latin economic and social development and fostered the growth of Latin instability and authoritarian government. The Latin American poor get poorer; and the rich, especially the foreign rich, get richer.

Because the U.S. multinational corporation has developed a global perspective, the U.S. government has had to develop a global foreign policy. The main concern of the multinational corporations is profits and economic hegemony; any economic development that takes place in the underdeveloped countries as a result of their activity is incidental. It is a myth that Latin America needs U.S. foreign investment, since the U.S.-owned multinational corporations mobilize most of their capital in Latin America through local earnings and loans, and since the export of profits from Latin America is greater than the net inflow of new capital. Rather, a strong case can be made that Latin American financial resources have been used to perpetuate foreign exploitation leading to the decapitalization of the Latin economies. Only if Latin America took the road of socialism—that is, nationalizing the financial, industrial, and agricultural sectors—could it begin to break out of underdevelopment and realize its economic potentialities.

NOTES

1. For the material in this section, I am largely indebted to Professor James O'Connor, who is preparing a comprehensive study of imperialism which will greatly add to our understanding of the subject.
2. Andre Gunder Frank, *Capitalism and Underdevelopment in Latin America* (New York: Monthly Review Press, 1967). See also his "Aid or Exploitation," in *Latin America: Underdevelopment or Revolution* (New York and London: Monthly Review Press, 1969).
3. Lloyd Best, "Size and Survival," *New World Quarterly* (Gurjana Independence Issue, 1966), p. 61.
4. Glaucio Ary Dillon Soares, "The New Industrialization and the Brazilian Political System," in James Petras and Maurice Zeitlin, *Latin America: Reform or Revolution?* (New York: Fawcett, 1968), pp. 186–201.
5. Dudley Seers, "Big Companies in Small Countries," *Kyklos,* XVI, No. 4 (1963).
6. *Survey of Current Business,* 46, No. 9 (September 1966), p. 40.

7. *Ibid.*

8. Mario Vera Valenzuela, *La política económica del cobre en Chile* (Santiago, Chile: Ediciones de la Universidad de Chile, 1961).

9. *Survey of Current Business,* 46, No. 9 (September 1966), p. 30.

10. *Ibid.*

11. *Ibid.,* p. 35.

12. *Business Latin America* (weekly report to managers of Latin American operations), May 25, 1967, p. 161.

13. *Ibid.*

14. *Survey of Current Business,* 46, No. 9 (September 1966), p. 35.

15. *Ibid.,* p. 38.

16. *Ibid.,* p. 35.

17. *Ibid.,* p. 37.

18. *Survey of Current Business,* 46, No. 6 (June 1966), pp. 36, 37.

19. David Pollock, "Development of Commodity Trade Between Latin America and the United States," *Economic Bulletin for Latin America* (ECLA-UN, Santiago de Chile), VI, No. 2 (October 1961), p. 59.

20. *Alliance for Progress Weekly Newsletter,* VI, No. 3 (January 15, 1968), p. 1.

21. Pollock, *op. cit.,* p. 62.

22. Fred Goff and Michael Locker, *The Violence of Domination: U.S. Power and the Dominican Republic* (mimeo), (New York: North American Congress on Latin America).

23. Kraig Schwartz, "The Socio-Economic Career Patterns of 30 Persons Who Helped Shape U.S. Policy Toward Latin America 1961–1965" (unpublished research report). The study is based on an examination of seventeen policy positions and the individuals who held them. The Department of Defense, the Department of State, and Presidential appointees are included.

24. The Foreign Assistance Act of 1961 as amended, Section 620(e)(1), in U.S., House, Committee on Foreign Affairs, *Regional and Other Documents Concerning United States Relations with Latin America* (Washington, D.C.: Government Printing Office, 1966), p. 143, quoted in J. P. Morray, "The United States and Latin America," in Petras and Zeitlin, *op. cit.,* p. 109.

25. *Ibid.*

26. *Alliance for Progress Weekly Newsletter,* VI, No. 7 (February 12, 1968), p. 3.

27. *Alliance for Progress Weekly Newsletter,* VI, No. 3 (January 15, 1968), p. 1.

28. *Ibid.*
29. *U.S. Statistical Abstract,* 1967, p. 827.
30. "The Fourth Year: The Role of Private Business," *Inter-American Affairs,* XX (Autumn 1966), p. 71.
31. *Ibid.,* p. 73.
32. Quoted in John Hickey, "The First Year: Business," *Inter-American Economic Affairs,* XVI (Summer 1962), p. 50.
33. *Ibid.,* p. 59, *passim.*
34. *Ibid.,* p. 64.
35. See Carl Oglesby, "Free World Empire," in Carl Oglesby and Richard Shaull, *Containment and Change* (New York: MacMillan, 1967), esp. pp. 83–97.
36. "The Fourth Year: The Fatal Barrier to Growth and Reform: Latin America's Economic Philosophy," *Inter-American Economic Affairs,* XX (Autumn 1966), p. 63.
37. *Ibid.,* p. 58.
38. *Ibid.,* p. 73.
39. Data drawn from *Aids to Business (Overseas Investment),* U.S. Department of State, Agency for International Development, Memorandum to Businessmen (Washington, D.C.: Government Printing Office, 1963), p. 44, and *Specific Risk Investment Guaranty Handbook* (revised), U.S. Department of State, Agency for International Development (Washington, D.C.: Government Printing Office, October 1966) pp. 50–51.
40. James Beckett, "Chile's Mini-Revolution," *Commonweal,* December 29, 1967, pp. 406–408; "The Fourth Year," in *op. cit.,* p. 68; James Petras, *Chilean Christian Democracy,* (Berkeley, Calif.: University of California Institute of International Studies, 1967).
41. *Specific Risk Investment Guaranty Handbook,* p. 41.
42. AID press release, March 14, 1966.
43. *Ibid.,* p. 5.
44. *Aids to Business,* p. 8.
45. *Specific Risk Investment Guaranty Handbook,* p. 13.
46. On Guatemala see Eduardo Galeano, "With the Guerrillas in Guatemala," in Petras and Zeitlin, *op. cit.,* pp. 370–380. On the Dominican Republic, see James Petras, "Dominican Republic: Revolution and Restoration," in Marvin Gettleman and David Mermelstein, *The Great Society Reader* (New York: Random House, 1967), pp. 390–413.
47. Report of the Consejo Interamericano de la Alianza para el Progreso (CIAP), *El esfuerzo interno y las necesidades de*

Chile, OEA/Ser. H/XIV, CIAP/178 (Washington, D.C.: Pan American Union, 1969).

48. *Alliance for Progress Weekly Newsletter,* VI, No. 4 (January 22, 1968), p. 1.

49. *Ibid.*

United States Policy
Toward Agrarian Reform*

One of the most striking characteristics of Latin America is its un-balanced social and economic development, as seen in the over-whelming economic-social-political power held by the few com-pared to the poverty and powerlessness of the many. Historically, the power position of elites in Latin America is rooted in agrarian-based societies, more specifically in land ownership. Thus social movements and political analysts concerned with the gross in-equalities in Latin America have of necessity focused on the issue of land reform. Upholders of the status quo, on the other hand, have sought to prevent or limit changes in land tenure by stressing economic factors affecting aggregate output. Neither proponents nor opponents of Latin American agrarian reform and agricultural development, however, can ignore the role played by the United States, the paramount political and economic power in the Western Hemisphere and a decisive force in shaping Latin American agri-cultural development. An analysis of the attitudes and policies of U.S. officials toward agrarian reform provides a basis for evaluat-ing the U.S. contribution to social change and the democratic re-structuring of Latin American society. We take as focus for our analysis the extent to which the United States has followed a re-distributionist or productionist approach to agricultural problem-solving. Specifically we intend to examine the following propo-sitions:

(1) that both the redistributionist (structural reform) and pro-ductionist (incremental change) schools of thought exist

* Written with Robert LaPorte, Jr. The authors wish to acknowledge the assistance of Jeffrey C. Rinehart of the Institute of Public Administration, Pennsylvania State University, in the preparation of this study.

among U.S. policy-makers, with the latter in the ascendancy since the Kennedy Administration;

(2) that this shift in approach has affected the type of programs and projects financed by the United States;

(3) that the productionist approach has been ineffective in significantly raising agricultural production, increasing production of food, and reducing Latin America's dependence on food importation;

(4) that the Alliance for Progress's original aim of radically restructuring Latin American agriculture has been repudiated.

The structural reform strategy for dealing with uneven development involves social mobilization, the institutionalization of political power, and the drafting and implementation of legislation to redistribute income so that benefits accrue more evenly.[1] The other view of Latin American development sees the solution largely in terms of "incremental" changes, based mainly on providing greater incentives to current investors. These two approaches are diametrically opposed to each other in terms of rationale, strategy, and "clientele," even though on occasion similar tactics may be adopted.[2]

Two Approaches: Redistribution vs. Incremental Change

In the societies of Latin America, agrarian reform has been very widely considered an important component of any policy of structural change. Agrarian reform, however, has been construed in sharply varying ways. To some it entails the distribution of large landholdings among the landless and small farmers. To others it means better utilization of existing tenure patterns to increase the products available for consumption and export. Still another view interprets agrarian reform as primarily involving improvement of transportation, communication, and storage facilities to expedite the flow of farm products to marketing outlets.

Even those who agree in favoring the redistributive approach may differ on whether agrarian reform policy calls for distribution of public or unused lands, or division of large private estates, or consolidation of small farms; and on whether the land is to be obtained through expropriation, taxation, confiscation, or a combination of these measures. Accompanying programs may or may not include technical modernization, increased educational facilities, diversification of products, and development of communications.[3]

In our use of the term, agrarian reform involves both a redistribution of political and social power and a fundamental reordering of the economic structure of the agricultural sector, since land ownership in Latin America involves social and political power in addition to the control of economic resources. Landholding and the style of life which accompanies it not only confer social status and prestige, but, through traditional paternalistic social relations and physical coercion, confer the power to control the political behavior of the peasants, who are thus little more than pawns in the hands of the large landholders. Possessing wealth, status, and the captive votes of the rural areas, the landowners are able to influence executives, legislatures, bureaucracies, and judiciaries. Through their control over political institutions they influence taxation, government expenditures, and the use of the police and army, all toward the end of perpetuating their own privileged position.[4]

Because changes in land tenure can have multiple effects on the distribution of political, economic, and social power, it is scarcely surprising that there is disagreement among scholars and political men over the employment of a comprehensive approach to agrarian reform. Some writers see Latin America's agricultural problems largely in terms of a more efficient use of the land and increasing technical capacity—in essence, as merely a matter of technology. The ends of such a policy would be to expand production and to secure a larger share of the export market. "Development" and reform would refer to the building of farm-to-market access roads, better marketing facilities, production of cheap fertilizers, importation of farm machinery, rationalization of credit, diversification of output to provide a better balance between supply and demand in the country and, perhaps, a broadening of the export base. Largely premised on the maintenance of existing land-tenure patterns, the only type of land distribution consistent with this policy would be the development of previously uncultivated areas. The underlying assumption is that the over-all growth of the agricultural sector will indirectly cause the income of small farmers and peasants to rise, along with educational and health levels. This strategy of modernization-from-above (the gradualist approach) argues that development can best occur through increased production *without* land redistribution. Those not receiving land in the countryside would migrate to the city as literate workers, thus supplying a labor market for industrial development.

Unfortunately, while intense exploitation of the peasantry and rural labor force has been commonplace throughout Latin America during the better part of four centuries, the landowners have not utilized the economic surplus to industrialize society. While in Europe, the Soviet Union, Japan, and even the United States, coercion of the agricultural population to extract the economic surplus was accompanied by rapid industrialization, this has not been the case in Latin America. Foreign investors and Latin elites have exported their earnings to the industrial capitalist world, invested in land, commerce, and real estate, and engaged in speculative activity. Historically the Latin American landowners have not matched Barrington Moore's description of the modernizers-from-above: they have exploited and coerced but they have hardly "developed."

Obviously, some elements or techniques of the two approaches are not mutually exclusive and could be integrated into a single program for agricultural development. The fact that the "client" group emphasized is different in each case, however, presents an insurmountable obstacle to such integration. The redistributionists, concerned with bettering the conditions of the majority of the agrarian population as rapidly as possible, stress land reform as a necessary precondition for agricultural development. For the productionists, on the other hand, the immediate needs of the rural populace are not primary; at best they may assume that these needs will ultimately be met by the increased production achieved through technical innovation. But the social forces that would be called on to implement the productionist approach suggest such a result is unlikely, for whereas the redistribution strategy depends on mobilization of heretofore ignored segments of the population, the productionists work through existing channels and institutions. Thus, while modernization-from-above may bring greater technical efficiency and raise production, it will not alter, but probably enhance, the economic, political, and social resources of the few who own land at the expense of the many who work it.[5] The modernization-from-below strategy of the redistributionists sees agrarian reform as an aspect of social change that will eradicate inequality in rights and income, thereby minimizing inequalities of access to the political system.

Agrarian Reform and Agricultural Development: U.S. Views, 1961–1968

The official U.S. view of agricultural development and agrarian reform in Latin America derives from three sources, the executive (President and executive staff), legislative (Congress), and the operating or administrative (Agency for International Development field staff). Although the Chief Executive has responsibility, in practice legislative intent as well as administrative interpretation play major roles in both shaping and implementing U.S. policies abroad. Even though conflict occurred over the formulation of U.S. policy on Latin American agricultural development/agrarian reform in the 1960's (there were structural reformers and advocates of gradual change among each of the three policy-determining groups), as well as over the implementation of policy in the field, a degree of consensus did develop early in the Kennedy Administration favoring "gradualism" and "production."

The statements of U.S. officials since the inception of the Alliance for Progress in 1961 reveal a gradual shift from the redistributionist to the productionist outlook. The extent of the shift can be clearly seen by contrasting the first Punta del Este Conference in August 1961, with the second, held in April 1967. In his message to the first conference, President Kennedy called for

. . . full recognition of the right of all the people to share fully in our progress. For there is no place in democratic life for institutions which benefit the few while denying the needs of the many, even though the elimination of such institutions may require far-reaching and difficult changes such as land reform and tax reform and a vastly increased emphasis on education and health and housing.[6]

The introduction to the Charter which was subsequently drawn up encouraged

> . . . programs of comprehensive agrarian reform leading to the effective transformation, where required, of unjust structures and systems of land tenure and use, with a view to replacing latifundia and dwarf holdings by an equitable system of land tenure so that, with the help of timely and adequate credit, technical assistance, and facilities for the marketing and distribution of products, the land will become for the man who works it the basis of his economic stability, the foundation of his increasing welfare, and the guarantee of his freedom and dignity.[7]

This section of the Charter explicitly stated that structural reforms, including "effective transformation . . . of land tenure," were necessary. The efficacy of technical assistance and infrastructure development in raising rural standards of living would be contingent upon these reforms.

The 1967 Punta del Este Conference, while paying lip service to the need to guarantee the *campesino* full participation in the economic and social life of his country, makes no mention of the prior necessity of structural changes:

> In order to promote a rise in the standard of living of farmers and an improvement in the condition of Latin American rural people and their full participation to economic and social life, it is necessary to give greater dynamism to agriculture in Latin America.[8]

These goals were to be realized by taking steps toward

> . . . increasing food production in the Latin American countries in sufficient volume and quality to provide adequately for their population and to meet world needs for food to an ever-increasing extent, as well as toward improving agricultural productivity and toward diversification of crops, which will assure the best possible competitive conditions for such production.[9]

Thus, by 1967, executive emphasis had clearly shifted from the structural reform goal of land redistribution to the productionist goal of increasing food output and thus securing a larger share of the world agricultural market. Modernization-from-below was shelved in favor of infrastructure development—in favor, that is, of providing incentives and subsidies to improve the efficiency of large landholders.[10] Limited expropriation of marginal and previously uncultivated land would provide a few new farmers with an opportunity to benefit directly in these changes.

While the contrast between 1962 and 1967 suggests a dramatic change in U.S. policy, the shift in fact took place slowly and can perhaps best be viewed over the entire five-year period. Events which marked this shift in policy occurred as early as 1962. From the beginning, Congressional opinion was generally hostile to the redistributionist policy of the Kennedy Administration. A report on agricultural development by the Subcommittee on Inter-American Economic Relationships of the Joint Economic Committee stressed the need for "increased agricultural productivity, and still more increased agricultural productivity." [11] The Subcommittee felt that land reform was a dubious means to use in improving agriculture. Echoing the traditional landowners' elitist mistrust of the common man, the Subcommittee spoke of the danger of the "illiterate or semi-literate cropper":

> It is frequently asserted, and even too frequently taken for granted, that an essential first step in increasing agricultural productivity and output of food and fiber for consumption and export in most of the South American countries lies in changing the landownership pattern.
>
> While the distribution of land to landless farmers may have justification on the grounds of equity and establishing the basis for free democracy, as land reform, the program ought not to rest exclusively on these grounds.
>
> The danger is that the illiterate, or semi-illiterate cropper on hearing of these plans will assume that he is soon to be freed from his traditional quasi-feudal role and have for his very own a plot in an Elysian field.[12]

As a result of their hearings and staff studies, the Subcommittee called for an "official clarification" of the meaning and objectives of agrarian reform in the context of the Alliance for Progress, stating that a review of U.S. policy was not only in order but imperative. They were especially concerned with minimizing the participation of the U.S. government. The Subcommittee set forth its own guidelines:

> The primary objective of agrarian reform measure *should at all times be increased agricultural productivity*. . . .

> Land reform is, thus, not exclusively a tenure problem but a problem of improved farming practices generally. . . .

> The objective of land tenure changes is not to be punitively directed against large landholdings or absentee landowners as such: on the contrary, existing property rights under law are to be respected. . . .

> The programing and administration of agrarian reform is, and must remain, an internal matter for each of the several nations. . . .

> Certainly the United States is not pressing for preconceived patterns of land tenure or agrarian reform; least of all can it undertake unilaterally to assure individual croppers of its support of ultimate landownership, no matter how seemingly meritorious cases may be. . . .

> As a first step in land reform and possible redistribution, the respective participating countries should look first to public lands and lands not presently under cultivation. . . .[13]

The emphasis was on: (1) production; (2) improving farm practices generally; (3) protecting existing property rights (including those of absentee owners); (4) undermining attempts to reorient U.S. policy away from support of the big landowners (whose tenure is an "internal matter"); and (5) use of public lands for broadening land ownership (apparently not an "internal matter"). Since nowhere in the Alliance for Progress Charter was land redistribution set down as a sufficient condition for modernization— it is always linked to technical assistance, increased credit, better education, and improved roads and marketing facilities, all of which are seen as factors in bringing about increased productivity —the Subcommittee's strictures were obviously intended to further limit the influence of the structural reformers. As a result, even in official definitions of the term "land reform," certain productionist themes are clear. For example, the Land Policy Statement, issued by the U.S. Agency for International Development (AID) on August 28, 1962, considered land reform to include only: (1)

natural resource surveys and inventories; (2) economic studies and research of land uses and tenure patterns in relation to productivity, efficiency, and social problems; (3) physical improvement of the land, e.g., via fertilizers, reclamation projects; (4) land-tenure adjustments through institutional changes in the adjustment of people to the land; (5) supervised agricultural credit; and (6) training and educational programs for officials and farmers.[14] AID was limited to providing capital assistance in the form of loans and grants to help defray certain administrative costs of land reform programs; that is, it could help finance the cost of supervised agricultural credit programs, land reclamation projects, and public facilities in areas where land reforms were being executed.[15] However, the Social Progress Trust Fund, instituted during the Eisenhower Administration and incorporated within the Alliance machinery, was explicitly barred from allocating funds for the purchase of agricultural land.[16]

AID's interpretation of Congressional intent regarding agricultural programs, its emphasis on support for discrete projects rather than broad reform programs, and the pressure of U.S. and Latin American landowning elites made it likely that the prohibition against the use of U.S. funds to purchase land would be carried out in practice. Assistance for gradual change (for example, credit and technical assistance given to colonists who settled new lands) continued. Executive as well as administrative accommodation to conservative pressure from Congress would seem to indicate that productionist values took precedence over those of the redistributionists at a very early stage. If this is the case, then the continuity in policy between the Kennedy and Johnson years is greater than suspected—in the direction of a more conservative agricultural development policy. There is considerable additional evidence to substantiate such a judgment.

The legislation authorizing the Alliance for Progress gave priority to agrarian reform measures. Title VI of the Foreign Assistance Act of 1962 directed the President to "assist in fostering measures of agrarian reform, including colonization and *redistribution of land, with a view to insuring a wider and more equitable distribution of the ownership* of land." [17]

The actual meaning of these general policy objectives was

clarified by Lincoln Gordon (then a consultant to the President's Task Force on Latin America and later Ambassador to Brazil and Regional Assistant Secretary under President Johnson). The agrarian reform policies which would be supported by the United States through the Inter-American Development Bank clearly flow from the strategy of modernization-from-above:

> *Senator Kuchel:* . . . It was suggested that by reason of the veto which the U.S. has in the two-thirds loan situation that we would be interested in the internal affairs of those countries when we made loans, perhaps to the extent of indicating our belief on land policy. Is that true?
>
> *Lincoln Gordon:* . . . I think it is a little more complex than that. . . . The idea is to try to force the owners, if they don't want to pay the taxes [on the land], to sell the land and make it available for ownership by smaller farmers as a result. This also seems to be a very useful kind of redistribution. Our thought is that the Bank would in such cases make loans available for helping the small farmer to get properly settled on the land. They would be for agricultural credit perhaps in certain cases it is for inaccessible land, for building access roads, for assistance to cooperatives in developing marketing and storage facilities for food and other agricultural crops and things of that kind.[18]

There are two typical themes in Gordon's statement. First, that land reform will be accomplished by taxing owners into selling unprofitable land. The idea of taxing owners in order to make them productive and efficient is certainly an important component of the productionist approach. But Gordon's notion that poor or landless *campesinos* will be in a position to acquire those lands which will be put on the market surely overlooks the obvious; other large landowners, and even industrialists not presently connected with the agrarian sector who want a hedge against inflation, are in a far better position to purchase land made available by the process he mentions. The second theme is that the external assistance given should be used for development of infrastructure. Later in his testimony, having made clear what he means by "agrarian reform," Gordon goes on to suggest that U.S. aid will be used as a political lever: "We obviously can't say we are going to dictate the land reform legislation of another country, but we are going to provide help when the right kind of legislation is forthcoming and refrain from providing help where it doesn't." [19]

The then (1962) Assistant Secretary of State for Inter-American Affairs, Edwin M. Martin, had a different set of priorities from those of land reform and other institutional changes:

> It is not possible to have a sound and constructive economic development program in a situation in which there is not a reasonable degree of political stability and political maturity. Unless you have a reasonable degree of political stability the normal course of business just won't be conducted. We've had a few examples quite recently of political instability and business just stopped. Unless it's a strong government which has the respect of the people, it will not be able to secure the sacrifices in money and personnel that are required to do a job of political and economic and social development.[20]

Martin's emphasis on the need for stability, the proper political climate for business, strong government, and "sacrifice" is made to order for the traditional conservative political system in Latin America. One can hardly imagine any situation where significant distribution of land takes place without some social dislocation, at least temporary "instability," flight of capital, and perhaps changes in government. It is beyond doubt that a number of the institutional changes stressed in the Charter of Punta del Este would have had a profoundly unstabilizing effect on many existing governments.

Because of the Alliance for Progress, the rhetoric of agrarian reform became respectable. Most liberal and conservative governments made appropriate symbolic gestures by passing agrarian reform laws which, however, were designed to be ineffective, or were not implemented. U.S. policy-makers demanded no more than gestures because they themselves were not convinced of the necessity of agrarian reform. Attempts to make extensive changes through existing political channels met with local resistance; the greater the political power held by the resistant economic groups, the more effective they were in preventing changes that would result in a redistribution of wealth. With his usual understatement, John Kenneth Galbraith made the obvious but frequently obscured point in 1951: "If the government of the country is dominated or strongly influenced by the landholding groups—the one that is losing its prerogatives—no one should expect effective land legislation as an act of grace. . . ." [21]

The policy statements cited above, which reflect a productionist approach, date from 1961 (Gordon's testimony) and 1962 (Martin's statement), both well before the end of the Kennedy Administration. A full-scale attack on the redistribution concept then appeared in the Clay Report of March 20, 1963. This report emphasized increased productivity, elite modernization, and the trickle-down approach to social improvement as the strategy to be encouraged among the recipients of U.S. aid. The recommended policies, largely derived from conservative economic theory, dictated goals such as monetary stability, balanced budgets, elimination of subsidies to government enterprises, and stimulation of private capital investment. The final recommendation spoke of the desirability of better land utilization to "increase income on the lower levels of society." The report's basic position was that

> Latin America must be encouraged to see its essential choice between totalitarian, state-controlled economies and societies on the one hand and an economically and politically freer system on the other, realizing that a society must begin to accumulate wealth before it can provide an improved standard of living for its members.[22]

The Clay Report clearly states the primacy of U.S. ideological and economic interests in the Cold War; development criteria which do not coincide with the interests of the propertied investor class are thereby dismissed as expressing the interests of the Communist bloc. Not all State Department officials, nor all of Kennedy's advisers, were in agreement with this rigid line, but the trend after 1963 was toward a much more conservative position. John Moors Cabot, a former Assistant Secretary of State for Inter-American Affairs, acknowledged the priorities and constraints imposed by U.S. corporate interests on U.S. policy: "Whereas our policy seeks to promote reform and social justice in Latin America, the need to protect our large economic stake injects a conservative note into our policies." [23]

The redefinition of U.S. policy to mesh with the demands of

the productionists can be seen in excerpts from two speeches of Teodoro Moscoso, the first Alliance coordinator:

> The people of the United States are not prepared to support a large scale effort which they think will result in the perpetuation of social and economic systems that are structured so as to benefit the few to the detriment of the many. . . . We are insisting on reforms as a condition of our material support to Latin America. We would rather withhold our assistance than to participate in the maintenance of a status quo characterized by social injustice. . . .

> Agrarian reform . . . (as a big chapter in the Charter of the Alliance) gave rise very quickly to the *misconception that all that was wanted or needed was the splitting up of the large landed estates* which were owned by a few wealthy men who also played a decisive role in controlling the political destiny of their countries. But it is not this simple . . . I prefer to speak rather in terms of modernizing agriculture. By that *we do not necessarily mean taking land away,* dividing it up and redistributing it, but *orderly reorganization,* including possible changes in land tenure, supervised credit and extension service, and farm-to-market roads. . . . This is the rational way in which the Alliance is tackling the problems of agriculture. It is the right way. . . .[24]

Subtle changes in the meaning of terms, shifts in emphasis and priorities, acknowledgment of difficulties and complexities—these highlight the shift from policies directed toward redistribution of land (and redistribution, therefore, of economic, social, and political resources) to policies that would maximize incentives for the existing elite. The rather strong productionist emphasis in Moscoso's statement suggests that the standard image of the Kennedy team as strong advocates of social reform under the Alliance may have been an exaggeration. Lincoln Gordon has noted:

> Some observers associate the loss of glamor in the Alliance with the death of President Kennedy, but the historical record cannot sustain the interpretation. The failure of the Alliance to catch fire as a political watchdog was already evident by mid-1962, and the atmosphere surrounding the São Paulo meeting of Economic Ministers in November, 1963, only a few days before the Kennedy assassination, was one of frank crisis, with many delegates audibly wondering whether the Alliance would survive another year.[25]

Whatever the initial assumptions behind the rhetoric of the original Alliance for Progress, it now appears that both U.S. and Latin American signatories of the Charter either were unprepared for the political pressures at home or were simply engaging in verbal rituals to exorcise the specter of Castro's agrarian reform, or perhaps both. From the early years, the modernization-from-above strategy predominated in the actions if not in the words of the Kennedy Administration.

President Johnson's policy followed in the same direction. On the third anniversary of the founding of the Alliance, he stated:

> Through land reform aimed at increased production, taking different forms in each country, we can provide those who till the soil with self-respect and increased income, and each country with increased production to feed the hungry and to strengthen the economy.[26]

A number of points emerge both from what Johnson stated and from what he omitted: (1) production is the overriding goal; (2) the payoff for the *campesino* is "self-respect" and increased income, not land; (3) the peasants will apparently continue tilling the soil for the *latifundista*. Thomas Mann, Johnson's Assistant Secretary of State for Inter-American Affairs, reiterated the productivity theme. While mentioning the abolition of the *minifundia,* Mann ignored the commitment to undertake the other half of the proposal in the Alliance Charter—the abolition of the *latifundia:*

> Archaic land tenure systems still exist which must be revised within the objective of increasing productivity. This means the elimination of plots too small to be viable as well as placing into production lands underemployed or idle. It also means supervised credit, extension service, research and all the other items of successful farming.[27]

Mann's visions of increased productivity and efficiency suggest that U.S. policy was largely designed to pressure existing elites to adopt measures to achieve these goals.

A variation on the productionist theme is the "national markets" program proposed by Walt W. Rostow, then chairman of the State Department Policy Planning Board and U.S. delegate to the Inter-American Committee of the Alliance for Progress (CIAP), the Alliance's principal coordinating body. Rostow's

prescriptions for solving the problems of the countryside emphasized a reliable and fair price for the landowners; more technical
assistance; credit at reasonable rates to help finance shifts to cash
crops, and improved farming methods and supplies of manufactured goods at reasonable prices.[28] On the national level, Rostow argued for a buildup of agricultural productivity, especially
in the higher-grade protein foods; improved marketing of agricultural products in the cities to guarantee reasonable prices in urban
markets; a shift of industry to the production of simple agricultural
equipment and consumer goods for the mass market; and the introduction of improved marketing methods for cheap manufactured goods, especially into rural areas:

> Applied, for example, to the Alliance for Progress in Latin Amer-
> ica, this strategy would give the whole enterprise a new cast, a new
> dynamism. It would not alter the need for improved methods of
> tax collection, for land reform in certain areas, for increased in-
> vestment in education, housing, and health. *But it would supply an
> operational objective in which private enterprise would have scope
> for real initiative and creativeness, a real basis for collaboration with
> governments, and a way of demonstrating to all the peoples its
> inherent virtues.* What greater reality could the Alliance for Progress
> have than if it began to yield a drop in food costs to the urban con-
> sumer; a shift in rural population to new, higher quality and higher
> productivity products; full utilization and rapid expansion in in-
> dustrial plant; and an enlarged flow of fertilizers, farm equipment,
> and industrial products to the villages at reduced prices.[29]

Rostow's exhortation for better marketing conditions seems more
suited to comforting the "true believers" of free enterprise than to
dealing with the issues confronting the underemployed and unemployed landless *campesinos* of Latin America. The benefits of
agricultural improvements within present-day society would increasingly become concentrated in the hands of those who already
control important social and economic resources. Rostow's account
furthermore fails to deal with the agro-commercial elites which
monopolize the marketing of produce and credits. They would,
of course, continue to flourish, given the free play of private enterprise that Rostow proposes. Capital-intensive farming, while it
might increase productivity, would also increase rural unemploy-

ment, driving tens of thousands of *campesinos* from the farm to urban areas where industry cannot provide adequate employment. Rostow's proposals were based on the familiar but faulty assumption that an "invisible hand" arranges the social order to everyone's satisfaction—a proposition which hardly fits with the historical experiences of those social classes disadvantaged by the free play of free enterprise.

In 1967, Congress gave official approval to the modernization-from-above strategy in a resolution which states in part:

> Whereas the achievement of this goal [self-sustaining growth] is in great part dependent upon an accelerated movement to integrate the economies of Latin American countries and a major effort to *modernize* the educational and *agricultural sectors,* with special emphasis on science and technology. . . . Further, the Congress recommends that the United States provide an increase in assistance under the Alliance for Progress for programs of educational and *agricultural modernization* and improvement of health. The nature and amount of such assistance is to be dependent on demonstrated need and adequate self-help within the recipient countries.[30]

Science, technology, and education were defined as the means for uplifting Latin America. Modernization no longer involved the reordering of the social structure. In the meantime, even the very existence of the problems was becoming less obvious to U.S. policy-makers—assistance was to be given in response to "demonstrated need." Furthermore, aid even for modernization-from-above was no longer to be so freely given—it was premised on the capacity for "self-help." The conventional prescriptions of the 1950's were once again the vogue. Policy-makers no longer expressed the urgency of the years immediately after the Cuban agrarian revolution. Kennedy's rhetoric of the early 1960's was increasingly displaced by greater emphasis on private enterprise and individual initiative, ideas supplied by those of his former advisers who continued to serve under President Johnson. U.S. policy-makers now seemed increasingly to think of Latin American agrarian problems in terms of food production: consequently they devised policies to increase production through improved technology, without much concern for the eventual distribution of either the food itself or the income derived from it.[31] In short, U.S.

policy embraced technical modernization without structural reform.

In 1965, Simon Hanson pointed to the end of the era of reformist rhetoric when he noted:

> The Latin Americans might still remember the social objectives envisaged in Kennedy's classic plea: "No society is free until its people have an equal opportunity to share the fruits of their own land." But the day of the dream was gone and the State Department hailing its departure from the land-distribution plan of land for the landless, put it flatly: "The main thing is to make available the range of services and supplies needed by farmers to increase their output." Achievement? [32]

The Triumph of Gradualism

Looking back from our current vantage point, the Alliance does not now appear to have ever been concerned with developing specific measures to implement a general redistributionist policy; at best, its rhetoric merely denounced "unjust" systems of tenure. Even during the Kennedy years the official pronouncements did not emphasize the expropriation of large landholdings, except in the case of the traditional haciendas, which were condemned because they were *inefficient operations*. Landless laborers on efficient plantations were not included in the redistributive plans of the Alliance. Intensity of land use as the basis for expropriation implied a special concept of social justice. What was crucial was not peasant needs but the owners' efficiency; accordingly, the expropriation of fully utilized large landholdings was unjust. The underlying premise is that "land fulfills its social function when it is fully used," regardless of how it is used and to whom the benefits accrue. [33]

The ambivalence in the Kennedy Administration on the redistribution-productionist issue was the basis for the subsequent easy transition to a completely productionist point of view. Only President Kennedy himself publicly spoke of redistribution without simultaneous reference to increased production and modernization of the rural sector. The most reasonable conclusion appears to be that U.S. policy-makers saw land redistribution merely as one more or less equal variable that could affect production, an economic issue and not a critical social issue.

The triumph of the "productionists" is reflected in the individual and collective attitudes of those U.S. officials responsible for implementing U.S. policy. The following statement by a senior AID official on the question of U.S. support for agrarian reform is typical:

> . . . everybody in the Agency [AID]—any economist— has argued himself out of it for a number of reasons. *First, land reform means a decrease in production.* Second, it means a disruption of marketing and credit and transportation. Third, it's just too costly. Fourth, and it's not said overtly, land reform is against the tide of history. History shows that the trend has been toward the consolidation of land . . . you can't resolve agricultural poverty. . . . Fifth, people are pessimistic about carrying the reform out. You just can't force vested interests to carry the load. . . .[34]

Another high-ranking official similarly commented: "The key is agricultural production. The mechanisms to do this are many. You can redistribute land and income, but the *first* fundamental thing to do is to increase production. . . ."[35]

In fact, the attitudes expressed in over forty in-depth interviews with the major AID officials connected with Latin American agricultural development programs support the idea that productivity is the fundamental and highest priority item in U.S. response to Latin American agricultural problems. In stressing productionist values, these officials revealed their hostility to structural reform.[36]

The Impact of the Incremental Approach

The test of any public policy is its effectiveness in fulfilling its objectives. The gradual-change or productionist approach to agricultural development in Latin America has had ample time to prove itself as a strategy for developing viable agrarian sectors in Latin American nations. To measure the success of this approach we have employed the same indicators as those proposed by the architects of this policy, namely the growth of (1) per-capita agricultural production, (2) per-capita agricultural food production, and (3) agricultural imports. The following tables reveal the results:

In terms of per-capita agricultural production during the Alliance for Progress years 1961–1968, the incremental approach has thus been a singular failure. By 1968, over half the Latin countries had failed even to maintain the 1961 level of per-capita food production. Over one-third of the Latin countries had experienced a *decline* of over 10 percent during this same period. Only one

Table 1

Indices of Per-Capita Agricultural Production,

by Country, 1961–1968

(1957–1959 = 100)

Country	1961	1962	1963	1964	1965	1966	1967	1968 (prelim.)
Mexico	100	106	104	109	114	111	108	111
Dominican Republic	94	93	90	86	77	78	73	69
Haiti	103	91	82	79	79	73	70	67
Costa Rica	105	101	97	88	88	96	98	106
El Salvador	115	111	120	119	101	102	108	97
Guatemala	108	120	121	115	128	113	117	112
Honduras	100	101	99	104	107	97	103	103
Nicaragua	113	128	135	164	145	148	142	138
Panama	95	91	91	98	109	105	103	105
Argentina	97	97	107	103	93	98	103	95
Bolivia	99	95	98	97	93	93	87	88
Brazil	104	101	103	91	115	100	104	98
Chile	95	90	96	97	95	94	94	96
Colombia	96	98	96	92	93	90	92	93
Ecuador	111	108	103	103	106	107	111	102
Paraguay	98	101	100	95	95	88	97	88
Peru	114	111	106	109	104	103	97	93
Uruguay	105	104	107	114	109	99	86	94
Venezuela	98	102	112	110	113	114	117	114
Latin America (19 countries)[a]	102	102	103	98	105	100	103	99

[a] Excludes Cuba, Guyana, Jamaica, and Trinidad and Tobago.

Source: Indices of Agricultural Production for the Western Hemisphere (excluding the U.S.), U.S. Department of Agriculture, May 1969, p. 4.

Table 2
Indices of Per-Capita Food Production,
by Country, 1959–1968
(1957–1959 = 100)

Country	1961	1962	1963	1964	1965	1966	1967	1968 (prelim.)
Mexico	101	106	105	111	115	117	115	118
Dominican Republic	92	93	87	84	77	79	73	71
Haiti	99	96	85	80	79	80	76	72
Costa Rica	98	100	92	96	87	91	93	102
El Salvador	97	104	103	95	96	105	100	105
Guatemala	100	105	110	106	108	108	104	106
Honduras	111	114	121	132	126	134	133	135
Nicaragua	94	91	89	99	111	105	103	106
Argentina	96	97	108	105	93	99	108	98
Bolivia	99	95	98	97	93	92	87	88
Brazil	105	108	109	108	121	113	118	114
Chile	95	90	97	98	96	94	95	96
Colombia	97	102	97	97	99	97	97	99
Ecuador	109	106	103	103	102	104	107	100
Paraguay	97	96	94	92	91	85	90	79
Peru	110	106	102	106	103	105	106	97
Uruguay	106	105	110	121	117	102	87	101
Venezuela	100	104	116	115	119	121	126	122
Latin America (18 countries)[a]	101	103	105	105	109	107	110	106

[a] Excludes Cuba, Guyana, Panama, Jamaica, and Trinidad and Tobago.
Source: Indices of Agricultural Production for the Western Hemisphere (excluding the U.S.), U.S. Department of Agriculture, March 1969, p. 9.

country achieved the 2.5 percent per-capita growth rate which economists assumed to be an adequate minimum. Finally, the two most populous countries of South America, Argentina and Brazil, suffered a *decline* in per-capita agricultural production between 1961 and 1968.

The performance of the Latin American countries in the area of food production was also dismal. The indices of per-capita food production show that almost half of the countries regressed in the period 1961–1968. Another third of the Latin countries showed

Table 3
Agricultural Imports 1961–1966
(millions of U.S. dollars)

Country	1961	1962	1963	1964	1965	1966
Argentina	85.0	76.6	59.8	97.3	112.7	110.5
Bolivia	17.8	25.8	27.6	26.9	26.4	24.0
Brazil	189.7	262.2	279.7	315.2	222.2	290.1[b]
Chile	97.2	129.4	176.6	172.2	146.0	166.2
Colombia	64.3	57.6	44.4	65.7	56.6	94.3[c]
Costa Rica	23.2	12.6	12.9	14.9	17.2	20.0
Dominican Republic	6.3	23.9	29.8	45.1	27.1	33.4
Ecuador	12.7	14.3	14.7	20.2	17.3	14.4
El Salvador	19.5	25.0	26.7	28.8	32.2	36.7
Guatemala	18.4	19.4	22.1	22.4	27.2	20.6
Haiti	5.4	6.9	7.6	6.8	8.9[a]	8.6
Honduras	8.5	9.4	11.4	12.5	13.4	17.4
Mexico	73.0	81.8	132.6	116.7	116.4	110.9
Nicaragua	7.6	10.7	10.2	14.3	17.1	19.3
Panama	18.2	18.8	18.6	21.6	20.9	22.0
Paraguay	5.9	6.3	6.2	6.8	6.8	6.7
Peru	76.1	83.6	88.3	96.9	121.4	134.1
Uruguay	28.6	25.6	24.4	29.1	20.4	44.5
Venezuela	186.6	172.7	174.5	176.1	179.4	148.1
Total (excluding Cuba)	944.0	1,062.6	1,168.1	1,289.5	1,189.6	1,321.8

[a] ERS estimate.   [b] 1967 = 338.3.   [c] 1967 = 69.6.
Source: Data were kindly provided by William Gasser, Chief, Western Hemisphere Branch, Foreign Regional Analysis Division of the United States Department of Agriculture, May 16, 1969.

little or no improvement. Only two countries, Nicaragua and Venezuela, achieved the minimum rates of growth projected in the Alliance for Progress. Stagnation and regression in the production of food may contribute to political insurgency and undermine attempts at industrial development.

In connection with declining production, between 1961 and 1966 Latin America as a whole has increased its imports of agricultural goods by 40 percent. Only two countries, Costa Rica and Venezuela, have lowered their dollar imports of agricultural goods through the substitution of local production. Because many of its agricultural products are geared to the export market, Latin America has failed to produce a diversified agricultural sector that can even keep up with the needs of its own population. These data give us some measure of the inadequate performance of the modernization-from-above strategy. The promise of efficiency and growth which were to result from the incrementalist approach has yet to be realized. If present trends are any indication of the future, social problems stemming from economic and political inequalities may be exacerbated rather than ameliorated by the continuation of current policies. The increasing dependence on food imports, with its increasing costs, will limit the purchasing power of the lower classes and the capacity to import capital goods needed for industrial development.[37] Declining living standards and urban migration without industrial employment could produce an explosive urban situation in the not too distant future. In brief, U.S. agricultural policy has failed to provide a viable alternative to the structural reforms advocated but not implemented during the early years of the Alliance.

Conclusion

It may well be that U.S. policy is primarily concerned neither with increasing production nor land reform, both of which, as we have seen, have been at one time or another stated policy goals, in which case it would be beside the point to evaluate the effectiveness of U.S. policy from either standpoint. U.S. policy-makers may have different criteria of success than those explicitly stated. From a political angle, for example, U.S. agricultural policy may be considered a success: it solidifies support among its traditional right-wing allies in the landholding elite. The productionist argument may be nothing more than code language for continuing support for and cooperation with the traditional landed oligarchy. Historical and statistical data conclusively show that the landowners have not substantially improved agricultural production or the condition of the agricultural population. Theoretical discussion concerned with production may in fact be nothing more than ideological apologetics for maintaining the political status quo.

The landholding elite has usually favored close relationships with the U.S., consistently lines up with the U.S. internationally, and supports U.S. business and economic penetration of Latin American society. The *quid pro quo* is U.S. support of the traditional landowners, rationalized in the form of discourses on productionist values. In a word, for U.S. policy-makers economic arguments seem to be subordinate to a different concern: the necessity of establishing counterrevolutionary alliances on a sound political basis.[38]

NOTES

1. Ernest Feder, "Land Reform in Latin America," *Social Order*, XI (January 1961), p. 2. It is interesting to note that two recent articles on Latin America in the Establishment-oriented *Foreign Affairs* (organ of the Council on Foreign Relations) make no attempt to analyze Latin American agricultural development. The articles are little more than apologies for present U.S. development policy in Latin America. See George C. Lodge, "U.S. Aid to Latin America: Funding Radical Change," *Foreign Affairs*, 47, No. 4 (July 1969), pp. 735–749; and Frances M. Foland, "Agrarian Reform in Latin America," *Foreign Affairs*, 48, No. 1 (October 1969), pp. 97–112.
2. The following terms are used interchangeably in reference to the structural reform school: comprehensive approach, distributionist or distribution strategy, modernization-from-below, redistributive or redistributionist policy or approach. Terms related to the incremental change school include: productionist, productionist approach, productivity theme, technical modernization, modernization-from-above, gradualist approach.
3. Victor Alba, *Alliance Without Allies*, (New York: Praeger, 1965), p. 194.
4. U.S., Congress, Joint Economic Committee, Subcommittee on Inter-American Economic Relationships, *Hearings on Economic Development in South America*, 87th Cong., 1st Sess., 1962, p. 12.
5. Increased mechanization of agriculture eliminates the need for manual labor and, consequently, decreases jobs in the rural sector, resulting in the redundancy of the rural laborer. Given the very limited absorption ability of the industrialization process, the

rural unemployed usually become the penny vendors and slum dwellers increasingly found in and around all the major metropolitan areas of Latin America.

6. John F. Kennedy, "Alliance for Progress, A Program for the Peoples of the Americas," *Department of State Bulletin,* XLV (August 28, 1961), pp. 355–356.

7. Charter of Punta del Este Establishing an Alliance for Progress Within the Framework of Operation Pan America, Title I, Section 6.

8. Declaration of the Presidents of America, Punta del Este: April 15, 1967.

9. *Ibid.*

10. U.S., Congress, Senate, Foreign Affairs Committee, Subcommittee on American Republics Affairs, *Survey of the Alliance for Progress: Problems of Agriculture* (testimony of William C. Thiesenhusen and Marion R. Brown), 90th Cong., 1st Sess., 1967, p. 2.

11. U.S., Congress, Joint Economic Committee, Subcommittee on Inter-American Economic Relationships, *A Report on Economic Policies and Programs in South America,* 87th Cong., 2nd Sess., 1962, p. 21.

12. *Ibid.,* p. 22. The last sentence of this quotation reveals the cynical contempt which many U.S. officials have toward the expectations for improvement held by many Third World people.

13. *Ibid.,* pp. 23–25. (Emphasis added.)

14. V. Webster Johnson and Baldwin H. Kristjanson, "Programming for Land Reform in the Developing Agricultural Countries of Latin America," *Land Economics,* 39 (November 1964), p. 357.

15. *Ibid.*

16. *A Report on Economic Policies and Programs in South America,* Article I, Section 1.04(a). The prohibition has been observed by AID as well.

17. U.S., Senate, Committee on Appropriations, *Hearings on the Inter-American Social and Economic Cooperation Program and the Chilean Reconstruction and Rehabilitation Program,* 87th Cong., 1st Sess., 1961, p. 64. (Emphasis added.)

18. *Ibid.*

19. *Ibid.,* p. 65.

20. Quoted in *U.S. News and World Report,* August 6, 1962.

21. J. Kenneth Galbraith, "Conditions for Economic Change in Underdeveloped Countries," *Journal of Farm Economics,* 33 (November 1951), p. 695.

22. Committee to Strengthen the Security of the Free World, *The Scope and Distribution of United States Military and Economic Assistance Programs* (Washington, D.C., 1963), p. 13. Known as the Clay Report.

23. *New York Times,* November 7, 1963, p. 19.

24. John C. Drier, ed., *Alliance for Progress: Problems and Perspectives* (Baltimore, Md.: Johns Hopkins University Press, 1962), pp. 94–95. (Emphasis added.)

25. Lincoln Gordon, "Punta del Este Revisited," *Foreign Affairs,* 45, No. 4 (July 1967), p. 635.

26. Quoted in Kenneth L. Karst, "Latin American Land Reform: The Uses of Confiscation," *Michigan Law Review,* 63 (December 1964), p. 327.

27. Quoted in Simon Hanson, "The Alliance for Progress: The Third Year," *Inter-American Economic Affairs,* XVIII (Spring 1965), p. 107.

28. Walt W. Rostow, "Deeper Roots for the Alliance for Progress," *Americas,* 17 (April 1965), p. 39.

29. *Ibid.,* p. 41. (Emphasis added.)

30. U.S., House, Committee on Foreign Affairs, *Support for a New Phase of the Alliance for Progress,* 90th Cong., 1st Sess., 1967, p. 2. (Emphasis added.)

31. *Survey of the Alliance for Progress: Problems of Agriculture,* p. 2.

32. Hanson, *op. cit.,* p. 76.

33. Ernest Feder, "Land Reform Under the Alliance for Progress," *Journal of Farm Economics,* 47 (August 1965), p. 658.

34. Interview with AID official, August 1968. (Emphasis added.)

35. Interview with AID official, September 1968. (Emphasis added.)

36. In the unstructured interviewing of forty AID officials in July–September 1968, we tried to approximate a disproportional stratified sample by focusing primarily on the separate subpopulation of officials involved in implementing Latin American agricultural development policy. For a discussion of the rationale underlying this approach see Hubert M. Blalock, *Social Studies* (New York: McGraw-Hill, 1960), p. 401. The principal subunits sampled within AID included: (1) Office of Capital Development; (2) Office of Program and Policy Coordination; (3) Congressional Presentations Office; (4) Rural Development Office. Among the interviewees were officials with field responsibilities in Paraguay, Chile, Peru, Panama, Ecuador, Guatemala, Bolivia, and the

Dominican Republic; ranks ranged from the lowest of the upper-management grades (General Schedule 9) to the higher (GS 17).

37. Agricultural export sector earnings have increased to the benefit of those who produce Latin American export specialities—bananas, sugar, coffee, etc., and not domestically consumed foodstuffs. Such increases tend to benefit U.S. interests since a large portion of this sector is foreign-owned.

38. Redistribution of land in and of itself may not lead to a revolutionary society, as Irish and Japanese experience can readily testify. However, given the present political alignments in Latin America, it is hardly possible that land redistribution will take place without the occurrence of a violent revolution led by a revolutionary socialist movement. In those circumstances the agrarian revolution would form an integral part of a social transformation that would seriously weaken the chances of a petit-bourgeois peasantry's reestablishing a traditional conservative society.

The Dominican Republic:
A Study in Imperialism*

Present U.S. foreign policy toward Latin America is both a continuation of, and a departure from, policy of the past. U.S. interference and intervention in the affairs of Latin countries, direct and indirect, have been a recurrent feature of that policy. What is new is the *degree* of *direct* U.S. involvement. In the Dominican invasion, U.S. policy-makers went beyond the previous planning, staging, and financing of coups by well-trained and obedient military juntas, to the large-scale use of U.S. troops in the hopes of salvaging the unpopular totalitarian wing of the Dominican army. In the Dominican Republic the army, traditional ally of the oligarchy and of U.S. policy-makers, had itself split, one section going over to the popular forces. With the breakdown of the traditional domestic apparatus of control, U.S. policy reverted to the earlier practice of "gunboat diplomacy" policy, becoming the substitute for the local elite as earlier it had intervened in order to create such an elite.

Another innovative feature of U.S. policy as reflected in the Dominican events is that the enemy was not Castroism or communism (nobody can take seriously the story handed out by Johnson of "53 communists running the revolution"), but a popular democratic revolution whose goals were part of the traditional liturgy of the "democratic left." The extremism of the new U.S. policy defines even this type of revolution as "subversive" and liable to brutal suppression by U.S. military forces.

The past activity of the United States in respect to the Dominican Republic has a discernibly totalitarian character: U.S. Marine occupations in 1904 and 1916, followed by the installation of Trujillo in 1930 through elections that had the rare virtue of compiling more votes than there were registered voters. U.S. protégé Trujillo,

---

* It should be noted that this essay was written in September 1966.

as the foremost anti-communist of Latin America, was applauded by most U.S. Congressmen—the Trujillo lobby was second in size only to that of Chiang Kai-shek. U.S. policy-makers looked aside when Trujillo murdered 50,000 Dominicans and 15,000 Haitian workers in two days in 1937, and hunted down and assassinated Dominican critics in exile, such as Jesús Galíndez in 1956. Trujillo's bloody purges of the Dominican population proportionally exceeded even Stalin's and Hitler's atrocities, yet were rarely criticized by U.S. spokesmen. Even after the Organization of American States passed a resolution in 1961 providing for economic sanctions against Trujillo, the United States violated those sanctions by maintaining the Dominican sugar quota and allowing the Sinclair Oil Company to deliver oil, thus continuing support of the totalitarian dictator.

It is a satisfying irony of Trujillo's end that it was precisely this tyrant's personal empire which offered the Dominican people their great opportunity to carry out a painless social reform after he was overthrown. When he was killed in 1961, 45 percent of the Dominican labor force was employed by the Trujillo family. He owned thirteen of the fourteen sugar mills on the island, controlling 85 percent of the total production of sugar, the main Dominican crop (prior to his death, it produced 48 percent of the total export earnings, which account for 24.5 percent of the GNP). One-third of the arable land, 71 percent of tobacco production, 68 percent of flour production, and 63 percent of cement production were in Trujillo hands, in addition to most of the Dominican industries. When Trujillo was killed this whole economic empire came under control of the state, without complicated expropriations and without disaffecting many people. This potent economic lever placed in Juan Bosch's hand the opportunity of immediately and substantially transforming the whole structure of a country with an annual per-capita income of less than $200 (less than $100 for the majority of the working populace) and a 60 percent illiteracy rate.

Juan Bosch

In December 1962, Juan Bosch was elected president with nearly 64 percent of the popular vote. He was the ideal president from the point of view of the Alliance for Progress, if one took seriously its declarations about social reform and democracy. Bosch's proposed program included an agrarian reform through the development of cooperatives; civil liberties; a moderate graduated income tax; a profits tax; separation of church and state; legal provisions for divorce; and a reduction of military expenses. Each measure infuriated some sector of the oligarchy: the church, which had collaborated with Trujillo, the military, which was still sustained by increased U.S. aid, and, most important, the "true believers" of free enterprise, who coveted the big Trujillo properties and were incensed over Bosch's refusal to denationalize them. Bosch did not get far with his program; workers on the state plantations got 4 percent pay raises, and a tax law (Law 5911) was passed, as was an agrarian reform law (Law 5879). But the Bosch program did not go much further than the enactment of these laws. A few parcels of land, 8 acres each, were distributed. Then the program stopped.

Bosch was overthrown primarily because his coercive apparatus was not consonant with his political program. He did not create an alternative source of power to replace the old Trujillo army, nor did he attempt to eliminate the old elites who were planning the overthrow of the government. Fearing the radicalization of the popular movement, Bosch neither attempted to strengthen the trade unions nor dared to call directly on the populace who were his electoral base. Above all, he did not develop armed popular militias and make a direct assault on the oligarchy. Bosch, the middle-class democrat, attempted to maneuver between his popular supporters and the old elite; his political style of bargaining and compromising among groups succeeded only in antagonizing the old elite while bringing few benefits to his followers. The old elites at once took the lead. An alliance of church, landowners, businessmen, and senior right-wing military officers crystallized around the charge that the Bosch government was communist. Meanwhile popular discontent with Bosch's indecision was growing.

By this point, United States sympathies with experiments in Latin American middle-class democracy were declining. Seven months after taking power Juan Bosch was overthrown by the totalitarian general Wessin y Wessin. The *New York Times* on October 5, 1963, stated that key members of the U.S. military mission in the Dominican Republic ". . . openly told their Dominican counterparts that they agreed with the characterization of . . . Juan Bosch as a pro-Communist." For this reason, it was said, the American officers implied to the Dominican military—notably Brigadier General Wessin y Wessin, prime mover of the rebellion— that the Pentagon would not stifle a new regime.

The Demonstration Effect

In 1961 Dominican officials estimated U.S. investment in the Dominican Republic at $250 million, a relatively small figure compared to U.S. investments in the rest of Latin America, and representing, moreover, only a small number of corporations. The principal investor is the South Puerto Rico Sugar Company, which owns 120,000 acres in cane, 110,000 acres of pasture with livestock, and 45,000 reserve acres, plus related industries including a railroad station and a dock. In addition, there are Mellon's Aluminum Corporation (852,000 tons extracted in 1963, profits estimated at 47 percent), United Fruit, and the First National City Bank. One instance will suggest what these corporations had materially to gain by the 1965 coup. In 1962, the vise of the Trujillo regime broken, the workers at South Puerto Rico Sugar engaged in numerous strikes. The company bitterly resisted, and though it eventually signed a contract, it was obvious that its interests, and "stability," could best be served by a military dictatorship. And, in fact, immediately after the Wessin y Wessin coup, U.S. corporations attacked the trade unions and reneged on some of the earlier concessions. When the contracts expired in early 1965, with the militant unionists excluded (they had been fired after Wessin's coup), the companies had a free hand in reducing real wages.

Nevertheless, profitable though the coup was in this sense, it is not short-run gains alone which can explain corporate support of the anti-Bosch alliance, or the disproportionate influence which a relative handful of corporations seemed to wield in the shaping of U.S. policy. Much more important was the corporate stake in preventing the spread of revolution throughout the hemisphere. The hostility to the Dominican revolutionaries which U.S. interests shared with their Dominican counterparts was not based on sharing profits with them in Santo Domingo, but rather on the fear of the "demonstration effect" which a successful socialist and democratic Dominican Republic would have on the rest of Latin America where they do have extensive investments and markets.

U.S. policy in the Dominican Republic has sinister overtones. As Theodore Draper asked in a letter to the *New York Times:* "What would the people of Europe have thought and felt if we had decided after Adolf Hitler's suicide in 1945 to back Air Marshal Goering as the man to save Germany from Communism? The analogy is not too inexact."

The choice which U.S. policy forces upon Latin America today is either revolution or militarization of public life. The social democratic alternative has been brutally rejected as unworkable in the Dominican Republic, as Bosch himself admits.

Revolution and Restoration: 1965–1966

Santo Domingo, with its rundown commercial area, and its daylight streets full of unemployed men and dilapidated wooden houses, looks like a hybrid of Harlem and a southern Negro shantytown. The difference is in the bullet scars on the buildings and the slogans on the walls: *FUERA GENOCIDAS, FUERA AGRESORES YANQUIS.* The houses destroyed by U.S. mortars still lie in ruins; most restaurant windows are still boarded up. Much of the destruction was wrought by the battle of June 15–16, 1965, when U.S. artillery and mobile units, including mounted machine guns, tried to carry out a U.S. general's boast that the revolutionaries' sector could be taken in two hours. After three nights and two days of fighting the U.S. Marines had advanced only two blocks. The ravages of the battle are still visible, but many Dominican freedom fighters are gone. In an interview with the author (August 25, 1966), former President Juan Bosch estimated that between three and four thousand Dominicans had been killed during and after the U.S. intervention. (During Balaguer's four-year term of office, hundreds of political opponents were murdered, many after they had been arrested.)

Today trade-union leaders do not venture out of doors without carrying a pistol as protection against likely attacks, while the Balaguer government has passed restrictive legislation to totally disarm the populace. Today anyone who was a Constitutionalist militant is hiding the fact, for it can be grounds for murder. After 8 P.M. the streets are empty; "peace and tranquility" are based on fear of the continued terror carried out by political gangsters who now have been revived and strengthened. Before dawn hundreds of unemployed line up outside the headquarters of the Partido Reformista (Balaguer's organization) and around government offices, waiting for nonexistent jobs. Typical of the style of the new government are the Red Cross posters plastered on all the buildings, boasting of service to "all the community." During the revolution, when this author, with a committee of doctors, called the Red Cross to get urgently needed plasma sent to the Constitutionalists, Red Cross spokesmen replied that they had to consult the State Department—and then refused to transmit the plasma to that side of the "community." A U.S. businessman told me that I should come to the Dominican Republic and get rich, especially now that all the new "projects" were getting under way with no taxes, cheap labor ($1 to $2 a day): "In the next five years this will be the best country in Latin America to make a fortune in."

The program of the Balaguer government gives every indication of being a businessman's dream. The proposed Austerity Law would lower salaries of public employees, freeze the wages of the working class, and prohibit strikes for at least one year—while placing no limits on profits. Prices of staple foods continue to soar. According to *Listin Diario* of August 22, 1966, the official price of regular rice is 14 cents a pound, of native beans, 16 cents. Trade unionists and workers claimed prices were actually much higher—beans 24 cents, "poor" meat 60 cents, potatoes 8 cents a pound. The lowering of real wages and the increase in prices reverses the central planks of the Balaguer campaign: lower prices and increased salaries.

The Political Truce Law would restrict party activities by not allowing public meetings except during the three months preceding the next election. Marches, assemblies, and public demonstrations in general would be prohibited. This would further atomize and demoralize the populace, cripple the parties of the opposition, and allow the Balaguer-controlled Congress to pass further anti-popular legislation without opposition—hence the term by which Balaguer's government is frequently referred to, the "legal dictatorship." On August 20, 1966, Balaguer signed a law that dissolves the state-owned Dominican Sugar Corporation, and makes the continuance of state ownership conditional on profitability, creating the possibility that enterprises could be turned over to private hands in five years. The Balaguer appointee on the new State Sugar Council, Gaitán Boucher, was a top executive of the U.S.-owned South Puerto Rico Sugar Company. On the other hand, Balaguer is not about to deprive himself of major economic resources for governing, as may be seen in the following episode. In August the Appeals Court of Santo Domingo dropped charges against a son-in-law of Trujillo, Martínez Alves, who had been dispossessed of the Trujillo patrimony. This ruling would have resulted in Martínez Alves becoming the principal stockholder of the majority of enterprises that are now state-owned. But Balaguer's Procurator General overruled the court.[1]

Balaguer has confirmed in their positions all the *trujillista* military officers whom the United States had rearmed and reorganized. The February 27 *Campamento* (the Constitutionalist garrison) is being totally dismantled, its officers being sent to study abroad or discharged and intimidated. Leading Constitutionalists who have been discharged from the army include Quiroz Pérez, Pericles Peralta Bueno, Leoncio Silverio, Polanco Algería, Marino Almanzar, González y González, Marte Hernández, Rodríguez García, and Major Calderon Cépeda. In addition, the G-2 bureau of the Military Intelligence Service has sent invitations to the remaining Constitutionalist officers and soldiers to visit its office, where they are subject to thinly veiled threats to life and position.[2] Much effort has been directed toward purging any possible dissident political force and creating a military completely loyal to the United States and to Balaguer.

In line with government policy, a considerable number of militant workers have been discharged by private and state enterprises: 695 workers from the Consuelo sugar central, 2,000 workers from public works, 624 from the San Cristobal works, 45 workers, including the trade-union leadership, from the Dominican Cotton Consortium, etc.

The political arrest of, and selective terror against, Constitutional leaders practiced under the provisional government of García-Godoy continue unabated. A few days before my arrival in late August 1966, Comandante Ramón Emilio Mejia Pichirilo, a Constitutionalist military officer, and Juan Bisonó Mera, an ex-Constitutionalist official in Villa Bisonó, were assassinated. Balaguer's "investigations," like those of García-Godoy, never discovered the murderers.

Other recent "unsolved" killings include a policeman of Constitutionalist sympathy, Anastasio Sosa, Guillermo Pelaez (14th of June leader), and some fourteen other persons in the month of August alone. Numerous arrests of Constitutionalist leaders continued to take place in Puerto Plata, Barahona, El Seibo, and the capital, Santo Domingo. Even the middle-of-the-road weekly *Ahora* commented sarcastically on the attitude of the government toward the continuing terrorism: "Nothing happens, because the authorities, including the First Executive of the nation, confine their responses to the traditional and inefficient 'investigations' that have always occurred." [3] "Always occurred" underlines the continuity of the present Balaguer regime with his earlier presidency under Trujillo.

The restoration of the old order was the primary aim of the U.S. invasion. The political gangsterism of Balaguer and of the military is the fruit of the U.S. intervention. The police-state legislation, the antiworking-class measures, and the totalitarian agencies and methods now in force are approved and to a large degree drawn up by the U.S. advisers found in the offices of every major ministry, from Financial and Commercial to Military Affairs, on the policy-making level.

A discussion of politics in the Dominican Republic today must be seen in terms of three phases: (1) the revolution of April 1965; (2) the U.S. military intervention and its aftermath; (3)the still continuing, complex process of restoring the old ruling classes in a permanently explosive socio-political milieu.

The physical presence of U.S. force was the prime instrument for the resurgence of *trujillismo,* both militarily and politically. The elections were held in a context where the rural 70 percent of the population was under military occupation and only one candidate was actually permitted access to the voters. The outcome of the election proper was determined by the events of the first days of the revolution and of the U.S. military occupation.

The April revolution began when a group of military officers led by Captain Manuel Pena Tavera of the February 27 *Campamento* rose in revolt against the corruption of military personnel and sought popular support. The initial call of the rebels was for a military junta which would rule for three months and then would permit free elections. The military did not "arm the people." Only about a hundred or so civilians received arms from the military; the arming of 6,000 other civilians was the result of popular assaults on armories, military stockades, and government buildings: as in all popular revolutions the people armed themselves. It was this fact of armed popular power which, together with the defeat of the pro-U.S. totalitarian military forces of Wessin y Wessin, caused Johnson to send in the Marines. The revolution began as an overwhelmingly urban mass movement involving the urban unemployed, the industrial workers, artisans, the self-employed, the lower-level employees, and the professionals. The top leadership was primarily professionals from the Partido Revolucionario Dominicano (PRD); the *comando* or command units were made up and led by Catholic trade unionists (CASC) and 14th of June and PRD militants. The U.S. force attacked and encircled the revolutionary forces, confining them to the city and preventing the effective mobilization of the countryside. The United States broke an agreement that it had made with the Constitutionalists, under the pretense that U.S. troops were establishing a zone of two blocks on either side of the U.S. Embassy to allow for the safe evacuation of U.S. citizens. Once the U.S. troops moved into the area they immediately extended the "passageway" into a noose around the Constitutionalist-held city. The trust placed in agreements with U.S. political-military forces indicated the predominance of the Boschists among the rebels.

As a consequence, the countryside was under American political-military control from at least the middle of May 1965, preventing the élan and solidarity of the popular forces in Santo Domingo from spreading throughout the country. The experience of a people's army defeating the tyrannical and parasitic forces of the ruling class, the program of popular reform, the arms and organization with which to confront the U.S. Marines—all these were absent from the countryside. Apart from the many areas where outright fraud was committed, Balaguer's greatest voting strength generally was found in those areas which the U.S. Marines had cut off from contact with the revolutionary forces, the areas isolated and under U.S. and Dominican military control. Hence the urban-rural split in the vote coincided with the origins of the revolution and geo-military positions after the U.S. invasion.

In reality there were two different but related "interventions" by the U.S.: a military intervention in April 1965, which established the bases for the political one that began in September and which reached its peak during the presidential election campaign. The first phase was accomplished through the use of overwhelming power—43,000 marines, and numerous tanks, helicopters, armed mobile units, weapons—and its lightning application to rebel population centers (northern Santo Domingo, Ciudad Nueva). Once favorable geographic positions were established, policy alternated between selected assaults and negotiations, each utilized to reinforce the other, the military actions exerting maximum pressure to force acceptance of U.S. negotiating terms. The United States was willing to bargain over the formation of a provisional government, but not about the Constitution of 1963, which went by the board. The Bosch-oriented leadership (supported by the small Dominican Communist Party, the PCD), fearing the continual threats of a massive U.S. attack, reluctantly agreed to negotiate for a provisional government on U.S. terms. The 14th of June Movement held out for the Constitutionalist demands. With close to 3,000 Dominicans killed and the city surrounded, the United States imposed the provisional government of Garcia-Godoy through negotiations that were not very different from blackmail.

With the installation of the provisional government, the process of demobilizing the popular forces and reconstituting the ruling elite was begun in earnest. The army, which had gone over to the Constitutionalists *en masse,* defected again out of fear or opportunism when U.S. troops landed, leaving only 1,000 soldiers who actually fought with the rebels. "Meat-grinder" tactics were now applied to the popular forces. During the period of the provisional government, over 280 Constitutionalist leaders and activists were killed; not one of the murderers was apprehended. (These figures, given to me by Caonábo Javiér, secretary-general of the Social Christian Party, were generally confirmed by most Dominican political observers.)

Selective rather than wholesale terror, the reduction of the political strength of the Constitutionalists in the armed forces, and above all the growth of an extensive network of economic-propaganda units, especially in the countryside and in government offices, began to introduce the carrot along with the military stick. The more involved U.S. political-action groups mentioned to me by the education director of the Christian-Democratic trade unions included CEDOECA (Dominican Center of Peasant Education), International Development Foundation, Community Development Organization, CARITAS, Peace Corps, Agency for International Development, and Civic Action Units (military).

Leaders of the Social Christian Party (PRSC), estimated that the U.S.-Balaguer group spent $13 million on the election. The idea of U.S. policy-makers was to establish a government subordinate to and dependent upon the United States while seeing to it that opposition political leadership was physically eliminated or neutralized. As "pragmatists," U.S. policy-makers took advantage of the existence of the political gangsters to further their policy goals.

In the meantime the popular forces and especially the trade-union movement went through a series of militant actions to try to stem the tide, including the general strike of February 1966. The American military and its determination to stay in the Republic at all costs provided the Dominican ruling class the guarantee that the strike could not be successful: there was a force beyond the Dominican Republic which could supply the resources needed to withstand popular pressure. The overwhelming presence of the now almost universally hated U.S. troops, and the inability of the Bosch leadership to propose any way out, began to have a reverse effect on the least political and most vulnerable sectors of the lower class: the women, the older people, the service sector (domestic servants, taxi drivers, etc.). Peace and price control, not Balaguer, were what most of these voters wanted; the will to resist among these strata had given way to the wish to subsist. The Balaguer coalition took shape in a situation marked by political assassinations and selective terror, military control, and the fact that Balaguer was in effect the only candidate in 70 percent of the country, the opposition being confined to the urban centers (Bosch was so frightened of being assassinated that he campaigned without ever leaving his house). In the city the Balaguer vote was composed generally of lower-class women with hungry children and of older male family heads; in the countryside, of intimidated peasants receiving politically controlled economic doles, and bombarded from radio and pulpit with intense anti-communist propaganda. In such a context "free elections" could not be "negotiated" with the United States; the vote operated simply as a means of legitimizing the superior economic and military power of the intervening U.S. policy-makers. The meat-grinder operation achieved its predetermined goal; Balaguer was "elected," authority was restored, and the United States had created the basis for its "democracy of the gallows."

The unfolding stages—revolution, invasion, and restoration—had profound effects on the lower classes, many of whom had previously had little experience in political matters. The short-run results may be the restoration of U.S. hegemony but the long-run effect is the creation of a great reservoir of popular anti-imperialist sentiment for revolutionary movements to draw on. The decisive age group is between fifteen and twenty-five years old. The period from 1961 to 1965 saw the emergence of a political generation distinct in every way from its "fathers": the "sons" who entered political combat at the end of the Trujillo epoch and who are indignant at their parents' subjection to the Great Benefactor. Many of the key revolutionary cadres both during and after the insurrection have been drawn from the unemployed children of the impoverished lower middle class. Young men from large families subsisting on the salary of a father who is a public employee, with no employment for themselves in sight and concentrated with their peer group in Ciudad Nueva—this group was in the forefront of the armed struggle. Prior to that point it had been virtually impossible for the political parties to organize them. Rafael "Fafa" Taveras, leader of the June 14th Movement, analyzed the political role of the unemployed as follows: because of the general economic insecurity and their own continual "mobility" (lack of regular employment), they do not form the nucleus of a political organization; but they are the sector of the population most easily mobilized for action. It is the under-twenty-five unemployed, politically trained during the last five or six years of struggle, who form the most explosive sector of contemporary Dominican society. In a population whose majority is under twenty-one, and with official and disguised unemployment between 400,000 and 500,000 (out of a population of 3.5 million), this sector is of significant social weight. The socio-political force of this group has virtually no electoral expression; it expresses itself only through popular mobilizations.[4]

The changes in the relationship of forces in the trade-union movement both during and after the insurrection and invasion are highly revealing. The union confederation with the largest membership, roughly 40 percent of the unionists in 1963, was CONATRAL —formed and financed by the U.S. Embassy and the AFL-CIO. The leftist Unión de Trabajadores Dominicano contained less than 5 percent of the unionists. The Social Christian unions, the PRD unions (Boschist), and the independents controlled the rest of the organized workers. During the revolution, CASC (Confederación Autónoma de Sindicatos Cristianos) and the newly formed FOUPSA-CESITRADO (led by PRD supporters with Marxist nuclei) played an important role in directing the insurrectionary commandos. The CONATRAL leadership supported the U.S. invasion and subsequently lost almost all of its union affiliates. CASC became the leading national confederation, especially in rural organization, while FOUPSA-CESITRADO became the second major trade-union force, controlling the big El Romano sugar central (13,000 workers), and the transport, construction, cement, port, electrical, and telephone workers. In total the leftist unions claim 100,000 members, more than five times their strength before the insurrection. More important, perhaps, the organization itself has changed. The PRD leadership under Miguel Soto has been replaced by younger revolutionary trade unionists led by Julio de Pena Valdéz, the new secretary-general.

The trade-union movement is bigger, stronger, and more militant than before the revolution. Valdéz relates[5] that prior to the U.S. invasion only the most politicized workers were interested in the problem of imperialism; now trade unionists cannot discuss even wages-and-hours questions without considering them in relation to the struggle against U.S. domination. The mass of trade unionists have become accessible and responsive to an anti-imperialist program and leadership. Among Dominican organized labor the United States has suffered a severe setback from which it will be hard to recover.

The rural populace remains divided between *minifundistas,* who tend still to be under the control of the church, the landowners, and the sugar workers, especially in the El Romano central, who have a long tradition of class struggle. While the majority of the peasantry was not actually involved in the revolution, many of the sugar workers joined the armed popular forces and took part in the two successful general strikes. The sugar workers receive from five to six pesos a day (1 peso = 1 dollar) but are unemployed at least six months of the year; the economic insecurity and geographical concentration of these rural workers facilitate political communication and produce the class solidarity and radical political culture so lacking as yet in the rest of the countryside. This class-conscious and combative rural proletariat could become an important base linking the revolutionary urban popular classes to the exploited poor peasantry.[6]

The "middle class" is divided into various strata, each with a differing outlook. The lower white-collar workers tend to orient generally toward the Boschist PRD and the PRSC (Partido Revolucionario Social Cristiano), and the younger groups toward the June 14th Movement. The professionals and upper bureaucracy tend to be divided among the PRD, the PRSC, and the Balaguer forces. The majority of the university students tend to be with the United Front of the Revolutionary Left (FRAGUA) which in turn is overwhelmingly sympathetic to the June 14th Movement. The results of the 1966 student government elections indicate the total absence of support for Balaguer and almost as little for Bosch: FRAGUA gained 53 percent of the vote, the Social Christian BRUC 41 percent, and the Boschist FURR 6 percent.

The margin of victory of the FRAGUA has grown, especially since the revolution, while Bosch and Social Christian support among the students has declined, the former precipitously. The experience of armed struggle against the U.S. Marines, in which many of the students were part of "commandos," appears to have strengthened the revolutionary tendency among the students. The absence of any coherent ideology in the PRD, its dependence on the personal leadership of Bosch, and its perpetual indecision make it less and less attractive to the new student generation, while the more dynamic and strongly anti-imperialist June 14th Movement is increasingly attractive to them. This tendency is reinforced by the fact that the post-Trujillo student body is being drawn more and more from the lower and poorer strata of the middle class. (Students of worker and peasant origin still form less than 1 percent of the student body.)

The ruling class in the Dominican Republic is not a "feudal" landowning oligarchy. The dominant class is primarily composed of export-importers, commercial agro-businessmen and the "pirate capitalists" in the military caste. The overwhelming majority of this group favored the U.S. intervention and was the social base that collaborated with the U.S.-directed Balaguer campaign. This ruling class, dependent on the United States and fully committed to U.S. hegemony, is linked through business contacts, privileged status, and shared values with the *trujillista* police and terrorist organizations, though it may disown specific actions such as political assassinations which compromise their U.S. counterparts or their own political position. The U.S. intervention saved this ruling class and hence its dependence on the United States is total. Over 60 percent of the Dominican economy is state-owned, the former private empire of the Trujillo personalist state. The future socioeconomic program of the ruling class is based on the gradual expropriation by private interests of these properties and of the franchises which had passed from the Trujillo family to the Dominican state.

Parties, Politics, and Consciousness

U.S. policy-makers have been using the "grass-roots" ideology of self-help and community development as a means of competing with the militant leftist and CASC trade unionists. "Community development" is employed as a means of consolidating the hierarchy of power and wealth by directing popular energies away from a confrontation with the controllers of wealth and power and by obscuring the nature of the class structure. One militant trade unionist referred to these operations as "community corrupters" because the marginal changes introduced attempts to weaken the social solidarity that builds organizations for struggle and structural change. The U.S. programs have not been too effective, since the leaders who have been coopted do not fight to better conditions, have not been selected through struggle, and compromise themselves by upholding "stability" against popular demands.

The four major political organizations in the Dominican Republic are the Partido Reformista (PR), the U.S.-financed and directed organization which backed Balaguer; the Partido Revolucinario Domincano (PRD), the liberal opposition directed by Bosch; Partido Revolucionario Social Cristiano (PRSC), the somewhat more reformist, Christian-Democratic group; and the radical-nationalist 14th of June Movement.

The Partido Reformista is not so much a party as an organization set up by U.S. policy-makers, with leadership largely recruited from the former Trujillo machine; Balaguer himself was the hand-picked president of the Great Benefactor in his last years. The PR "activists" were largely recruited from lumpen elements, the older unemployed or semiemployed of the service sectors who saw a chance to get jobs or earn fast money. The military and the rural clergy, mostly Cuban exiles and expatriates from Franco's Spain, provided informal electoral organizations along with the U.S.-directed community development organizations. The social forces behind PR were clearly the ruling class, U.S. and Dominican. PR's one aim was to legitimate through "free elections" its *de facto* return to power via U.S. bayonets. The "Balaguer mass" never was nor is today represented in a party, either formally or informally. The Partido Reformista was an ad hoc organization, constructed for a single purpose, and has never developed a structure or a program. The only contact today between the "activists" and PR is the line of jobhunters in front of the so-called party office. Given this lack of firm political organization, it is understandable why the police, the army, and restrictive legislation are playing such a decisive role. The other side of the coin is Balaguer's attempt to demobilize and atomize the politicized urban populace through a ban on public meetings, restrictions on the parties, prohibition of strikes, and general constraint on union activity through the wage-freeze law. In addition, of course, these policies directly benefit the social classes which Balaguer serves, strengthening their control and increasing their economic benefits. Balaguer has also utilized the plums of patronage to coopt elements from the right wing of the PRD. Two PRD leaders have entered Balaguer's cabinet, Minister of Finance Antonio Martínez Francisco and Minister of Industry and Commerce José Antonio Brea Pena. Both were, and some say still are, on Bosch's national committee. The combined use of repression and cooptation to destroy political opposition resembles the "salami tactics" used by Stalin in Eastern Europe during the postwar years.

Bernard Fall has analyzed an extreme application of this totalitarian strategy practiced by the United States in Vietnam. He wrote: "The new mix . . . is one of technological counter-insurgency—if you keep up the kill rate you will eventually run out of enemies. Or at least armed enemies. Of course the whole country will hate you but at least they won't resist you. What you will get is simply a cessation of resistance—an acquiescence in one's fate rather than a belief that your side and your ideas have really prevailed." [7] In this sense U.S. policy had the same goal in the rural areas and among the urban women and older poor of Santo Domingo: the use of overwhelming force produced both acquiescence, as shown in their vote for Balaguer, and undying hatred for the United States.

The Partido Revolucionario Dominicano is a personalistic party, almost totally dominated by Juan Bosch and primarily geared to electoral activity. Though its leaders are mainly middle-class professionals, they are generally oriented by modern neo-capitalist ideas. The electoral base of the PRD is largely composed of the urban poor, the industrial workers, public employees, professional groups, shopkeepers, small (and a few larger) manufacturers. It lacks a clear ideology. It is vaguely for a welfare state, mildly anti-imperialist but having strong links with the pro-imperialist "Pepe" Figueres, Muñoz Marín, and Leoni groups in Latin America (the self-styled democratic left—neither democratic nor left). The political position of the more conservative PRD leadership usually predominates in periods of parliamentary activity. And the result is that the class conflicts in society reemerge in the conflicts between the militant PRD masses and the party. In 1963, after Bosch was elected, the sugar workers demanded that he live up to his election pledges and deal with their economic needs. Bosch only finally agreed to negotiate when the workers threatened to close down sugar production. Likewise, one reason why the rural peasantry did not take the risk of voting for Bosch was that he never made any gesture to relieve their rural misery as he had promised to do in 1962–1963. The Bosch congressmen are continuing this pattern. Deputy Ambriorex Díaz (PRD-Santiago) in 1966 introduced an amendment to a proposed rural minimum-wage law empowering Balaguer to set the minimum wage below two pesos a day in areas where owners couldn't afford to pay the standard because of unproductive land.[8] Similarly, William Nova Rosario (PRD) opposed overtime pay. Thus, the PRD leadership defends the profit interests of the small and medium businessmen against the demands of the hungry rural workers.

The result is that Bosch's personal prestige has declined because of his own and the PRD's debility during the coup of 1963 (he refused to prepare or lead the populace against it), the insurrection of 1965 (he asked State Department permission to lead the April revolution while U.S. Marines were landing), and the election of June 1966 (he was afraid to leave his house to campaign). The party leadership's definition of itself as a bourgeois collaborationist opposition has disoriented its popular base, exposing it to the appeal of other, more political forces. The nonexistence of PRD student support and the sharp decline in its trade-union support are indicative of growing disillusion with the PRD among the more politicized Dominican popular forces; these may be omens of a more general exodus.

A sector of the Balaguer coalition, the Military Police Intelligence (IPM) and the air force, want Balaguer to act more forcefully against the opposition. This group has begun to intensify their plotting. Signs reading *Wessin Si, Balaguer No* and *Balaguer es Comunista* are generally the work of this group. These ultras are said to have a list of five to six thousand "communists" who are to be eliminated. The fear which the PRD has of this group appears to be one reason for their collaboration with Balaguer.

The Partido Revolucionario Social Cristiano is a party overwhelmingly made up of middle-class professionals, public employees, small businessmen and students, with little penetration into the working class. Its program does not appear too much different from that of other Christian-Democratic parties. Because of the U.S. invasion, however, it has developed an anti-imperialist consciousness that one finds all too rarely among Christian-Democrats in the rest of Latin America.

Much more involved in grass-roots organizing and with a wider influence among the populace is the Confederación Autónoma de Sindicatos Cristianos, the Christian-Democratic trade-union movement. Probably the largest and most influential confederation at the moment, CASC has grown considerably both in numbers and militancy because of its active participation in the armed resistance against the U.S. Marines. CASC leaders like Henry Molina and Francisco Santos played important roles in directing the revolutionary commandos. The strength of CASC appears to be growing most rapidly in the countryside, where it has sixty to eighty unions organized in FEDELAC (Federación Dominicano de Ligas Agraria Cristiano). According to the CASC education director, its trade-union schools have been more and more oriented toward training rural organizers.

Though CASC is an ideologically oriented union and has a working alliance with PRSC, there is a definite syndicalist tendency in its orientation to the working class: in practical terms unionism is perceived as the major vehicle for mobilizing and defending working-class interests. CASC is both militant and reformist: militant in confrontations on economic struggles and less clearly radical on the larger political issues—except on the question of the U.S. presence. The revolution and the invasion had the result of causing the older conservative Catholics both in PRSC and CASC to leave,[9] with the result that those who remained and the new members recruited during the struggle have strengthened the militant wing, especially of CASC.

The combativeness of the workers who form the CASC cadres is tempered, however, by their strong commitment to Catholicism, and through this channel comes the major anti-communist influence. The single most important factor preventing these workers from turning their anti-imperialism and class consciousness into a revolutionary socialist commitment is their ideological link with the Catholic hierarchy and doctrine. While liberal Catholic spokesmen encourage trade-union activity and organization, the overwhelming stress is on working within Western progressive liberalism, which involves militant anti-communism and avoidance of popular mobilizations for social revolution.

During the three phases of recent Dominican political history, the papacy and the Dominican church hierarchy took somewhat different approaches. The overwhelming majority of the Dominican clergy sided with Balaguer, the Dominican ruling class, and the United States. Papal Nuncio Emanuele Clarizio attempted to mediate between the conflicting forces and during the election the Vatican took the position that Catholics could vote for any of the candidates. The Papal Nuncio, Clarizio, gives the impression that he tends to favor a moderate Social Christian position rather than a total commitment to the Balaguer forces. The appointment of Bishops Roque Adames and Juan Antonio Flores have strengthened these moderate liberal elements. The necessities of the armed struggle thus appear to have had the effect of overcoming some of the more conservative tendencies and influences among Catholics, but they may well emerge again in the coming period.

The 14th of June Movement originated in the late 1950's as a grass-roots student-based organization dedicated to the overthrow of Trujillo. The plan was discovered and many of the revolutionaries were tortured and executed. The June 14th Movement became a symbol of the resistance to Trujillo and grew rapidly in the period following Trujillo's fall. Under the influence of the Cuban Revolution, the leadership took a turn toward guerrilla warfare after Bosch was overthrown, and many of the top leaders, including Tavarez, were killed. As the June 14th Movement leaned toward open support of the Cuban Revolution, sectors of the professional middle class defected; with the sudden turn away from mass struggle to guerrilla warfare the leadership lost contact with important popular sectors in or around the movement. Since 1963, however, the June 14th Movement has again been growing rapidly in numbers and cadres. Bosch estimated that the June 14th Movement had 800 followers in 1963 and has 12,000–15,000 in 1966.

Besides being the major force in the universities, the June 14th Movement appears increasingly influential in the second largest trade union, FOUPSA-CESITRADO. The April revolution and the armed resistance accelerated the influx of new members, especially from the impoverished and radicalized lower middle class (self-employed, artisans, and lower-level public employees), who constitute the primary social force in the June 14th Movement, and are predominantly oriented toward radical nationalism with a focus on the expulsion of all U.S. influence and the expropriation of the foreign investors. Throughout 1966 intense discussions have been taking place in the Movement on basic political and ideological questions: the nature of Dominican society, the dynamics of revolution, and the strategy for taking power.

Rafael Taveras, a leader of the June 14th Movement, sees the petty bourgeoisie becoming a revolutionary force because of its growing impoverishment and the limits imposed by U.S. imperialism. Concerning the immediate program of the Movement, he says they hope to mobilize the large, explosive sector of unemployed young workers and sons of the lower middle class. Taveras seems to favor mass mobilization politics; at the same time there appears to be a group in the Movement which is considering guerrilla warfare in the countryside. Such an orientation would probably be disastrous, given the relatively unpoliticized nature of the countryside and the existence of a revolutionary consciousness among

broad layers of the urban populace. The combination of nationalism and urban mass politics would seem to be the most fruitful
strategy for immediate gains—barring wholesale political assassinations. The restrictions that Balaguer will impose on the functioning of the parliamentary opposition and on the reformist trade
unions should confirm the revolutionary perspective of June 14th
and create a broader ground for activating the mass. Taveras notes
that the possibilities for democratic reforms in the Dominican
Republic are few, and hence he projects the future in terms of
"revolution or dictatorship." The major weakness of the June
14th Movement has been its internal heterogeneity, ideological in-
definiteness, and lack of working-class cadres. But in recent months
it has been moving closer to class politics, especially in light of insurrectionary experience. June 14th militants view the limits both
of the revolution and of their own role in it as resulting from their
inability to organize the major mass force in the revolution, the
urban working class. According to Taveras, the working class
formed the backbone of the revolution but lacked the "party of the
class to direct the struggle and hence the revolutionary energies
were dissipated by the parties of the middle class (PRD, PRSC)."
Ideological clarification and the consolidation of the organization
appear, however, as necessary prerequisites to the forming of such
a party.

A revolutionary strategy must recognize that in the Dominican
Republic the revolutionary movement of April 1965 took the form
of a classic social revolution rather than rural guerrilla warfare. It
was an armed uprising emanating from the urban centers and
based to a large degree on the trade unions, the urban employed,
and the university and secondary school students. In Santo Domingo the high urban unemployment rate, the cleavage in the traditional base of elite power (the army), and the availability of a
highly mobilizable urban population provided the opportunity for
an urban-based mass insurrection. The presence of an occupation
force exacerbates all the latent hostilities generated by externally
supported national-capitalist exploitation and provides a unifying
theme—anti-imperialism. In this sense the Dominican Revolution
resembles the European Resistance during the Nazi occupation.

Of the two small communist parties, the pro-Chinese Movimiento Popular Dominicano (MPD) appears the more active and has influence in the June 14th Movement. The pro-Soviet Partido Comunista Dominicano (PCD), is much smaller and tends to orient its activities toward supporting the "progressive" sectors of the PRD, accusing the more militant June 14th Movement of being "petty-bourgeois socialists." [10] Neither group has much direct influence; both must rely on coalitions with the other parties, especially with the June 14th Movement. They are plagued by lack of cadres, lack of ideological sophistication among their new members, and ideological divisions. Recently the MPD split into two factions, each publishing a journal with the same name, *Libertad,* and apparently the same politics. While the MPD and PCD grew as a result of the revolution and its aftermath, the great majority of the newly radicalized populace entered into the more grass-roots national-popular June 14th Movement.

With illiteracy still over 60 percent, with at least one-third of the labor force of Santo Domingo unemployed, with 400,000 peasants lacking sufficient land to live on, with 200,000 school-age children out of school, and with potable water available for only 5 out of every 300 peasants, the need for profound structural changes is obvious. The reemergence of the old ruling class, the restoration and strengthening of the old piratical military-capitalist caste by the United States, can only serve to set the stage for a new confrontation. Balaguer's restrictive legal measures are aimed at containing the challenge of the organized forces. Meanwhile, as the emptiness of Balaguer's promises of reform is revealed by rising prices and political assassination, the popular unrest checked by the U.S. onslaught is slowly beginning to express its strength. Behind the seeming acquiescence and fear there is in the popular consciousness a profound hatred of the totalitarian military and their U.S. counterparts.[11] There is a growing maturity in revolutionary political consciousness among the trade unions, the political militants, and the young unemployed. The balance sheet of U.S. policy in the Dominican Republic indicates that the "stability" it so brutally imposed is only a transition to a new confrontation.

NOTES

1. *Listin Diario,* August 22–26, 1966.
2. El LJ4 (organ of the Movimiento Revolucionario 14 de Junio), August 20, 1966.
3. *Ahora,* August 29, 1966, p. 66.
4. From an interview with Taveras.
5. In an interview with the author in August 1966.
6. The *minifundia-latifundia* pattern prevails in the Dominican Republic: 86 percent of the landholders (392,000) own only 19 percent of the land, while .9 percent of the landowners (4,400) own 46 percent of the cultivated land, 20.6 million hectares.
7. Bernard Fall, "This Isn't Munich, It's Spain," *Ramparts.*
8. *Listin Diario,* August 24, 1966.
9. One right-wing split-off group, the Partido Demócrata Cristiano (PDC), later supported Balaguer during the election.
10. *El Popular,* August 8, 1966.
11. U.S. white and Negro soldiers were equally brutal and equally condemned. Black Dominican workers asserted that when they told North American Negroes to go back to the United States to fight for their own rights, the Negroes responded, "Will you pay me $400 a month?" Conservative civil rights spokesmen who advocate "coalition" with the Democratic Party in order to obtain promises of improvement in the immediate economic position of the North American Negro cannot and do not offer any effective political challenge or opposition to their "coalition" partners, e.g., Lyndon B. Johnson, on crucial foreign policy matters. On the contrary, it is not unusual for Negro leaders to support this policy. No one put it better than Staughton Lynd when he said "coalitionism" today is "coalitionism with the Marines."

Imperialism:
A System of Control

Imperialism can be looked at as a system of domination and control by one nation over another in order to maximize profits. In the present period of global strategies and commitments, however, this is too narrow and simple a conception of the problem. It underestimates the development of institutions whose policies and scope of involvement span continents. It overlooks the degree to which the components of a social system interact and are interdependent; the complex functioning of the modern capitalist state requires a number of activities which are both autonomous and interdependent. These activities, generated by economic, political, social and cultural institutions, extend outward toward the semicolonial societies (the misnamed "Third World") and inward into the structures of the metropolitan society.

Imperialism is a global system of power. Though its impact can be localized in a particular society in a particular time, imperialism as a system cannot be understood by examining any one single event at a particular time and place. The consequences and operations of imperialism must be measured in terms of *cumulative* impacts in *many* localities. The local event in a given time period must be understood in this geographically extensive and historical context.

Imperialism is not merely a system of exploitation causing deprivation of the population and societal underdevelopment, though those are certainly major effects of the activity of the metropolis. Imperialism is also a system of rule. Rulership implies authority. The central activity of political authority is making decisions that protect vital interests. Imperialist rulers defend their interests through policies framed to sustain the system over time—i.e., framed in strategic terms. In some cases the rulers will tolerate an unfavorable situation in a particular area; in other cases, where strategic interests are involved, they will mobilize all their resources to insure an outcome advantageous to themselves. Imperialism as a system of rulership, in other words, also involves tactical adjustments. The promotion of economic growth or stability in "showcase" areas, for example, is not incompatible with imperial political goals. Bourgeois social scientists who generalize upon such tactical adjustments to prove the benign influence of the metropolis are functioning as ideologists rather than scientists when they leave out of account the cost of subordination and the overall negative development pattern within the colonial areas.

Imperialism as a system of rulership with a global perspective is not a totally centralized enterprise. The resources and organizational structure of the metropolis are insufficient to permit it to impose its hegemony on all continents simultaneously. This requires accommodation and the creation of regional authorities with discretion to act for the larger interests. The favored nations which act as the strategic envoys of the metropolis—the subimperialist powers—may not always experience the hardships imposed by the imperialist countries and hence may not exhibit the features of a classical semicolonial country. Usually the subimperialist nation will evince characteristics of an imperialist and a colonial country both, as befits its intermediary position in the global imperialist system.

Imperialism is not reducible to a single component, so that a discussion of so-called "economic imperialism" is nonsense. Imperialism is a multidimensional phenomenon whose components are in dynamic interplay. The political, economic, military, social, and cultural institutions, policies, and policy-makers act complementarily to reinforce each other's contribution to the maintenance of metropolitan power. "Voluntary" student and intellectual associations are used by the U.S. government to transmit values among the educated classes of the Third World to facilitate the acceptance of U.S. economic penetration. Likewise, attempts are made to convince students and cultural groups that socialism and freedom are incompatible—that only under a "free enterprise system" can they develop a democratic society and avoid the "pitfalls of totalitarianism." The revelations in 1966 and 1967 concerning CIA-financing of the overseas activities of the AFL-CIO, the National Student Association, the Congress for Cultural Freedom, etc., are only the most recent examples of the functioning of the noneconomic components of the empire which complement economic expansion.

The complex interplay of the components of imperialism can be illustrated if we glance at one component and notice the multiple directions in which it manifests itself. The economic institutions of imperialist domination in general are of two types, public and private, linked through private activity and governmental policy. For example, public economic activity takes the form of governmental policy underwriting foreign investment, promoting compacts between semicolonial governments and private enterprise, guaranteeing investment against nationalization, and enforcing compliance through both the control of loans and the financing of debts incurred by the semicolonial country. The public and private economic components of imperialism are not confined to "investments" (including loans, credits, etc.), but involve control over trade, markets, and raw materials. Control over these economic dimensions in turn results in the need for other kinds of control: not merely over quantity of goods or income accumulated, but over access to strategic resources essential to a multitude of economic operations in the metropolis (i.e., tungsten, uranium).

Notwithstanding the multidimensional character of imperialism, some components are more important than others. In terms of both differential costs and benefits, the private economic sector takes priority over the public. The government's economic policies and activities frequently, though not always, function to furnish subsidies to private investors; loans to semicolonial countries, for example, are used to finance exports and to promote private investment. Contrary to the argument of bourgeois social scientists that imperialism is unprofitable—an argument proceeding from the mistaken use of the "nation" rather than the interested investors as the unit of analysis for measuring profitability—it is profitable in a specific class sense, which should be the major consideration of any "cost-benefit analysis" of imperialism. Government expenditures to finance overseas expansion are paid for by wage and salaried workers; the profits of economic expansion accrue to the stockholders.

The historical development of imperialism reveals the interconnection between present policy and past activity, future interests and present stakes in given outcomes. Imperialism is a historical phenomenon; current policy decisions only become meaningful when considered in a temporal context. The historical perspective highlights the key variables operating in a particular policy decision. Empirical analysis of policies can only be made in a framework which includes the global commitments of the imperial center and the historical development of interstate relations.

As a historically determined phenomenon subject to attrition or extension, imperialism has a dynamic character. The word "imperialism" does not denote some activity or set of individuals disliked by "poor nations." Nor is it an omniscient and omnipotent force, an eternal nemesis. The power of the metropolis exists in a "field of forces." Hegemony is not imposed outside of the multifarious relations of mutually interdependent social systems; imperial domination or the dissolution of empire is the result of outcomes of social struggles, and decisive shifts in political, social, economic and cultural relationships. Imperialism can only be understood in relational, historically specific terms.

The options available to political decision-makers involved in the intricate web of imperial-satellite relations are circumscribed by the historical context: the political origins and complex commitments of the political actors. Interstate relations of a specifically imperialist-satellite type are not static givens resulting merely in poverty, exploitation, and underdevelopment; dynamic and unstable social forces are engendered. Opposing political forces are created, organized, and disciplined, and domination is not total but countered by popular resistance—the satellites are not passive but contain human agents with consciousness who through political action create the basis for alternative systems.

Patterns of Intervention:
The United States and Latin America

Intervention can be defined as the deliberate use by one nation of military, political, or economic force to secure its own desired ends in respect to the target nation.

The notion of intervention does not include those national policies which affect another nation merely by virtue of the complex interdependency between the two nations. Dependent nations, of course, are by nature more vulnerable to external changes, planned or inadvertent, than more autonomous nations. The vulnerability imposed on the Latin American nations by their external dependence makes them more susceptible to intervention by the United States. One important factor contributing to their susceptibility is the existence of linkage groups—American investors, Latin military officials trained in the United States, etc.—that reside or carry on business in Latin America but owe allegiance to or depend on the United States for support.

U.S. intervention has taken many forms. It may, as in Vietnam, take the form of massive military intervention to establish a client state likely to accept Washington's international policies. Or it may take the form of a threat to withhold loans or credits, or to change the import quota of one-crop exporting countries, in order to influence a policy of a government on a specific issue, or to promote U.S. investor interests.[1]

Intervention, Annexation, and Indirect Rule

While it is only since World War II that U.S. foreign policymakers have actively attempted to make the governments of Asia and Africa conform to the global aims of the United States, this is not the case with Latin America. Latin America has for at least a half a century been recognized as belonging to the U.S. "sphere of influence." [2] This has meant that U.S. policy-makers have played a predominant role in matters of Latin American trade, economic development, and foreign relations. Beginning as early as the middle of the nineteenth century the U.S. government has pursued an interventionist policy with a variety of policy goals. In the Mexican province of Texas and later throughout the southwest and far west, U.S. colonists settled and soon became the advance guard of annexationist movements. Before the turn of the century armed U.S. military forces occupied Cuba and Puerto Rico and threatened to become involved elsewhere, also for annexationist purposes.

In the twentieth century, however, a substantial shift in U.S. policy occurred; control over Latin economies and legal restrictions on the sovereignty of Latin nations became the policy objectives of U.S. decision-makers. Outright annexation was replaced by indirect rule—the establishment of semicolonies. Military intervention generally occurred in the countries bordering the Caribbean: Mexico, Nicaragua, Colombia, Panama, the Dominican Republic, Haiti, etc. The necessity of repeated military interventions indicated both the precarious nature of the unpopular regimes installed by previous interventions, and the U.S. policy-makers' lack of expertise in creating administrative machinery to effectively control and repress popular movements.

In the early 1930's this situation began to change. The Somoza, Trujillo, and, to a lesser extent, Batista regimes, which were outgrowths of U.S. military or diplomatic intervention, were able to capitalize on the assistance of U.S. advisory missions to establish effective mechanisms for control; dictatorial rule over their populations in one case lasted thirty years (Trujillo) and in the other continues to this day (Somozo). Batista was in and out of office over a twenty-five year period.

Control and Manipulation: The Good Neighbor Years

The 1930's marked the appearance of a new pattern of intervention, based to a certain degree on the success of the previous types. Annexationist intervention in the nineteenth century had brought large areas of Mexican territory into U.S. possession. The social and economic costs were relatively cheap, and the benefits were high: the annexed territory contained excellent resources— e.g., gold, oil, grazing and farm land—more than sufficient in terms of the entrepreneurs available to exploit the new conquest. The military interventions were also successful (only partially so in the case of the Mexican Revolution) in establishing governments which were generous to U.S. investors and also followed U.S. policy in the international arena. By the 1930's, when favorable boundaries and governments had been established, the policy of intervention was characterized chiefly by efforts to stabilize the status quo and consolidate past gains by excluding external competition. The Good Neighbor Policy befriended governments in the Caribbean which were largely creatures of U.S. policy, whose economies were shaped to U.S. needs, and whose main preoccupation was to stay in power.

The worldwide crises during the 1930's also deeply affected the interventionist capacity of the United States. The ability of the U.S. government to intervene has not been always and everywhere the same. Despite the fact that Washington strongly opposed the Mexican government's expropriation of North American oil interests, intervention was not feasible because of the strong popular backing of the Cárdenas government, the U.S. preoccupation with the impending global confrontations in Europe and Asia, and the existence of an organized opposition to military intervention within the United States. On the other hand, in the case of the Cuban social revolution of 1933, the United States managed, through nonrecognition of the reformist Grau government and support for Batista, to preserve the status quo and U.S. economic and political hegemony. The manipulation of politico-economic and diplomatic measures, and the threat, rather than the actual use, of overt military force to maintain hegemony, characterized U.S. policy in the period during and immediately after World War II. The overwhelming economic and military power of the United States forestalled any major crises. Latin governments, anticipating U.S. reactions, failed in most cases to pursue vigorously nationalist policies. In summary, the pattern of U.S. interventionist policy until the early 1950's can be understood as the result of cumulative favorable outcomes in which successful military intervention and annexation prepared the ground for more flexible types of intervention: politico-economic mechanisms of control and manipulation of elites.

The Policy of Indirect Military Intervention

Starting with the 1954 U.S.-directed military coup in Guatemala, the United States began to use a multiplicity of policy instruments for interventionist purposes. Such diplomatic and economic pressures as an anti-communist resolution aimed at isolating the Arbenz government at the Tenth Inter-American Conference at Caracas in 1954,[3] the cutting off of economic assistance, etc., were followed by U.S. organization of a largely Guatemalan military force to realize U.S. policy ends. This policy of indirect military intervention, a modification of the earlier, direct approach of U.S. military occupation bolstered by U.S. economic and diplomatic pressure, was successful in realizing U.S. political and economic goals, i.e., defending U.S. investors' property and installing a government which supported U.S. international policy. Success in Guatemala encouraged the U.S. government to organize and direct the Bay of Pigs invasion by U.S.-based Cuban exiles in 1961, for the same ends. The Cuban government's ability to defeat the invaders led to a rethinking of U.S. interventionist strategy.

Intervention in the 1960's

While U.S. policy-makers continued to operate through indigenous elites to maintain the status quo in Latin countries, they realized that certain innovations in interventionist strategy were needed. One key event which appears to have shaped new policy directions was the 1962 Cuban missile crisis. The U.S. military blockade of Cuba, backed up by the explicit threat of nuclear warfare on a global scale, was a successful form of intervention, at least in the short run: it allowed the United States to intervene in Cuban political life to the extent of controlling the type of military resources the Cubans would be permitted to acquire from the Russians for defense purposes. More significant in the larger perspective, the effectiveness of a direct military threat—including its success in forcing the Soviet Union to back down despite Cuban objections—encouraged U.S. policy-makers to use a direct military approach again in subsequent situations likewise considered to be critical. The evolution of U.S. policy in Vietnam, the shift from indirect military intervention (aiding a client government) to direct military intervention on a massive scale, is one instance. Closer to home, the same shift can be observed in respect to the Dominican Republic.

When in 1965 it appeared that the client military junta and its supporters in the Dominican Republic were unable to stem the tide of popular revolution even with U.S. military aid (indirect military intervention), the United States turned to massive direct military invasion, rationalized *post hoc* by President Johnson with the claim that civil wars were now international. In practical terms, unilateral U.S. intervention in the Dominican Republic laid the basis for possible future acts of a similar kind in Latin America. The impotence of the Latin and North American political opposition encouraged U.S. use of direct military means, and thereby accelerated the institutionalization of U.S. hegemony in the hemisphere. The growing importance which U.S. policy-makers attach to the idea of a continental police force—the euphemistically titled Inter-American Peace Force—capable of intervening in any country where the status quo is endangered, indicates that U.S. interventionist strategy is still being refined, albeit still in terms of direct military intervention.

The lesson seems to be that success invites replication; it is accurate to speak of an intervention multiplier effect, with particular patterns of intervention dominating in particular periods and political contexts. But the patterns should not be interpreted in an overly schematic way, for we find a continuity in types of intervention from one period to another, and in some cases a pattern of alternate types, depending on specific political circumstances.

If we were to range the types of U.S. intervention on a spectrum of "overtness" we might categorize U.S. interventions in Latin America over the last fifteen years as follows:

Type of Intervention	*Country*
Direct military intervention	Cuba 1962 Dominican Republic 1965
Indirect military intervention	Guatemala 1954 Cuban invasion 1961
Direct economic intervention	Cuba 1960 Dominican Republic 1961
Economic manipulation (loans, credits, debt payments, grants utilized as policy instruments)	Throughout Latin America
Political and diplomatic manipulation (training and indoctrinating of military personnel, recognition of governments, etc.)	Throughout Latin America

Differential Cost/Benefits of Intervention

In evaluating the consequences of intervention, we must take account of two points: in calculating "benefits" we must distinguish between benefits as defined by U.S. policy-makers and economic interests, and benefits as defined by the needs of the interested nations. This approach rejects as absurdly simplistic, misleading, and ideologically biased, the notion that what are perceived as benefits by U.S. interest groups are necessarily good for the rest of the hemisphere. A major preoccupation of U.S. policy-makers who rely on interventionist techniques is insuring that Latin governments support U.S. policies in the Cold War and maintain favorable economic conditions for U.S. commercial and investment groups. The rhetoric of democracy which accompanies intervention is more often than not a rationalization for acting on behalf of these interests. In calculating benefits resulting from U.S. interventionist policies, the real interests and ideological rationalizations involved must be clearly distinguished. If we analyze accordingly the four cases of U.S. military intervention, direct and indirect, that have occurred in the hemisphere in the last fifteen years, we will find the following:

Guatemala (1954): *Low Cost:* Economically, and in terms of social costs: few American casualties.
High Benefit: Overthrow of reform government; restoration of land to United Fruit; installation of government that clearly supports U.S. policies to the extent of lending itself as a training base for attacks on Cuba, etc.

Cuban blockade (1962): *High Cost:* Global mobilization in preparation for nuclear confrontation.
High Benefit: Withdrawal of missiles; isolation of Cuba from rest of hemisphere and successful reassertion of U.S. hegemony in Western Hemisphere; successful use of massive military force to change defense policy of Soviet ally and to cause Russian retreat from commitments.

Cuban invasion (1961): *High Cost:* U.S. prestige placed in support of defeated invaders; U.S. politically identified with invaders.
No Benefits: Loss of prestige; loss of political support in Latin America and within Cuba; strengthened revolutionary Left in Latin America; eliminated possibility of recovery of $1 billion in U.S. investment in Cuba.

Invasion of Dominican Republic (1965): *Low Cost:* Relatively inexpensive economically and in terms of troops lost; merely verbal opposition by Christian Democrats and liberals in North and South America.
High Benefits: Eliminated from power nationalist reform group which based on armed populace might have followed a more independent foreign policy and a more restrictive domestic policy vis-à-vis U.S. investors; election of president favoring U.S. business and U.S. foreign policy; populace disarmed and old military apparatus restored.

In three out of the four cases intervention has been a successful tool of U.S. policy, restoring a favorable political environment for business interests and creating conformity with U.S. international policies.

From the point of view of the great majority of the population residing in the intervened countries the balance sheet looks somewhat different. In Guatemala substantial areas of land that were distributed to peasants were returned to U.S. investors; trade unions were dissolved; little has been done in the way of education, health, and welfare. Politically, Guatemala has since 1954 been ruled by military dictators or militarily controlled civilian governments, aided by right-wing terrorist vigilantes who caused upward of 3,000 deaths between 1966 and 1969 alone.[4] In the Dominican Republic several thousand civilians were killed, and the old economic and military elites returned to power in the course of dissolving the popular militias and physically eliminating selected Constitutionalist rivals. Elections under military tutelage resulted in the entrenchment of the supporters of President Balaguer, who had also served as president under the Trujillo dictatorship. Massive unemployment, highly inequitable land distribution, and low levels of literacy continue.[5]

As these illustrations suggest, the consequences for the intervened nation of indirect or direct U.S. military intervention against leftist reform regimes are largely negative in terms of both socioeconomic development and political freedom. The pattern that emerges from past U.S. intervention in Latin America is one in which high benefits to the U.S. coincide with largely negative consequences for the intervened nation. The history of pre-World War II interventions in the Caribbean countries, direct and indirect, suggests a similar pattern. The result has been dismal for the intervened nations. U.S. intervention has probably contributed in a major way to the low position of most of these countries on various scales of social, economic, and political development.

In terms of benefits to U.S. policy-makers and economic interests, it should be noted that short-term payoffs may result in serious losses in the next generation. For example, the successful intervention in Cuba in the mid-thirties resulted in temporarily stabilizing a status quo favorable to the United States. However, it may have created conditions for a more radical social revolution in the 1950's by postponing many of the social reforms that popular forces were demanding. The same may now be happening in the Dominican Republic and Guatemala.

Types of Intervention and the Status of Latin Nations

U.S. use of its various modes of intervention corresponds to the different political relationships between the United States and the intervened nations. In a somewhat schematic categorization we can classify these relationships as follows:

Type of Intervention	*Status of Intervened States*
Direct and indirect military intervention.	*Colonial and annexed territory:* Puerto Rico, the southwest states incorporated in the U.S., e.g., Texas, etc.
	Semicolonial or indirect rule: Cuba 1900–1958, Guatemala 1954–present, Haiti 1900–1933, etc.
Direct economic intervention and routine economic and political manipulation and pressure.	*Client states:* Venezuela, Colombia, Brazil 1964–present, Costa Rica, Haiti, Ecuador, Paraguay, Bolivia 1964–present, Panama, Mexico until 1910.
	Dependency: Chile, Mexico, Argentina 1945–1955, Uruguay, Brazil 1950–1964.

A number of observations are in order: the Caribbean area is still subject to direct and indirect U.S. military intervention. As a consequence, with the exceptions of Cuba and Mexico, these are countries that remain under direct or indirect U.S. rule; the remaining Latin American nations are largely client states. The countries subject to indirect rule are those in which the selection of key government officials was accomplished in the physical presence of the U.S. troops. The client states, on the other hand, nominally select their own officials, but these are filtered through political and social selection processes to insure their acceptability to the United States. U.S. officials have a variety of other means by which to affect Latin American policies, influence the choice of elected officials, and establish the boundaries within which political leaders can act. One obvious and important lever for intervention is the loans which the United States can offer to countries which have trade deficits and which are thus in constant search for ways of refinancing past debts. U.S. influence in the international financial agencies can add further weight to its policy demands upon

Latin nations. It is therefore not surprising that client state leaders largely direct their economies to serve U.S. economic needs—e.g., guaranteeing U.S. investments, maintaining one-product export economies—and consistently vote with the United States in international policy matters.

The U.S. ability to intervene through routine channels to effect policies favorable to U.S. economic interests is illustrated by the resolution of the conflict between the Boston Panama Company and the government of Panama.[6] The Boston Panama Company owned 500,000 acres of land, an area one-half the size of Rhode Island, and only utilized 5,000. The Panamanian government, applying a tax law on uncultivated land, eventually asked for a $2 million payment. The Boston Panama Company refused to pay the sum and conferred with U.S. government officials on ways to avoid complying with the law. Communications from the U.S. corporation were sent to the Department of Commerce's International Bureau and to Senator Russell Long, informing them of the corporation's economic interests, the probable effect of the outcome of their case on the rest of the investment community in Latin America, particularly on the role of private investors as envisioned in U.S. development policy for Latin America. Senator Long and Jack Behrman of the International Affairs Section of the Department of Commerce sent letters to the State Department. Political pressure was exerted on the Panamanian government through threats to cut off loans in accord with the Hickenlooper Amendment to the Foreign Aid Bill of 1962. In a matter of weeks the Panamanian government acceded to the demands of the corporation. In the process it was revealed that the President of Panama, Mr. Chiari, was on the board of directors of a processing plant operated by the Boston Panama Company. Such U.S. intervention through economic pressure and cooptation of members of the political elite is far more common and important in shaping Latin American policies to U.S. needs than military intervention.

The political pressures exerted through official bureaucratic and diplomatic channels in the Boston Panama case were preceded by similar activities involving the International Telephone and Telegraph Company in Brazil. In fact the Boston Panama executives leaned heavily on the procedures utilized by ITT in its successful dealings with the Brazilian government. As in Panama, the Brazilian government sought to improve the use of economic resources, in this case the communication system which under ITT had failed to meet the increasing needs of Brazil's fast-growing cities. Brazil attempted to nationalize ITT's property, offering a monetary compensation. Refusing the sum offered, ITT turned to the State Department which, as later in Panama, used the threat of the Hickenlooper Amendment to arrange a favorable settlement for ITT.[7] Both the Brazilian and Panamanian governments were in extremely vulnerable financial situations and were dependent on U.S. financial assistance.

Through numerous close ties with high military officials in Latin America via training schools, exchange visits, military assistance and advisers, the United States can indirectly veto potential presidential candidates perceived as threats to what U.S. policy-makers consider critical interests. The channels through which policy is habitually set and personnel chosen help the United States to intervene without appearing to intervene: it is done as routine activity via established institutions by public officials, elected or self-selected depending on what the particular tradition may be in each particular Latin country. The interlocking of public and private interests does not involve any secret conspiracy by an evil cabal. The frame of reference is generally known by the political actors and is accepted as a matter of fact.

The dependent nations in Latin America are largely the more developed nations, which generally select their own public officials and contain a sizable domestic middle class. Apart from that, however, they are heavily dependent on U.S. corporations or government for foreign exchange earnings, loans and credits, imports, markets for exports, military alliances and training of officers. Politically they support U.S. positions in international affairs except in regional matters adversely affecting domestic elites, or occasionally on questions of direct military intervention.

The recent agreement between U.S. copper corporations and the Chilean government is a case in point. In the course of a discussion with one of President Frei's top economic advisers we asked why Chile had not made an effort to nationalize the highly profitable mines instead of granting tax cuts and buying into one of the least profitable mines. The Chilean official answered that he thought that nationalization was a good idea—but that it could not be done because the Chilean government was several hundred million dollars in debt to the United States. If we nationalize, he continued, your government will demand immediate payment, and if it is not forthcoming, we may have your navy and Marines in Valparaíso as in Santo Domingo. The hypothetical sequence of events which this Latin official described fits in well with our discussion of the routine type of politico-economic intervention, with one modification: manipulation and nonmilitary intervention appears to be backed up by the implicit or explicit threat of a more direct sort of intervention. In this case and in the multitude of day-to-day administrative policy choices which confront Latin officials, there need be no person or group representing U.S. interests on the premises to keep watch. Rather the imperial presence is incorporated into the political culture of a client state like Panama or a dependency like Chile. The fact that politicians are socialized to accept certain alternatives as the rules of the game itself constitutes a form of intervention.

Among the client states and the dependencies the pattern has been for the United States to rely almost exclusively on routine, nonmilitary techniques in influencing and shaping the policies and makeup of regimes. It should be added, however, that this restraint may be the result of the success so far achieved by these limited means. Should limited measures prove inadequate, the United States probably would turn again to unilateral military intervention. On this point we have the testimony of President Kennedy, who asserted immediately after the failure of the U.S.-directed invasion of Cuba in 1961:

> Let the record show that our restraint is not inexhaustible. Should it ever appear that the inter-American doctrine of noninterference merely conceals or expresses a policy of nonaction—if the nations of this hemisphere should fail to meet their commitments against outside Communist penetration, then I want it clearly understood that this government will not hesitate in meeting its primary obligations which are to the security of our nation.[8]

NOTES

1. The Hickenlooper Amendment is one example of the economic sanctions available to the United States. The use of it and of a variety of other economic measures was threatened in the conflict between U.S.-owned International Petroleum Company and the Peruvian Government in the 1968–1969 period.
2. Gordon Connell-Smith, *The Inter-American System* (New York: Oxford University Press, 1966), Chs. 1 and 2.
3. Tenth Inter-American Conference, *Documents of the Plenary Sessions.*
4. See Eduardo Galeano, *Guatemala: Occupied Country* (New York: Monthly Review Press, 1967).
5. See James Petras, "Dominican Republic: Revolution and Restoration," in Marvin Gettleman and David Mermelstein, *The Great Society Reader* (New York: Random House, 1967), pp. 390–412.
6. The information is gathered from private correspondence.
7. John Hickey, "The First Year: Business," *Inter-American Economic Affairs,* XVI (Summer 1962).
8. Associated Press, April 20, 1961.

The Rockefeller Report
on the Americas*

On October 31, 1969, President Nixon delivered a major policy speech to the Inter-American Press Association outlining his Administration's orientation toward Latin America. As Nixon pointed out, his proposals were "substantially shaped by the report of Governor Rockefeller." The Rockefeller mission was initiated by the Nixon Administration as a means of formulating ideas on policy to deal with Latin American problems. A close reading of Nixon's address and the *Rockefeller Report* reveal a convergence of viewpoints, a surprising unity of purpose and outlook. Thus the *Rockefeller Report* is not merely another study but an important document that reflects the thinking of influential policy advisers and that is likely to shape the concrete measures taken by the Nixon Administration. An analysis of the *Report* is thus extremely important in understanding the direction of U.S. policy and the meaning of specific actions.

The Search for a New Policy

The Rockefeller mission to Latin America, the subsequent report to the President, and Nixon's policy speech all are attempts to discover a new post-Alliance for Progress policy. The goals set forth in the early Alliance documents are as far as ever from realization: instead of democratic governments, autocratic military regimes rule over most of the area; the large landowners still dominate agriculture; the rate of growth during the decade was not only lower than the Charter of Punta del Este's 2.5 percent per year but also lower than the average growth rate of the 1950's. Ex-

---

* *The Rockefeller Report on the Americas* (Quadrangle Books: Chicago, 1969).

ternal resources for development amounting to $2 billion yearly were more than balanced by the outflow of payments for debts, profit remittances, etc. Even one of the founding fathers of the Alliance, Harvey Perloff, concedes that "the accomplishments of the Alliance since 1961 have been poor indeed." [1] There is thus almost universal consensus that the Alliance was a failure. The question remains: with what does the Nixon Administration propose to replace the "democratic revolution" enunciated in the Alliance?

The Report: Prescriptions for the Status Quo

While the Rockefeller mission was being organized, Latin American leaders met in Viña del Mar to produce a position paper entitled "Consensus of Viña del Mar." This document called for elimination of trade barriers, reduction in freight rates, liberalized terms for loans, more Latin elite participation in development decisions, etc. No proposals for internal reform were included. In short, the Latin elites were asking for more consideration from the United States in their efforts to develop their societies and maintain control. The elite recommendations to promote development from above, i.e., without structural changes or popular participation, appear to have influenced the *Rockefeller Report*.

The Rockefeller mission to Latin America was planned at a time when regimes politically friendly to the United States were numerous, but also at a time when populist-nationalist opposition to these regimes was growing. In this political context, U.S. policy-makers were searching for measures to stabilize a politically favorable status quo which was marked by serious economic and social problems. Rockefeller's *Report* provides U.S. policy-makers with a series of proposals designed to produce more flexible instruments and organizations to keep the Latin American economies afloat and to strengthen the economic elites. The over-all purpose of the *Report* is to facilitate the consolidation and expansion of U.S. economic and political interests in the area.

The *Report* appears to contain both reform and conservative proposals, with the emphasis on the latter. Some of the recommendations are aimed at toning down some of the more visible excesses of U.S. economic/political exploitation. The most important proposals from the point of view of political power are those aimed at strengthening the machinery of repression: what emerges from the proposals for change is a model for a developing police state. In language reminiscent of the early 1950's, the *Report* noted that "it is plainly evident that . . . [communist] subversion is a reality today with alarming potential." [2] This is the same trick that Joe McCarthy used—the self-evident truth: there is an international communist conspiracy discernible to all except those vulnerable to subversion. The prime mover of the conspiracy is not Castro and Marxist forces (which, however, have "joined for acts of subversion, terror and violence in the cities") but the Soviet Union, which is behind the Cuban terror." [3] The *Report,* basing its tendentious assertions on the presence of Soviet ships in Havana, notes: "This Soviet performance in Cuba and throughout the hemisphere is to be contrasted to the official Soviet government and Communist Party protestations not only of peaceful co-existence but of disassociation from Castro and his program of terror in the American republics." [4] This improbable view is put forth at a time when the Soviet Union is providing credits and commercial assistance to a number of U.S. client states and when the Latin American Communist parties have everywhere denounced armed revolution. Chastising Nixon's predecessor, Johnson, for being soft on communism, the *Report* states: "Clearly the opinion in the United States that communism is no longer a serious factor in the Western Hemisphere is thoroughly wrong." [5] A major spokesman of the Eastern Establishment discusses revolutionary politics in Latin America within the same conspiratorial framework popular with backwoods Southern reactionaries. Throughout the account, whether discussing young people, labor, or the church, the turn toward radical politics is always presented as being in large part due to "subversive penetration."

The *Report*'s discussion of the alternative routes to development is dogmatic, simplistic, and colored by wishful thinking, asserting that the choice is between a "pluralistic form of government which will enable individual talent and dignity to flourish," and one that is "radicalized, statist and anti-U.S." [6] Either the regimes are for the United States or they are against it; there is no third alternative. To insure that the "right" path is chosen, the *Report* suggests that the Latin military be indoctrinated at U.S. training bases in the "fundamental achievements of the U.S. way of life." [7]

While socioeconomic problems are mentioned in the *Report* they are never connected to the social order which generates them, and the prescriptions for dealing with them involve strengthening the coercive forces which uphold that social order: more police and military training; more arms and military equipment to suppress internal opposition; easier access to large-scale armaments.[8] Condemning current levels of U.S. collaboration with conservative military regimes as insufficient, the *Report* goes on to recommend more "realistic efforts . . . on an effective hemisphere-wide basis." [9]

The *Report* quaintly reveals its affinity for authoritarianism by noting that "the question is less one of democracy or a lack of it than it is simply of orderly ways of getting along." Throughout the *Report,* the right-wing military and civilian dictatorships which oppress the Latin people and whose policies are largely responsible for stagnation and poverty, and wholly so for severe political repression, are referred to as "free nations," "democratic governments." Political forces bent on changing those oppressive conditions and institutions are in Rockefeller's terminology "enemies" —the "covert communist forces" who "exploit" these factors.[10] The *Report* is based on a conspiratorial view of Latin American politics bordering on paranoia—a madness which, however, has a calculated policy purpose: to strengthen the U.S. commitment to the military, to the buildup of the coercive apparatus, and to an outlook which encourages direct U.S. military intervention when and if needed.

The obvious sympathy for right-wing extremism found in the *Report* may have been influenced somewhat by Rockefeller's hostile reception upon arrival in most Latin countries, or perhaps it was the cancelled invitations; one cannot discount completely the factor of hurt pride and personal peevishness. Moreover, in Rockefeller's case more is at stake in the general hostility shown to him than a loss of face: the Rockefeller interests are an important investor group in Latin America. The mass popular demonstrations were directed at those investors like Rockefeller who

plunder the continent. The threat that popular-national movements represent to Rockefeller's personal interests merely reinforced his perception of the threat that they represent to the larger
U.S. investment community. It is within this matrix of personal
pique, private interest, and class-ideological conviction that the
extreme repressive measures proposed by the *Report* must be understood.

Reforms to Prevent Change

The organizational changes proposed in the *Report* flow from
its political perspective: the emphasis is on centralizing and ra-
tionalizing the structure of policy-making in order to allow for
rapid and uniform action capable of dealing with emergencies.
The kinds of changes which the *Report* suggests make the U.S.
presence less visible but not less real; see for example the *Report*'s
strong endorsement of U.S. private capital and its emphasis on
the need to provide a favorable investment climate.

The emergence of client regimes obviates the need for unilateral
action; hence the *Report* stresses multilateral action, in which
friendly client regimes are to jointly share the burdens of policing
and administering the empire. Conceding that U.S. interests have
not always treated the Latin elites well, the *Report* recognizes
the need to subsidize these impotent social forces in order to maintain a friendly neighborhood of client states. The U.S. has not
heretofore assumed full responsibility for its hegemonic position.
As a result the client regimes have not received an adequate share
of the benefits and are in danger of losing ground to the "covert
enemy." The *Report* is thus particularly concerned that the Latin
elites receive a larger share of the returns.

Specifically, the *Report* calls on the United States to revise
some of its tariffs and quotas to increase Latin trade, especially
in manufactured goods. This may have some negative impact on
the most backward and inefficient sectors of the U.S. economy,
but it will clearly benefit the large manufacturing subsidiaries of
U.S. multinational corporations which now predominate in most
Latin countries. In other words, the trade liberalization policy
proposed by the *Report* coincides with the denationalization of

industry in Latin America and becomes a means of expanding U.S. overseas enterprises by providing optimal world conditions: low taxes and labor costs abroad and profitable markets in the United States. The *Report* proposes that prices of Latin commodities be stabilized. U.S. consumers, largely wage and salaried workers, are to subsidize the Latin and U.S. *latifundistas* and plantation owners. Given the authoritarian nature of current Latin American societies and U.S. material support of the police who uphold them, the benefits of liberalized trade and subsidies cannot be broadly shared.

U.S. aid to bolster the sagging satellite economies has largely seeped back into U.S. pockets; much of it has served to finance short-term impact programs and to secure the political positions of friendly politicians. Aid has had little or no impact in promoting dynamic long-term Latin American development. The *Report* suggests that high interest rates and other overcharges, including the obligation to use U.S. freighters, be eliminated. But, the restrictions on the spending of U.S. loans, previously confined to purchases of U.S. goods, are to be liberalized only to the extent of permitting purchases "within the Western Hemisphere." [11] The price competitors with U.S. producers, however, are not found in Mexico, Paraguay, Bolivia, Brazil, or Argentina but in West Germany and Japan. The latter countries, which can consistently undersell U.S. capital-goods producers, are still excluded.

The debts which the Latin elites have incurred and the drain of earnings out of the country by foreign investors have made the economic position of Latin regimes very precarious. The *Rockefeller Report* suggests that debt payments be deferred where client elites face serious problems in keeping their economies afloat.

According to the *Report,* Latin industries are to develop as adjuncts of U.S. industrial development. "Specializing" in the technologically backward and low-paying industrial areas, they can supply the United States with cheap consumer products while importing goods from the more sophisticated industrial enterprises of the north. The *Report* refers to this institutionalization of inferiority and dependence as a "more efficient division of labor." [12]

In the last third of the *Report* there is a series of tables and graphs documenting the social problems of Latin America. The omissions are glaring: there is no discussion of agrarian reform, i.e., land redistribution. Nixon and Rockefeller are completely oblivious to the problems of millions of landless peasants. The erroneous and simplistic notion is put forth that increased production will improve the lot of everyone. Studies have shown that the expansion of commercial agriculture has merely displaced agricultural laborers, increased the earnings of the landowners, and accentuated social inequalities. The profound problems of health, education, and welfare which the *Report* describes are not linked to the socioeconomic institutions and policies of the Latin "democratic nations." Nor is any attempt made to discuss the contribution of overt and covert U.S. military, economic, political intervention and policies to the perpetuation of these explosive social and economic conditions, an omission especially significant in light of the *Report*'s recommendations that the police powers be strengthened against "insurgent forces," more accurately the social forces who would be looking for some social improvements.

Conclusion

The post-Alliance Latin American policy of the Nixon Administration will be largely geared toward consolidating the current configuration of political and economic forces within the hemisphere. Changes in the areas of trade and aid will be marginal and will reflect the pressures which will be forthcoming from the Latin elites who are feeling the pinch in their own societies. The transfer of technological innovations, to the extent that it takes place, will primarily depend on the large privately owned U.S. multinational corporations.

The strategy of conserving the status quo will be challenged on the margins by newly emerging "elite nationalists" who will increasingly press for greater trade with Europe, the Communist countries, and Japan, and for better terms from the United States. It is not inconceivable that the Nixon Administration may be forced to make concessions to these "elite nationalist" regimes providing that there are not simultaneously changes in property relations within society. A system permitting foreign exploitation and fostering a rigid class hierarchy based on a modernized police-military apparatus and securely within the U.S. orbit is the "model" which the Nixon Administration hopes to consolidate and nourish in Latin America.

NOTES

1. Harvey Perloff, *Alliance for Progress: A Social Invention in the Making* (Baltimore: Johns Hopkins University Press, 1970).
2. *The Rockefeller Report on the Americas* (Chicago: Quadrangle Books, 1969), p. 34.
3. *Ibid.,* p. 35.
4. *Ibid.*
5. *Ibid.*
6. *Ibid.,* p. 33.
7. *Ibid.*
8. *Ibid.,* pp. 63–65, *passim.*
9. *Ibid.,* p. 61.
10. *Ibid.,* p. 60.
11. *Ibid.,* p. 86.
12. *Ibid.,* p. 101.

IV

Criticism
of Studies
# of Latin America

Latin American Studies
in the United States:
A Critical Assessment

Central Assumptions and Strategies in Current Research

A tacit, yet central assumption of many students of U.S.-Latin American relations is the idea that Latin American social and economic development is in harmony with United States interests.[1] Further, some go so far as to state that conflict between the United States and Latin America is a function of irrational Latin attitudes toward the United States (Yankee-baiting, xenophobia, etc.).[2] Others suggest that a misperception of U.S. interests combined with a generous portion of "errors" by well-meaning U.S. policy-makers is behind some of the antagonisms.[3] Balanced between Latin misunderstanding and U.S. errors are the neat formulas calling for "closer cooperation" issued by the U.S. or, from the Latin side, for "more concern for Latin problems." [4] The problems are thus set afloat in the sea of "common concerns" which engulf the two areas and provide the basis for joint action or at least discussion. Issues are removed from the context of power relations and attached to a set of policy formulations which encompass the supposed desires of both parts of the hemisphere.[5] Yet the intensity of North American liberal rhetoric is matched by the impatient demands of Latin America's impoverished millions. The social scientist, seeking to come to grips with reality, must confront the facts of mass discontent, poverty, and exploitation in Latin America.

"Harmony-of-interest" adherents generally employ one or more of three research strategies: (1) separation of the human or social condition from the basic structure of the society; (2) separation of the "structural problems" from the existing political agencies of change; (3) projection of political guidelines meant to solve the problems, contain discontent, or stabilize the situation while allowing United States policy to appear progressive.

Incrementalists: Maximizing the Marginal

The first approach, while taking cognizance of the basic destitution in Latin America, also discovers "hidden unused" resources which, if developed, would offer a beginning toward overcoming that destitution. The incremental approach uncovers virtues in even the most oppressive conditions (e.g., inflation, which exhausts the masses in the endless pursuit of subsistence, gives the elite room to develop, and leads to stability).[6] Acceptance of the status quo becomes the first step toward change. This theory minimizes any conflicts within the society or between the United States and any part of the elite.

Seeking virtues in the stagnant society which might actually lead to change while blessing existing alliances is an ideological solution often used by U.S. policy-makers. It requires no modification of established arrangements—simply imaginative discoveries of what can be done with the current elites. By setting aside any discussion of the social forces necessary for structural changes, this kind of analysis focuses almost exclusively on policy proposals unrelated to structural conditions or the actual behavior of elites. Taking the period from World War II to the present, the actual functioning of elites in country after country has produced economic stagnation and the perpetuation of glaringly inequitable land and income distribution, widespread malnutrition and hunger, disease and illiteracy, greater class differences, and sharper social conflict. Political authoritarianism and instability have become the hallmark of Latin countries.[7] The social scientist of the status quo imagines himself in the Department of State directing loans and other assistance southward on the journey of progress.[8] The temporal sequence extended, the loss of dynamism becomes part of a large historical picture in which continuous stagnation becomes the background of that journey. More than advocates of any other approach, the incrementalist accepts on sheer faith the convergence of United States and Latin American interests in Latin development.

The Structuralist: Ethnocentricism in Development Studies

The structuralist approach concentrates on examining the relation between human conditions and society through the institutional structures. The researcher, his values drawn from North American experience, constructs a model based on an idealization of U.S. institutions. He separates out for criticism those institutions and problems which do not correspond to his preconceived model, e.g., the "traditionalist" sector, the "feudal" landed aristocracy, and the military, which are condemned as unproductive and inefficient. He condemns the anachronism of paternalistic social relations in an age of collective bargaining. Totally distorting history by ignoring the West's occupation and plunder of continents, its use of violence, slavery, and exploitation, the researcher presents Western development as a model for evolution through stages and usually ends with a call to the landowner for "self-reform." [9] Uneasy about overt relations between the United States and "traditional" groups, the researcher may caution his colleagues in the State Department about over-identifying with a declining group, or even appeal to them to reorient policy. But he does not seek to find out why throughout history no serious conflicts have developed between U.S. policy-makers and the "traditional" groups over the question of exploitative social relations. Nor is serious consideration given to the "adaptive" behavior of modern United States corporations—i.e., their frequent borrowing of traditional methods of social control.[10] Above all, for this research approach, problems are localized in the "community"—village or slum—and thus can be considered apart from the areas in which decisive U.S. interests are involved. The methodological separation of specific analytic units, such as the traditional landowner, becomes an ideological weapon when these units are not put back into relation with the dominant system of power, urban interests, and intersystem relations. By attacking traditional landowners in isolation from other phenomena, the researcher plays the role of both structural critic and loyal defender of his homeland, spokesman for the "expectant peoples" and exponent of liberal democracy.

Policy Guides: Social Science as Ideology

The third and more heterogeneous group, the "policy guides," recognize the unstabilizing impact that U.S. policy has on Latin America. Some of the writers even predict catastrophes ahead unless certain demands are met.[11] U.S. neglect of the Latin American continent is the common concern of this group: a somewhat puzzling concern given the continued control and saturation of the Latin American internal market by U.S. exports (over one-third of all U.S. machine exports are absorbed by it), the continued control and extraction of primary goods and profits, and the establishment of military schools for large numbers of Latin military personnel. Among this group, the activist wing conceive of themselves as, and in fact frequently are, advisers to the State Department.[12] Additionally, they are spokesmen for a political potpourri in Latin America calling itself the "democratic left," and are likewise influential in promoting a "democratic alternative" to communism. While in practice nearly all these "democratic movements," once they have attained power, have perpetuated existing inequalities and repressed popular forces, the scholars of this point of view in theory accept the need for revising organizational structures to incorporate sectors of the populace. Because of the political orientation of this group (its close relation to the State Department and the Latin regimes) and their desire to influence policy, their writings are full of impressionistic descriptions interspersed with exhortations to U.S. policy-makers. Strident apologies are offered for the corruption and failure of "democratic left" regimes, coupled with energetic denunciations of those who unequivocally condemn these failures as "extremists," "terrorists," etc. Lack of any systematic analysis leads the policy-guide adherents to borrow concepts from the structuralist and incrementalist schools and lump these with appeals to stolid State Department officials to participate in social revolution.

In place of analysis, one is offered descriptions of social sectors in terms of their relation to the author's program.[13] The middle sector, for example, is likely to be described as embodying not only progressive goals but the political know-how ("realism") necessary to realize them. Historical description, often based on somewhat tendentious interviews, tends to confirm the same characteristics and to set the stage for the author's presentation of his highly schematized program and the next level in the "democratic revolution." [14]

Some Misconceptions of Key Problems

Both the scholarship and the ideology of these schools employ certain widely used concepts derived from a nonconflict model of U.S.-Latin American relations.[15] The assumption of "harmony of interests" precludes analysis of social problems and internal conflicts, and projects a set of concepts which buttress this fundamental assumption. Typical are such categories as developed-underdeveloped nations, and modern-traditional societies.

The developed-underdeveloped descriptive concept is very common in literature dealing with U.S.-Latin American relations. While it is interesting to note in quantitative terms how one country compares with another, this framework does not allow for analysis of the decisive power relations between the two, the degree of control that one exercises over the other, and how this feeds one system and drains the other. The causal sequence is aborted: the factors which produce basic quantitative differences are ignored and only the effects of this basic dominant-subordinate relation are revealed, compared, and considered relevant. The dynamics of intersystem relations, the interrelation between the dominant industrial countries and the subordinate primary producers is almost totally lost when the focus is on discrete problems in a static comparison of the developed and underdeveloped nations.[16] The underlying theory of "harmony of interests" suggests a static, one-dimensional, quantitative analysis which leaves out or minimizes conflict and hence the real concern of governmental policy-makers.

The needs of the subordinate countries differ from those of the industrialized countries which control major decisions affecting the former's development.[17] The control by U.S. business of Latin imports, exports, technology, and finances is well known. When President Johnson, as a matter of course, sent the FBI to investigate and uncover "communism" in the Dominican Republic, and when members of the CIA explained to the public on a television program ("The Science of Spying") how they organized the overthrow of the Guatemalan government, permeation by the United States of the Latin military and police became public knowledge.[18]

These two factors, force and economic resources, generate sufficient leverage to contain the ruling political groups within bounds which U.S. policy-makers consider permissible. Conflicts nonetheless emerge precisely because key sectors of the opposition in Latin America are not institutionalized and find a powerful base in the popular thrust against the military-administrative-economic straitjacket of U.S. policy. This "lost" dimension—the intersystem decision-making process[19]—must be made explicit in any consideration of development. Likewise, the question of control over decisions is intimately related to the ability of the subordinate countries to mobilize resources for development. The central conflict (U.S. dominance versus Latin American developmental aspirations) is over the two major necessities of development, control over natural resources and over the internal market. The two major failures in Latin countries, their inability to develop a dynamic internal market and a dynamic industrial sector, are related to the fact that they have had little control over decisions directly affecting these areas.[20] The central conflict in U.S.-Latin relations is between social forces within Latin America which are trying to assert such control, and attempts by the United States to maintain its dominant position.

U.S. proposals for the formation of an inter-American army,[21] the invasion of the Dominican Republic, and violent opposition to the Cuban Revolution, as well as the Latin American opposition to these U.S. policies, are all responses to the question of development in the broadest sense of the word. Those forces in Latin America concerned with maximizing the use of internal resources for national socioeconomic growth clash with U.S. policy, which is premised on maintaining control over decisions affecting the Latin market and primary products, in order to further the growth and expansion of the U.S. economy. Hence, concepts such as "developed" or "underdeveloped," which preclude consideration of conflict, cannot cope with the most relevant issues at their source.

The incrementalists, structuralists, and policy guides alike believe in the sincerity of the U.S. government's periodic declarations of concern for Latin development; this leads them to consider the problem in a "constructivist"—that is, uncritical—way: how can more hospitals, schools, and the like be encouraged, how can more value be added, how can prices be stabilized? Important as answers to these questions are, they cannot be arrived at without reference to the decisive control exercised by the United States over key Latin American resources and the resulting effects on the national developmental process. This indicates the multiple limitations inherent in the use of static, quantitative, comparative concepts.

Historical Perspective: A Lost Dimension

The distortion imposed by this sort of analysis is multiplied by the use of unilinear conceptions of historical development.[22] The First New Nation ideology, which transfers a given type of development from one period to another that is totally different, and which imposes the characteristics of the one on the other, overlooks the relations of domination and subordination which the first nations impose on the latter.[23] More to the point, it overlooks the degree to which the development opportunities (colonies, export markets, etc.) which obtained earlier no longer exist for the developing nation, but have become positive advantages and weapons for maintaining dominance by the already developed country. The cumulative disadvantages of today's subordinate countries, in a context of established centers of industrial power, impose radically new patterns for development.[24]

Paradoxically, the development criteria for the First New Nations become the ideology sanctioning the containment of the new insurgent developmental forces. The dogma of unilinear-historical development is both a model of frustrating dynamic growth (as a political doctrine, this is expressed in the "democratic-capitalist model" based on U.S. experience) and a faulty conceptual framework for examining the potentialities and necessities inherent in the development of the subordinate countries in the contemporary world.

Jousting Windmills: Sectoral Conflict

U.S. social scientists specializing in the subordinate countries, particularly the structuralists, make frequent reference to two sectors, the modern and traditional.[25] As pointed out earlier, U.S. policy is usually presented as geared to promoting the former and eliminating the latter. Taking their cue from this overt orientation, the social scientists proceed to analyze each of the two sectors—leaving aside the key problem: the extent to which the modern sector is conditioned by the existence of the traditional one. More concretely, instead of contrasting communication and popular political participation in each area and then devising typologies of the modern, transitional, and traditional as a method of coming to understand development,[26] it is more useful to examine the degree to which participation in the modern sector has been based on the perpetuation of a closed system in the traditional sector, as in Brazil, Chile, etc. Further, in light of recent happenings, the dynamics of development and concrete historical events suggest that when there are strong indications that this relation is going to change, the "modern" sector acts in a very "traditional" fashion, that is, it suppresses participation.[27] The political, social, and economic interrelations between the traditional sector and the modern, the fact that the leading elites are integrated through family ties,[28] individual relationships, or by the impersonal forces of the market, indicates the practical uselessness of making the analytic distinction.

The lack of conflict between the modern and traditional elites (based on the interlocking of personnel and the overlap of interests), the existence of a traditional sector with a constant supply of readily available mobile cheap labor for the city, and the easy exploitation resulting in high profits and an outlet for investment by enterprising entrepreneurs from the modern sector indicate the integration of both sectors. In Latin America "traditional social relations" found in the modern sector are used, with occasional modification, to maximize profits and maintain the modern system of production. The extensive use of domestic services, cheap hand labor, the violent opposition to independent industrial unionism,[29] and the demand by the entrepreneurs that the state control the unions reflect the continued domination of traditionalism in the city, including the industrial sector.[30] Modernity is not a geographical question, but a class question. Modern living and conveniences for whom? In Latin America there exists a stratified modernity coterminous with the strata controlling the economic resources of the country. Traditionalism and modernity vary according to the levels of analysis of the socioeconomic system. One can discover modernity at the level of the productive unit (techniques) and yet find traditionalism at the level of social relations (worker-owner).

The interpenetration of modernity and traditionalism is the typical form of modern capitalist development and of command relations in the subordinate countries. It is usually manifested in the development of modern production techniques side by side with the maintenance of traditional social relations in order to keep labor docile or under control. The decisive conflict hence cannot be as the "dualists" would have it, between a modern sector and a traditional sector, but between those dominant classes having access to modern life through their socioeconomic power and those subordinate classes exploited through traditional social relations. A perspective capable of analyzing societal development within Latin America today as an integrated whole would focus on these patterns of interdependence and interrelation within an international framework of subordinates and superordinates.

Social Change and Neo-Positivistic Fallacies

Popular concepts used to describe the subordinate countries have changed with time, probably more because of political considerations than for reasons of analytical clarity; the harsh-sounding "backward countries" became the mildly deprecatory "underdeveloped countries," which gave way to the more affirmative "developing countries." The new rubric indicates that as more countries established native political regimes, the connections between the dominant powers and the new elites of the subordinate countries demanded a positive characterization. The social scientists of the dominant countries supplied the demand: the nations ruled politically by the new elites still subordinate to the old metropolitan centers were renamed "developing areas." [31] To continue using earlier terms would be to point up the abortive nature of the transfer of decision-making from the metropolis—by merely handing over political and not economic control. This in turn would highlight the growing socioeconomic gap between the subordinate and dominant countries.

As a descriptive conception, the idea of "developing countries" underplays not only this growing gap[32] but the instability, stagnation, and hence growing political authoritarianism of these regimes.[33] The impact of these combined social-economic-political factors on the development process makes the regimes of the subordinate nations susceptible to violent overthrows, which may reinforce the tendency toward regression, as, for example, in Brazil and Bolivia.[34] The weight of these crises and the historic import of the subsequent shift away from development play no role in the concept of "developing nations." [35] Just as the idea of "revolution" does not preclude the concept of counterrevolution, likewise the concept of "development" should include the idea of regression. And it would be a mistake to take account of the regression concept merely by subsuming it within a general developmental framework as an incidental factor or as part of the "cost" of development.[36] Events in Chile, Paraguay, Brazil, Argentina, Colombia, Haiti, Bolivia, Ecuador, Guatemala, and Uruguay have shown that the concept of political, social, and economic regression can describe historical patterns much more accurately than the concept of "developing countries." [37]

Comparative analysis which takes "development" in the general affirmative sense (increasing industrialization, rising standard of living) as a given, belies an optimism which assumes that "necessity is the mother of invention." On the contrary, needs can persist without any significant changes or attempts to satisfy them, as has been the case in many of the subordinate countries. In this sense the concept of "transition" or "nations in transition" should be related to both poles, regression and development. The impact of historic events, such as violent shifts in power toward antidevelopment groups, or decisions by the elites of the dominant powers to utilize force in establishing antidevelopmental policies,[38] can decisively change the direction and rate of economic and social development. The political variables can become negative factors in the historical process. What appear as abstract processes of social and economic development—which determine "political modernization" can, under the impact of decisive historical events and decisive shifts in political decision-making and power, become in turn subject to the determinants of the new national and old international decision-makers. Analysis of national economic and social and political development must be subsumed within an international framework of subordination-dominance. The consequence of focusing exclusively on "national variables" in the subordinate countries is that too often the international variables break like thunder over one's head and the neat cross-sectional correlations are destroyed.

NOTES

1. In broad fashion these assumptions, along with a plea for more U.S. "understanding," can be found in the following partial list of sources:

   A. A. Berle, *Latin America: Diplomacy and Reality* (New York: Harper and Row, 1962).

   H. E. Davis, *Government and Politics in Latin America* (New York: Ronald, 1958).

   Lincoln Gordon, *A New Deal for Latin America: The Alliance for Progress* (Cambridge, Mass.: Harvard University Press, 1963).

   Lewis Hanke, *Modern Latin America: Continent in Ferment* (Princeton, N.J.: Van Nostrand, 1959), 2 vols.

   John Johnson, *Political Change in Latin America: The Emergence of the Middle Sectors* (Stanford, Calif.: Stanford University Press, 1958).

   William Whatley Pierson and Federico Gil, *Governments of Latin America* (New York: McGraw-Hill, 1957).

   J. Fred Rippy, *Globe and Hemisphere: Latin America's Place*

in the Post-War Foreign Relations of the United States (Chicago: Regnery, 1958).

William S. Stokes, *Latin American Politics* (New York: T. Y.
Crowell, 1959).

Frank Tannenbaum, *Ten Keys to Latin America* (New York:
Knopf, 1963).

In addition, the U.S. Senate itself has published a lengthy docu-
ment, *United States–Latin American Relations: Compilation of
Studies Prepared Under the Direction of the Subcommittee on
American Republics Affairs of the Committee of Foreign Re-
lations,* 86th Cong., 2nd Sess. (Washington, D.C.: Government
Printing Office, 1960).

One of the few sources occasionally questioning this main-
stream assumption was the *Hispanic American Report* (no longer
published). See, for instance, its discussion of the support by the
U.S. labor movement of Latin American company unionism:
Hispanic American Report, XV (October 1962), p. 702. In an
earlier period, prior to World War II, under the general editor-
ship of Harry Elmer Barnes, a series of well-developed studies on
imperialism was published.

2. A quotation from John Johnson's *Continuity and Change in
Latin America* (Stanford, Calif.: Stanford University Press, 1964)
is illustrative. He writes: "Nationalism, especially in the negative
sense of a tendency to hold someone else responsible for a people's past failures and current difficulties runs like a bright thread
through the complex pattern that has been developing in Latin
America since the end of the nineteenth century" (p. 14). Johnson also employs the easy method many scholars have adopted
for disposing of the problem of imperialist domination—putting
it in quotation marks: "Politicians began to win votes by associat-
ing the traditional ruling elites with a decadent European culture
and with foreign elements who were 'victimizing' Latin America"
(p. 14). According to this account, alliances between the U.S.
business community and "traditional" elites exist only in the slogans of ambitious politicians; high profits extracted by foreign
investors appear as something cooked up to win votes. This of
course assumes both that the politicians are simply opportunists
who paint false pictures of foreign concerns and that voters are
incapable of perceiving the benign social role played by foreign
business elements. Both assumptions are part of an elitist attitude
toward the Latin nations and their citizenry. More important, in-

sistence on these assumptions precludes any thorough examination of the objective basis for the Latin attitudes: the actual associations between the traditional elites and foreign elements and their "contribution" to the nation and lower income groups. For such a discussion of the economic basis of Latin American anti-imperialism, see Robert F. Smith, *The United States and Cuba: Business and Diplomacy, 1917–1960* (New Haven, Conn.: Yale University Press, 1960), and Maurice Zeitlin and Robert Scheer, *Cuba: Tragedy in our Hemisphere* (New York: Grove Press, 1963).

3. See Tannenbaum, *op. cit.*, and Hanke, *op. cit.*

4. See the speeches at the OAS conference in Rio de Janeiro, November 1965, especially the presentation by the Chilean and U.S. delegations: *La Nación* (Santiago de Chile), November 21, 1965, p. 25.

5. Roberto Campos, the Brazilian economic director of the Castelo Branco dictatorship, taking a "realistic" view of power relations, accepts the fact of U.S. power and domination of the hemisphere and builds his "development perspective" within this power relation. Hence, for example, his promotion of U.S. investment even at the expense of what is called "marginal inefficient" Brazilian enterprises. See *Ultima Hora* (Santiago de Chile), January 16, 1966, p. 2. This of course has alienated sectors of Brazilian private enterprise, especially those which are not subsidiaries of U.S. firms.

6. Albert O. Hirschman, the most candid and conscious exponent of this approach, states: "I am trying to show how a society can begin to move forward as it is, in spite of what it is. Such an enterprise will involve a systematic search along two closely related lines: first how acknowledged, well-entrenched obstacles to change can be neutralized, outflanked and left to be dealt with decisively at some later stage; secondly and perhaps more fundamentally, how many among the conditions and attitudes that are widely considered as inimical to change have a hidden positive dimension and can therefore unexpectedly come to serve and nurture progress." *Journeys Toward Progress* (New York: Greenwood, 1963), pp. 6–7. See especially his discussion in "Inflation in Chile," pp. 159–233, for an application of his method. See also Anibal Pinto's *Chile: Una economía difícil* (Mexico City: Fondo de Cultura Económica, 1964), for a Latin American adaptation of this approach.

7. At best some countries like Brazil experienced short bursts of economic growth, accompanied by a virulent inflation and followed by economic stagnation and political authoritarianism. Mexico, which has shown steady economic growth, is a country in which growth was preceded by a violent prolonged revolution, not by elite maneuvers to maintain a basically untenable structure. The typical cases of countries whose elites utilized the incrementalist approach—Colombia, Uruguay, Chile, Argentina, and Peru—failed to achieve substantial social and economic improvements and have experienced increasing political insurgency.

8. Hirschman places great importance on his potential usefulness as policy coach: "More important, if it [his idea] could be instilled into the policymakers it would sharpen their perception . . . enhance their resourcefulness." In "pleasantly" noting this "convergence of a private research interest with a pressing public need," Hirschman also accepts the fact that the U.S. is "involving itself into the policymaking process of other countries to a hitherto unheard-of extent." *Op. cit.*, p. 7.

9. See W. W. Rostow, *Stages of Economic Growth* (New York: Cambridge University Press, 1960).

10. Interestingly, it was a nonacademic journalist who has written one of the better books on U.S.–Latin American relations and who presents abundant examples of U.S. exploitation of Latin America. See John Gerassi, *The Great Fear in Latin America* (New York: Macmillan, 1965).

11. Any one of the yearly productions by Robert Alexander will stand as typical; one might look at *Prophets of the Revolution* (New York: Macmillan, 1962) or *The Struggle for Democracy in Latin America* (with Charles Porter; New York: Macmillan, 1961). See also Gerald Clark, *The Coming Explosion in Latin America* (New York: McKay, 1963), Theodore Draper, *Castro's Revolution* (New York: Praeger, 1962), Johnson, *Political Change in Latin America* (cited above), Harry Kantor, *The Ideology and Program of the Peruvian Aprista Movement* (New York: Octagon, 1953), and Gary McEóin, *Latin America: The Eleventh Hour* (New York: P. J. Kennedy, 1962).

12. One should include Arthur Schlesinger, author of the "White Paper on Cuba" and of a USIS pamphlet entitled *La revolución permanente* (1965), in this group of Latin Americanists. See Zeitlin and Scheer, *op. cit.*, for a documented critique of the

"White Paper" and its falsifications and mishandling of documents.

13. See, e.g., Johnson, *Political Change in Latin America.*
14. See Robert Alexander, *The Bolivian National Revolution* (New Brunswick, N.J.: Rutgers University Press, 1958).
15. A note of caution on the utility of a conflict model for analyzing dynamic factors (revolution, counterrevolution, etc.) at critical junctures. The point is not that a conflict model will necessarily bring out the direction of change; conflicts can be resolved in varying ways, depending on many factors, such as the relationship of forces or material and political preparation. A conflict model is a necessary but not sufficient basis for analyzing any specific outcome: it provides the framework through which one can approach the field of forces. Needless to say, an overexuberant commitment to a particular outcome can lead even a "conflict theorist" to make totally false predictions based, for example, on an impressionistic treatment of the relationship of international and national forces. Probably an extreme case was that of the author whose book on a revolution in the making in Brazil was published precisely at the time when a counterrevolution was taking place in that country. See Irving Louis Horowitz, *Revolution in Brazil: Politics and Society in a Developing Nation* (New York: Oxford University Press, 1964).
16. Ivan Vallier, "Recent Theories of Development," in *Trends in Social Science Research in Latin American Studies,* a conference report published by the University of California Institute of International Studies (Berkeley, Calif., March 1965). Vallier points to the significance of the intersystem relations in constructing a theory of development in Latin America. "The relationship between socio-economic development in these countries [Latin America] and their modes of involvement in the international or world system (economic, political, religious, etc.) provides material for conceptual and theoretical thinking. Although the international dimension is not being entirely overlooked in recent theories . . . the major stress has been placed on the country as the unit of analysis" (p. 24).
17. Paul Baran's excellent study, *The Political Economy of Growth* (New York: Monthly Review Press, 1957) deals with this. An interesting attempt at relating the intersystem variables can also be found in Merle Kling, "Towards a Theory of Power and Po-

litical Instability in Latin America," *Western Political Quarterly,* XI, No. 1 (March 1956), pp. 21–35.

18. This is not to underplay important relationships between national socioeconomic groups and military power. For a fascinating discussion, see José Nun's "A Latin American Phenomenon: The Middle Class Military Coup," in *Trends in Social Science Research in Latin American Studies.* He notes that ". . . in many cases, Latin American middle classes are threatened by the oligarchy or by the working class and voting is one of the principal instruments of this threat. Therefore, the army . . . in the majority of the countries comes to the defense of the threatened sectors and allows for political instability in defense of a premature process of democratization. Middle classes are then confronted with a double fear: fear of the problem and fear of the solutions . . . there are enough reasons to see the Latin American middle classes as factors of political instability, whose instrument is the army and whose detonator is precisely the democratic institutions which these sectors appear to support. This is a peculiar Latin American phenomenon that may be called the middle class military coup" (p. 56).

19. Fernando Cardoso in a preliminary paper, *El proceso de desarrollo en América Latina* (Santiago, Chile: Instituto Latino-Americano de Planificación Económico y Social, 1965), besides pointing to the inadequacy of conceptions of development as a "national" phenomenon, focuses on the international context of decision-making and the degree of dependence/autonomy that national decision-makers have in relation to the rest of the world.

20. In *Chile, una economía difícil,* Anibal Pinto points to some of the added difficulties in countries which have already taken up the "easy" opportunities for economic development through import substitution. This book, however, has two important weaknesses: one is the suggestion that basic problems may be overcome by reorienting entrenched interest groups which have shown little interest in fulfilling the roles which Pinto proposes for them; the second is the facile dismissal of the possibility of profound political changes which would underwrite the more dynamic orientation which Pinto considers so important. In this sense, the book is both utopian and conservative.

21. The text of Dean Rusk's speech at the November 1965 Rio de Janeiro Conference of Ministers reaffirmed, however, that the

United States will continue to intervene unilaterally in Latin American countries.

22. Glaucio Soares has dealt at length with this conception in "Economic Development and Political Radicalism" (unpublished Ph.D. dissertation, Washington University, St. Louis, Missouri, 1963).

23. See Seymour Martin Lipset, *The First New Nation* (New York: Basic Books, 1963).

24. For further discussion see "The Middle Class in Latin America," above, p. 37.

25. Daniel Lerner, *The Passing of Traditional Society* (Glencoe, Ill.: The Free Press, 1958).

26. *Ibid.;* and with a somewhat different focus, Karl Deutsch, "Social Mobilization and Political Development," *American Political Science Review,* LV, No. 3 (September 1961), pp. 493–514.

27. In Brazil, when Goulart attempted to broaden suffrage and introduce other social reforms, the biggest protest demonstrations were in the large urban centers and were composed primarily of the modern middle class.

28. Ricardo Lagos has done some important research on the integration of the economic elite in Chile; see *La concentración del poder económico* (Santiago, Chile: Editorial del Pacífico, 1965). Note especially Part II, pp. 93–159.

29. A recent U.N. document on industrial entrepreneurs in Latin America indicates that their acceptance of trade unions is coupled with a greater demand for greater state control. In other words, most entrepreneurs think in terms of corporate unions. Further, in the present context, what the entrepreneurs accept is the weak, highly fragmented trade-union structure, in which, with a few exceptions, each factory has its own union and 85 percent of the labor force is not organized in truly independent trade unions. The U.N. document observes that "a strong proportion of the entrepreneurs support the idea that the state must increase its control over the workers' organizations, above all in relation to the petitions for increase in salaries and the right to strike." United Nations, Economic Committee on Latin America, *El empresario industrial en América Latina* (E/CN. 12/642, 1962), pp. 16–17.

30. A survey study of the Chilean entrepreneurial elite shows that over 82 percent are for maintaining the present system of fragmented unionism or for increasing state control in order to further restrict basic activities. Less than 15 percent are for giving more

freedom to the trade unions. *El empresario industrial en América Latina,* pp. 42–44.

31. Gabriel Almond and James Coleman, *The Politics of the Developing Areas* (Princeton, N.J.: Princeton University Press, 1960); and M. Millikin and D. Blackmer, eds., *Emerging Nations* (Boston: Little, Brown, 1961).

32. United Nations, Economic Commission on Latin America, *Estudio económico de América Latina, 1963* (E/CN 12/696/Rev. 1, New York, November 1964), especially Ch. II, "La evolución del sector externo en la económia latino-americana en el período 1960–63," pp. 32–40.

33. United Nations, Economic Commission on Latin America, *Social Development of Latin America* (Mar del Plata, Argentina: May 1963).

34. For material dealing with regression in Latin America, see my article "Brazil Since the Coup," *New Left Review,* No. 34 (November–December 1966), pp. 72–78.

35. See C. Wright Mills, *The Power Elite* (New York: Oxford University Press, 1956), for an interesting discussion of the importance of historical events in modern political analysis.

36. For this positivistic viewpoint, see Johnson, *Political Change in Latin America*; Hirschman, *op. cit.;* and Victor Alba, "Latin America: The Middle Class Revolution," *New Politics,* I (Winter 1962).

37. Gerassi's *The Great Fear in Latin America* contains material tending to support this position.

38. Guatemala, on the verge of initiating a significant program of social reform, found itself the victim of precisely such a power play, and Mr. Nixon and Allen Dulles have pointedly taken credit for the effort. What they have not mentioned is the regression since the CIA-engineered coup of 1954. See Mario Monteforte Toledo, *Guatemala—Monografía sociológica* (Mexico City: Universidad Nacional Autónoma, 1959).

U.S. Congressional testimony in reference to the Brazilian military takeover indicates that the United States is heavily involved in making such decisions affecting even the largest of Latin countries.

The Dominican Revolt:
A Case Study of American Policy*

This study is an expanded version of Theodore Draper's earlier articles which appeared in a variety of magazines. At the time of publication a number of commentators and liberal Senators (including McCarthy and Gruening) hailed his essays as first-rate research on the subject.

Draper's discussion of the 1965 Dominican revolt is a narrowly conceived study of a particular aspect of U.S. policy: an analysis of the rationalizations presented by several highly placed policy-makers for their intervention against the Constitutionalist forces. Draper combines the reports of several journalists with the results of his own investigation and proceeds to show that the policy-makers consistently lied about the nature of the revolution and therefore about the reasons for which they were intervening. That is about as far as Draper's account takes us.

Little effort is made to relate this intervention to past U.S. interventions in the Caribbean; nor to connect it to general U.S. policy or economic and strategic interests in the area. The lack of any historical and contemporary context allows Draper to criticize particular policies of particular policy-makers while continuing to maintain his fundamental commitment to U.S. politics and to anti-communism. He avoids any systemic attempt to interrelate policies and link them to institutional and structural variables. More important, Draper's criticism of U.S. policy is based on opposition to a particular kind of intervention—against what he perceived as an anti-communist liberal regime. Implied throughout his

---

* Theodore Draper, *The Dominican Revolt: A Case Study of American Policy* (New York: *Commentary*/American Jewish Committee, 1968).

discussion is the notion that intervention in other circumstances might not be so morally repugnant.

At no point does Draper attempt to analyze the real reasons behind the falsehoods of statecraft. There is nothing new in the fact that diplomats lie. The point is that U.S. policy-makers themselves were not taken in by their own lies; they were acting and speaking from a specific political perspective. There is a consistent pattern in U.S. policy toward the Dominican Republic which Draper fails to discover. The result is that his account is quite inadequate and superficial in explaining *why* the United States chose the policies it did. About two-thirds of Draper's discussion is devoted to showing that the communists were not in the leadership of the revolution—thus refuting the official rationale for the U.S. intervention. But he never goes beyond this to ask: what then were the real interests served by U.S. intervention?

In analyzing the events surrounding the shifts in U.S. policy Draper never grasps the interplay between the changes in the nature of the revolution and the measures adopted by U.S. policymakers. With a monumental simplicity not characteristic of President Johnson and his advisers, Draper describes the struggle in the Dominican Republic as between Bosch and the supporters of liberal democracy on the one hand and the military who were attempting to install a dictatorship on the other. He fails to discuss the crucial change in the nature of the participants on the Constitutionalist side, especially after April 27. By that date thousands of unemployed and working-class Dominicans had received arms. The struggle of the pro-Bosch military group plus its allies among the bourgeois political leaders against the old *trujillista* military apparatus was transformed.

Draper's failure to analyze the significance of the transformation of the Dominican revolt from a military coup against Reid Cabral led by pro-Bosch military officers into a mass popular social upheaval prevents him from explaining the real basis of U.S. foreign policy, not only in the Dominican Republic but in other countries. Facing assaults from the U.S.-supported Dominican air force and army led by General Wessin y Wessin, the rebels decided to arm the civilians. From April 25 onward, armed civilians and army units patrolled the city together. By April 27 thousands of civilians had been armed.[1] One writer, Frederick Richman, concluded after lengthy interviews with State Department officials that "the decision to arm civilians perhaps more than any other rebel action, branded the rebel movement in the eyes of the State Department as Communist-dominated." [2] Based on interviews with James Johnston, assistant to Undersecretary of State for Economic Affairs Thomas C. Mann, and Harry Schlaudeman, State Department Desk Officer for the Dominican Republic during the crises, Richman found that "the more ideological State officials saw it [the decision to arm civilians] as 'standard Communist practice,' while the more pragmatic viewed the civilian armament as creating an anarchic situation which the Communists could exploit to their advantage. As one aide (Johnston) put it, the revolution was no longer 'controlled' and the risk of the Communist takeover should the revolution succeed correspondingly rose." [3] It was at this point that the United States decided to send in the Marines; the word "communist" in the operational code language of the State Department means: mass popular revolution that may have social as well as political consequences. When the armed populace outnumbered the pro-Bosch military, there was a real possibility of the revolution going beyond the limited middle-class political reforms espoused by Bosch. It was on this basis that the policy-makers of U.S. imperialism intervened— they couldn't risk "another Cuba" now that the revolution had burst the confines of bourgeois hegemony. Theodore Draper's profound hostility to radicalism, his strident defense of Bosch and of liberal politics in general cause him to select facts more in the manner of a defense lawyer than as a social scientist concerned with understanding a revolutionary event. His account, far from illuminating the forces and motivations shaping U.S. policy, presents us with a grotesque caricature which, however, fits the liberal middle-class prejudices and biases of *Commentary* magazine.

Draper's failure to consider the change in the social base of the revolution is matched by the irrelevancy of his criticisms of the Johnson Administration for squashing what he continued to view as a liberal revolution. President Johnson and his advisers were correct in foreseeing that the armed populace would not be satisfied with a parliamentary façade and the election of a president who had allowed the *trujillista* army to expand during his term of office. The armed Dominican populace could indeed provide a real base for a social revolution that would be independent of U.S. corporate, political, and military domination. This is what Johnson and his associates correctly perceived and what Draper refused to discuss.

In part Draper's study is an apology for Juan Bosch. Bosch's most incredible shortcomings, blunders, and miscalculations are turned into virtues by Draper. For example, throughout his discussion of Bosch's political career Draper points out that he did not utter "anti-American" (i.e., anti-imperialist) speeches. Draper cites this supposed virtue to lend weight to his argument that the Bosch forces were essentially "democratic." [4] During his presidency Bosch heard rumors that the Pentagon was plotting with the Dominican military to overthrow him but "for lack of proof [*sic*] did not complain." Draper goes on to note: "Until he was utterly dismayed and incensed by the U.S. intervention last April [1965], Bosch had scrupulously refrained from making any anti-U.S. allusion, even in the most trying circumstances. . . ." [5]

That is, Bosch was silent when, under Kennedy, U.S. military aid increased and a U.S. Military Assistance Advisory Group trained three new companies of "counter-subversive troops"— which were instrumental in overthrowing him. [6] The military's share of the budget increased from 25 percent under Trujillo to 40 percent and the number of military men increased by 10,000. [7] Bosch "refrained" from exposing U.S. imperialism's support of the Reid Cabral dictatorship, and preferred to rely on the U.S. Navy to offset the *trujillista* gangsters who overthrew him rather than attempt to organize the popular forces. In short, Bosch must bear heavy responsibility for the influence that the United States exercised during his term of office. His failure to recognize the imperialist role of the United States played into the hands of the Dominican right wing and hardly prepared the Dominican people for the terror bombings, armed assaults, and eventual occupation that were in fact the result of the initial U.S. intrusion. His unwillingness to align with the revolutionary Left and his responsiveness to pressures from some of his close associates to join the coalitions and elections imposed by the U.S. occupation further disoriented the struggle for Dominican freedom. [8]

It was only after the provisional government and later the Balaguer regime murdered many Dominican revolutionaries that Bosch, in exile, began to publicly and forcefully attack U.S. imperialism. Unlike Bosch, Draper still refuses to recognize the interrelationship between specific policies and the general counterrevolutionary thrust of U.S. imperialism. Without too much reflection, much less evidence, Draper throws out the idea that there were significant splits among policy-makers and that the State Department was divided. The liberals in other words lost a policy outcome but the system as it stands is still capable of developing "democratic alternatives."

U.S. imperialist policy is not the product of a struggle between good guys in the State Department and bad guys in the Pentagon but directly reflects the corporate interests represented by major policy-makers. From their point of view it made sense to lie about the nature of the revolt, to send in the army to set up a number of puppet juntas, to restore the *trujillista* army—and to repress the armed populace demanding political freedom and a social transformation. Draper's discussion of surface issues fails to illuminate the underlying social forces that shape the past, present, and future struggles in the Western Hemisphere.

NOTES

1. *New York Times,* April 27, 1965, p. 2.
2. Frederick Alexander Richman, "The Dominican Intervention: A Case Study in American Foreign Policy" (Honors Thesis, Department of Government, Harvard University, 1967), p. 41.
3. *Ibid.*
4. By equating criticism of imperialism with "anti-Americanism," Draper demonstrates the ignorance that frequently accompanies unreflecting nationalism. A social system is not the same as a nation. It is Draper's essential "pro-Americanism" that causes him to identify democracy with the United States and makes him oblivious to the fact that the U.S. occupation of the Dominican Republic empties the notion of democracy of any substance.
5. Draper, p. 36.
6. John Bartlow Martin, *Overtaken by Events: The Dominican Crisis*

From the Fall of Trujillo to the Civil War (Garden City, N.Y.: Doubleday, 1966), p. 353 *passim*.

7. *Ibid.*

8. The role played by self-styled "democratic socialists" from the United States in talking Bosch into participating in the elections is a sordid one. This visit was financed by the U.S. government whose agencies and military forces controlled the countryside. The pro-U.S. military forced Bosch to confine his electoral campaign to making tape recordings of his speeches in his home. The outcome of this farcical election was blessed by Theodore Draper's co-religionists Norman Thomas and Bayard Rustin upon their return to the United States.

Revolution in the Revolution?*

Despite basic weaknesses in Debray's discussion it is necessary to acknowledge a number of valid points. Debray correctly points to the Latin American leftists' lack of military knowledge and their preoccupation with junkets to "international democratic organizations" at the expense of national concerns. Second, he effectively destroys the notion that the revolutionary vanguard in Latin America is necessarily the "Marxist-Leninist party" (read: pro-Moscow or Maoist groups) and properly calls for a new analysis of revolutionary politics free from the influence of Russian and Chinese dogma and based on Latin American reality. Debray's prescription to the non-Communist revolutionaries (nationalists, Catholics, Socialists and Marxists) is that it is a "right and duty to constitute themselves a vanguard independently of these parties." Third, Debray presents an accurate (but all too brief) sketch of the ossification and bureaucratization of the Communist parties in Latin America (again, both pro-Moscow and Maoist) for whom ". . . the political organization has become an end in itself." He correctly points to the negative results of the sterile schisms and sectarian squabbles among "revisionists," "Marxist-Leninists," and "Trotskyists," etc., which afflict the Latin American revolutionary movement. Debray notes that these divisions do not reflect national problems but the international policies of external powers. His description of how, for a time, the Communist Party manipulated the guerrillas in Colombia, Guatemala, and Venezuela is excellent.

When polemicizing against corrupt, inert, bureaucratic parties, Debray is a perceptive critic. However, what he offers in their place is less than adequate since he deliberately avoids even a rudimen-

* Régis Debray, *Revolution in the Revolution?* (New York: Monthly Review Press, 1967).

tary political analysis of developments in Latin America. (This omission is rationalized on the ground that he is seeking to overcome the destructive politics of the pro-Soviet and the Maoist parties.) Instead, a series of formulas for action is substituted for political analysis; the problems of revolutionary struggle are defined in "military insurrectionary" terms. Debray writes: "Revolutionary politics, if they are not to be blocked, must be diverted from politics as such." But blocked by whom? To answer this crucial question demands political analysis because it requires a critical study of the relation of Stalinist politics to revolutionary struggles, from local manipulation to international politics. Indeed, by avoiding serious political analysis, Debray deprives his proposed military activity of any rational meaning and there cannot be any coherent explanation of the current political impasse of the guerrilla movement or any light shed on the underlying causes for the reversals suffered by the revolutionary movement in Latin America.[1] Thus, when he attempts to come to grips with guerrilla defeats he ascribes them to individual mistakes, inexperience, and to being part of a larger historical perspective—a convenient excuse for avoiding difficult, concrete political analysis.

For Debray, improved military tactics and individual "determination," "awareness," and "certainty" are sufficient to make a successful revolution. This argument, lacking any substance, falls back on tendentious analogies with the "Cuban case," largely based on personal communications from Fidel Castro during the Sierra Maestra period. Debray's advocacy of guerrilla separation from the mass appears to be an attempt to make a virtue of the isolation of the initial guerrilla movements. Yet how is it possible to generate "all forms of struggle" by the "initiative" and "mobility" of a guerrilla group which is isolated from a mass base and located in remote *focos*?

In his sometimes virulent polemic against mass, organized revolutionary politics, Debray focuses on a specific tactic, the use of armed self-defense by Bolivian miners. Here, he grossly oversimplifies a complex situation with the shallow observation that the miners' unequivocal defeat "proves" that the policy of self-defense was wrong. One could similarly argue: the Bolivian guerrillas were wiped out, *ergo*. . . . That, of course, is no way to discuss serious political problems. Debray trivializes major political questions: the defeat of the Bolivian miners is ascribed to an ideology ("Trotsky-ism") while guerrilla defeats are due merely to poor tactics. Debray, unlike a Bolivian revolutionary, does not have to answer to a work-ing-class constituency and evidently he feels free to offer the miners hollow platitudes and thundering commands. But what is a mass working-class movement to do when it has to protect jobs and un-ion to keep everyone from starving: turn to armed self-defense or wait until guerrillas "take the initiative"? Debray's answer is to criticize those movements having some contact with the masses while holding high his abstract Revolutionary Strategy—so high that it is neither related to popular problems nor relevant to the living social forces which create a base of support for revolutionary struggles. Likewise, Debray's dismissal of the economic demands of workers as reformism is nonsense; economic struggles in Latin America become political precisely because the ruling class is so dependent on the state.

Accepting the isolation of the guerrillas from the mass, Debray develops the idea that mass support is a function of the develop-ment of guerrilla firepower and offensive strength, rather than view-ing the relationship as a dialectical process in which the guerrilla struggle is an outgrowth of mass struggle, assisting the mass move-ment and, in turn, strengthened by it.

In one sense, it appears that Debray has overreacted to the be-trayal of Communist Party politics: *all* parties, politics, and mass struggles are rejected in favor of guerrillas, elites, and military tactics. But Debray has more in common with the Latin Commu-nists than he would like to think. Both Communist collaboration with the bourgeoisie and Debray's *guerrillerismo* reflect an unwill-ingness to involve the masses in revolutionary struggles or to build movements and parties that truly reflect and defend their interests. Debray's gratuitous insults of Bolivian revolutionaries and the Peruvian peasant leader Hugo Blanco are reminiscent of Stalinism.

Thus, despite references by some writers to Debray's "romanti-cism," he is really an organizational man, at least in his writings. He reduces complex social and political processes to simple organ-izational formulae. This "theoretician of revolution" brushes aside as too "theoretical," questions dealing with the moving forces of society, their levels of struggle, the issues around which they fight. For Debray, ". . . the nub of the question is not theoretical, it lies in the forms of organization through which the Socialist Revolution will be realized." [2] Because of this superficial approach Debray completely fails to recognize the important political activity of Blanco in Peru and Yon Sosa in Guatemala: their work in organizing and politicizing masses of previously isolated and exploited peasants. When Debray does attempt to make a specific criticism he commits the elementary mistake of not checking out his sources. Drawing on a document from the Rebel Armed Forces (FAR)— when it was under Communist Party influence—in order to attack Guatemalan guerrilla leader Yon Sosa, Debray accuses him of denying the importance of the peasantry in the revolution (Yon Sosa has spent years in peasant organizing), of underestimating military tactics (Yon Sosa has been fighting arms in hand for seven years), etc. Debray repeats these silly lies which even the FAR (minus its pro-Soviet wing) no longer believes: how else explain FAR cooperation with Yon Sosa today?

Instead of writing polemical diatribes against the tiny Posadas sect which wormed its way into one of the Guatemalan guerrilla units, Debray should have faced a more serious problem: the absence of an analysis and theory of Latin American development within the guerrilla movement, a failure which left it to types like Posadas to provide alternatives to the bankrupt Stalinist dogma of collaboration with the national bourgeoisie.

To justify his elitist conceptions Debray attributes the stranglehold of Latin American reformist bureaucrats over mass organizations to the limited consciousness of the masses. Along with impressionistic bourgeois journalists, Debray suggests that cleavages between mass organization leaders and the rank and file exist only in a feverish Trotskyist imagination. With this superficial view it becomes easier for Debray to see the struggle in terms of guerrilla units against the state, since the masses are "initially passive" and their "protection depends on a favorable military outcome." Debray does not know that many Latin American reformist leaders develop organizational interests and methods separate and apart from the members and then bureaucratically impose their views on the organization, and that given a favorable opportunity the masses, including those found in the most developed countries of Latin America, have shown enormous combativeness.

Throughout Debray's account one finds a preoccupation with "security" and a distrust of everyone. The working class is "reformist"; trade unions are "economist"; cities are bourgeois; peasants can't be trusted. If all this is so, on what basis does one construct a revolutionary organization? Even on the level of revolutionary techniques and tactics Debray is badly informed. He rejects "armed propaganda" as ineffective, leading to disaster. Yet, Montes, leader of the FAR (a group which Debray continually praises), effectively used armed propaganda.[3] Debray's error was to equate "armed propaganda" with speeches and faith, when in fact it involved activities such as expropriation of land, retributive justice to terrorist landlords, etc. The only specific suggestion he offers to win over the peasantry is "combativeness"; he never discusses what the guerrillas fight *about*. Without a program and specific socioeconomic reforms, the struggle between the state and the guerrillas would appear to the peasantry as a squabble between two parties equally alien to them.

There is a certain sophistry in Debray's mode of arguing. In criticizing armed propaganda, he asks: "How have the inhabitants rid themselves of their class enemies?"—as if recruitment of peasant militants is not part of the process of eliminating class enemies. By asking the same ultimatist question about Debray's proposal for suicidal "direct confrontations with the military"—will one attack on a military convoy rid the peasantry of its class enemy?—one can evoke the same negative answer. Debray's mindless military action becomes the route for bypassing the complex political work that accompanies armed revolutionary struggle. Fortunately, his prescriptions have been rejected by the Guatemalan guerrillas.

For a book which specifically states that it is based on the Cuban experience there is precious little serious study of the social forces which enabled the Cuban Revolution to succeed. Debray's account is a distortion of Cuban revolutionary experience. He divorces military aspects from political questions as though the Revolution's success was determined merely by Castro leading 200 fighters against 5,000 soldiers. But contrary to this mythical notion, there were organized forces in the cities, towns, sugar *centrales,* and universities that directed men and material to the mountains and to the streets. The student directorate, the July 26th Movement, and the militant trade unionists provided massive urban support for that revolutionary struggle.[4] If Latin American revolutionaries imitated Castro's "military confrontation" with Batista, as Debray advises they should, without the national, urban Cuban political conditions, it would result—and has already resulted—in tragic disaster.

Debray's pragmatism, his narrow vision, and his ill-informed discussion of tactics without any understanding of the socio-political context lead him mistakenly to consider military tactics apart from the concrete social conditions existing in each Latin American country.

As noted earlier, Debray believes it impermissible to subordinate the guerrillas to a party. His argument is based primarily on the experience of armed struggle in Venezuela, Colombia, and Guatemala. More specifically he discusses the relation of a guerrilla movement to a party, the Communist Party, which was intent on dismantling the guerrilla operations. The question he does not confront is: what should be the relationship of a guerrilla movement to a non-CP party committed to revolution (not coexistence), which has an apparatus for conducting an armed struggle? And if such parties do not exist and guerrilla struggle begins, should one make a virtue of this weakness as Debray does? Because he does not recognize the absence of a revolutionary organization as a weakness, and because he equates all parties with the Communist class-collaborationist parties, he feels free to condemn the urban area which produces such parties as a "bourgeois" trap for revolutionaries. What Debray does not realize is that the reason it is a trap for revolutionaries like the Peruvian guerrilla Héctor Béjar, or the Venezuelan Fabricio Ojeda, is that there was no urban revolutionary underground and that the Communists at best ignored them and at worst cooperated with the police. It is not the city or the urban party that is at fault, but the unfavorable relationship of social forces and, more specifically, the failure of the existing leftist organizations to develop a revolutionary policy.[5] Armed with empty abstractions, Debray distorts the important role which the urban populace has already played in revolutionary struggles (Dominican Republic 1965, Cuba 1959, Venezuela 1958, Bolivia 1952, etc.) and which it must play in the future.

Shifting from the question of party to that of leadership, we find Debray repeating the same errors. He argues that the abandonment of the guerrillas was due to the urban location rather than the policies of the leadership. Debray should know better: when the Venezuelan CP recalled its guerrillas, both urban and rural party leaders quit. It was not the bourgeois ambience or psychology of the city that brought the Venezuelan CP leader Petkoff down from the mountains. Debray covers up basic political differences between social revolutionaries and pro-Soviet class collaborationists with psychogeographical mystifications. Because of this corrupt relationship between the CP and the guerrillas, Debray opts for self-reliant guerrillas and makes a virtue of isolation from centers of urban radicalism.

Debray proposes to reduce infiltration by reducing contact with the cities to a minimum. He has already spoken of the untrustworthiness of the peasants, polemicized against armed propaganda, against peasant unions, against self-defense by trade unions and independent republics, against vanguard parties. The question is, aside from Debray, whom does one recruit?

In practice, the Bolivian *fracaso* revealed that without trained cadres in the city and country, a substantial group of undisciplined and unreliable activists were recruited along with honest revolutionaries to the guerrilla movement, with disastrous results. Ralph Schoenman's analysis speaks to this point:

> As to the guerrilla: the guerrilla seemed to be comparatively cut off from the traditional left formations. And one consequence of this is that in the cities and in the mines there was an absence of struggle which related to what the guerrillas were doing. In the cities very little is known of the Liberation Army.
>
> The absence of an underground paper or leafleting or political activity, psychological warfare in support of the guerrilla, the absence of these things was an important contributory factor to the isolation of the guerrilla.[6]

In Debray's scheme of things, military operations and tactical knowledge of military operations are given priority over gaining mass support. The result is that isolated, purely military victories do not lead to political gains or to weakening the central state power. Given his mountain mystique, Debray had little or nothing to say to the millions of workers of Chile, Argentina, Uruguay, and the Dominican Republic where the urban populace is much more militant than those in the rural areas. He offers no political strategy for struggle to Venezuela's huge urban slums, Peru's sugar plantations, etc.

Mistrust of the masses and ultravoluntarism are both elements in Debray's demand for an authoritarian organization. Debray proposes to "put an end to . . . congresses . . . assemblies at all levels." Democracy is "paralyzing"; it is the cause of the Debrayan vice called "excessive deliberation," which "hampers executive, centralized, and vertical methods." What if leaders, who are only too often misinformed, make incorrect decisions? What if lower cadre possess insights that lead to a wiser course? Does democratic or autocratic organization further the revolutionary movement in such cases? Debray does not provide any evidence that a "technically capable executive committee centralized and united, a revolutionary general staff" is better equipped to lead a revolution. He just assumes it, as a matter of principle.

A study of the history of revolutionary movements leads one to reject these elitist precepts. Dynamic revolutionary leadership can only emerge through class struggle and vigorous discussions and cannot resemble the ultracentralized organization espoused by Debray. Debray's type of leader breeds an atmosphere of dependence and intellectual sterility in a movement that usually disappears with the leader.

For Debray, who lacks a coherent theory of revolution, a handful of committee leaders can "set the 'big motor' of the masses" turning—a slight variation of the discredited old theory of an elite electrifying the masses through bold actions, an approach which has cost Latin American revolutionaries dearly.

By reducing armed struggle to guerrilla struggle, by equating guerrillas with an uprooted and isolated elite, by focusing almost exclusively on the military rather than the political aspects, Debray predetermines the outcome: defeat.

NOTES

1. Debray has shifted his viewpoint since he wrote *Revolution in the Revolution?* because of his discussion with Che and his experience with the Bolivian Stalinists, who apparently played an important role in aiding in the suppression of the guerrilla movement. In an open letter written from prison and published in *Le Nouvel Observateur,* November 7, 1967, Debray stated:

   "In light of the experience of the Bolivian comrades and of my last conversations with Che, I will undoubtedly modify *Revolution in the Revolution?* on important points where I am not completely in agreement with him, and I will strengthen other parts, broadening their meaning (the condemnation of the CP, for example, that Che found extremely chickenhearted). But it will be necessary, taking into account the difficulties encountered by the guerrilla movement in Bolivia, to point out the role of chance factors, the betrayals by individuals (unpredictable) and of the party (the latter was predictable but not to the degree and with such cunning), and of the very conception of revolutionary struggle put in practice with intransigence."

   See *Marcha* (Montevideo), November 24, 1967, pp. 21–22. Accounts from Bolivia suggest a close working relationship between the Barrientos dictatorship and the pro-Moscow CP, which was the only party among leftist and nationalist parties whose leaders were not arrested. See "Report from Bolivia Underground," *The Militant* (New York), November 24, 1967, p. 4; also "Interview with Ralph Schoenman," *World Outlook,* November 24, 1967, p. 959.

2. Apparently consistency is not one of Debray's strong points. Elsewhere he writes: "The penalty for a false theory is a military defeat. . . . the butchery of tens and hundreds of comrades and men of the people."

3. See Eduardo Galeano, "With the Guerrillas in Guatemala," *Ramparts,* September 1967, pp. 56–59, and an extended version of the same article in James Petras and Maurice Zeitlin, *Latin America: Reform or Revolution?* (New York: Fawcett, 1968), pp. 370–380.

4. For a detailed empirical analysis of the mass working-class support of the Cuban Revolution, see Maurice Zeitlin, *Revolutionary Politics and the Cuban Working Class* (Princeton, N.J.: Princeton University Press, 1967).

5. The importance of urban support of the guerrillas based on a vanguard party was cited in a thorough and perceptive analysis of the defeat of the Peruvian guerrilla struggle: see Silvestre Conduruna, "Las experiencias de la última etapa de las luchas revolucionarias en el Peru," *Vanguardia Revolucionaria* (Lima), No. 5 (1966).

6. *World Outlook,* November 24, 1967, p. 958.

Poder y clases en el
desarrollo de América Latina*

In recent years Latin American and U.S. social scientists have written a great deal about Latin American social classes, especially the middle class. Graciarena's collection of essays is one of the best and should be read alongside the work of Véliz, and Nun.[1] Of special interest are the chapters which deal directly with class and politics. An additional bonus is the excellent critical discussion of the activity of U.S. sociologists in Latin America and the role of their Latin American counterparts.

Graciarena exhibits great skill not only in criticizing existing analytical schemes—the abstract models that are irrelevant to understanding specific historical developments in Latin America—but in developing a counter approach that proposes to investigate problems growing out of the constellation of forces shaping the Latin American political experience within a coherent model of conflict politics.

There are a number of critically important issues that Graciarena raises from a fresh perspective. One such issue is the central role played by the state in Latin American political development. Unencumbered by concepts derived from U.S. political science ("interest group theory," "pluralism," "party politics," "congressional government," etc.), Graciarena convincingly argues that it is the bureaucracy which plays a major role in maximizing opportunities, allocating societal resources: in a word, he notes the decisive impact of politics on economic development.

Graciarena's account of both the historical and contemporary factors which have influenced the behavior of the middle class is excellent. His account of the different phases in middle-class

---

* Jorge Graciarena, *Poder y clases en el desarrollo de América Latina* (Buenos Aires: Editorial Paidos, 1967).

politics, and the shifts in policies, is a more accurate description than the views which claim for the middle class either a completely innovative or completely status quo orientation.

Despite the general perceptiveness of these essays, however, they contain some weaknesses. Graciarena's discussion of the white-collar worker as part of the conservative middle class may be valid for Argentina and Brazil, but in Chile and perhaps Uruguay certain occupational groups (bank employees, teachers, health workers, etc.) have shown great militancy, elected Marxist union leaders, and participated with blue-collar workers in common struggles.

Graciarena generally views political radicalism as largely a product of the continuation of "traditionalism." A careful examination of recent history upholds the opposite view: Latin American radicalism is associated with modernization and development; the advance of modern capitalism (especially in its imperialist form) makes exploitative social relations transparent to the worker, eliminating the paternalistic obfuscations that blurred class exploitation in the "traditional system." Urbanization, commercialization, literacy, and industrialization all have had the effect of radicalizing and politicizing oppressed class strata: exposed to new ideas and capable of understanding and transmitting them, the "modernized" oppressed groups begin to realize the social and political potentialities of organization and struggle. The decomposition of the older propertied classes and the expansion of the class of salaried workers have resulted in the creation of new strata which at times align themselves with radical political groups.

Graciarena, drawing his lessons only from past Argentine experience, too easily dismisses revolutionary politics as a phenomenon confined to intellectuals. In many parts of Latin America, capitalist expansion through foreign-owned enterprises resulted in permanent large-scale unemployment of class-conscious sugar workers, as in Cuba; in Chile and Bolivia capitalism organized and concentrated industrial workers in homogeneous occupational communities that became centers of Marxist working-class politics. The development of capitalist social relations and wage payments in rural Cuba and Chile and the increasing commercialization of agriculture in Peru coincided with the growth of mass support for revolutionary politics; it is not always a phenomenon of the urban intelligensia.

In contrasting political experiences in Latin America to those in the United States and Europe Graciarena understates the role of violence and exploitation and the degree of instability in the West in order to highlight them in the Latin nations. His account omits key political events in the development of the advanced capitalist countries: the rise of fascism (Germany, Bulgaria, Hungary, France, Italy, Spain) which eliminated opposition and created incentives and opportunities for investors; imperialism, regional hegemony, and conquest, including genocide, which provided the inexpensive flow of services and goods that dynamized their economies. Graciarena's discussion includes liberal stereotypes that describe European and U.S. politics in terms of "consensus." In 1968, 125 cities in the United States experienced violent black uprisings in one day, and ten million French workers walked off their jobs in a demand for structural change, yet we are given to understand that in the capitalist West consensus politics, self-sustained growth, and the end of ideology reign supreme. The apologetic writings of Daniel Bell, Raymond Aron, S. M. Lipset and Walt W. Rostow have unfortunately influenced Graciarena's account of Western development. He errs in accepting the liberal thesis of the peaceful evolutionary character of change in the advanced capitalist countries. If the Latin American businessmen whom Graciarena contrasts so unfavorably with those in the United States and Europe had the opportunities and protection afforded by an imperialist state, would they not be more "risk-oriented" and dynamic? Graciarena's account understates the problems *within* the advanced countries, as well as the problems that their imperialist policies create for the entrepreneur in underdeveloped countries.

But my major criticism is that throughout Graciarena's thoughtful discussion of the socio-political forces shaping Latin American political development (the "marginals," the middle class, etc.) he leaves out an important, if not decisive influence. The United States has become increasingly involved in internal Latin politics not only in the Caribbean but in the large countries of the Southern continent. U.S. policy-makers, and through them U.S. social forces, shape investment and financial policies through their control and manipulation of loan-granting agencies such as the International Monetary Fund, Inter-American Development Bank, the World Bank, etc.[2] The U.S.-dominated American Institute of Free Labor Development indoctrinates thousands of Latin American trade unionists. U.S. military schools have been vehicles of value transmission to at least 20,000 Latin American military officials. U.S. private investors have in recent years taken over many large industries in the more advanced Latin American countries. In short, U.S. personnel are a major determinant of Latin American development. North American officials and investors do not act outside, but within, the Latin social structure. Yet there is little if any detailed discussion in Graciarena's book of the multidimensional impact that U.S. imperialism has on the behavior of Latin American social classes, its effects on the distribution of power and the pattern of Latin American development.

Graciarena does discuss in a limited way the exploitative role of U.S. academics in Latin America and the policies of the International Monetary Fund, and this is good. But the analysis should go deeper and consider which social classes act autonomously and which are dependent on and/or dominated by U.S. policymakers and interest groups. For example, on my recent visit to Chile, I found that much of what passes for national planning was designed and influenced by U.S. personnel who were largely funded by the Ford Foundation. Even cabinet appointments in some countries are determined by U.S. officials, as former Bolivian Minister of Interior Argüedes has revealed. A discussion of power and social classes in Latin American development is not complete unless it integrates into the discussion data concerning U.S. penetration and influence. We need a model of stratification that takes account of the "international variables."

Despite these criticisms Graciarena's book does provide us with useful insights concerning the behavior of social classes in Latin America. What is needed now is a number of empirical studies of Latin American countries in order to verify or invalidate Graciarena's suggestive propositions; for example, to examine in detail the legislation of several middle-class governments in specific issue areas like education, welfare, and development, etc.). Graciarena's book provides a theoretical groundwork based on a solid understanding of Latin American reality which, if combined with empirical research, would produce some fascinating studies from the new generation of Latin American scholars.

NOTES

1. José Nun, "A Latin American Phenomenon: Middle Class Military Coup," in Petras and Zeitlin, *Latin America: Reform or Revolution* (New York: Fawcett, 1968), pp. 145–185; Claudio Velíz, ed., *The Politics of Conformity* (New York: Oxford University Press, 1967).
2. General Valdivia, a member of the ruling military junta in Peru, in 1968 revealed that the International Monetary Fund threatened to deny the Peruvian government a $75 million standby credit "unless Peru restores the properties of I.P.C. [International Petroleum Corporation]." Other agencies putting pressure on the General included the Agency for International Development, the Inter-American Development Bank, and the World Bank. See the *New York Times* for December 8, 1968.

Internal Security
and Military Power*

This book is concerned with the problems of internal security within Latin America, with the Latin American military's role in dealing with this problem, and, most important of all, with an analysis and discussion of those U. S. policies and institutions which have attempted to define both the security issue and the role of the military for the Latin Americans. In the concluding section the authors pass a critical judgment on U. S. policy, considering the U. S. role as harmful for democratic development.

Prior to discussing any other question about internal security and military power in Latin America, one must ask: what are the interests to be secured and to what type of social structure is military power wedded? And dealing in particular with the military programs of the United States for securing Latin America, one must investigate the historical context—the origins, development, and nature of U. S. involvement in Latin America. This procedure enables us to better understand the goals which U. S. policy-makers are currently pursuing. It also allows us to evaluate the program and goals of those forces which oppose U. S. policies.

The authors of *Internal Security and Military Power* accept the publicly stated goals of U.S. policy as if those goals actually guided the decisions of policy-makers. Those goals are basically three: (1) opposition to subversion; (2) support for constituted authority; (3) promotion of economic growth and social reform. Within this framework, the authors suggest that U.S. policy-makers face a dilemma: U.S. support for the Latin military in pursuit of public order and certain forms of economic development in practice

---

* William F. Barber and C. Neale Ronning, *Internal Security and Military Power* (Columbus, O.: Ohio State University Press, 1966).

means the repudiation of social reform. This is indeed a dilemma if the official statement of goals is taken at face value. The United States is then seen as the helpless victim of a native elite rather than its willing accomplice. The dilemma dissolves, however, when one observes, as Barber and Ronning do not, that U.S. policy encourages economic growth and social reform only insofar as these are compatible with U.S. property interests; supports constituted authority only when it upholds these interests; and defines as subversion any serious popular challenge to the status quo.

In recent years a number of scholars have pointed out a number of cases which illustrate the economic basis of the U. S. global policy.[1] More pertinent to our discussion of Latin America, however, is the considerable number of scholarly works which have documented in detail the expansionist nature of U. S. policy.. In the pre-World War II period, before Cold War scholarship defined the issue as one of hemispheric defense against the Communist Threat, many scholars seriously considered the issue of the United States threat to Latin American development.[2] Cold War academicians have conveniently ignored these early scholarly studies in order to push the U.S. government's line. These studies clearly point to the economic basis of U.S. concern for hemispheric security and internal defense of current Latin social systems. In this sense Barber and Ronning are typical products of Cold War scholarship: they ignore the essentially exploitative basis of past and present U.S. efforts to promote the military as an agency of civic action.

In the development of the United States the army not only provided engineers to build bridges, as Barber and Ronning mention, but exterminated the indigenous population to provide living space for the expansionist-minded capitalist farmers and industrial interests. The army not only made the useful surveys mentioned by the authors, but colonized and annexed by violence one-half of Mexico. In short, if we take into account *all* dimensions of the history of U.S. military-civic action, we are alerted to aspects of current U.S. policy in Latin America which do not illustrate the sort of progress that Barber and Ronning advertise.

Two chapters, the fourth dealing with "Administrative and Planning Agencies," and the fifth on "Training," are useful for understanding the U.S. government's counterrevolutionary effort in Latin America. The authors provide a detailed description of administrative and planning agencies: their members, functions, and scope of activity. This section also contains a good description of coordination between the Pentagon and State Department, in which the latter, contrary to popular liberal mythology, appears to exercise foremost authority. Against the prevailing assumption that major policy differences exist between Pentagon and State, Barber and Ronning describe how the two institutions interchange personnel and programs. The key unit appears to be the office of the State Department's deputy assistant secretary of politico-military affairs that guides, coordinates, and maintains liaison with the Defense Department and the military services on politico-military matters and relationships.

Two questions have been raised concerning Latin American politics: Why have Latin American revolutionaries chosen the methods of armed struggle? How does the United States control and influence Latin American politics?

An important part of the answer to the questions can be found in Barber and Ronning's account of the wholesale involvement of the United States in training, financing, and indoctrinating *thousands* of Latin military and police officials. According to the authors, U.S. policy-makers organize and train a broad array of repressive forces and supply them with plans and programs to physically destroy threats to "constituted authority." U.S. financial aid and programs of military-civic action have not promoted economic development and social reform, but they have provided U.S. policy-makers a lever of direct influence over Latin affairs: the authors describe a number of Latin military officials trained in the United States who have seized power, destroyed the opposition, and been warmly received by the U.S. government.

Full credit for the development of these policy orientations and practices belongs to former President Kennedy. As this study shows, in almost every policy area and agency the big push came from the Kennedy brothers. The Kennedy-sponsored Special Group (SG) set up the Inter-American Police Academy to train police to suppress mass protest activity; SG established the Internal Defense Plans for each country; SG established the "Country

Team" collaborative process which was a means of coordinating all U.S. agencies in a foreign country around a common counter-revolutionary strategy. The authors credit the liberal wing of the Democratic Party, notably Senators Fulbright, Church, and Morse, with taking the lead in promoting and extending worldwide counterinsurgency through civic action and regional police forces. The Kennedy Administration was responsible for modernization of the repressive apparatus.

The United States government operates numerous specialized training schools and courses to teach U.S. and Latin military officials how to defend the empire. In June 1962 the State Department began a series of counterinsurgency courses entitled "National Interdepartmental Problems of Development and Internal Defense." The Air Force set up a Special Air Warfare Center for counterinsurgency in Florida; the Army has established a Special Warfare Center at Fort Bragg; the Marines have their own training and indoctrination schools. In addition, there is the Military Assistance Institute in Virginia. The biggest training operation takes place at the U.S. Army School of the Americas, from which 16,000 Latin Americans had graduated by the end of 1964. For educating the Latin military elite there is the Army Special Warfare Center and School and the Army Civil School at Fort Gordon, Georgia. In addition, there are specialized training units like the Inter-American Geodetic Survey, the Mobile Training Teams, Air Commando Teams, and others. The courses which indoctrinate middle- and senior-grade Latin officers—the book contains an extensive summary—are becoming increasingly sophisticated; the officers now study insurgency in the specific political, economic, and social contexts in which it occurs. With the introduction of such careful organization and planning, Kennedy laid the groundwork for the ascendancy of the military in Latin America and for stabilization of U.S. power in the hemisphere. (The more immediate needs of U.S. corporate capital, however, were not ignored in the process: one "training goal" of the various institutes is to "further the sales of United States produced military equipment to meet valid country requirements.")

Through the author's discussion of U.S. planning and organization, both by the Special Group and by the Country Team, we come to a better understanding of the pervasive influence exerted by the United States on politico-military developments in Latin America. If the Latin countries—both the so-called "democracies" and the dictatorships—were not U.S. satellites in the past, they are rapidly becoming so. This study provides some concrete examples of U.S. influence over what are euphemistically referred to as the "Latin counterparts" of U.S. military officials. Discussing a pamphlet on civic action written by Colonel Julio Sanjines Goita, Bolivian dictator Barrientos' ambassador to the United States, Barber and Ronning point out that Sanjines had "obviously . . . absorbed some of the ideas of the U.S. civic action planning." The pamphlet's prologue was written by Colonel Truman Cook, then Chief of the U.S. military mission in Bolivia. It was published by AID. The authors also mention a Guatemalan officer who "had just returned from attending the Information Training School conducted at Fort Slocum, New York. Probably as a consequence each issue of the military magazine carried extensive articles and photographs of civic action projects." In general, the authors note: "The experienced observer of Latin America can detect in the speeches of its leaders and the publications issued by its defense departments, the ideas and arguments advanced by U.S. spokesmen for civic action. The same ideology and the same phrases are utilized."

As liberals who accept the reformist rhetoric of civic action, the authors use a makeshift cost-benefit analysis to argue that: (1) military-civic action is a highly inefficient and costly means to exploit resources for development and reform; the output is low relative to the amount of inputs—civilians could produce more output more cheaply; (2) politically the program has strengthened authoritarian regimes in Latin America. Accepting the official objectives of the military training program and civic action doctrine as "economic development" and "responsible government," Barber and Ronning are forced to conclude that U.S. policy has failed. They never consider the possibility that what they label "costs" are in fact counted as benefits by U.S. policy-makers, and that from the point of view of U.S. expansionist and business interests, military-civic action has been quite effective. Certainly it did its job well in the 1920's and 1930's: Trujillo and Somoza were generous to U.S. corporations and consistently supported U.S. international policies. It is hard to believe that the program's present aims are any different.

The continuation and extension of military civic-action programs by U.S. policy-makers suggests that they are interested in maintaining past relations and policies, not in basic reforms. Their criterion in shaping policy for Latin America is the degree to which it insures that Latin countries will defend U.S. economic interests and support U.S. international goals. The failure to help Latin America achieve economic development and social reform is simply a corollary of U.S. success in empire-building.

NOTES

1. See, for example, David Horowitz, *The Free World Colossus* (New York: Hill and Wang, 1965); Carl Oglesby and Richard Shaull, *Containment and Change* (New York: Macmillan, 1967); Robert F. Smith, *The United States and Cuba: Business and Diplomacy, 1917–1960* (New Haven, Conn.: Yale University Press, 1960); Maurice Zeitlin and Robert Scheer, *Cuba: Tragedy in Our Hemisphere* (New York: Grove Press, 1963).

2. E.g., Bailey W. Diffie and Justine Whitfield Diffie, *Porto Rico: A Broken Pledge* (New York: Vanguard Press, 1931); Charles D. Kepner, Jr., and Jay H. Soothill, *Banana Empire: A Case Study of Economic Imperialism* (reissue; New York: Russell & Russell, 1967); M. M. Knight, *The Americans in Santo Domingo* (New York: Vanguard Press, 1928); Margaret C. Marsh, *Bankers in Bolivia: A Study in American Foreign Investment* (New York: Vanguard Press, 1928); Parker Moon, *Imperialism and World Politics* (New York: Macmillan, 1926); Scott Nearing and Joseph Freeman, *Dollar Diplomacy* (paperbound reissue; New York: Monthly Review Press, 1969).

Pentagonism:
A Substitute for Imperialism*

Juan Bosch has written a book which purports to supersede
Lenin's description of imperialism as the last stage of capitalism.
"Pentagonism" describes a capitalist state which no longer needs
to exploit colonies but which expands and realizes profits by ex-
ploiting its own population through continual reproduction of war
material. Citing the growing size of the military budget, and more
specifically the proportion allocated to the Pentagon for war contracts, Bosch deduces that Pentagonism has replaced the earlier
capitalist-imperialist ruling class.

While military expenditures have indeed been a fundamental
factor in stabilizing the corporate economy, this has not replaced
the overseas expansion of U.S. capitalism but rather has complemented it. Bosch does not discuss the enormous growth of U. S. corporate investments abroad and the singular growth of the U. S.-
based multinational corporation in all areas of the globe. Secondly,
that the U. S. corporate ruling class has not become the subject of
the Pentagon, as is attested by the recall of Westmoreland, the reorganization of the Pentagon under McNamara, and the decision
by former President Johnson to engage in an Asian land war despite military advice to the contrary. Bosch's discussion of U. S.
politics is another version of the theory of two policy-making centers: the Pentagon devises a militaristic foreign policy while the
State Department proposes a nonmilitaristic one. Despite the obvious fact that all the initiatives to expand U. S. involvement abroad,
from the Dominican Republic to Vietnam, came from the Executive—that is, from the spokesmen for corporate capitalism—Bosch

---

* Juan Bosch, *Pentagonism: A Substitute for Imperialism* (New York:
Grove Press, 1968).

implies that "Pentagonism" was "really" responsible, though he presents no evidence whatsoever. The subordination of the military to U. S. corporate capitalism and its interests continues: the expansion of U. S. corporations abroad still defines the major thrust of U. S. foreign policy, and the Pentagon still functions to maintain the empire against popular revolutionary challenges. Bosch fails to show how the Pentagon gained autonomy from corporate capitalism; nor does he specify how it took over the decision-making machinery.

Bosch mistakenly attributes to Lenin the view that imperialism is manifested through military conquest and not through international economic, political, and social domination. Colonialism, Bosch should know, is only one form of imperialism.

The idea that the military is the source of external expansion was first systematically argued by Schumpeter and has been presented more recently by Richard Barnet. Unfortunately their attempts to explain how and why the military came to dominate policy are weak. Like his predecessors, Bosch falls back on psychological explanations, i.e., national character. But psychological drives can take any number of political directions, depending on what alternatives the social system and the economic institutions encourage. In Schumpeter, Barnet, and Bosch the psychological explanation is no explanation; the militarist psychology and military responses abroad are both rooted in the organization of society and more specifically in the nature of the economic system.

The value of Bosch's book is not in what it tells us about U. S. politics, but what it tells us about the author. Juan Bosch was, in the early 1960's, very close to the Kennedy Administration in Washington and allied with the self-styled "democratic left" in Latin America. A supporter of welfare capitalism, he cooperated with Kennedy's Alliance for Progress as an alternative to a Cuban type of social revolution. In 1963 Bosch, after winning an electoral majority in 1962, was overthrown by a U. S.-supported military junta; hundreds of millions of dollars in U. S. funds were poured in to prop up the Reid Cabral junta; when it was overthrown by a violent popular insurrection that demanded the restoration of Bosch's Constitutional government, the United States ordered the bombing of the civilian population and sent in 40,000 Marines. The terror and assassinations which ensued left their mark. Because of his experiences Bosch lost some of his illusions about the efficiency of parliamentarianism and elections as vehicles for social change; he shed his illusions about U. S. democracy; he lost confidence in most of his U. S. and Latin American liberal and social-democratic friends who betrayed him and collaborated with the United States during or after the occupation. This book is Bosch's attempt to come to grips with the failure and bankruptcy of his own past and that of his associates. Bosch, now self-exiled, has come to realize that U. S. imperialism has no conscience; and that in a crisis and under pressure from imperialism the "democratic left" will side with the Marines. Old comrades like Costa Rica's Figueres, Venezuela's Leoni, Puerto Rico's Muñoz Marín, and the North American A.A. Berle did not lift a finger. Norman Thomas and Bayard Rustin were part of the observation team sent to give cover to the U. S. sponsored elections that provided a legal facade for Bosch's ouster. *Pentagonism* is Bosch's attempt to describe the historical and social forces that have corrupted liberal ideals in U. S. society.

Latin American Radicalism*

Latin American Radicalism claims to be a "documentary report on Left and nationalist movements." Instead we find a collection of articles by U. S. and Latin American writers and academics who run the gamut from State Department advisers, through Kennedy liberals and Latin American bourgeois nationalists, to revolutionary socialists. What are the criteria for considering State Department and Alliance for Progress advisers like Rosenstein-Rodan, John J. Johnson, and Raul Prebisch equipped to prepare "documentary reports" on left and nationalist movements in Latin America?

This book is really three collections by three editors who have very little in common in terms of their political outlook, writing style, or their treatment of the subject they ostensibly are writing about. Irving Horowitz is responsible for the weakest section, Part I, "The Socio-Economic Pivot." In this section there are a number of studies, mostly by liberal scholars, which analyze a variety of subjects, from international politics to military institutions, which have no clear relationship. Essays of varying quality discuss the Alliance for Progress, the Latin American left wing, the Central American Defense Council. Though entitled "The Socio-Economic Pivot," the section contains no analysis of such a major social force as the peasantry and peasant movements, or of such a major social issue as agrarian reform in any of the countries where it has recently been attempted (Chile, Peru, Bolivia, Cuba). In a word Horowitz fails as an editor to establish any connection between the theme and the essays.

Horowitz's own two essays are good examples of the wordy and vacuous writing that C. Wright Mills so aptly criticized. For example, in "The Norm of Illegitimacy: The Political Sociology of

---

* Irving L. Horowitz, Josue de Castro, John Gerassi, eds. (New York: Random House, 1969).

375

Latin America," Horowitz writes: "Finally, each paper, in its own way, illustrates a concern with the norm of illegitimacy, the non-functional, nonequilibrated basis of political rules, economic policies and social systems that for the most part currently define the areas as an authentic entity over and apart from any of its national or regional parts." As a matter of fact, none of the essays in Horowitz's section except his own is specifically concerned with the normative aspects of political rules. Moreover, his essay is unsuccessful in its own right, an attempt at reconciling Marx and Max Weber which does justice to neither.

Weber's discussion of legitimacy relied on psychological, legalistic, and traditional formulas to explicate its meaning. Marx rooted his notion of legitimacy in the class character of society; in Marx's analysis of class societies, legitimacy was largely an artifact of the ruling class. Hence, legitimacy in a class society was always a relative phenomenon which did not exist independently of the class interests that it served. The Weberian notion, or at least Horowitz's discussion of legitimacy, reflects an empty formalism that perceives legitimacy as a neutral political substance whose value is extrinsic to the class interest that it rationalizes. Horowitz's essay fails to convey an idea of the *social* basis of legitimacy. Is it proper to regard liberal capitalist regimes elected in exploitative class societies as "legitimate"? If so, is this based on normative or juridical considerations? Horowitz is not clear on so basic an element of his theme and thus the rest of his discussion is obscure.

Part III, edited by John Gerassi, does contain a number of documents which are reports on left and nationalist movements, all of them, however, written from one perspective, that of the *fidelista* guerrilla movements. Gerassi includes excerpts from the writings of Camilo Torres, Debray, Castro, Guevara, and Fabricio Ojeda. He omits revolutionary socialists and nationalists, like Hugo Blanco, Francisco Juliao, the left Peronists, and Leonel Brizola, who propose an alternative revolutionary approach, armed struggle through mass organization. Likewise, though they are attacked directly or indirectly throughout the book, not one document or article is included to present the pro-Moscow Communist Party point of view, despite the fact that this tendency dominates the labor movement in Chile and Uruguay.

In the middle section, the Brazilian liberal Josue de Castro gathers together a number of informative articles, including studies of U. S. relations with the Dominican Republic, colonialism in Puerto Rico, and nationalism in Brazil. The dominant theme, the over-all negative impact of U. S. economic, cultural, and military policies, is adequately developed. Unfortunately there is little serious analysis of the determinants of U. S. policy; nor is there a systematic investigation of key policy-makers and their relationship to corporate and military institutions.

The book's unfocused and evasive character is epitomized in the collaborative introduction to the whole volume. The editors hedge all their political bets and fail to identify the prime targets of the Latin American anti-imperialist movements: ". . . the basic international need is for political revolution; and that would entail the expulsion of foreign imperialism. Whether in fact this two-pronged attack by the left on what they perceive to be the sources of continental misery will succeed or whether the analysis they offer is too simplistic to provide a satisfactory program or prognosis, remains to be seen."

Perhaps it is this studied disengagement from the issues that allowed the editors to put this book together in the first place.

Parasitism and Subversion *and* Capitalism and Underdevelopment in Latin America*

Over the past several years an enormous quantity of books on Latin America has appeared, an endless stream of volumes full of tedious clichés about revolution, irrelevant criticism of poverty, gratuitous (and sometimes subsidized) policy advice to indifferent U.S. officials, and ill-informed sensational journalism. Many of the new authors simply repeat or rehash arguments and descriptions from equally badly written and poorly researched earlier work.

Andreski's work is no exception. The standard formula for writing a book on Latin America is (1) to point out the problems (poverty, inequality, underdevelopment, injustice); (2) to contrast development in Latin America with the development of the "healthy Western democracies"; (3) to identify the villans in Latin society, enumerate their personal vices, and contrast these culprits with the efficient heroes of the Western world; (4) to proclaim the need to emulate the productive, efficient Western elites or suffer the torments of Totalitarian Revolution.

This approach allows the author to play two roles simultaneously —the social critic and reformer vis-à-vis Latin America, and loyal supporter of the West, or, more often, of the United States. The major tactic of this approach is to ascribe the problems of Latin American development and motivation to "feudalism," "traditionalism," or "Hispanic culture," thus evading the problems posed by the impact of five centuries of private enterprise.

---

* Stanislav Andreski, *Parasitism and Subversion: The Case of Latin America* (New York: Pantheon, 1966); Andre Gunder Frank, *Capitalism and Underdevelopment in Latin America: Historical Studies of Chile and Brazil* (New York: Monthly Review Press, 1967).

378

According to Andreski and a horde of U.S. Latin Americanists, Latin landowners who pay low wages and exploit their workers for profits are not like their counterparts in California or Texas—they are "feudalists" acting out the Spanish heritage. Latin military personnel defending the existing elites and suppressing popular revolts are not like U.S. soldiers and military advisers defending sugar cartels in the Dominican Republic or banana companies in Guatemala—they are avaricious, power-hungry men. Latin capitalists using the state to suppress strikes, finance their investment, and legislate protection from foreign competition are not like their U.S. counterparts who maintain high tariffs, enjoy government protection of monopolies, and receive government war-contract handouts—for the Latins are "parasitic capitalists." In a word, the author's attempt to draw a line between "parasitic" and "productive" capitalism fails; the attempt to use the former to explain the stagnation and poverty in Latin America and to advocate the latter as a cure is futile. The author himself acknowledges this when he casually notes the role of the foreign ("productive") investors in Latin America: "The drawbacks of these units of agriculture [North American companies] lie neither in managerial inefficiency nor in unwillingness to invest but in the disregard for the long-term interests of the local inhabitants . . . for the sake of making big profits quickly." Instead of extending his term "parasite" to his fellow Westerners he admonishes them for not showing "a greater sense of social responsibility." Andreski shies away from identifying the villain of stagnation as private enterprise for private profit.

The author has done little serious research into the complex pattern of Latin American social and economic development. He fabricates a picture of Latin America based on the Original Sin of the Spanish Conquest and then describes contemporary problems in terms of the heritage and attitudes of the remote past. The growth of an industrial bourgeoisie in Latin America, the expansion of significant middle strata and of a professional army, the organization of labor and Marxist parties around the new industrial-urban complexes, the emerging socio-political movements of the peasantry based on their interaction with centers of radical political organization, the promotion by the United States of a hemisphere-wide network of military and economic organizations to contain revolution, the middle class's close alliance with and increasing dependence on the military and its willingness to support military dictatorships to preserve its position, the linkages between land-owners and "modern" businessmen, the formation of partnerships between "parasitic" Latin businessmen and "productive" U.S. firms for mutual protection—none of these new developments which actually determine present-day Latin politics are analyzed in terms of how they produce "parasitism" and "subversion" in Latin America.

At times Professor Andreski relies on some silly notions to explain Latin American problems: dictatorship in Guatemala is inevitable because Guatemala is an "uncivilized republic." His attempt to explain stagnation by population growth is undercut by his own data: the two countries with the lowest birth rates, Argentina and Uruguay, are among the countries with the lowest rate of economic growth. On the other hand, Mexico, which has one of the highest birth rates, also has a high growth rate. Because he lacks a coherent theoretical framework, Andreski resorts to the useless device of arranging his social facts in that standby pattern, the "vicious circle," thus avoiding any serious analysis of the structural determinants of those social facts.

Among the factors that Andreski conjures up to explain poverty and stagnation are climate, geography, Hispanic determinism, the "lust" and "unbridled egoism" of the Latins, and their penchant for violence. Throughout his book Andreski compares Latin America to the United States and Europe, always to the detriment of the former. Adopting a lofty moral tone, Andreski criticizes the Latins for their treatment of the Indians, blithely ignoring the fact that the Latins at least did not liquidate the Indians as did the North Americans. In comparing Latin American political development with that of the West, he excoriates the Latins for their violence, having apparently forgotten that the West produced a Hitler and a Lyndon Baines Johnson. He ignores the centuries of destructive conquest by the Western "democracies" of England, France, Belgium, and now the United States. The violence in Latin America is considerable but it is not at all comparable to the violence generated by the science and technology of the Western "democratic" systems. The most concentrated act of political violence in Latin America in recent years was not committed by the "lustful," "violence-prone" Latin Americans but by the U.S. Marines in the Dominican Republic.

Parasitism and Subversion is a bad book but, difficult as it is to believe, not much worse than most of the books turned out yearly by U.S. academicians and journalists.

The book by Andre Gunder Frank, in contrast, is an exceptional work. It is a serious attempt to study the interplay of historical and contemporary structural factors which perpetuate underdevelopment in Latin America. The theme is to clarify "how . . . the structure and development of capitalism, . . . long since fully penetrating and characterizing Latin America, . . . generated, maintain[s] and still deepen[s] underdevelopment."

Frank's essays challenge three interrelated tenets in the mythology of Latin American development studies: (1) that the problems of development are largely domestic problems of capital scarcity; (2) that feudal or traditional institutions are largely responsible for impeding saving and investment; (3) that this economic system is sanctioned and protected by the concentration of political power in the hands of rural oligarchies. Rejecting analytic categories largely derived from the experience of Western capitalist development centuries earlier, Frank's historical analysis of the determinants of economic behavior and social stratification in Latin America leads him to focus on international economic relationships as the basic variable. He identifies the metropolis/satellite relationship as the key to studying the process of underdevelopment in Latin America.

By a careful examination of the commercial and agricultural interaction between two Latin countries, Brazil and Chile, and the West beginning in the sixteenth century, and by tracing the economic relationships of the national metropolis, the regional centers, and the hacienda, Frank shows that (1) the key factor influencing the poor performance of the Latin economies was their integration through subordination to the world capitalist market; (2) the major determinant of low rates of investment in Latin America was the expropriation by the West of the economic surplus to finance its industrialization; (3) a basic consideration influencing the behavior of the Latin property owners was profit maximization, not merely "conspicuous consumption"; (4) production was geared toward the market, not toward self-sufficient manors; (5) the market and the structure of ownership, not "traditional values," dictated the rate of productivity. Frank effectively destroys the myth of the feudal past so often cited and exploited by U.S. scholars as a means of defending capitalist development as a dynamic "democratic alternative" to Latin American stagnation. Frank's economic analysis poses a political problem that is perhaps even more important from the point of view of contemporary Latin American political development. The major social factor in Latin American political and economic development has been and still is the private entrepreneur, whether he is in agriculture, commerce, or industry. The contemporary problems of economic stagnation and social rigidity are a result of their activity for the past four centuries. The question arises: how can this same group that perpetuates misery overcome it? Not so long ago the Alliance for Progress was heralding a peaceful, democratic social revolution to be led by these same middle sectors. Perhaps the growing reliance by U.S. policy-makers on the military to safeguard Latin America from popular revolution is a recognition of the hard fact that Latin American and U.S. private enterprise can neither develop the Latin economy nor stabilize their rule.